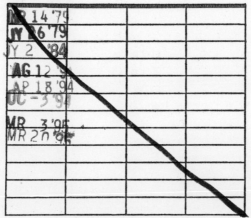

THE EXCEPTIONAL CHILD

A FUNCTIONAL APPROACH

McGRAW-HILL SERIES IN SPECIAL EDUCATION
ROBERT M. SMITH, Consulting Editor

Cartwright and Cartwright:
DEVELOPING OBSERVATION SKILLS

Smith:
CLINICAL TEACHING: Methods of Instruction for the Retarded

Smith:
INTRODUCTION TO MENTAL RETARDATION

Smith and Neisworth:
THE EXCEPTIONAL CHILD: A Functional Approach

Worell and Nelson:
MANAGING INSTRUCTIONAL PROBLEMS: A Case Study Workbook

THE EXCEPTIONAL CHILD

A FUNCTIONAL APPROACH

ROBERT M. SMITH
The Pennsylvania State University

JOHN T. NEISWORTH
The Pennsylvania State University

with chapters by

CHESTON M. BERLIN, Jr., M.D.
Professor of Pediatrics and Pharmacology
The Milton S. Hershey Medical Center
Pennsylvania State University

ALAN O. ROSS, Ph.D.
Professor of Psychology
State University of New York, Stony Brook

McGRAW-HILL BOOK COMPANY
New York   St. Louis   San Francisco   Auckland   Düsseldorf
Johannesburg   Kuala Lumpur   London   Mexico
Montreal   New Delhi   Panama   Paris
São Paulo   Singapore   Sydney   Tokyo   Toronto

THE EXCEPTIONAL CHILD
A FUNCTIONAL APPROACH

3 4 5 6 7 8 9   K P K P   7 9 8 7 6 5

This book was set in Elegante by Rocappi, Inc.
The editors were Stephen D. Dragin, Janis M. Yates, and Susan Gamer;
the designer was Nicholas Krenitsky;
the production supervisor was Judi Frey.
The drawings were done by J & R Services, Inc. Photographs by James Lukens.

Library of Congress Cataloging in Publication Data
Smith, Robert M   date
    The exceptional child.
    (McGraw-Hill series in special education)
    Includes bibliographical references and index.
    1.   Handicapped children—Education.   I.   Neisworth,
John T., joint author.   II.   Title.
LC4015.S6   371.9   74–20736
ISBN 0-07-058975-5

CONTENTS

PART III COMPLICATIONS OF EXCEPTIONAL CONDITIONS

FOREWORD

In characterizing the current developments in special education as a revolution, the authors of this significant introductory textbook are taking cognizance not only of the profusion of new ideas that are revolutionizing the education and training of exceptional children but, also, of the emergent philosophical approach, which may well be termed humanist, on which the developments are based. In the innovative programs described and discussed by the authors, the focus of special education is the child rather than the category of handicap. Thus, the authors make no attempt to define *handicapped children* in terms of children's characteristics, as other writers have done in the past; instead, they define *special education* in terms of its capability to intervene in the education of children who have special needs. This introduction to special education, consequently, is not just a minor updating of old materials; it is fundamentally new, a different approach to the education and training of exceptional children.

The new focus of special education is the beginning of an exciting chapter in the history of the education of persons with exceptionalities. That history, if told from the point of view of handicapped children, is a shocking story of massive neglect, denial, and rejection. The efforts to provide education for them were first systematized in Europe about a century and a half ago with the establishment of asylums for deviant persons. In the United States, the efforts culminated in the latter half of the nineteenth century with the establishment of special residential schools for various categories of handicaps. Not all handicapped children were eligible for the schools, however, and there were not enough schools to enroll all who were eligible.

At about the turn of the century, a few public school systems in large cities initiated special classes and day schools. They were modeled after the residential schools' curriculums and were staffed by teachers who were trained by those schools during summer sessions or brief sojourns. Until the close of World War II, the "special class" movement grew slowly. Then, and for about the next twenty-five years, a virtual explosion occurred, as if to make up for the centuries of neglect. Programs in special education in the public school systems doubled and doubled again in all parts of the nation. By 1970, about seven times more children were being served in special classes than had been served in 1945, and seven times more colleges were turning out special teachers in special education. There were no great technological breakthroughs to account for this busy period of development, however. The goading force was the organization of parents of handicapped children. The expanded programs were enlargements of the old model in which children were categorized by handicaps.

In the busy quarter of a century from 1945 to 1970, the categorical programs led to the development of broad special education departments in school districts and in colleges and universities. For the first time, it became possible for workers in special education to look at the commonalities of children across the categories. More similarities than differences were found. Many special educators came to the realization that the categorizing and labeling of children by handicaps was an unnecessary factor in making educational decisions for the children.

Since the turn of the century, the steady trend in special education has been one of progressive inclusion—that is, of bringing special programs and exceptional children out of isolation and including them in one environment for all children of the community. It has been demonstrated that many exceptional children function as well or better, with a little extra help, when they are able to associate in classrooms and community activities with their nonexceptional peers. The question therefore arose: Why not restructure the mainstream of education to accommodate as many exceptional children as possible without displacement to special settings? Many school systems around the country answered the question by substantiating the viability of mainstreaming mildly to moderately handicapped children. The movement has entailed a restructuring of the traditional role of the special teacher which is reflected in the changing teacher-training programs.

The story, obviously, is far more complex than the brief summary given here, but perhaps enough of it has been told to explain the erosion of the old models and the current period of what the authors of this book call revolutionary change. Dependence on categories to make educational decisions is becoming a practice of the past; administrative arrangements are altering rapidly; new relations with regular education are being negotiated; and new approaches to individualizing educational diagnosis and decisions are being installed. Although the explosion of 1945–1970 is waning, a new, more reflective, and more productive period seems to have begun for special education.

Periods of transition are difficult and risky for textbook writers because so much is going on at the same time. Yet rapid change requires acknowledgement in the literature. It is especially important that students receiving their first orientation to a field through basic textbooks start out with a valid topical view of emerging ideas and practices. Professors Smith and Neisworth, in this book, have had such students in mind. They have confronted the entire context of special education in rapid transition with scholarly insight and personal courage.

Maynard C. Reynolds, Ph.D.
Professor of Special Education
and Chairman, Department of
Psychoeducational Studies
University of Minnesota

PREFACE

Public education in America has been founded on the proposition that educational opportunities must be provided to all children who can benefit from them. Earlier in our history, this meant the exclusion of most children who currently are referred to as "exceptional" or "handicapped." Such children, it was thought, could not profit from the facilities, personnel, materials, and methods employed within the regular public school. It seemed logical, then, for these "uneducable" children to be shut off from public school services. But the conception of who can benefit from schooling changes as our knowledge and technology change. In medicine, for example, many of the "untreatable" conditions of yesterday are routinely managed today. Similarly, the profession of special education is constantly expanding its ability to provide strategies and materials for educating the rejects of the past. Today's public school typically includes many exceptional children who bear an array of labels and who qualify for a variety of placements and services.

Special education has grown rapidly but not always productively. We have made many mistakes, but the net effect of special education—in concert with parent organizations, social legislation, and scientific advances—has been to bring us to a new era in our perspective and educational intervention with children. We now consider that American public education is truly universal and that *all* children have a right to education, regardless of alleged or real limits to their educational potential. New concepts of human development give greater emphasis to the role of environment in preventing and treating disability. Advances in learning theory and technology make teaching more a precise applied science than a well-intentioned but ineffective art.

These trends and the children involved in them are the concern of this book, which is intended primarily as an introductory text for students in special education. Because the text includes considerations of medicine, psychology, and sociology, students in nursing and child development will also find it germane to their interests. Furthermore—and this is of prime importance—the recent emphasis on integrating exceptional children into regular educational settings ("mainstreaming") makes an introductory text of this nature valuable to the regular educator, who will be encountering more and more "special" cases in the classroom.

Assisting children and their families to prevent or overcome developmental difficulties is a complex and challenging mission. While special educators must focus specifically on the content and processes of educational intervention, the contributions of medicine, psychology, sociology, and other disciplines are crucial to a more comprehensive understanding and treatment of atypical children. We have provided, therefore, three chapters dealing with information from disciplines allied to special education, contributed by two eminent specialists: Cheston M. Berlin, Jr., M.D., Professor of Pediatrics and Pharmacology, The Milton S. Hershey Medical Center, The Pennsylvania State University (Chapters 3 and 4); and Alan O. Ross, Ph.D., Professor of Psychology, State University of New York at Stony Brook (Chapter 9). Their presentations help provide the wider spectrum of knowledge necessary to the contemporary special educator, and we are especially grateful to them.

We are pleased to thank the many students and colleagues who lent assistance in the various phases of our work. In particular, we are grateful to James Lukens, Peter Picuri, Ellen Swartz, Carol Stoltz, Ronald Madle, John Greer, Marci Hanson, Robert Algozine and Delbert McEwen for their contributions. Secretarial help on the manuscript has been most supportive, and special thanks go to Diane Bloom, Lorraine Kulbicki, Sharon Shefcheck and Karen Connelly.

We are also indebted to our many colleagues, both within special education and from allied fields, who encouraged us in our attempt to develop this noncategorical introductory text.

Robert M. Smith
John T. Neisworth

THE EXCEPTIONAL CHILD

A FUNCTIONAL APPROACH

I
THE STATUS
AND NEW
DIRECTIONS OF
SPECIAL EDUCATION

Special education is undergoing a period of revolution. Old concepts, philosophies, practices, organizational configurations, and stated goals are yielding to new ones. Whenever this takes place, entrenched patterns coexist for a while with newly emerging ones; but the old patterns finally give way to more modern views bolstered by scientific findings and empirically verifiable theories. Not all that is traditional is cast aside, however; indeed, some traditional formulations gain validity from new inquiry and reassessment. This is the case with special education, which is in a state of transition and development with respect to concepts of disability; ideas about how and why exceptional children are assessed, grouped, and treated; the role of special educators; and the interaction between science, technology, humanistic philosophy, and social policy.

There is little doubt that this stage of transition and development, with its conflicts, ambiguities, and uncertainties, will remain for some time. Nevertheless, there is a distinct tendency toward accumulation of scientific fact and unanimity of professional opinion which is giving special education new stability, optimism, and energy. The study of special education is a study of a changing field; the student must be familiar with both its status and its new directions.

1
SOME CONTEMPORARY CONCEPTS

STUDY TARGETS

1 Cite three general trends that contribute to the current revolution in special education.

2 List at least five speculations on the implications of trends for the training of special educators. Include in this list courses, experiences, or both that reflect these trends.

3 List and briefly summarize five criticisms of the "disability approach" to classifying exceptional children.

4 Enumerate the ten new directions in special education that are emerging in response to social and philosophical issues and dissatisfaction with traditional educational programing for exceptional children.

5 Describe three professional roles that a special educator could assume in addition to the traditional role of classroom teacher.

6 Write a short paragraph on the differences between the definition of "special education" and the definition of "exceptional children."

SPECIAL EDUCATION: A CHANGING FIELD

If you are, or are preparing to be, a special educator, you are involved in a profession that is undergoing rapid change. Advances in social philosophy, learning theory, and technology have produced a continuing revolution which makes it difficult but exciting to be a special educator. It is important to understand this dynamic context and its implications before attempting to define and delimit "special education." New concepts of the causes of human behavior, the determinants of development, and definitions of "normality" and "deviation" are part of a tranformation in social philosophy that is giving special education new emphasis and optimism. Historically, human development and competence were held to be primarily, if not exclusively, a function of internal, predetermined regulation. Ontogeny (individual development) was believed to be predestined and inevitable: the result of a biological master plan. Particularly as regards disability and abnormality, there has been a philosophy of fatalism; as a result, it was believed that special education, therapy, and other services could serve only to ameliorate, contain, or care for the many unfortunate conditions that frustrate development.

Through a series of transformations, a modern philosophy has emerged that sees normal human development as a continuous process involving interactions between an individual's biological makeup and the environment. That is, the content, direction, rate, and outcome of individual development result from a complex interplay of "nature" and "nurture." Extending this view of normal development to "abnormal" or "defective" development has enormous implications for special education. Intellectual, emotional, social, sensory, and physical deficiencies do not reside exclusively with the individual and are not exclusively the result of a defective constitution. Rather, such deficiencies are the product of constitutional characteristics interacting with environmental variables. Constitution and environment affect each other, and neither is static. Such a position implies that special education may be conceived of as planned ontogenetic intervention designed to reduce, eliminate, or preclude deficiencies. A contemporary philosophy of special education, then, rejects the idea of merely caring for or maintaining those with deficiencies, or helping them to adjust; instead, it emphasizes prevention and correction. Thus, retarded or distorted development and physical handicaps are not conditions simply to be managed, tolerated, subdued, or patched up; they represent problems to be reversed, drastically reduced, or compensated for, with the goal of successive steps toward normalization. In our present state of knowledge there are, of course, many problems of children that cannot be "normalized." Even with these cases, however, the goal must be progressive improvement in the *direction* of normal functioning.

Advances in learning theory and technology have contributed to the emergence of this optimistic philosophy. For many years it seemed that experimental and educational psychology had little relevance to practical application or intervention. Theories were propounded, theorists argued among themselves, and laboratory studies were conducted and reported: but this held little interest for the practitioner. Within the past 10 years, however, there has been movement toward more objectivity and pragmatism in the broad area of teaching and learning. For example, psychologists have discovered, codified, and implemented principles of learning and demonstrated that problems of learning and adjustment can be predicted and controlled. At first, only the most severe problems of institutionalized persons were the subject of experimentation. Rapidly, however, the success of the principles and procedures involved led to widespread application to increasingly various problems, persons, and situations.

The theoretical and empirical contributions have provided the basis of new techniques for fostering the growth of each child's capabilities. New assessment procedures, medical and psychoeducational, allow more accurate evaluation of the instructional needs of children. Instructional practices have become more efficient, more effective, better documented, and better assessed. For example, special education is making more and more use of behavioral objectives, programed instruction, motivational management procedures, and competency-based curricula. Instructional materials complementary to learning principles are being developed. Hardware (teaching machines and other electrical and mechanical gadgets) and software (such as programed texts) are changing the role of the special educator.

As a result of these and other trends, there is—understandably—a great deal of debate and some conflict within special education over issues such as terminology and definitions, diagnostic criteria, placement and grouping of children, type and sequence of teaching methods and materials, and training and certification of teachers.

Indeed, special educators are examining the fundamentals on which the profession has been organized and has functioned. For instance, by 1950 twelve categories of exceptional children had been identified: the educable mentally retarded, the trainable mentally retarded, the emotionally disturbed, the socially maladjusted, the speech-handicapped, the deaf, the hard of hearing, the blind, the partially sighted, the crippled, the chronically ill, and the gifted. As will be pointed out in Chapter 7, these categories are based on actual or presumed causes or "conditions." Through a variety of diagnostic procedures and a system of inference, children have been assigned to a category. Thus, for example, "mentally retarded" children were viewed as categorically different from all other groups. On the basis of such supposed uniquenesses, "special" instructional techniques and materials were sought to serve the needs of each category of children. Even separate "psychologies," descriptive of each category, were offered.

This classification scheme has been criticized by special educators as inappropriate and badly focused. The major points of criticism on this issue are the following:

1 *The categories are educationally irrelevant.* Relatively little educationally pertinent information is conveyed by the categorical descriptions. Calling a child "emotionally disturbed," for instance, does not provide the special educator with any specifics regarding the child's instructional needs. Does he read, write, use language adequately, pay attention, dress himself, follow instructions, adhere to safety regulations, move about competently, get along with others, and learn and remember information adequately? Does he show any significant physical deviation? These and more questions must be asked about any child who bears any categorical label. If the child did not carry the label "emotionally disturbed" but instead carried the label "learning-disabled," the teacher would still be without the specific information mentioned. Thus, categorical labels based on the origin of a disability or the general "condition" of a child have been found to be of little assistance to educators.

2 *Categorical groupings overlap; children do not fit neatly into single categories.* Most children in special education settings have multiple problems. Many children, for example, have a below-average learning rate along with problems of mobility, social adjustment, language development, or self-management, or various combinations of these. Likewise, children with severely reduced vision or hearing frequently also have problems of social adjustment and learning. Simply stated, one problem leads to another. Trying to fit a child into the one "most appropriate" category has led only to jurisdictional disputes, administrative maneuvering, and academic quibbling while the child waits for help.

3 *Categories label children as "defective," implying that the cause of the educational or developmental deficiency lies only within the child.* Due consideration has not been given to the proposition that functional problems are a product of a person interacting with an environment. According to the "interactional" point of view, a deficiency resides neither with the person alone nor with the environment alone. Educational problems result from an imperfect match between the characteristics of a person and those of the surroundings in which he must function. The proper focus must be on the *performance* problems of children; categorical labels must not be used to "explain" poor performance. Labeling children rather than specific deficiencies of performance creates negative expectations and stereotypes. Children with only a few attributes of a particular category may be presumed by teachers to have many or all of its characteristics. Accordingly, teachers and others may behave differently toward a child because of a label, and thus bring about their negative expectations.

4 *Special educational instructional materials and strategies are not category-specific.* With few exceptions, good procedures and materials for intervention are generalizable across categories of children. Principles for motivating learning, for instance, do not change with the "type" of child; likewise, good procedures for teaching reading are effective with all children and should vary only to handle individual differences, not categorical differences.

5 *Preparation of teachers along traditional categorical lines results in redundancy of course work and barriers within the profession.* For example, specialists in mental retardation and specialists in emotional disturbance have established their own journals, professional organizations, and conferences despite the fact that they must deal with common developmental and educational problems. Such categorical training programs unfortunately encourage disputes among professionals regarding diagnosis (e.g., is a child mentally retarded or emotionally disturbed?) which qualifies a child for categorical services.

6 *Finally, patterns of funding for special education have perpetuated the categorical approach.* University training programs and school systems are hesitant to diverge from categorical practices lest their funding be endangered. For example, since money is available for training teachers of the mentally retarded, university and college programs tend to maintain courses (including "special methods") and a special faculty to conform to the requirements of funding agencies, even if faculty members in a training program may be philosophically opposed to the traditional categorical approach. The paradox here is that special educators and funding agencies are caught in a self-perpetuating cycle where each blames the other for not refocusing the system toward more contemporary, preferred practices.

The issue of categorizing exceptionalities along traditional lines is fundamental and influences the direction of professional training programs and school practices. There are, however, other equally crucial propositions that have traditionally been a part of special education. The belief that exceptional children should be educated in self-contained classrooms segregated from other youngsters; the notion that every child should be routinely given an intelligence test before being included in or excluded from a special education program; the belief that a physician should give his opinion in *every* case of suspected exceptionality, as a part of the placement practice; and the concept "once deviant, always deviant"—all these are currently being challenged from many quarters. Changing views about society's responsibility to exceptional children, buttressed by promising research on the causes, assessment, and handling of handicapping conditions, have supported the arguments of special educators who challenge these fundamental beliefs and practices.

Early integration of all children can help them learn to appreciate each other.

During the early 1970s a dramatic movement was begun within special education in response to these issues. Special education has recently been taking some important new directions: (1) Categories based on causes and medical conditions are being replaced by groupings based on educationally relevant dimensions (e.g., problems related to attention, following directions, coordination, social interaction, academic achievement, and communication). (2) Exceptional children are being placed in nonsegregated settings as close as possible to the mainstream of regular students. (3) The normalization of exceptional children has been established as a goal of special education (i.e., children are to be placed in, or returned to, settings that require normal levels of functioning on their part). (4) Robotlike or perfunctory psychometric testing is being de-emphasized as a necessary and sufficient condition for receiving special education services. (5) The role of the teacher is becoming more dominant in the educational diagnosis of and intervention for exceptional conditions; physicians and psychologists are assuming more of a consultive role. (6) Educational services are being provided to all children irrespective of their degree of disability or presumed potential. (7) There is increasing emphasis on early intervention to redirect or prevent potential major debilitation. (8) Formal and continuous training is being provided for all professionals and paraprofessionals who are responsible for exceptional children. (9) There is greater emphasis on providing continuity of services between school and home (including education of parents) and between school and postschool programs. (10) New funding possibilities are emerging, not tied directly to disability categories.

CAREERS IN SPECIAL EDUCATION

The traditional role of the special educator has been that of a teacher of exceptional children in a self-contained classroom or special school. Special education classes have been segregated from the mainstream of regular education. The children enrolled in them have been grouped according to the traditional disability categories. The special educator has been responsible for conducting a program of education almost parallel to the regular class program, but presumably specially tailored for exceptional children. This restricted concept of the role of the special educator has given way to broader and more varied ideas of the times, places, and goals of special education services. More and more the special educator is being called upon to design and implement educational programing for preschool children to remediate, reverse, or prevent disabilities. At the other extreme, there is a growing emphasis on developing systematic postschool opportunities for young people and adults with special needs.

In addition to their role as teachers in self-contained classrooms, special educators are increasingly being called upon to serve as consultants to regular class teachers, to parent-training programs, and to administrators. Because educational opportunities are being made available to more children from preschool to adolescence, and these experiences are provided in almost all possible settings within the school environment, special education personnel are assigned to a wider range of situations than has heretofore been the case. Similarly, eligibility for special education services is no longer restricted to children who exhibit only extreme deviations of "clinical" proportions. Relatively normal youngsters with singular learning problems, difficulties in motivation, or conduct problems are often referred to a special educator. The day is rapidly approaching when both children and their teachers will readily seek the advice of a special educator without hesitation or fear of invoking clinical or pathological connotations.

As you ought to suspect, a wide range of careers is possible in special education: teacher's aide, resource-room specialist, consultant to regular class teachers, diagnostic and remedial specialist in certain subjects or skills (e.g., reading, arithmetic, language), counselor to parents, recreation specialist, supervisor and program administrator, researcher, teacher trainer in special education. The most recent data are those for special education teachers employed by public schools. As late as 1970, it was estimated by the U.S. Office of Education that 124,000 special education teachers served in public school programs for nearly 3 million exceptional children. Considering the present and future need for teachers of exceptional children with mild disabilities alone, and assuming that philosophy and programs will remain the same, Gallagher (1971) estimated that the need for teachers could not be met during the next century. The emerging philosophy of exceptional children and their instructional needs will, moreover, increase the need for professional personnel.

DEFINITIONS

The way most authors in the field of special education have chosen to define exceptional children can be illustrated by the following three definitions.

An exceptional child is

a child who deviates from the average or normal child (1) in mental characteristics, (2) in sensory abilities, (3) in neuromuscular or physical characteristics, (4) in social or emotional behavior, (5) in communication abilities, or (6) in multiple handicaps to such an extent that he requires a modification of school practices, or special educational services, in order to develop to his maximum capacity [Kirk, 1972, p. 4].

An exceptional pupil is so labeled only for that segment of his school career (1) when his deviating physical or behavioral characteristics are of such a nature as to manifest a significant learning asset or disability for special education purposes; and, therefore, (2) when, through trial provisions, it has been determined that he can make greater all-around adjustment and scholastic progress with direct or indirect special education services than he could with only a typical regular school program [Dunn, 1973, p. 7].

The exceptional child shall be considered to be one whose educational requirements are so different from the average or normal child, that he cannot be effectively educated without the provision of special educational programs, services, facilities, or materials [Gearheart, 1972, p. 2].

Of course, it is important to know something about the prominent characteristics of those to whom professional attention is being directed, and this is obviously the point of the prevailing definitions. That is, most definitions have focused on attributes, deficiencies, or defects of the child. A slightly different perspective is to focus on *what is done to the youngster educationally* rather than on the extent and character of his deviations. Advocates of the latter orientation hold that focusing the definition on exceptional characteristics of children can lead to (1) inappropriate labeling of the child, and thereby to making the child a scapegoat (i.e., blaming the child for his problems), (2) imprecision in delineating the prominent instructional needs of each individual child (i.e., calling a child "mentally retarded" does not lead to a specification of instructional needs), and (3) emphasizing the management of problems without overt concern for the prevention of future disorder or the elimination of circumstances that promote handicaps.

The following definition is proposed in order to minimize these weaknesses. It shifts the emphasis from characteristics of the child to manipulation of educational variables for intervention. Thus, we have defined "special education" rather than "exceptional children."

> Special education is that profession concerned with the arrangement of educational variables leading to the prevention, reduction, or elimination of those conditions that produce significant defects in the academic, communicative, locomotor, or adjustive functioning of children.

Here, we have emphasized the major goal of special education. If a child's performance suggests continued deficiencies, the basic problem for the special educator is to determine the most appropriate arrangements of relevant educational variables. The definition is educational—it does not focus on medical, constitutional, or hidden reasons for deficiencies in performance. It embraces functional areas of performance, all of which can be directly observed and objectively measured. It implies that special education should be as concerned about the prevention of disabilities as it has traditionally been about the reduction of disabilities. It suggests that a child can be "exceptional" at one time and not at another, or in one situation but not in another. And finally, criteria are suggested concerning what constitutes a "significant deficiency" in one or more of the functional areas. It is our belief that this concept is specific to the environment and will vary with the environment. Local conditions, community norms, and prevalent expectations for performance should be used to make this determination.

We urge you, then, to view special education as an emerging applied science for designing and delivering intervention with the goal of normalization for all children.

THE ORGANIZATION OF THIS BOOK

It would be premature, and indeed not possible at this time, to discuss all the implications of the vast changes taking place in special education, for the field has not yet stabilized. This book, written during a period of rapid transition, attempts to bridge the gap between the traditional content and organization of an introductory text in special education and the emerging ideas about the structure and content of the profession.

The traditional introductory test has focused on problems of exceptional children within distinct disability categories. Thus, for example, evaluation devices, teaching methods, psychosocial problems, and learning characteristics of emotionally disturbed children have been discussed separately from these same topics as applied to mentally retarded children. Similarly, each category of children has been considered in relative isolation from the others. As a result of this organizational pattern, students have considered becoming teachers of the mentally retarded, *or* the cerebral palsied, *or* the brain-injured, *or* the emotionally disturbed, and so on, as if there were separate and distinct pedagogies for each type of child.

The new focus in special education, which this book attempts to reflect and promote, is that there are common concerns, instructional procedures, materials, and goals that cut across the various disability groupings. Children labeled "mentally retarded," "emotionally disturbed," "neurologically handicapped," "learning-disabled," "blind," "deaf," etc., overlap considerably with respect to factors that have direct relationship to special education. Good instructional practices, founded on sound principles of learning, when properly implemented, are effective for all children, whatever their form and degree of disability. This book attempts to describe the content common to the various exceptional conditions.

Regardless of these similarities, of course, there are peculiar clusters of characteristics and problems related to specific disabilities. Blind and deaf children demand some highly specific methods and materials, for instance. These and other procedures are presented in the category summaries included in Part V.

In Part I, there are two chapters that set the scene for the special educator. This chapter has provided a broad overview of the state of transition in special education. Details of and evidence for the points brought out here will be discussed throughout the book. This chapter has emphasized, in a more general manner, the prominent and emerging trends, issues, philosophical changes, state of reorganization, career options, and theoretical and technical advances which characterize contemporary special education; and it has considered existing definitions, and proposed a definition, of the special educator's object of concern.

Chapter 2 gives a synopsis of the major special education categories as traditionally organized: each brief sketch is given more detailed treatment in Part V. Additionally, Chapter 2 notes the major dimensions of interrelationships among the disability categories and the reorientation that is currently taking place. The common elements referred to in Chapter 2 are pursued in greater depth in Parts II, III, and IV.

Part II consists of four chapters, each directly linked to disabilities. Chapters 3 and 4 focus on the causes, or etiology of exceptional conditions. (Professor

Berlin, a pediatrician, has broadly delineated the reasons why children develop disabilities, from a medical perspective.) There is also a discussion of the various psychosocial conditions that are known to foster exceptionalities. These chapters emphasize the preventive procedures that can be taken to reduce and eliminate primary and secondary disabilities. Chapters 5 and 6 consider the assessment procedures that are currently used to evaluate children and to describe their characteristics and levels of functioning. (Again, Professor Berlin has approached this subject from the perspective of a physician.) Chapter 6 deals with the diagnosis of psychological, social, and educational variables.

Part III deals with three major clusters of complications and issues that often arise as a result of a child's being different. Chapter 7 considers the complexities of the classification practices that have traditionally been employed to organize special education. These methods of classifying exceptional children have led to the practice of labeling and grouping youngsters in ways that have precipitated additional handicaps and imprecision in preferred management procedures. These complications, and the additional burdens on the child, seem to be produced more by the labels that have been used, and the interpretation given to those labels, than by the disability itself. Alternatives for classifying special education problems, which avoid the hazards of traditional labeling practices, are presented: these options are based on educationally relevant variables.

Chapter 8 discusses the somatopsychological complications that stem from the visibility of deviant physique or functioning. How one is viewed by others—and how one perceives that others view him—frequently adds to the problems of being exceptional. Obviously, a missing limb or severely limited vision contributes to impaired functioning in the average environment; but the *reactions* of others to such a disability frequently generate further limitations and handicaps, not the least of which is the impact that they have on the individual's self-esteem. Suggestions are made for reducing the primary deficiency as well as its visibility, and, thus, the somatopsychological complications.

Chapter 9 deals with a relatively neglected area of concern in special education: family problems. In this chapter, Professor Alan Ross discusses the range of complicating factors that are often found in the family setting of the exceptional child. Problems of anxiety, guilt, embarrassment, rejection, and bewilderment on the part of parents and siblings are considered along with specific recommendations for their resolution. Practical procedures are offered to parents for the rearrangement of family interaction.

Each of the issues discussed in Part III is pertinent to all forms of exceptionality, regardless of origin and degree of severity. As you study these chapters, you will also note that the problems and issues presented are equally relevant to the school and the home.

Part IV—"Special Education Intervention"—addresses itself to four major topics germane to all categories of exceptional conditions, however classified.

Chapter 10 deals with instructional procedures common to all effective teaching. While there are some highly individualized teaching procedures for certain specific education problems, valid psychoeducational principles and practices are, for the most part, applicable in most instructional circumstances. These strategies must be mastered by the special educator in the early stages of training. Chapter 11 presents an abridged selection of devices and gadgetry available to the special educator for minimizing the consequences of disabling conditions and promoting more normal functioning. Ranging from artificial limbs to complex electronic apparatus to simple homemade devices, these prostheses when properly used can be an important part of the special educator's armamentarium.

Chapter 12 ("Settings for Special Education") and Chapter 13 ("Community Services and Resources") represent extensions of the preceding two chapters. They discuss alternatives for special education programing as a whole. Chapter 12 focuses on the available range of facilities and plans in most school systems, criteria for making decisions regarding placement, the need for flexible programing as regards options for placement, and the general objective of approaching normalization for all children through appropriate sequencing of placement assignments. Chapter 13 emphasizes the array of resources and services available within the community that special educators should draw upon to augment and support the school's efforts. A number of benefits are achieved when there is close cooperation between the school and services and personnel in the community, not the least of which is the opportunity for effecting a smooth transition for the child as he moves to postschool programing and attempts to become more naturally integrated within the community.

Part V presents outlines of exceptionalities as traditionally classified. This material constitutes a body of information that has heretofore characterized the organization and content of special education. It is included in order to provide the student with details of special education as traditionally classified. Unique causes of a condition, prominent theories of the origin and treatment of the condition, the number of people so classified, unique terminology associated with the problem, the history of activity among special-interest groups, and other historic and current features associated with a category are summarized. Instead of presenting the information discursively, we have given it in much the same format as the popular college outline series. It is hoped that the form of presentation will facilitate and focus the study of pertinent factors in the various areas of disability. Students just entering the field of special education should have basic knowledge of the traditionally classified areas of disability. We have given this information in the form of a brief summary so as to place greater emphasis on what we view as the central thesis of the book—the common concerns of special educators. We emphasize that this is a study and reference section, and we encourage you to refer to appropriate portions of these outlines as you read related chapters in other parts of the book. For example, as you read the two chapters on assessment you may want to refer to the sections of Part V dealing with the presumably unique assessment procedures and materials that have been developed for specific disability areas. Once you have become acquainted with the common concerns in Parts I, II, III, and IV, you will be better prepared to appreciate the commonalities and differences that exist across the various disability areas.

At the close of each of the first four parts, we suggest some projects that call for application of the information presented. These projects are more than mere exercises or drills; they should foster your active, meaningful involvement in the field. Your understanding of the material will be enhanced by your participation in these projects. Some require involvement by your colleagues; some must be done "on location."

2

CONVENTIONAL CATEGORIES OF EXCEPTIONAL CHILDREN

STUDY TARGETS

1   Read each overview, refer to the relevant section in Part V for more detail, and use the Glossary to assist you in developing a list of key words and concepts pertaining to each area of exceptionality.
2   Generate ten true-false questions for each disability area and exchange these questions with another student to test your comprehension of the material.
3   After reading the chapter, list at least seven areas of functioning in which there is a high probability of overlap among categories, e.g., language fluency or social interaction with adults.

Exceptionalities can be viewed from various perspectives; two of the most prominent are exemplified in Table 2-1. At the heads of the columns we have listed several of the major traditional categories of disabilities. Each has been further divided into several subgroups. Most of the professional literature, the

TABLE 2-1 TRADITIONAL CATEGORIES OF DISABILITY

Areas of Generic Concern and Commonality	Mental Retardation			Behavior Disorders		Communication Disorders				Language			Physical Disabilities				Learning Disabilities: Academic		
	EMR	TMR	SMR	Emot. Dist.	Soc. Mal.	Artic.	Cleft Palate	Voice	Stut- tering	Dev. Delays	Sensory Aphasics	Exp. Aphasics	C.P.	Locomo- tion	Musc. Dystro.	Perc. Motor	Reading	Writing	Arith.
1. Causes of Exception-alities a. Familial b. Social c. Psychological d. Medical e. Hereditary etc.																			
2. Characteristics of Ex-ceptional Conditions a. Physical deformity b. Motor disorders c. Communication problems d. Social-effective functional defects etc.																			
3. Diagnostic Practices a. Interdisciplinary b. Individual assess-ment c. Data collected over time d. Performance com-pared with self or others e. Early identification etc.																			

4. Complications of Exceptionalities
  a. Family
  b. Somatopsychological
  c. Psychosomatic
  d. Inept or inappropriate schooling
  e. Erroneous or biased conclusions from diagnostic data
  etc.			

5. Instructional/Management Procedures
  a. Use of general principles of learning
  b. Focus on prevention
  c. Employment of prosthetic devices
  d. Mobilization and use of community resources
  e. Focus on normalization
  f. Variable placement
  etc.			

6. Nomenclature, Frequency, Definitions, Theories Concerning Cause and Management, Use of Drugs, Prognosis, etc.			

orientation of professional and lay groups, and college and university programs in special education (as well as in allied fields) have focused on characteristics *within* each of the groups. This perspective is based on the proposition that children called "mentally retarded," for example, are more alike within that category than any of them is similar to any children called "emotionally disturbed," and so on. Although it is true that there is a body of basic literature in each of the disability areas (see Part V), the belief that they are discrete, relatively independent, and mutually exclusive cannot be supported.

There is, then, substantial overlap among the disability groups in areas such as those listed on the left. For example, constitutional and environmental difficulties pertain to all categories of disabilities. Likewise, motor disorders, unusual physical characteristics, family problems, diagnostic and evaluative practices, emphasis on preventing secondary disorders, and certain management procedures are relevant to children in all of the traditional disability categories. As mentioned earlier, the field of special education has moved rather dramatically in the direction of considering that the fundamental generic issues pertain to all exceptional children. At the same time, one should not lose sight of the fact that just as it is foolish to characterize all mentally retarded youngsters on the basis of group characteristics, it is equally presumptuous to assume that the generic phenomena apply to all.

This chapter provides an overview, or advance organizer, for the traditionally classified disability areas that are detailed in Part V. Secondly, woven into each summary are brief commentaries that highlight the commonalities among exceptionalities from the special educator's point of view. Thus, the two major objectives of this chapter for the student are (1) to prepare you to review the detailed accounts about exceptional conditions that appear at the end of this book in Part V; and (2) to alert you to look for the areas of common concern among categories and to appreciate their interrelationship.

PROBLEMS OF LEARNING

The most fundamental focus of concern for a special educator is the development of skills and children's use of them to solve problems. Anything that interferes with children's learning or acquiring skills and information or applying the skills and information learned is of vital interest to teachers. It is clear that children differ greatly in their rates of learning, memory capabilities, skills in interrelating information with new knowledge, sensitivity to environment, receptivity for learning, and facility to generate adequate responses to problems.

Certain children exhibit a generalized depression in learning in contrast to other youngsters of the same age. Traditionally, they have been labeled "mentally retarded" if their performance is significantly below that of their peers. The criterion for what constitutes a meaningful deviation from the "norm" is a point of debate among professionals within and among disciplines. This debate has led to some confusion regarding the establishment of subcategories within the broad field of mental retardation, as well as at the opposite or "gifted" end of the continuum. Not only has there been lack of clarity in the upper and lower boundaries for the subcategories, but at a more basic level those disciplines that have had a historical interest in the problems of individuals adjudged to be mentally retarded disagree on which dimensions to use in determining if the condition exists (or existed). Attorneys, educators, physicians, pharmacologists, sociologists, and mental health specialists approach the problems of the mentally retarded from different perspectives and, thus, could be expected to have divergent opinions regarding what constitute the most appropriate criteria for defining the condition.

This very same problem sweeps across the other categories and fosters confusion and inconsistency in communication among professionals and members of the laity. Moreover, lack of agreement on the very fundamental factors that dictate if a condition exists or not has led to labeling children in increasingly more vague ways, e.g., "minimal brain-damaged," without adequate documentation and often with serious, deleterious consequences. The most frustrating and serious result of problems related to definition and the inconclusiveness of criteria is that the labels tend to bias therapists, teachers, and others in ways that serve to restrict the child's progress in important areas of learning.

The causes for a general depression in learning ability (mental retardation) are varied and complex. It is clear that professionals disagree widely regarding the relationships that are thought to exist between certain constitutional and environmental circumstances and the various expressions of mental retardation. It has been estimated that upwards of 80 percent of those youngsters of school age identified as mentally retarded exhibit the "condition" for reasons that cannot be adequately documented. As with many of the other areas of exceptionality, mental retardation is very disproportionate among various segments of the population. More children from lower socioeconomic strata are defective in functioning than children in higher social classes. The relative influence played by poor prenatal care, weak constitutional origins, and the various environmental stages of development and functioning is an area of intense study, for it is clear that the fractioning out of the various contributors to intellectual retardation and other conditions will eventually lead to sophisticated preventive procedures. This, clearly, is a domain of common concern in all areas of deficiency.

Specialists in mental retardation, as well as those in other areas of concern, are constantly faced with substantial problems related to the measurement and evaluation of variables pertaining to exceptionalities. There are difficulties in determining which of the vast multitude of tests to use, what kinds of data to collect, what basis of comparison of a child's performance to use, which interpretation is most accurate, what the child should be called, and, of great importance, whether the examiner is a competent diagnostician. Whether a youngster is called "mentally retarded"—and will have to face a multitude of complications, ineptnesses, social-psychological problems, erroneous conclusions, and biased perceptions by others—is often inextricably related to the skill of an examiner, the appropriateness of the measuring instruments, and the truth of the conclusions reached. This same set of problems occurs throughout all disciplines concerned with exceptional persons and conditions, and the consequences of a wrong judgment or conclusion are equally severe and long-standing. In the field of mental retardation the complex problems just mentioned occur time and time again.

In a very general way, the performance problems that the mentally retarded exhibit are more resistant to change than deficiencies in single skills. The retarded typically show low-frequency behaviors in those areas in which they have previously failed, e.g., in many of the academic subjects, because so often they lack opportunity in their early years for gaining those skills required to be successful in school and society and for learning developmentally important behaviors. As a result the retarded often exhibit socially inappropriate and developmentally obstructive behaviors. Self-stimulation, personal abuse, communication problems, stereotype behaviors, and withdrawal are examples of behaviors that have been learned by mentally retarded persons in the absence of an environment that is properly focused and planned. Institutions for the retarded are notorious settings for the development and maintenance of such unfortunate behaviors.

Compounding the problems of the mentally retarded is the high incidence of other disorders. Motor problems, speech and language weaknesses, and social-personal problems head the list. These become more serious and frequent in children who are considered trainable or severely retarded than in those considered educable. For youngsters with physical deformities or cosmetic defects, psychological complications inevitably arise because of the complex social consequences of such obvious deviations. Along with these somatopsychological problems, the mentally retarded and their families often suffer severe distress. These complications exacerbate the basic learning difficulties of the mentally retarded and, in a real sense, magnify the management and instructional problems. For example, a retarded child who experiences constant failure in school and embarrassment before his peers is a candidate for significant behavior and adjustment problems. For many such children, then, the layer upon layer of problems that result serve to blur the proper "assignment" of the children to a "category."

There is clear unanimity of feeling among professionals that mentally retarded children are not a homogeneous group and, therefore, should have an instructional program that is individually appropriate. The range of their educational needs is as broad as that of any other group of youngsters. Although there is a wide diversity of opinion regarding which of the many psychological theories is most easily translatable for use in educational programs for the mentally retarded, most special educators agree that a number of general principles of learning have special pertinence and are particularly effective when properly implemented. Examples of these principles are reinforcement of success, proper sequencing, programing in small steps, teaching for application, and practice.

The concept of "normalization" has emerged as a central theme throughout special education and especially in the field of mental retardation. The attempt to integrate exceptional youngsters into the mainstream of society has several points of origin. First, dramatic changes were reported in the performance of severely mentally retarded persons through the use of systematic instructional programing. Second, certain segments of society became concerned and vocal about the poor treatment many institutions for the mentally retarded were providing their residents. Third, research confirmed the suspicion held by many people that certain commonly accepted practices in the education and management of the mentally retarded were, in fact, making the functional condition worse because of unfortunate attitudinal, pedagogical, and social circumstances. Finally, behavioral scientists became convinced, upon the urging of parent groups, that one cannot expect "normal" functioning from a retarded person when he lives in an abnormal environment. These situations have led to a veritable renaissance in thinking concerning how best to deal with the problems of mental retardation.

The field of learning disabilities is a relatively recent addition to special education categories. Although historically there have been pockets of serious interest in and inquiry into the causes and characteristics of and the appropriate therapeutic procedures for dealing with wide performance discrepancies in certain children, special educators did not evidence an intense and all-abiding interest in such children until the early 1960s. It was only after the publication of several classic texts on this general subject and pressure by parent groups that organized professional interest developed. The concomitant publication of several promising diagnostic tests that alleged to pinpoint specific areas of performance disability (mainly in the academic subjects), with accompanying instructional activities designed to remediate the deficiencies, gave impetus to the movement, which before then had been focused within certain of the medical specialties.

As has been true in many relatively new fields of inquiry, professionals have not agreed on some basic concepts. For example, the literature reveals wide differences in definitions: some believe that brain damage is a necessary condition for a child to be classified as "learning-disabled," others choose not to include social or personal deviations within the category, and still other special educators hold the belief that special education embraces all learning disabilities. Obviously, the definition is the key to other considerations, including incidence, characteristics, identification, prevention, and therapeutic approaches. Without agreement on whom we are talking about, it is virtually impossible to agree on how many there are and what characteristics they exhibit. This inconclusiveness, of course, is typical of most fields of inquiry during stages of early formulation and development.

In spite of the problems related to such new areas, there is general agreement that children with learning disabilities exhibit a performance discrepancy of significant magnitude in one or more academically related areas. In contrast, their level of functioning in other fields is usually approximately equivalent to that of children of the same age. Mentally retarded children, in contrast, function poorly in most, if not all, academic and psychosocial areas. The major literature in the field of learning disabilities does not focus only on academic problems; there is a definite orientation toward considering some of the early weaknesses in perceptual-motor skills and language skills that are presumed to be the building blocks on which subsequent academic prowess is founded. Many of these competencies, however, while logically pertinent, do not have close and consistent theoretical bases and have not been empirically validated. Indeed, they stand as hypotheses, although a great deal of the literature on learning disabilities is presented in a fashion suggesting that they are established.

The diagnostic approaches that are used to evaluate the various nuances of mental retardation are quite close to those used in the field of learning disabilities. An interdisciplinary approach has been recommended. Great emphasis has been given in the past to an intensive medical evaluation. There has been, however, a gradual movement away from this orientation toward a more task-oriented, functional assessment that emphasizes the specific "molecules of performance" that make up the subject areas in which the child seems deficient. The fundamental principles of assessment of mental retardation and of learning disabilities are very similar, as are the problems of evaluation mentioned earlier: test validity and reliability, test bias, comparative data, and the effectiveness of the tester.

The basic causes for learning disabilities are unclear, although there is general agreement that poor early school experiences, emotional problems, inept child-rearing practices, diseases, and accidents are major contributers to the problem. Prenatal and perinatal complications are probably related in certain instances, but the exact relationships are unclear.

Finally, the best methods and procedures for dealing with children with learning disabilities are not agreed upon. Numerous points of view and philosophical propositions have been advanced in favor of one approach or another. Most of these strategies have not been tested enough to be proved valid. Unquestionably, lack of clear definition of the types of children and the characteristics that fall under the rubric "learning disabilities" is at the heart of the inconclusiveness and imprecision that currently characterize this field.

ADJUSTMENT PROBLEMS

There are two very broad categories of adjustment problems: emotional disturbance and social maladjustment. Almost everyone experiences instances of maladjustment in his lifetime. These transitional problem periods are normal if they are relatively brief and infrequent. They may very well be situation-specific, that is, related to a certain trying or disturbing event, place, or person.

Hence, there is no clear line of demarcation between normal and abnormal personal-social behaviors. "Emotional disturbance" is a general term that is used to include numerous imprecisely defined conditions such as "mental illness," "psychosis," "neurosis," "schizophrenia," "phobia," "obsessions," "compulsions," "autism," and so on. Each of these categories of disturbance has characteristics that separate it from the others. Fundamentally, children who exhibit emotionally disturbed behaviors are excessively aggressive, withdrawn, or both. Their central problem usually is not violation of social rules or the mores and folkways of the culture; they are, however, usually very unhappy people.

Social maladjustment, in contrast, involves behavior which violates rules. The behavior may be acceptable within the context of the child's subculture, but not in society at large. In fact, within the child's immediate social milieu rule-violating behavior (e.g., throwing stones at school windows) may be rewarded.

According to research, there is no single most vulnerable period in a child's development for the fostering of emotional disturbance. No doubt during those periods in which major familial, social, or physical changes, or a combination of these, occur, the child is more susceptible than at other times. The first days in school, the beginning stages of verbal communication, periods of intense competition in school, and adolescence are all landmark periods during which greater pressures are experienced by children. Hypothetically, at least, they could set the stage for emotional maladjustments.

As was mentioned in the preceding section, imprecision in the definition of a phenomenon makes clear assessment impossible in other important areas, such as frequency of the exceptionality, its characteristics, its diagnosis, and its treatment. The broad area covered by the term "behavior disorders" suffers from the same definitional ambiguity as "learning disabilities," with all of the related consequences. The statement that upwards of 12 percent of children in school have significant behavior disorders really has little meaning without an agreed-upon functional definition of the term. There is a belief that emotional disturbance occurs less often in lower social-economic situations than in the middle and higher categories. The reverse seems to be true for social maladjustment.

The behavior symptoms attendant on adjustment problems are multitudinous. Checklists have been developed to aid in alerting teachers to conduct and personality problems; however, for most teachers extreme behaviors by a child stand out to such an extent against the backdrop of a class of youngsters that such lists are superfluous. Teachers and diagnosticians are usually not guilty so much of under- or over-referral of children suspected as having adjustment problems as of playing psychiatrist and dealing with the reasons they postulate for the child's strange behavior as if they are fact. This procedure only leads to labeling, an exacerbation of the existing problems, achievement disorders, and other types of complications. There is no question that adjustment problems have multiple etiologies, but the presumed genesis of any child's emotional or social disorder is clearly outside the expertise of most school personnel.

The treatment and management of behavior disorders by teachers and psychologists within the environs of the public school have taken many tacks. Individual versus group therapies, behavioral versus drug intervention, psychoeducational versus psychoanalytical procedures, and arranged versus ecological procedures have been espoused and implemented according to the personal perspectives of the professional personnel on the scene. Each method has its advocates, and all have histories of success and failure. There is no debate on the need for increasingly relevant research on each of these and other methodologies.

The field of behavior disorders is fraught with great imprecision, perhaps more than most other areas of exceptionality. This imprecision is not surprising, since the whole area of personal affect and social interaction has historically been explained by theories that themselves were vague. Special educators have become increasingly concerned about these areas since the late 1950s, mainly as a result of having recognized that adjustment problems seem more prevalent among exceptional children, in combination with other disabling conditions, than in other groups of youngsters. There appears to be a double disability, with emotional disturbance being especially prominent. Some have chosen to label this as "emotional overlay." These observations by teachers, then, have contributed to a real interest among special educators in more precise definition, more accurate observation and diagnosis, and more effective ways to prevent or treat the various adjustment problems that schoolchildren exhibit.

SENSORY PROBLEMS

Serious auditory and visual disorders are less common among exceptional children than are the previously discussed areas of disability. Approximately 5 percent of school-age children have hearing levels lower than the normal range in at least one ear, and of this group one out of ten requires a special educational program. The literature reveals that various dimensions and criteria have been used to classify auditory disorders. The location of the problem (outer ear, middle ear, or inner ear), the degree of hearing impairment (as measured by an audiometric evaluation), the age at onset (before or after birth), and the types of auditory disorders (conductive, sensory-neural, central, or psychogenic) illustrate the range of possibilities for establishing categories. By far the most helpful and frequently used classification system for special education purposes is degree of hearing loss. This has more functional relevance and is tied directly to hearing behavior, which, in turn, provides specific information on the nature of a child's special educational needs.

Hearing disorders can be traced to the same basic sources as other disabilities. Prenatal, perinatal, and postnatal difficulties can affect any or all of the three major segments of the auditory system. Some are effectively managed by medical intervention, short- or long-term, while other auditory problems cannot be prevented, reversed, or medically ameliorated. Psychological and social difficulties frequently attend hearing disorders and often serve to worsen the consequences of the hearing problem itself. Deaf people, for example, are often hesitant to try speaking. When they do speak, they exhibit a characteristically unique pattern of speech and language that signals abnormality to the listener. The reactions of listeners to deaf speech can be extreme enough to influence the hearing-impaired person in very negative ways. Some have trouble in personal and social areas; others are influenced in their academic functioning.

Relatively sophisticated approaches have been developed by audiologists and otologists (M.D.'s) to observe and measure the characteristics of the auditory system. Technical advances in this field are impressive and have led to major changes in past practices and philosophies. For example, because of progress in physiological audiometry, infant hearing tests are much more valid and reliable than has been true in the past. Advances in microsurgery of the ear have also proved extremely effective in reversing significant auditory disorders.

Instructional programs for children with hearing defects require highly skilled professionals. The most immediate issue of concern, quite logically, is to help the hearing-impaired child to develop acceptable skills in expressing ideas and competence in understanding what others are communicating to him. There is controversy among special educators on the proper focus for this instruction. Some emphasize training in oral expression, while others emphasize manual language. Consequently, pockets of professional groups in different parts of the country confine themselves to one or a combination of these approaches. Debate also appears in the literature and at professional meetings on the most appropriate location for educating hearing-impaired children and youth. Some believe that residential schools provide the best milieu. An equally vocal group of professionals hold that these children should be educated within the public schools.

It has been estimated that between 0.1 percent and 0.4 percent of children of school age have significant visual disorders. This is the smallest group of exceptional children. A standard classification system has been adopted by almost all professional groups who have an interest in visual defects. The legal definition of blindness is used to dictate the types of social services for which the blind can qualify. It has little meaning educationally, and so special educators have chosen to classify as blind those who cannot read print. The partially sighted are youngsters who can read print with special low-vision aids.

The causes for visual disorders parallel the causes of the other disabilities that involve clear organ dysfunction. Accidents, poisoning, infections, tumors, hereditary difficulties, and nutritional deficiencies stand out as major contributors to visual problems. There are a multitude of types of visual defects. Problems with the areas surrounding the eye, refractive errors, muscle imbalance and failure, defects in the receptive mechanism, cataracts, glaucoma, and albinism are among the most prominent forms of ocular difficulties. Each has different causes and demands unique medical intervention.

Teachers have an important place in the early diagnosis of potential visual problems in young children. As problems are suspected more elaborate screening devices can be used to assess the validity of the teacher's hunch. These tests measure visual acuity, depth perception, possible muscular problems, and the child's range of visual field. The child's response, then, could lead to his being referred to an ophthalmologist.

COMMUNICATION PROBLEMS

Speech is the way humans make sounds; language is human verbal expression. Both fall under the broad rubric "communication" and collectively constitute the area of disability that involves the highest percentage of children. Estimates on the incidence range from 5 percent to over 10 percent of school-age children.

The way speech and language develop normally is fairly well documented in descriptive accounts. The very earliest stages are reflexive vocalization, babbling, vocal play, lallation, and echolalic utterances, which play important roles in the character and strength of subsequent communication capabilities. At around a year of age, the child's first words appear—usually single-syllable, consonant-vowel combinations, as in "ma-ma" or "da-da." Each month thereafter new, more complex words appear in the child's repertoire. At age 2, under facilitating circumstances, nearly 300 words can be expressed in combinations and in appropriate ways. As youngsters grow older, their skills in making complex speech sounds and their vocabularies increase dramatically. Under normal circumstances, a 6-year-old child has a comprehension vocabulary of more than 2,000 words.

Especially during the early stages of development, speech and language develop simultaneously. If something occurs to impede their development during this crucial early period, both will be deleteriously influenced. Perhaps the greatest source of difficulty in this respect is a child's being around poor or inadequate models. When adults either do not speak to their youngsters or err in their patterns of speech and language, children will not learn to communicate properly. Other functional causes for communication disorders are poor teaching methods, emotional problems, fatigue, and low energy levels. Problems with the organs involved in verbal communication, as well as those of the central nervous system, can interfere with the establishment and enhancement of speech and language. Hearing loss, brain or nerve damage, seizures, pathology of the vocal cords, problems with the soft or hard palate, swollen adenoids, paralyzed oral structures, growths, and glandular dysfunction are associated with organic weaknesses or malfunctions. These organic deficiencies may result from prenatal, perinatal, or (perhaps) postnatal conditions.

Speech defects are typically classified in terms of (1) articulation problems (sound omissions, substitutions, distortions, or additions), (2) disorders in rhythm or speech flow (stuttering or cluttering), (3) voice deviations (quality, pitch, or volume), (4) cleft palate, (5) cerebral-palsied speech, and (6) those speech defects directly related to hearing problems. Professional speech personnel have over the years developed special types of evaluative procedures to screen for and comprehensively assess the relevant nuances of the various speech disorders. Each type of evaluative procedure, of course, is intimately related to the particular theory to which its author subscribes, as are any treatment approaches that stem from the same points of view. Part V provides a reasonably comprehensive review of the prominent perspectives related to speech disorders for both diagnosis and treatment. The diversity of opinion in these areas among eminent speech pathologists should be studied carefully in order to gain a full appreciation of the state of this very large and important area of special education.

Children with language problems have difficulty dealing with the system of linguistic symbols. This can be manifested in numerous ways, including failures in understanding the meaning of what is said or written, difficulties in relating the meanings of words to the information the child has previously acquired, weaknesses in expressing meaning to others through the written or spoken word, problems in focusing on specifics or in formulating generalizations, disorders of auditory or visual recall, or combinations of any of these.

This area has gained increasing attention during the 1960s as a result of great advances in the field of psycholinguistic testing. The Illinois Test of Psycholinguistic Abilities has been instrumental in fostering research, development, and experimentation in the broad area of language. Specialists in the field of learning disabilities have chosen to include language disorders as part of their general area of expertise. The field is still in a relatively embryonic stage and in serious need of rigorous and extended research and experimentation. Thus it affords numerous opportunities to students who are interested in moving into an area of special education that is undergoing great change at this time.

MOTOR DISORDERS

At birth a physician looks for certain motor behaviors in the infant that together serve to indicate that the child is reasonably healthy. Sucking, swallowing, grasping, the contraction of pupils in reaction to bright lights, and several forms of reflexive behavior are signs that suggest a normal pattern of motor behavior in a newborn. As the child moves toward the first birthday, he makes a tremendous advance in his motor performance. Certain of his basic reflexive behaviors become less obvious, he reaches in response to objects, he moves from side to side and exhibits control of his head and upper body, the fine coordination between fingers and thumbs develops rapidly, and the rudiments of locomotion skills become obvious. Ages 2, 3, and 4 constitute significant landmark periods, during which the child gains ever-increasing control of his body and becomes skilled in executing complex motor behaviors.

As they grow older, most children begin to take on adultlike characteristics in their locomotion. They are typically able to run, skip, hop, jump, and climb steps with facility. Ages 6 and 7 are periods during which the youngster demonstrates relatively mature patterns in fine motor skills, such as in writing, in throwing, and in a wide spectrum of locomotor activities of substantial complexity.

Many motor disorders occur as a result of problems that exist either during the prenatal period or during the process of birth. Relatively few are the result of postnatal difficulties, such as some unusually traumatic experience like amputation, brain tumor, poisoning, or a serious blow to the head.

Of all the types of motor disorders, cerebral palsy is the most common, affecting approximately 1 to 3 per 1,000 school-age youngsters. The original problem is not with the child's muscles; the motor disorder is caused by brain damage that has affected the motor areas of the brain in either a specifically focused or a generalized fashion. The inability of the child to use his extremities and other motor systems results in further complications, weaknesses, and disabilities through disuse. Muscles contract, fibers become excessively tense, and additional deformities result.

There are various forms of cerebral palsy, each of which is theoretically characterized by unique symptomatology. Most astute diagnosticians are able to differentiate whether a given cerebral-palsied child is spastic, athetoid, ataxic, with tremor, or rigid in spite of the fact that the presumably unique characteristics of each in reality overlaps with some of the others. As in the other disability areas, there is enormous variability among children in the degree to which they are involved, the presumed time of onset, the number and location of the extremities influenced, and the extent to which other systems are involved. Cerebral palsy illustrates in an obvious and dramatic way the great difficulty in logically or pragmatically classifying children according to the traditional disability groups and the lack of meaning that such categories have for special education. What is the point in debating whether a child who has hearing problems, is speechless, walks with difficulty, and has trouble learning is mentally retarded, cerebral-palsied, or deaf? Most complex patterns of disability simply cannot be separated into such neat categories. In fact, the cerebral-palsied are so heterogeneous that the category itself has almost no meaning for education and rehabilitation.

These propositions notwithstanding, over the years varied, thoughtful, and consistent attention has been given by several of the professions who have traditionally had concern for the cerebral-palsied child. Speech and hearing specialists, physical therapists, and occupational therapists have led the way in the social and behavioral sciences in designing treatment and management programs for the cerebral-palsied. The theories advocated are as numerous as they are diverse in point of view. For the most part their collective, common focus seems to be on helping the youngster with the problem gain more strength and independence in muscle functioning. Some attack the problem by dealing with the muscles themselves, while other more extreme perspectives suggest working on the child's higher neurological centers. Medical-surgical procedures are used in varying degrees to provide support, remedy deformities, and facilitate the increased usage of the child's motor capabilities.

There is no standard special education program for cerebral-palsied children. Their instructional needs are idiosyncratic, dependent on their characteristics, background, and ambitions. And, of course, the types of special education options available in a community will dictate to a very great extent how well the youngster's educational requirements can be met.

Epilepsy is a condition caused by neurological disturbance that results in seizures of varying intensity and frequency. Motor dysfunction accompanies the seizures in most cases. Muscles become stiff and contract, and violent muscular jerking may occur. In some instances only certain sections of the body may be influenced. The condition occurs rather infrequently (in 1 per 1,000 school-age children), it usually results from early brain damage during the prenatal or perinatal period, and the major treatment is drug therapy. The condition is a perplexing one for many teachers, and especially when the teacher is unaware of how best to deal with a child's seizure.

Spina bifida occurs with the same frequency as epilepsy. The defect is congenital (present at birth) and is characterized by an opening in the child's spine. Neural tissue frequently protrudes and this results in varying degrees of paralysis of the legs. Bladder and sphincter control are often lost.

Muscular dystrophy is a progressive disease in which the muscle tissues degenerate into fat. There are several types of muscular dystrophy. The cause is thought to be hereditary, and because no successful treatment is available the patient usually dies at an early age.

Motor disorders are also the consequence of such infrequent conditions as polio, clubfeet, congenital amputation, and curvature of the spine. The patterns of deviation range from complete to very mild involvement, and remediation in most of the cases can significantly improve the child's level of functioning.

Several evaluative devices have been developed to assess motor development in children. Some of these instruments are for very young children and can be used to detect significant delays in development. Data so collected, then, are used to decide what kind of procedures can be taken to prevent an exacerbation of the condition and, hopefully, to reverse its consequences.

The whole area of motor disorders exemplifies the generic character of exceptionalities. The psychosocial complications, the multiplicity of deviations that are frequently present, the time of onset and the reasons for the disabilities, the process involved in assessment and diagnosis, and the varieties of therapies used are broadly similar to the other forms of exceptionalities we have briefly described. Most exceptional youngsters have functional problems that are complex and that interact among themselves and with the environment in unique ways. It is most important that the special educator recognize these core issues and focus particular attention on factors that have pertinence to the establishment of instructional programs.

SUGGESTED PROJECTS FOR PART I

1 Talk to a university special education instructor, a special education class-room teacher, and several students who do not major in but have heard of special education. Ask them to define "special education." From your interviews, determine the divergence as well as possible common elements in the definitions.

2 This project is one you can begin now and continue throughout your reading of this text. Construct a large chart similar to the one presented in Chapter 2. Make sure the columns and rows are wide enough to create sufficiently large cells in the chart for written entries. As you read the text, begin to fill in the spaces in the chart with appropriate, summarizing terms. For example, you might enter "Rh incompatibility, inadequate nutrition, birth damage" and other such terms in the space created by the intersection of the "Mental Retardation" (TMR subhead) column and the "causes" (medical subhead) row. As you do this throughout your reading, you will be summarizing and detecting interrelationships and differences among the disability categories. Probably, you will wish to alter your entries as you learn more terms and information.

ANNOTATED RESOURCES FOR PART I

Holt, John. *How Children Fail.* New York: Dell, 1964. (Paperback, 223 pages; introduction by Allan Fromme.) This popular book, written much like a diary, is composed of a series of memos and observations of classroom experiences with elementary school children from a teacher's perspective. The contents are divided into four topics: (1) "Strategy"—describing ways children attempt to meet or dodge demands that adults make of them in school. (2) "Fear and failure"—describing the interaction of children with fear and failure and their effect on learning. (3) "Real learning"—delineating differences between what children appear or are expected to know and what they actually know. (4) "How schools fail"—analyzing ways in which schools foster dysfunctional strategies, increase children's fears, stifle learning and creativity, and generally fail to meet the real needs of their students. Holt provides candid examples of classroom interactions to substantiate his criticisms of conventional education and proposes an open classroom and individualized learning as alternatives.

Kanner, Leo. *A History of the Care and Study of the Mentally Retarded.* Springfield, Ill.: Charles C Thomas, 1964. (144 pages and index.) Written in the style of a historical narrative, the book traces chronologically interest and developments in the care of mentally retarded persons. The book describes the first written mention of mentally defective persons (i.e., idiots, fools, imbeciles, dunces) in Greek and Roman literature, the Bible, the Talmud, and the Koran. The works of Pereire, Itard, Guggenbuhl, Seguin, and Howe mark the beginning; from there the history of the study of mental deficiency is traced geographically from Europe to the United States. The remaining chapters are devoted to a description of early periodicals on mental deficiency, the shifting orientation of institutional care, special classes in public schools, quantitative determination of intellectual adequacy, and eugenics and mental retardation. The final chapter updates developments to the 1960s. This is an excellent historical text and presents a broad sociological perspective of the changing patterns of social concern for and care of retarded people.

II
CAUSES AND ASSESSMENT OF EXCEPTIONAL CONDITIONS

When they perceive in a person deviations or variations from what is considered to be normal, most people are interested in knowing what's wrong with the person. Inevitably, the second question they ask is, "Well, why does he have the problem?" or "What caused it?" And then, close on the heels of these questions they ask how bad the problem is and whether or not something can be done about it.

Man has devoted enormous energy and resources to searching out reasons for the occurrence of various phenomena. Among the most interesting areas of inquiry for centuries has been the study of himself and especially the reasons for the various differences among people. There have been enormous swings from genetic to environmental back to genetic rationalizations throughout the ages to explain the major reasons for individual deviations in humans. As theories are advanced and their postulates tested, new theories become predominant and change the philosophical positions of scientists, only to undergo subsequent assessment.

The major orientation of special education has properly been the provision of educational help for children who deviate in some significant way from most other youngsters. Nonetheless, special educators have also been concerned about causes. Evidence of this exists in the types of courses that have been offered in teacher training programs, the heavy medical focus of many fundamental textbooks in special education, the employment of medical terminology in describing and explaining educational problems, and the heavy emphasis given to the need for *each* exceptional child to have a comprehensive medical (often including a neurological) examination on a routine basis. Special educators are in disagreement over the extent to which prospective teachers should learn about medical issues related to exceptional conditions. Some assert that a detailed understanding of biology and the pathology of physical and medical deviations is vital to a well-rounded training program. Others argue that such study is irrelevant for special educators.

Part I presented an overview of the causes, prevention, and assessment of organic malfunctioning. We feel that it is important for special educators to have this overview of medical information as well in order to appreciate the circumstances giving rise to constitutional difficulties. These chapters provide teachers with an awareness of the complexities involved in the medical aspects of exceptionalities and clearly suggest that such problems are within the physician's domain of responsibility. Further, the medical chapters suggest the important role of environmental factors in contributing to exceptionalities. For instance, nutritional problems are within the medical domain but are also clearly environmental and social.

The chapter on psychosocial bases of exceptional conditions provides an overview of conceptions of development with emphasis on developmental disabilities. It discusses several classes of environmental variables that apparently are responsible, alone and in combination, for causing or amplifying handicapping conditions or both. The chapter on psychosocial and educational assessment focuses on the broad strategies special educators employ in evaluating a child's educational status and needs. Emphasis is placed on assessing both the child's performance and the unique characteristics of the environment within which he functions. The considerations included in this chapter are broad enough to be applied to the full range of handicapping conditions in children.

3
MEDICAL BASES OF EXCEPTIONAL CONDITIONS *

* By Cheston M. Berlin, M.D., Professor of Pediatrics and Pharmacology, The Milton S. Hershey Medical Center, The Pennsylvania State University.

STUDY TARGETS

1 Make a table that lists preconception, postconception, and perinatal problems that can occur in the mother and lead to potential problems or handicaps for the child. Adjacent to each problem identify at least one procedure that could be taken to prevent or remedy the condition.

2 List four diagnostic procedures that physicians can use to ascertain the condition of the fetus during the prenatal period.

3 Outline the five factors during the process of delivery that relate to its complexity and the robustness of the infant at birth.

4 Give the dimensions used in conducting an Apgar evaluation of an infant.

5 Write a short essay in which you discuss the prominent postnatal conditions that could cause handicaps in children and the steps that a family could take to minimize their occurrence.

Physicians throughout history have been interested primarily in treating illness. Even in the most recent years in our country, emphasis has swung away from the spectacular achievements in basic biomedical research (of the 1950s and 1960s) to the problem of the delivery of health care, mostly the treatment of the ill. There is evidence that the development of the health maintenance organization (HMO) will increase interest in the *well* patient and, most importantly, in the *prevention* of disease. With the development of vaccines and antibiotics, the scourge of infectious disease, formerly the cause of most of man's medical disasters, has been met, and although certainly not conquered, considerably subdued. Our society is now facing two large problems: chronic disease and the prevention of conditions which may lead to lifelong medical and social handicaps. In our concern for the development, birth, and rearing of children, we now realize that if we can prevent birth defects, mental retardation, metabolic disorders, and behavior disorders, the child also deserves to have an optimal environment in which to grow.

Best estimates indicate that there are about 5 million people in the United States who may be mentally retarded. "Mental retardation" is best defined as *inadequate* intellectual functioning for independent functioning in society. Between 1 percent and 3 percent of all newborn infants (about 120,000 per year) will have a handicap that will place them in this group. An equal number of infants are born each year with significant congenital medical conditions capable of causing other types of medical or social handicaps or both. A great deal has been learned concerning the *causes* of these conditions; more must be learned about their precise mechanisms; and much more must be learned about their *prevention*.

PRENATAL CAUSES OF HANDICAPPING CONDITIONS

PRECONCEPTION

We must look further into the past, beyond prenatal conditions to *preconception*. This is particularly important for the female. The female is born with her lifetime complement of ova; no more will be formed during her life. Hence the ova of a 20-year-old woman attempting pregnancy have lain dormant for 20 years. About 2 million primary (first stage) ova are present in the ovaries of the newborn female. Only about 25,000 of these are usable at the time of puberty. Since only one ovum is expelled each month during the menstrual cycle, only about 350 to 400 ova will be available for fertilization during the entire reproductive cycle of the female. During the 20 years that the ova are dormant prior to attempts to reproduce, ample opportunities exist for these germ cells to be damaged.

The formation of sperm cells in males is entirely different. Not until puberty does an active process begin which results in mature sperm capable of fertilizing ova. These sperm are continually made in the pubescent and adult male; hence potentially damaging events will affect only a small number of the total output of a male. Nonetheless, dangers do exist for the male as well as the female.

Heredity obviously determines a large part of the nature of the developing fetus and the newborn. We know that the genetic material is contained within the nucleus of the cells (sperm and ova) in structures called "chromosomes." Human beings have forty-six of these chromosomes arranged in twenty-three pairs; twenty-two pairs have identical partners and are termed the "autosomes"; one pair determines the sex and are called the "sex chromosomes." Errors in both groups exist and may result in profound handicaps. They will be described later. In the maturation of each germ cell (sperm and ovum), the amount of genetic material is halved so that at fertilization each germ cell contributes one half of the chromosome pair; the fertilized ovum thus has a full complement of chromosome material. One half of each pair comes from the mother and the other half from the father.

Hereditary characteristics are dependent on the genetic information on these chromosomes. Characteristics such as skin color, height, and possibly intelligence are dependent on information from many genes and are termed "polygenic characteristics." Specific conditions such as sickle-cell anemia, phenylketonuria (PKU), and cystic fibrosis are errors in single pairs of genes.

Any exposure which might alter genetic material may not only injure the individual himself but may also be passed on to his offspring. Figure 3-1 illustrates a possible scheme for identifying the consequences of genetic damage.

If the genetic material (DNA) is changed (mutated) three consequences may occur: (1) The damage is so severe that all life processes (metabolism) stop, and the cell dies. (2) The damage is repaired. Information is now available that human cells (like bacterial cells) possess the ability to repair this damage. Perhaps human cells do this constantly throughout the life of the individual. (3) The mutation persists. If the mutation involves the gonadal cells (ova and sperm), there may be difficulty getting pregnant (sterility) or staying pregnant (abortion or miscarriage; the fault may be with the sperm as well as the ovum), or the fetus may have one or more congenital anomalies. If the body cells are affected, the changes *could* lead to the development of malignancy or, if the cells belong to a fetus, the production, again, of a congenital anomaly. In animals (not yet demonstrated in humans) significant genetic damage (e.g., exposure to ionizing radiation) causes premature aging of cells.

All of these changes may be passed on to subsequent generations. Because the human generation time (20–25 years) is so long, the long-term effects of genetic damage are not yet well defined. For example the data being collected on the survivors (and their progeny) of the atomic bomb blasts at Hiroshima and Nagasaki are just now entering the second generation. It now appears that in the survivors the risk of developing solid tumors (discovered in the decade 1960–1970) is increased as well as the risk for developing leukemia (discovered in the decade 1950–1960).

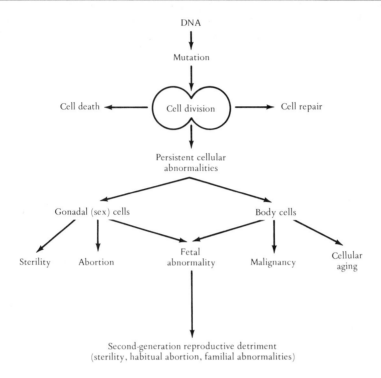

FIGURE 3-1   Schema for identifying consequences of genetic damage.

Currently the information connecting prenatal exposure to drugs, chemicals, or radiation and the occurrence of birth defects is scanty and based largely on animal models. Animal models are not an accurate indication of human biology—e.g., thalidomide is not nearly as toxic in rats as it is in humans.

The same comments apply to preexisting (chronic) disease in humans. Two prominent exceptions are diabetes mellitus (sugar diabetes) and chronic renal (kidney) disease. Women who have diabetes have more difficulty getting pregnant, staying pregnant, and having normal babies (see below). Women with chronic renal disease (which may be undetected *until* pregnancy) have similar problems, although they do not have as many problems getting pregnant as women with diabetes. Men with these two diseases do not appear to have significant reproductive problems, but they have been studied less extensively.

POSTCONCEPTION

The two major areas of concern after conception has occurred are providing the best possible fetal environment and protecting the fetus from direct exposure to potentially damaging influences. Table 3-1 summarizes these influences.

TABLE 3-1   POSTCONCEPTION INFLUENCES ON THE FETUS

Maternal Condition: Interfering with Optimal Fetal Environment	Direct Danger to Fetus
Anemia	Infection
Chronic renal disease	Rubella (German measles)
Diabetes	Syphilis
Cancer	Toxoplasmosis
Hyperemesis (severe vomiting)	Cytomegalic inclusion disease
Nutrition	Herpes
Infection	Tuberculosis
Rh problems	Radiation
Toxemia	Drugs/chemicals

Maternal disease conditions

Chronic renal disease

In mothers with chronic renal disease the placenta fails to function effectively to provide nutrients to the baby. The precise mechanism is unknown. The placenta is smaller than normal and frequently has areas of degeneration and calcium deposits. The baby does not grow properly and, when born, is smaller (and more scrawny) than expected for his gestational age. The pregnancy may be stormy, with high blood pressure (hypertension), edema (retention of water), and presence of protein in the mother's urine. Premature birth (with attendant problems) is common. The danger to the mother may be great around the time of delivery: hypertension and edema may cause a condition known as "toxemia," which when severe may lead to convulsions (eclampsia) and threatens the lives of both mother and fetus. The successful conclusion of such a pregnancy demands meticulous medical supervision and the full cooperation of the patient.

Diabetes

A similar problem exists with the diabetic mother. When pregnancy occurs (sterility may be a problem), spontaneous miscarriage in the first trimester is common. Later in pregnancy strict regulation of the mother's diabetic state is mandatory. In spite of the best possible management the infant may face a considerable array of problems. Premature birth occurs commonly, not only naturally but as a result of early deliberate induction of birth, which may be medically necessary to prevent fetal death. The pregnancy may have to be terminated as early as the eighth fetal month (8 weeks early) and almost always by the ninth fetal month (4 weeks early). These infants run an increased risk of the development of a serious respiratory difficulty (hyaline membrane disease). In addition the baby may have problems with blood sugar just after birth because of overactivity of his pancreas (increased output of insulin). This occurs in response to wide fluctuations in the mother's blood sugar. These babies run an increased risk of the occurrence of congenital abnormalities. Many of the pregnancies must be terminated by Caesarean section, which offers additional hazards (operation and anesthesia) to both mother and infant.

Toxemia

Edema, hypertension, and protein in the urine during the last trimester of pregnancy are evidence of a syndrome called "toxemia." If the condition is severe enough, the blood pressure becomes extreme and convulsions may occur. This condition is known as "eclampsia." Although some of these mothers may have identifiable kidney disease, many do not and the condition may occur without warning. This is only one of many reasons for careful prenatal care. The danger to the fetus is twofold: normal growth may be impaired (because of insufficient placental nourishment) and the treatment, especially at or near the time of birth, may affect the baby. For example, one of the drugs used in the treatment of toxemia-eclampsia is magnesium sulfate. The magnesium ion crosses the placenta easily and quickly. It may (in high enough concentration) seriously depress the newborn's breathing and heart action.

Rh disease

One of the most exciting and satisfying advances in pediatrics and obstetrics has been the description (1932) and definition (1940) of the Rh blood group, and the treatment (1946) and prevention (1964) of Rh disease. All this has been accomplished within the period of 32 years. Humans have many blood types. Although the ABO system (i.e., types A, B, O, and AB) is the major one, there are over twenty other groups, of which the Rh (named after the rhesus monkey, in which it was discovered) is the most important. About 85 percent of Caucasians and almost 100 percent of Negros are Rh "positive" (they have the type); 15 percent of Caucasians are Rh "negative" (do not have the type). Should an Rh-negative woman become pregnant by an Rh-positive man, there is a good chance that the baby will be Rh-positive, like the father. During the first part of any pregnancy there is invariably "leakage" across the placenta from baby to mother of a small number of the baby's red blood cells. This may be enough to stimulate in the Rh-negative mother the production of antibodies against the Rh factor. These antibodies cross the placenta to the baby, attach to the fetus's red blood cells, and render them very unstable and subject to easy destruction.

If this sensitization has occurred and the mother makes sufficient antibodies to cross the placenta, two effects occur. The first is destruction of the baby's red blood cells. This may cause an anemia so severe that the fetus may die from severe anemia and attendant heart failure. The second effect is that destruction of red blood cells releases free hemoglobin (normally carried to the blood stream within the red blood cell) into the circulation, which is promptly broken down. A product of this breakdown is a compound called "bilirubin." All red cells have a definite life span of 120 days. Destruction of these cells and the disposition of the freed bilirubin presents no problem to normal children and adults. It is handled easily in the liver and is excreted, mostly through the bile and hence out with stools (a minor amount is excreted through the urine). The presence of bilirubin in the fetus is not serious, as it crosses the placenta and is well handled by the mother's liver. However, because of the large amount of bilirubin freed in the sensitized newborn and the immaturity of liver function in newborns, large amounts build up in the blood. This bilirubin is very soluble in fats, and since the fat content of brain tissue is very high, significant amounts may be deposited in the brain. This bilirubin is toxic and causes a condition called "kernicterus" ("yellow kernel," so named because the areas of the brain will be stained yellow). Kernicterus causes a clinical condition very similar to some forms of cerebral palsy, with spasticity of certain muscle groups and mental retardation.

Kernicterus may be treated by early removal of the bilirubin by changing the infant's blood (exchange transfusion). This procedure has now been developed to the point where risks are very small. Multiple transfusions may be required; in extreme cases ten to fifteen, usually less than three or five. It is now possible (at much greater risk) to provide the infant with new blood while he is still in the uterus. This must be done when evidence of severe sensitization exists at a time when the fetus is too young to be delivered (before 32 weeks' gestation). A small amount of adult red blood cells are given to the baby by the insertion of a needle through the mother's abdomen, through the uterus, and into the baby's abdominal cavity. Blood is well absorbed by the abdominal cavity, and this added blood will prevent the fetus from dying of severe anemia and heart failure. This procedure is technically very difficult and the hazards to both mother and baby are high.

Prevention of any disease is always safer and easier than treatment. Mothers who have been sensitized by having an Rh-positive baby have in their serum a detectable antibody against Rh-positive red cells. This antibody, which belongs to the gamma globulin class, can be highly purified by laboratory methods. It has now been conclusively demonstrated that giving this antibody (vaccine) to Rh-negative mothers immediately after they have their *first* Rh-positive baby or a miscarriage of an Rh-positive fetus will prevent Rh disease in the next pregnancy. (First pregnancies rarely cause Rh disease even if the fetus is Rh-positive. If the disease does occur in a "first" pregnancy, then prior sensitization has probably occurred, either by a miscarriage or the administration of mismatched blood.) This vaccine was first introduced in the mid-1960s and has resulted in a virtual disappearance of the disease. However, there are still cases occurring in mothers who were sensitized before the vaccine was available or who failed to receive it after a pregnancy or miscarriage or who have unknowingly received Rh-positive blood.

Rh disease is not the only cause of increased bilirubin in newborn infants. The list of causes is very long and includes infection, incompatibility in other blood groups (especially the ABO groups), drugs, and prematurity. These cases can usually be handled by the judicious use of exchange transfusions or exposure of the infant to high-intensity light, which hastens the destruction of bilirubin in the circulation before it is absorbed by brain tissue.

It has been estimated that there are at least 200,000 infants per year in the United States who risk developing Rh disease. That we are now in a position to prevent all cases of Rh incompatibility between mother and infant must rank with the development of the polio vaccine as one of the great achievements in pediatrics in the last 20 years.

Nutrition

Perhaps the most important and controversial issue in producing a healthy baby is the nutrition of the mother. There is now abundant experimental evidence in animals that failure to provide adequate caloric intake and adequate protein to the mother has profound effects on the offspring. These effects are in two areas: body size and brain development. It is now known that the growth of a fetus is of two types—first (in time): an increase in the number of cells of the body (hyperplasia); second: an increase in cell size (hypertrophy). Later in pregnancy and during postnatal life, growth occurs chiefly by an increase in the *size* of cells—i.e., very few new cells are made; the existing cells simply get bigger. If the mother is deprived of calories, protein, or both, the offspring are small; and if the deprivation is severe enough, they remain small. This is critical where the brain is concerned. The sensitive phase appears to be the increase in number of cells (hyperplasia). Poor maternal nutrition results in a fetal brain (as well as other organs) with a markedly reduced number of cells. This number *cannot* be increased by postnatal feeding: there appears to be a point during gestation after which attempts to reverse the effects of malnutrition are fruitless. This fact has been demonstrated in experiments with animals but is less well documented in humans. The chief reason for this is that populations likely to be undernourished are also likely to live in socioeconomic conditions detrimental to the growing infant. Most human studies have focused on areas in Central and South America. Mothers in these studies are deprived of adequate protein and calories and do give birth to infants with significantly reduced birth weights compared to well-nourished populations. Autopsy studies are few as yet but do show that the brains of infants whose mothers were undernourished are smaller and do have fewer cells than the brains of infants whose mothers were not undernourished. However, follow-up studies of infants born to malnourished mothers are inconclusive because such children live in an environment in which infectious disease, poverty, malnutrition, and psychological neglect are common and important factors in the child's intellectual development.

The current literature on the problem of malnutrition during pregnancy and its outcome is becoming increasingly voluminous. Much of the work has been done on animals, but some tentative conclusions with regard to humans can be made.

1 The most important factor seems to be the mother's state of nutrition *before* pregnancy. The better nourished she is prior to conception, the less effect malnutrition has during pregnancy. There was a severe famine (indi-

vidual intake less than 750 calories per day) in parts of Holland during 7 months of 1944–1945. A recent study of males (age 19 at time of study) whose mothers were pregnant in 1944–1945 showed no difference in mental performance between the group whose mothers were malnourished during pregnancy and the group whose mothers were in another part of Holland which did not suffer so severely.

2 Birth weight is related to weight gain by mothers during pregnancy.

3 Birth weight is related to placental weight. Small placentas may be caused by poor nutrition, smoking, infections, and chronic maternal disease.

4 In humans, the spurt in brain growth probably extends from mid-pregnancy to the postnatal age of 2 years. Interference with this spurt of growth at *any* time within this range *may* cause a permanent decrease in brain size which *may* lead to suboptimal mental performance. It is also widely believed that, within limits, adequate nutrition may compensate for deprivation if instituted before the end of the spurt in brain growth. There is an optimal time to guarantee adequate brain growth; this opportunity may occur only during a short period of time.

5 Postnatal influences, especially environment and socioeconomic conditions, may be the major factor determining whether and to what extent malnutrition affects intellectual function. Good nutrition is not a guarantee that all will be well; but it is a start and is, logistically and financially, comparatively easy to achieve. Table 3-2, for example, illustrates how prudent buy-

TABLE 3-2   COSTS OF PROTEIN IN FOOD

Food	Protein Content (%)	Cost per 1/3 RDA (Cents)
Milk—powdered	3.5	8.5
Cottage cheese	19.5	9.2
Dried lima beans	20.7	9.7
Peanut butter	26.1	10.0
Tuna, canned	29.0	17.0
American processed cheese	23.0	19.0
Milk—whole	3.5	19.0
Milk—skimmed	3.5	19.0
Chicken	20.3	20.0
Eggs	12.8	22.0
Hamburger	22.0	23.0
Fish	18.7	23.0
Natural cereal	12.0	25.0
Rib roast	24.0	31.0
Frankfurter	11.7	34.0
Steak—porterhouse	23.0	36.0
Pork chops	23.0	39.0

RDA (Recommended Dietary Allowances) per day is calculated as 60 grams for women and 65 for men. With three items from the first ten foods on the list, total day cost for an adequate intake can be less than 60 cents. Costs based on prices in August 1973.

ing may purchase the most protein at least cost (it may be necessary to educate parents in this regard).

Direct dangers to the fetus

Infection

Since 1960 it has become apparent that of the infections that cause damage to the fetus, four intrauterine infections are responsible for the most damage. These four are rubella (German measles), syphilis, toxoplasmosis, and cytomegalic inclusion disease (CID).

Rubella is a virus infection which causes very mild disease in children or adults but catastrophic results in the fetus if maternal infection occurs within the first 3 months of pregnancy—the earlier in these 3 months, the more certain and more severe the damage. It may cause fetal death or leave the infant with a mild hearing loss. The outcome is more likely to be somewhere between these extremes. Virtually every organ system can be involved, singly or in combination. The most common defects are mental retardation, cataracts, hearing loss, congenital heart disease, and small stature (height and weight). Once the mother becomes infected with the virus, spread to the fetus cannot be prevented. The chance of having an affected offspring is so high if infection occurs early in the first trimester (at least 60 percent in the first month) that many parents will choose to have a therapeutic abortion. Rehabilitative procedures are certainly possible and may be quite effective: eye surgery, glasses, hearing aids (not very effective as the deafness is due to nerve damage, not conductive damage), and surgery for the congenital heart disease. Fortunately, we can prevent this tragedy completely: the rubella vaccine is effective and safe. Every woman of childbearing age should know whether she has had rubella. She can find out through a simple blood test (rubella titer). A history of having had rubella is unreliable: many viruses unrelated to rubella may produce similar symptoms. If the blood test shows that the woman has *not* had rubella she should receive the vaccine. This vaccine must not be given to pregnant women and pregnancy should be avoided for 2 months after administration of the vaccine. The determination of the rubella status should be part of the health supervision of all adolescent girls or should be included in the premarital examination. Rubella babies should become as rare as acute poliomyelitis.

Syphilis is an infection caused by a bacterium called a "spirochete" (because of its corkscrew shape under the microscope). When infection is present in the mother, the spirochetes cross the placenta and invade all fetal tissue. Fetal infections probably occur after the fifth month of gestation. Syphilis is a particularly treacherous disease because initially all organ systems may be involved (including the brain) and this involvement may not be apparent until years have elasped. The time of the appearance of some symptoms may be judged from the size of the infecting inoculum transferred across the placenta from mother to fetus. With a heavy infection, the infant may exhibit (during the first 2 months of infancy) persistent watery nasal discharge, enlarged liver and spleen, skin rash, eye changes, and bone changes (seen by X ray only). Very frequently these symptoms are ignored or are entirely missed, and the child appears at a later age with well-established destructive lesions which may involve *any* organ system, especially the brain.

Like rubella this disease is 100 percent preventable. Unlike rubella it is also treatable should an infant be born to an infected mother. Blood tests for the presence of syphilis must be done on all pregnant women; they should be done on *each* pregnancy and are best performed twice during pregnancy. A woman with a negative blood test in her first trimester of pregnancy may be infected during her seventh month with disastrous consequences to the fetus.

Newborn infants should have their cord blood tested and if the test is positive, they should receive treatment. Penicillin is still very effective and the drug of choice for both mother and infant. Early treatment will usually prevent permanent damage.

Toxoplasmosis may be a relatively mild illness in adults: slight fever, malaise, occasional skin rash. The illness is similar to a mild case of infectious mononucleosis. Affected infants are born with significant involvement of the brain and eye. Serious mental retardation may result. The only prevention possible is the avoidance by the mother of any infectious disease in other people (especially children). There is a drug treatment currently under investigation at several medical centers; it is too early to predict whether such treatment will prevent permanent damage.

Cytomegalic inclusion disease is very similar to rubella. However, maternal illness may not be apparent. The infant may have severe involvement of the brain and eye; other organ systems are usually not involved. No prevention (except avoidance of infection) and no treatment are known.

Research work is being done which may lead to the development of vaccines for both toxoplasmosis and cytomegalic inclusion disease. Should they become available, all four of the common prenatal infections will be preventable or treatable, or both. A large proportion (perhaps the majority) of cases of significant mental retardation will disappear. The incidence of these prenatal infections may be as high as 1 in 700 to 1 in 1,000 in some populations.

Two infections occur not during pregnancy but during the actual process of birth. These are herpes and tuberculosis. Herpes is best known as the virus responsible for cold sores or fever blisters (at the corners of the mouth and around the nostrils). Another type causes ulcers on the genitalia and is liable to affect the infant as he comes down the birth canal. The brain is severely affected and hence this disease in newborns is rapidly fatal; should recovery occur, the damage is profound. Herpes in the newborn may be prevented by recognition of the disease in the mother (good prenatal care) and delivery of the child by Caesarean section.

If a mother has active tuberculosis, the infant must be separated from the mother after birth and closely observed for signs of tuberculosis. The mother must be treated and the infant repeatedly tested. Should tuberculosis occur, prompt treatment with drugs is effective. Should the infant acquire tuberculosis and not be treated, the illness may be severe and may terminate in tuberculosis meningitis (infections of the membranes lining the brain and spinal cord).

It should be appreciated that all the above infectious agents multiply very well in fetal and newborn tissues. The diseases are more severe than in adults, and should the infant recover, permanent damage may be profound.

Radiation

Exposure of pregnant animals to large amounts of radiation in the form of X rays predictably causes severe congenital anomalies in the offspring. The evidence for humans is less sharp, particularly with regard to what amounts are hazardous. Exposure to large amounts in the human has caused bone defects and microcephaly (small head and, invariably, mental retardation). There is vigorous debate over how much exposure is dangerous. For example, some investigators claim the exposure of the pregnant mother to a single abdominal X ray significantly increases the chances of the infant's acquiring a malignancy. These arguments are based on the statistics in thousands of cases. However, there is argument about whether the type of statistical analysis used is correct. Nonetheless, everyone agrees that the pregnant woman should avoid *all* X ray exposure unless *absolutely* necessary. This would include routine chest and dental X rays.

Because of the tragic experience of Hiroshima and Nagasaki we know that exposure to *atomic* radiation is also hazardous to the fetus. Pregnant women close to the center of the explosion had a very high rate of spontaneous miscarriage. A high percentage of the babies subsequently born alive had microcephaly. It is still too early to determine what long-term effects this exposure might have. It is important to realize that a major cause of our ignorance of any environmental effect on either mature or fetal man is the long human generation time: 20 to 25 years. For example we are now in the second generation after Hiroshima. It may well take a hundred years of careful observation to determine how damaging a chemical or an X ray may be.

The effects of other types of radiation—e.g., cosmic rays, microwaves, low-frequency radio waves—are completely unknown. They appear not to have a significant effect at doses recently studied in both man and animals.

Drugs and chemicals

The list of drugs which are definitely known of a certainty to cause structural fetal damage are to date few. They are listed in Table 3-3. Most of these compounds are known to interfere chemically with the genetic material (DNA). The first four drugs are used in the treatment of various malignancies. It was established very early in the development of these drugs that they could cause fetal damage. Case reports are not common because most women with cancer do not become pregnant, and if they do, they frequently are unable to complete the pregnancy. However, the drug Methotrexate is now being used

TABLE 3-3   DRUGS KNOWN TO CAUSE FETAL DAMAGE

Drug	Medical Use	Damage
Methotrexate	Treatment of cancers	Multiple bony anomalies
Busulfan	Treatment of cancers	Multiple anomalies
Aminopterin	Treatment of cancers	Miscarriage; any major congenital anomalies may occur
Cyclophosphamide	Treatment of cancers	Abnormal digits and palate
Thalidomide	Sedative	Anomalies of heart, eye, ear, limbs, kidney, intestinal tract
Diphenylhydantoin	Epilepsy	Cleft palate (risk twice normal)
Progestational compounds	Prevention of miscarriage	Masculinization of female baby
Diethylstilbesterol	Prevention of miscarriage	Risk of female baby's developing vaginal cancer in young adulthood

to treat a skin condition called "psoriasis." This condition does not interfere with pregnancy and the patient may "forget" she is taking a drug.

The thalidomide story is an unparalleled catastrophe of human pharmacology. This drug was developed as an effective and safe sedative (which it is). It was distributed widely in Western Europe in the late 1950s and early 1960s. A very small amount was distributed in this country for clinical trials. In 1960 and 1961 there were published many disturbing reports of children born with a heretofore rare abnormality called "phocomelia"—absence of part (or parts) of a limb (or limbs); the remaining limb (or limbs) may be disfigured. The limbs resembled flippers. Other defects are known: deafness, abnormal ears and eyes, congenital heart disease, abnormal kidneys, and narrowed intestinal tract. Connection was rapidly made with maternal ingestion of thalidomide during early pregnancy. In fact, the "critical period" of ingestion is extremely narrow: between the thirty-fifth and fiftieth days from the beginning of the last menstrual cycle. Only two animal species are similarly affected by this drug: the rabbit and the monkey. It is difficult or impossible to produce congenital abnormalities in any other animal. This tragedy may result in the requirement that any drug which may be given during pregnancy must first be tested in the monkey. Thousands of these babies were born in Europe before the connection was determined. The drug was never officially on the market in the United States. Thus, there are less than twenty affected American babies and many of these were born in families who acquired the drug while in Europe. It appears that this drug is virtually 100 percent capable of causing fetal damage if ingested during the critical period. Only one infant is known who escaped damage when his mother ingested the drug during the critical period.

Besides the chemical compounds listed in Table 3-3, there are many other drugs of which suspicion is high but definite proof lacking. Everyone does agree that the safest course is to avoid, whenever possible, the ingestion of *all* drugs and exposure to any chemical, whether prescribed or purchased over the counter.

Genetic defects

Earlier in this chapter mention was made of the critical role of genetic material (DNA). This material is the chemical material in chromosomes. It determines not only what information is passed on to daughter cells during cell division but also directs the chemical processes within the cells. The human embryo begins with the fusion of ovum and sperm. When they divide, each daughter cell should receive an equivalent amount of genetic material. This is made possible by the doubling of the chromosomes just prior to cell division, with equal numbers going to each daughter cell. If this fails to occur the result is unequal distribution of genetic material, which may be disastrous to the embryo. Abnormalities arising in this fashion are classified as "chromosomal abnormalities."

Although each daughter cell may receive equal *amounts* of genetic material (equal numbers of chromosomes), the genes transmitted may not be normal. Very small deviation from normal, perhaps only a single small chemical alteration, may cause a severe disease (e.g., sickle-cell anemia). The group of diseases caused by abnormal genetic material are known as "metabolic errors" (inborn errors of metabolism). This name is used because the normal chemistry (metabolism) of the cell is altered by the inability to provide or dispose of a critical biochemical or protein.

Chromosomal errors   Each human cell possesses 23 pairs of chromosomes (the total number is 46). There are 22 pairs of structurally identical chromosomes (as seen by the microscope—a rather crude tool for genetic investigation). These are called "autosomal" chromosomes. One pair has nonidentical halves: one member is the X chromosome (female), the other the Y chromosome (male). The combination of two X chromosomes (XX) determines a female; XY determines a male. YY is unknown. For identification, the chromosomes are placed in groups according to their configuration. (See Figure 3-2.)

Should cell division (during embryo growth) result in an unequal distribution of chromosomes, one cell will contain, for example, 47 chromosomes, the other 45. If this occurs very early, e.g., during maturation of the ovum before fertilization, then all further cells will have the same abnormal number of chromosomes. As an example, an ovum (or sperm) just before fertilization should have 23 chromosomes (1 from each pair) to match with the 23 from the sperm (or ovum). Suppose the ovum has 24: 1 complete pair plus 22 single chromosomes. Fertilization occurs with a normal sperm (23 single chromosomes). The fertilized egg (which now begins to produce daughter cells) has 24 plus 23 or 47 chromosomes: one "pair" has 3 instead of 2 chromosomes (called

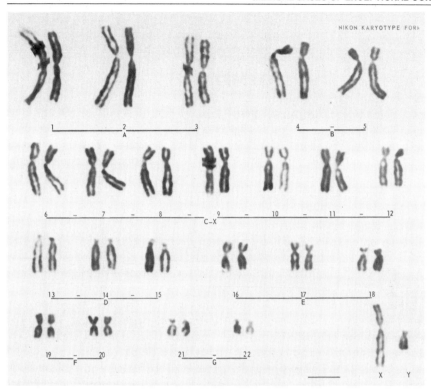

FIGURE 3-2 Chromosome groupings (karyotype).

"trisomy"). If this occurs in Group F, a mongoloid child results. There are now many examples of patients with chromosome numbers in excess of the normal 46. Only a few common ones will be mentioned.

Group D—3 chromosomes
Group E—3 chromosomes
Group G—3 chromosomes

These patients have severe structural anomalies.

Group D and Group E trisomy show very severe changes usually incompatible with life past the immediate newborn period, although a few may survive to 1 year of age.

Group G results in mongolism (or Down's Syndrome). The major components of this syndrome are typical facies due to folds (epicanthal) of skin over the medial aspect of the eye, a round face, a flattened head (especially in the back), and depressed bridge of the nose. The patients have very poor motor tone (they are "floppy") during infancy. They are small for their age. Mental retardation is virtually always present although its severity varies widely. A large proportion have congenital heart disease. Numerous other structural problems may be present. These children always need special medical and educational care. It is not possible to predict in infancy the degree of permanent retardation: requirements for schooling may change in a single individual's life span.

A fertilized ovum may contain fewer than 46 chromosomes. The only one of clinical importance is the female "pair" of sex chromosomes. If one of these is missing, the resulting "pair" of sex chromosomes has only one X chromosome. Although these children appear to be female, their ovaries are not developed; they are infertile and puberty does not occur. The latter fact is frequently what brings them to the physician. The administration of sex hormones will allow the sexual maturation to occur, but infertility is permanent. The therapeutic induction of sexual maturation is critical for psychological well-being in these patients and allows gender identification. Mental retardation does occur in a number of cases.

The sex chromosomes contain numerous other errors resulting in 3 or more chromosomes. A Y chromosome must be one of these chromosomes to confer maleness. Most individuals with 3 or more sex chromosomes both are sterile and have some degree of mental retardation.

Although the number of chromosomes may be normal there may be changes in their structures—e.g., breaks, rings, and pieces missing. The consequences may not be obvious, but these changes are a source of great concern because of animal and bacterial experiments that do show changes in subsequent generations. This explains the concern over exposure to ionizing radiation and certain chemicals, which in certain doses are known to disrupt the normal chromosome. The best rule for preventing possible problems is to permit as little exposure as is consistent with medical needs.

Metabolic (chemical) errors   Chromosomal errors result from defects in chromosomes visible with the microscope. This means that substantial amounts of genetic material are abnormal and it is not surprising that the defects are profound. However, there may exist very small defects in genetic material "visible" only at the molecular level; these defects usually result in the inability of the individual to carry out successfully the normal chemical processes of life. The system for providing energy for these processes is known as "metabolism." Since the defects are inherited (wholly or in part), the group is known as "inborn errors of metabolism." These inherited metabolic errors now form a large group—perhaps nearly 2,000. They involve errors in every aspect of the body's chemistry: proteins, amino acids, fats, sugars, vitamins, bile salts, and hormones. Table 3-4 lists a few of the more common inherited metabolic errors.

Many of these metabolic errors can be treated—e.g., insulin for diabetes, special diet for PKU and galactosemia, and blood transfusions for the large group of hemoglobin disorders. Early diagnosis and treatment is mandatory to prevent permanent changes. PKU is an excellent example. A simple blood test (Guthrie) is available for diagnosis in the newborn period. If the disease is

TABLE 3-4   COMMON INHERITED METABOLIC ERRORS

Disease	Compound Involved	Consequence
Phenylketonuria (PKU)	Phenylalanine (too much)	Mental retardation, seizures, eczema.
Sickle-cell anemia	Hemoglobin (wrong one made)	Poor delivery of oxygen to tissues. Abnormal red blood cells are easily destroyed by body and clog blood vessels.
Tay Sachs disease	Ganglioside (fatty substance in brain)	Excess stored in brain. Deterioration of all brain function leading to death in first or second year.
Diabetes	Insulin (protein) not made	High blood sugar. Possible early development of degenerative changes in nearly all body tissues.
Galactosemia	Galactose (sugar) increased in blood	Mental retardation, cataracts, liver disease.

confirmed, prompt institution of a diet low in phenylalanine (the compound which is not properly handled and which accumulates) will, in most cases, prevent mental retardation. With other diseases, such as Tay Sachs disease, treatment does not exist and attention is currently being focused on prevention.

For a small number of metabolic diseases, currently about thirty-five, it is possible to detect whether a woman is carrying an affected fetus. Amniocentesis is a procedure whereby a small amount of amniotic fluid is withdrawn from the uterus through a needle in the mother's abdominal wall. Chemical analysis of this fluid and the cells suspended in this fluid can determine if the fetus is affected. If it is, therapeutic abortion may be elected to terminate the pregnancy. The ethical issues involved in this area are enormous and beyond the scope of the discussion here. These issues plus the rather small number of diseases which can be so identified argue very strongly for another approach to prevention or treatment, or both.

PERINATAL CAUSES OF HANDICAPPING CONDITIONS

The process of birth is the single major challenge to the newborn. In a matter of minutes he must surrender his fetal protection in the uterus for the hostile outside environment. The processes of labor and delivery and the adaptation to self-support are a time of maximal danger. Damage that occurs during this period is frequently severe and irreversible. All of the conditions that have been discussed previously are dependent on prenatal events. The following problems occur during or after the birth process.

PREMATURITY

This is an unfortunately common event occurring between ten and twelve times per 1,000 births. Many factors are known which predispose to prematurity.* These include maternal illness (diabetes, kidney disease), more than one fetus, previous pregnancy resulting in a premature infant, Rh sensitization, incompetent cervix, and premature rupture of membranes. Trauma is rarely a cause. Very often the cause is not apparent. Premature infants born at between thirty-five and thirty-seven weeks' gestation have an excellent outlook. As prematurity increases, the immediate complications become more of a problem, especially the most common cause of mortality and morbidity in all newborns: hyaline membrane disease. This disease affects the lungs and is caused by the formation of a membrane between the lung capillaries and the tiny air sacs (alveoli), which markedly interferes with the passage of oxygen *into* the blood and carbon dioxide (waste) *out of* the body. The amount of oxygen in the baby's blood may fall to very low levels, causing brain damage which is not reversible. Before the late 1960s, the results of treatment of severe hyaline membrane disease were discouraging. Mortality was high and survivors frequently had brain damage of varying degrees. In one of the most exciting advances in pediatrics in the last 30 years, a breathing method has been developed which allows not only markedly increased salvage of these infants but very encouraging follow-up results in the neurological status of these infants. In spite of this procedure, prevention is obviously preferable. One very simple prevention measure is prenatal care. Adequate prenatal care was shown in a recent Pennsylvania study to cut the prematurity rate by a factor of 3—from 35 to 6 cases per 1,000 births.

Infants born *later* than their due date (postmature) are also at risk, but for a different reason. They rarely have lung problems but may have marked difficulty with their blood-sugar levels. Blood sugar is a very necessary source of energy for the brain. Low blood sugar can be as devastating as low oxygen content in the blood. However, even postmature infants without detectable decreases in blood sugar may have neurological problems in later life—especially learning disabilities. Adequate monitoring of blood sugar is mandatory for such infants.

A third group of infants is born with birth weight much lower than expected for their gestational age (small for date). They may also have blood-sugar problems and are at increased risk like the postmature babies. For example an infant born at term normally weighs about 3,000 grams (6½ pounds). An infant "small for date" (term baby) may weigh 2,000 grams (4½ pounds). This implies marked difficulty with placental nutrition; it may occur with or without maternal disease. These infants also must be closely moni-

* A premature infant is usually defined as a baby born at less than thirty-seven weeks' gestation (normal gestation is forty weeks). Mothers may be uncertain or incorrect about their last menstrual period; the determination is then done on physical examination of the infant. Any infant of less than twenty-six weeks' gestation is considered "immature" or "previable."

tored, especially for decreases in blood sugar. Early feedings may help prevent problems.

A fourth group of infants is very large for their gestational age. A term baby of a mother who is a diabetic may weigh 4,500 grams (10 pounds) or more. They are also at increased risk for low blood sugar. This may be due to the baby's increased circulating insulin in response to the diabetic mother's high blood sugar. Often the mother does not have diabetes or even prediabetes and the cause is obscure. These infants can be well managed with early feeding and careful following of blood sugar. If they have a smooth neonatal course, they appear not to be at increased risk for later problems.

MECHANICS OF LABOR
Uterine contraction should be a smooth process. The fetus must continue to receive its blood supply from the mother during labor; prolonged or severely irregular contractions will compromise this blood flow. Obstruction to the outlet of the uterus (fibroids) if severe will necessitate delivery by Caesarean section. Should the placenta be abnormally placed over the cervical outlet, immediate Caesarean section is mandatory to prevent a catastrophe.

PRESENTATION OF THE FETUS
This refers to the position of the fetus within the birth canal. Head first is the most common and safest presentation; but the head should be so positioned that the top (vertex) comes first. Face or brow presentation may result in very high forces being applied to the head, with resultant skin and occasionally intracranial bleeding. Breech presentations (rump or feet first) need special handling. Transverse presentations (long axis of baby is at right angles to the outlet), if not corrected to a head or breech, demand Caesarean section.

LOCATION OF PLACENTA
If the placenta lies over the outlet, as mentioned above, immediate Caesarean section is necessary to avoid massive bleeding—a disaster to mother and infant alike. A partial placental praevia may also cause significant bleeding if the margins are torn before the baby is safely out.

RUPTURE OF MEMBRANES
The membranes surrounding the fetus must, of course, be ruptured before delivery can occur. In fact, this rupturing frequently stimulates the onset of labor. Rupture usually occurs near the time of delivery or within the previous 24 hours. The amniotic fluid thus released is normally a clear, amber-colored fluid. It is also an excellent culture medium for bacteria. Prolonged rupture of the membranes (longer than 24 hours before delivery) places both mother and infant at high risk for infection. This infection may cause very serious and irreversible damage to the baby, as will be explained later. If a fetus is subjected to unusual stress within the uterus, he may respond by defecating. The

content of the bowel at this time of development is a black substance called "meconium." Meconium-stained amniotic fluid is green-black in color and signals intrauterine distress and hence a high-risk delivery.

ANALGESIA AND ANESTHESIA

Drugs given to women in labor and delivery for relief of pain are nearly all depressants of brain function. Because they all cross the placenta with ease, the fetus also receives and is influenced by them. Should the dose be sufficiently high, or the period from administration to birth sufficiently short, the infant's central nervous system will be depressed. He may not be able to breathe on his own and will then require an antidote, prompt respiratory support, or both.

MULTIPLE BIRTHS

Multiple pregnancies do carry increased risk to the offspring, primarily in the area of prematurity. Twins are more likely to be born prematurely than single fetuses and thus be subject to all the risks of prematurity (see above). In addition one twin may "steal" most of the placental nutrition and be significantly larger than the other. The smaller twin is at increased risk for a number of problems. The "steal" may affect blood supply during labor and one twin will be anemic, the other plethoric. Both are hazardous conditions: anemia may be severe enough to cause circulatory failure, and plethora may be severe enough to cause clotting within blood vessels, especially in the brain.

CONDITIONS IN THE INFANT
Fetal monitoring

Technology now exists to monitor the status of the infant during labor. With relatively simple means both the fetus's heart rate and intrauterine pressure can be continually monitored. When disturbing patterns occur certain maneuvers can be used or the delivery speeded up, or, if necessary, prompt Caesarean section can be performed. This technique has been invaluable in the prevention of neonatal problems.

During the actual process of delivery of the infant all of the above are important. In addition, the application of forceps may be necessary. Forceps are used commonly and usually skillfully. However, it must be recognized that since they are applied to the head, very hard pressure or twists may cause physical damage to the face, the nerves outside the cranium, and the brain and upper spinal cord. Likewise, the use of anesthesia during this final part of the birth process may cause significant depression of the central nervous system, since the infant alone will be responsible for handling the anesthetic agent. Caesarean section represents a distinct hazard because of the use of general anesthesia; most sections are well performed in less than 10 minutes' anesthesia time.

Apgar scoring

In an attempt to evaluate the status of a newborn's response to adaption to extrauterine life, Dr. Virginia Apgar in 1953 developed a series of five clinical observations which would indicate the well-being of a newborn infant. They are:

1 Heart rate
2 Respiratory effort
3 Muscle tone
4 Reflex irritability
5 Skin color

Each response is graded 0, 1, or 2 (0 = "absent," 2 = "normal") for a total score of 10. The evaluation is done at 1, 3, and 5 minutes after delivery. A score of 7 or under is cause for concern; low 1- and 3-minute scores might indicate problems in the immediate newborn period. A low 5-minute score, especially if below 5 has now been shown to be associated with a significant increase in abnormal neurological findings at 1 year of age. This large study is ongoing and further data will indicate how well the Apgar score may indicate increased risk for possible handicapping situations.

NEONATAL CAUSES OF HANDICAPPING CONDITIONS

The following are the more common problems that might occur after birth to cause permanent damage to the infant. Most of these have been mentioned above:

1 Age of the fetus
2 Size of the fetus (considering age)
3 Effects of maternal disease (e.g., lowering of blood sugar in the infant of a diabetic mother)
4 Hyaline membrane disease
5 Rh disease
6 Infection
7 Metabolic disease (inherited disease, liver or kidney damage)
8 Bleeding (deficiency of various clotting factors)

It is evident that division into preconception, prenatal, perinatal, and neo-natal condition can be artificial. Many illnesses exist throughout more than one of these time periods. It is useful to remember that they all (especially those causing brain damage) may operate through one ultimate mechanism: inability of the young, growing, and vulnerable central nervous system to receive adequate energy for normal chemical processes. In brief there are three basic mechanisms of this damage: lack of oxygen, bleeding into the brain and spinal cord, and direct physical damage. It should also be apparent that with proper medical attention most of these problems can be prevented or greatly minimized. The following procedures will ensure the best possible outcome of a pregnancy:

1 Adequate and early prenatal care
2 Screening for possible infectious disease
3 Good maternal nutrition *before, during,* and *after* pregnancy
4 Avoidance of drugs and chemicals during pregnancy
5 Judicious use of medications during labor
6 Close supervision of the newborn

POSTNATAL CAUSES OF HANDICAPPING CONDITIONS

Late detection of handicapping conditions does not always mean that the biologic result occurred *after* birth. Usually it means late recognition of a condition present before or since birth. However, certain conditions do occur after birth and may have severe consequences, even death. By far the most common is physical trauma. Accidents have always been by far the commonest cause of death in children of all ages; they are also the commonest cause of permanent disabilities. The resulting handicap is every bit as real as that of the child brain-damaged at birth. It is also usually more preventable. These accidents usually cause damage to limbs, head, or spinal cord. The rehabilitation of the children thus damaged requires an intensive multidiscipline team approach.

A smaller number of children suffer permanent disability from diseases—e.g., infection, degenerative nerve diseases, and late onset of genetic disease. Proper child health supervision has eliminated many of the scourges—e.g., there is now no excuse for a child's contracting acute poliomyelitis. We are thankful that there are now fewer than twenty cases of polio per year in this country. Measles is a severe disease, seldom fatal but frequently crippling. The vaccine should, if widely used, eliminate this disease also. Prompt, judicious use of antibiotics should control most of the bacterial illness that may lead, if untreated, to permanent disability—e.g., meningitis and rheumatic fever. The degenerative diseases are not approachable by any means yet known. Genetic diseases, such as muscular dystrophy, are still puzzles. Much more research will be needed to put the pieces into place.

Two especially common handicapping conditions should be mentioned to illustrate many of the above points.

Cerebral palsy is a term used to describe brain damage resulting in spasticity of muscles and (usually) coexisting mental retardation. The cause is usually direct physical damage or deprivation of oxygen to the brain. The cause may be set early in pregnancy with poor nutrition or at the time of delivery with a very hard labor and forceps damage. The range of damage may be great—

from severe disability requiring total care to slight spasticity in one limb. There is also dissociation of the muscle involvement from the mental damage. Some children are so severely crippled as to be unable to walk or even push a wheelchair; yet they may not be truly retarded. The term has fallen into disuse among some pediatricians, because it is vague and because better understanding of the causes has resulted in more precise diagnostic labels.

"Hyperactivity" is a term which should be reserved for the child with extreme motor activity, poor or absent attention span, marked learning difficulties, and a great degree of responsiveness to the use of stimulant drugs (such as amphetamine). Its cause is unknown. Organic brain damage in these children is not usually detectable. Nervous, fidgety children do not have this problem and the widespread use of drugs for this type of "hyperactivity" is to be deplored. The diagnosis should be made by a pediatrician conversant with this problem and not the parent, the teacher, or the school nurse.

The explosion of medical knowledge within the last 30 years has equipped us with very powerful tools to prevent most of the handicapping conditions of childhood. Great strides have already been made in the elimination of certain diseases. Sophisticated expertise is available to the pediatrician and the obstetrician to identify and treat potentially damaging illness. We need only two conditions to assure each developing child of the most fertile social, intellectual, and physical environment: continued research into the unsolved problems, and provision of known medical solutions to all parts of the population.

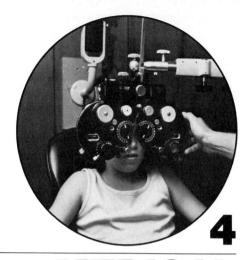

4

MEDICAL ASSESSMENT OF EXCEPTIONAL CONDITIONS *

STUDY TARGETS

1 In a series of short sentences, list the factors that physicians consider when taking a history during a medical assessment, and briefly describe the reasons for considering each.

2 Prepare an outline for an oral report to be given to a group of students just entering college in which you (a) list the major dimensions involved in the physical assessment of a child by the physician, (b) specify the general signs that lead to the suspicion that an abnormality may exist, and (c) conclude with a brief statement about the relevance of the medical assessment to special education.

Usually, the family physician or the pediatrician is the first professional consulted in the medical investigation of a handicapping condition. The assess-

* By Cheston M. Berlin, M.D., Professor of Pediatrics and Pharmacology, The Milton S. Hershey Medical Center, The Pennsylvania State University.

ment begins with a careful history. The patient is then examined. Finally, tests—both laboratory and achievement tests—are ordered, depending upon the findings of the history and the physical examination.

THE HISTORY

The medical history of an individual has always been very crucial to medical care. It directs the physician both to possible diagnoses and to avenues of further investigation. In some instances a careful history can directly result in the diagnosis.

FAMILY HISTORY

A handicapping condition may have had its beginnings before the conception of the patient. Questions must be asked concerning the family history of any diseases. Genetic disorders, although they occasionally appear for the first time in the patient being investigated, may be discovered in near or distant ancestors. Is consanguinity present? Frequently a distant common relative may be discovered or a mother and father may discover that their families originally came to America from the same small town in Europe. A family tree is an excellent way to take a history; when possible, it should be extended back at least three generations. Specific questions must be asked about miscarriages, early infant deaths, odd-looking individuals, and the occurrence of mental retardation. In many families these are considered skeletons in the closet and often information must be obtained laboriously.

PREGNANCY

Often events occurring during the pregnancy can provide clues for the focus of medical assessment. Was the pregnancy unusual? Was there bleeding or infection? Was birth weight low? Were any drugs taken during pregnancy? Was there exposure to potentially toxic drugs? A "yes" answer to any of these questions helps the physician in conducting and ordering tests for conditions that may have their basis in circumstances surrounding the pregnancy.

LABOR AND DELIVERY

Because so many handicapped children result from perinatal difficulties it is particularly important to ascertain the details of birth and the newborn period. Was labor prolonged (over 12 hours) or unusually difficult? Were the membranes ruptured more than 24 hours before onset of labor—predisposing to maternal and fetal infections? Was there any significant bleeding before or during delivery? How much analgesia and anesthesia were necessary? Was there difficulty getting the baby to breathe? How long did the baby have to stay in the hospital? Was jaundice (yellow skin) present? Was the baby blue? Was there any Rh incompatibility? Did he need oxygen? Are Apgar scores available? A low 1-minute Apgar suggests depressed functioning of the infant.

A low 5-minute Apgar places the infant at increased risk for neurological problems at 1 year of age.

GROWTH AND DEVELOPMENT

One of the best estimates of the well-being of a child is growth, both height and weight. Children will grow at rates which are surprisingly constant from child to child. Growth charts are available (Figures 4-1 and 4-2) on which height and weight may be plotted against age. The resulting curve follows a percentile, the latter derived from long-term follow-ups of "normal" children. Most children will grow in the channels between 25 percent and 75 percent of the normal population. The percentile is not by itself important. Normal children may be between the 3rd and 97th percentile; they are obviously small or large for their age. It is only a decrease or increase in the *rate* of growth that alerts the physician to a possible change in nutrition, hormonal balance, or metabolic processes. Any type of illness may cause depression in growth: chronic infection (tuberculosis), thyroid disease, intestinal malabsorption of foodstuffs, and an inadequate emotional environment. A few illnesses may even cause sudden abnormal spurts of growth. Failure of a child to maintain a consistent rate of growth may be the first clue to the physician that the child may have a problem.

The acquisition of skills at definite ages (developmental landmarks) is perhaps the most sensitive measurement the physician possesses. Within certain age ranges infants learn these skills in a predictable sequence. Table 4-1 lists the landmarks and the ages at which some of these are accomplished. More extensive lists are available. Some list gross motor skills; some fine motor skills; others are a measurement of socialization. In early infancy, the range of normal is very wide. Even at 1 and 2 years of age, considerable variation is permissible. This explains the reluctance of physicians to label a child as "slow" or "retarded" unless there is obvious significant delay in many of these landmarks.

SCHOOLING

The first indication that a child may not be developing normally may be in school performance. Even in kindergarten the child's adaptation to and performance of routine tasks such as coloring, identification of left and right, and simple drawing may alert the teacher to a potential or actual handicapping condition. Early identification is crucial to prompt evaluation and meaningful suggestions for appropriate special educational intervention.

SOCIAL HISTORY

Many children with a relatively typical medical history do poorly in competitive situations, such as school. The reason may be a very unstable social environment. The physician dealing with children is very much oriented to the critical role played by emotional factors in the child's development. In-

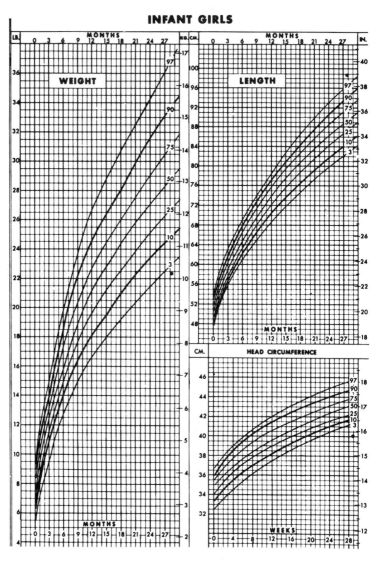

deed, there is a syndrome, now well described but not well explained, called "failure to thrive." The failure usually has a nonorganic background. "Maternal deprivation" or "paternal deprivation" describes the same clinical syndrome. The home environment is so deficient in providing stimulus and response opportunities and interpersonal reinforcement (as discussed in Chapter 5) that the child fails to develop in all areas: mental, physical, and social. The problems presented by such a background are considerable and are frequently unsurmountable. Broken home, divorce, death of a parent, neglect or abuse of a child—all are too frequent. The successful solution is difficult and time-consuming and requires a team approach involving the physician, the

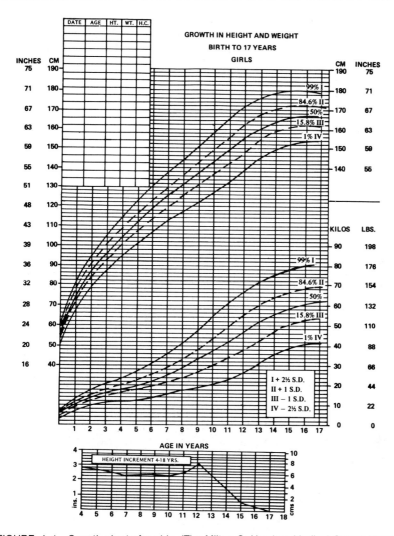

FIGURE 4-1 Growth charts for girls. (The Milton S. Hershey Medical Center Hospital.)

parent or parents, teachers, social workers, and others, such as a psychiatrist, relatives, and the family pastor and lawyer.

In the absence of obvious medical conditions, difficulties in social adjustment may be traced (even in the well-balanced family) to a single traumatic event—e.g., the death of a close family member or multiple geographic moves. Given a secure home situation this problem can be met with a well-carried-out counseling program.

Of particular importance is the identification of traumatic episodes occurring during crucial periods in the child's development. The period from birth to about age 2 (infant to toddler) is a time for identification of self as opposed

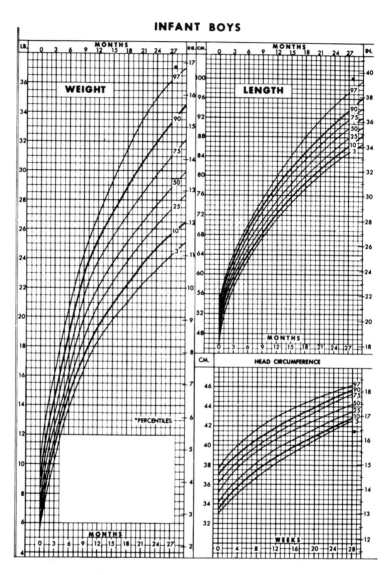

INFANT BOYS

to the rest of the world. The preschool period from age 2 to age 6 is a time during which children differentiate between male and female and take on appropriate sex roles. Also of importance in this period is the increasing growth toward independence—e.g., accepting separation from parents, independent play, and formation of personal friendships. The period of time from age 6 to age 12 is typically characterized by rapid physical growth, good health, expansion of social contacts, increasing concern for personal appearance—but all the while the maintenance of strong parental attachments. Any

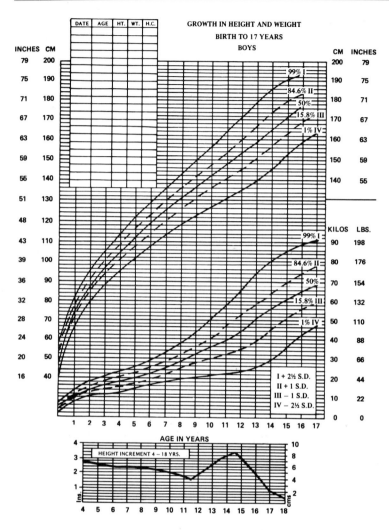

FIGURE 4-2 Growth charts for boys. (The Milton S. Hershey Medical Center Hospital.)

major disruptions in the family, such as the death of a parent, may be of disproportionate traumatic impact during this age period. It now appears to many pediatricians and psychologists that this is a most critical time. Preliminary observations of emotionally disturbed young adults indicate that many of them have suffered significant "losses" during this period.

The teenage years have their own, now well-known, problems to be faced: sexual development, decisions about vocation, self-image, and independence from parents. The physician is alert to this time and appreciates the significance major social events might have in the individual's development.

TABLE 4–1   MAJOR DEVELOPMENTAL LANDMARKS

Age	Gross Motor	Fine Motor	Socialization
Birth	Startle response: Moro		Eyes—fixes briefly on bright red object.
1 Month	Lifts head off table while prone.		Watches face.
2–3 Months	Lifts head to 90° angle from table.		Smiles/laughs.
4–5 Months	Rolls back to stomach.	Grabs object.	
8–9 Months	Sits with support and briefly without support. Stands briefly with support.	Transfers object from one hand to other.	Fear of strangers.
10 Months	Pulls self to standing position. Attempts to get toy placed out of reach.	Pincer grasp.	"Da-da"/"Ma-ma." Plays "peek-a-boo."
12 Months	Cruises—walks holding on to furniture.	Plays pat-a-cake.	May have several words in vocabulary.
18 Months	Walks well.	Rolls ball.	Indicates wants. Mimics parents' work (household chores).
2 years	Walks backwards and upstairs.	Kicks ball. Takes off clothes. Scribbles with pencil.	Start of play with peers. Toilet training may start.
2½ years	Runs well.	Throws ball overhand.	Combines two words.
3 years	Jumps in place.	Rides tricycle.	Able to attend nursery school. Partial to complete toilet training is achieved.

PHYSICAL EXAMINATION

The physical examination must be complete. The following is a survey of the areas examined by the physician, in the order he usually follows.

GENERAL APPEARANCE

The physician is attentive to how appropriate a response the child gives for his age—e.g., an 18-month-old should *not* be cooperative. Is the child well cared for? Is there evidence of unusual bruising, cuts, old scars? Height and weight are absolutely critical as discussed previously under "Growth and Development."

VITAL SIGNS

The vital signs include temperature, pulse, respiration, and blood pressure. Of these, the latter is the most important for alerting the physician to possible

chronic disease. Children never have elevated blood pressure without significant medical problems. Of these problems, kidney disease is the most common.

SKIN

Because the skin and the nervous tissue (brain and spinal cord) develop from the same embryonic tissue (ectoderm), lesions of the skin may be the first clue to abnormalities of the brain. Areas of change in pigmentation are particularly important.

The presence of unusual numbers of bruises in unaccustomed areas (face, back) may raise suspicion that the child has been abused or may indicate diseases of the blood and bone marrow.

HEAD

The physician measures head circumference to determine if it falls within the normal range for the child's age. In general the head grows because the brain grows. The actual circumference is not as important as is the maintenance of a *rate* of growth. A very small head (less than the third percentile) is not always an indication of mental retardation, but in a child whose development is not normal, it certainly greatly increases suspicion that the brain is not growing normally.

There are volumes available on facial appearance as an indication of the presence of a serious medical condition. With most of these syndromes (a term meaning a constellation of findings similar from patient to patient) mental retardation of varying degrees is present. A few examples are Down's Syndrome, gargoylism, Sturge-Weber (large birthmark over the face and also over the underlying surface of the brain), and hypothyroidism (cretinism).

EYES

The following ocular abnormalities may indicate the presence of systemic medical disorders: wide-set eyes, cataracts, dislocated lens, or changes in the pigmentation of the retina. Vision must be screened in children capable of cooperation (usually age 4 and older). Many learning problems are due to poor vision, and improvement is dramatic with appropriate lenses. Muscle balance is important: the eyes should move together (conjugate gaze). With severe muscle imbalance (strabismus) vision may be markedly impaired.

EARS

The presence of repeated episodes of middle-ear infections may result in the chronic accumulation of fluid within the middle-ear chamber. When hearing is impaired in the young infant, speech and language development will be delayed. There are also congenital causes of partial or full deafness. Since children with hearing loss do not learn to speak, a screening audiogram is important. Special techniques have been developed to assess hearing in very young infants (age 1 year).

The presence of malformed or low-set ears, or both, suggests structural abnormalities in other organ systems, especially the kidney. Many patients with chromosomal problems have ear abnormalities.

MOUTH, THROAT, AND NECK

Abnormalities to be looked for here are mostly concerned with infection. Carious teeth, chronically infected tonsils, and continuous enlargement of the lymph nodes (glands) may indicate infection which needs further investigation and appropriate correction.

The neck must be palpated for abnormalities of the thyroid gland. Ordinarily this gland is not felt in children. If enlarged, it may suggest either overactivity or underactivity.

HEART AND LUNGS

Attention here is focused on determining those conditions that may indicate chronic lung disease (e.g., asthma) or heart disease (congenital or rheumatic). Children with involvement in either of these areas risk significant handicapping conditions. They are rarely retarded, but their physical activity may be so restricted that serious emotional consequences interfere with development, school progress, or both.

ABDOMEN

Enlargement of the liver, the spleen, or both may indicate the presence of a "storage disease." These diseases are characterized by abnormal accumulation of certain biochemicals which interfere with the functioning of the organ. Several of these diseases may also involve the brain.

GENITALIA

Many chromosomal disorders have as part of their clinical syndrome ambiguous genitalia (i.e., assignment of sex is difficult). Abnormal genitalia indicate a serious medical situation in two respects: (1) other abnormalities must be sought, and (2) the social and emotional consequences to the patient and his family may by themselves cause considerable handicapping unless a definite assignment of sex can be made immediately.

EXTREMITIES   (Including Musculoskeletal System)

Extra digits or deformities of the extremities may be associated with severe handicapping conditions. The abnormal limbs of the children whose mothers took thalidomide are examples. Very frequently abnormal extremities indicate defects in other organ systems (especially heart and kidney). Abnormal size of limbs or abnormal proportion of limbs in relation to body and head size are present in many syndromes. Retardation is frequently also present.

NERVOUS SYSTEM

Examination of this part of the body is perhaps the most important in determining not only a diagnosis but also the degree, if any, of developmental retardation that exists. Because young infants do not cooperate and follow directions, this examination is often best done by observation. Important points are (1) type and symmetry of locomotion (crawling, walking, running, hopping, skipping); (2) ease and coordination of movement of each side of face and body; (3) responses to sounds, sights, and other stimuli; (4) pupil size and reaction to light; (5) reflex response on each side of the body; and (6) performance on single tests of balance.

Perhaps the most valuable investigatory tool possessed by the physician is observation. This is particularly valuable if the situation is not artificially contrived. The best situation is watching the child at play. Experienced pediatricians can make surprisingly accurate estimates as to the presence and degree of any handicapping condition by watching the child play for 30 minutes.

Many of the above points of assessment can be made only by the combination of several observers. The team approach to diagnosis is crucial. Parents, teachers, and family must be consulted for information on the child's actual performance level. The primary physician consulted for an evaluation may feel it is necessary to seek further consultation depending on his own findings. Consultants may include a psychiatrist, a pediatric neurologist, a speech therapist, and specialists in the eye and the ear.

LABORATORY TESTS

There are numerous laboratory tests available to the physician for support in determining the diagnosis in a child with a potential handicap. Only a few of the important ones will be mentioned. These are, in addition to the routine examinations used for normal health maintenance:

Chromosome analysis. This test both counts the number and allows examination of the structure of the genetic material. It should be performed only on children who, in addition to mental retardation, have abnormalities in various body structures (e.g., cleft palate, abnormal fingers and toes) because it is expensive and time-consuming and requires highly trained technical personnel.

Examination of blood, urine, or both for excess of normal body chemicals or presence of abnormal compounds should include analyses of glucose (sugar), certain fats, and amino acids (the building blocks of proteins).

Hormones. Those related to the thyroid, pituitary, and gonads are especially critical to development and should be examined if appropriate.

X rays. The maturation of the bones is an important indicator of general body development. Bone age can be determined by X rays of the wrist and knee and may alert the physician to a discrepancy between skeletal and chronological age that will be an aid in the diagnosis of exceptionalities.

It remains for the physician to synthesize all of the areas of evaluation that have been discussed. He must also evaluate the opinions of other consultants (if obtained) and consult with parents, teachers, and social workers. The diagnosis is only the beginning: an estimate of the degree of handicapping would then permit an adequate plan of education and rehabilitation. The complexity of these problems of special education demands the involvement of all members of the child's world to ensure the most successful program.

CONCLUDING REMARKS

Obviously, significant medical problems can be key issues and obstacles to optimal educational progress. Indeed, it appears that special educators have been too often preoccupied by medical and quasimedical terminology, diagnoses, and procedures. Medical knowledge is important to the special educator only insofar as it relates to educational problems. Special educators are not junior physicians, psychiatrists, or geneticists; but they should be aware of the important role played by medical factors in educational development, be alert to at least the gross signs of physical involvement, and most importantly, have adequate sensitivity to call on medical specialists as required.

5

PSYCHOSOCIAL BASES OF EXCEPTIONAL CONDITIONS

STUDY TARGETS

1   Define the major characteristics of the four positions on development (preformationism, predeterminism, environmentalism and interactionism). Hint: What role do heredity alone, environment alone, and both in combination play in each of the four points of view?

2   List four broad environmental conditions that contribute to disabling conditions in children.

3   Define punishment and list four reactions children might give to severe or persistent punishment.

4   Summarize, in your own words, the interactionist position with respect to child development.

5   Briefly describe several feasible strategies for intervention designed to minimize or prevent developmental disability.

We shall begin this chapter with a caution: the psychological, social, and educational factors related to disability surveyed in this chapter should not be seen as distinct and isolated from the biomedical variables previously discussed. Development is a process continuously influenced by the total complex of factors accumulated throughout an individual's history. One's previously established constitutional and behavioral characteristics, whatever their origin, interact with current variables and are influenced by them. Thus, genetic, medical, emotional, intellectual, and other aspects contribute to the status of an individual and combine to form a "package" that interacts with subsequent variables. No two persons have exactly the same composite; accordingly, no two individuals are affected in precisely the same manner by the same event. Therefore, as we summarize psychological, social, and educational variables related to exceptionalities, bear in mind that these are divided from biomedical variables only for convenience of discussion.

What determines the development of disabilities? Are they genetically or environmentally produced? Can disability be remediated or "cured"? Are mental retardation, emotional disturbance, and learning disabilities discrete and independent? Are they reversible? Does the age of onset of a disabling condition determine permanence or set limits to its changeability? Answers to these questions, indeed even the asking of such questions, depend heavily upon one's view of the determinants of development. Clearly, if one believes that development is predetermined or preset at conception, then his interest in the reversibility or modification of development would be minimal. Likewise, if one believes that disability is almost entirely environmentally produced, then his questions basically focus on how and when—*not* on whether—developmental problems can be rectified.

FUNDAMENTAL HISTORICAL POSITIONS ON DEVELOPMENT

One's perspective on the fundamental determinants of development is bound to influence the magnitude, intensity, direction, and nature of his attempts at educational and therapeutic intervention. Teachers, family counselors, social workers, institutional personnel, and others who believe disability is static and inherent will behave much differently than persons who expect and work for significant changes in disability. In this section, we shall provide an overview of four basically different views of development that have varying implications for intervention. The first three views, "preformationism," "predeterminism," and "environmentalism," are of historical significance and represent extreme positions stressing the rather exclusive operation of biological or environmental factors. The fourth view, "interactionism," is presented as the most currently acceptable position on development.

PREFORMATIONISM

A preformationist approach to development actually denies any qualitative developmental process. The view, antiquated and of historical interest only, holds that all an individual is or ever will be is preformed at conception. All bodily characteristics, talents, interests, and competencies are "signed, sealed, and delivered" at the moment the sperm fertilizes the egg. "Development" is nothing more than increase in size; the environment has no role whatsoever. Progressively and inevitably, the individual "unfolds" on an immutable, pre-set schedule. New features and characteristics of the person are merely the result of predestined fate.

During past centuries, when the preformationist view was dominant, the child was seen as a miniature adult. It was believed that all adult traits were present in the child but were simply less pronounced. Even the paintings of this era depicted children as little men and women. Formal education and training were reserved for children of families that were of "quality" ancestral soundness.

It seems clear that the preformationist view of developmental disability was rather straightforward. Developmental retardation, disturbed behavior, and other disabilities not attributable to clearly exogenous factors (e.g., physical insult) were simply the result of "defective stock." Little or nothing could be or was done, since the defect was believed to be inborn and static.

PREDETERMINISM

Promulgated and given impetus by J. J. Rousseau (1712–1778), the predeter-ministic position replaced former developmental theories and became the dominant view for about a hundred years up to the early 1900s. Predetermin-ism, like preformationism, asserts that all characteristics and proclivities are locked up within the child from birth. Predeterminism differs from the older view, however, in two important ways. First, Rousseau and those who shared his view, such as J. H. Pestalozzi (1746–1827) and Friedrich Froebel (1782–1852), recognized qualitative changes in development. Ontogeny—i.e., individual development—was seen as much more than quantitative alteration. Individual differences and similarities in qualitative developmental changes were documented; childhood was seen as important in its own right and quali-tatively different from adulthood.

Various qualitatively different "stages" in the progression of development were described and said to be somewhat universal for all children.

Second, predeterminism departed from preformationism in recognizing some degree of environmental influence. Essentially, the environment was seen as providing the enabling conditions for predetermined development. "Innate potentials," "latent talents," and "natural goodness" would invariably unfold according to a natural (genetic) master plan. Rousseau emphasized the corrupting influence of the environment. If only we could provide the child with free and permissive surroundings, then his capacities would emerge in undistorted and full expression. The unstructured child-centered models in education, counseling, and therapy prominent in the last several decades seem obviously rooted in a predeterministic tradition.

While predeterminism considers the environment, it does not ascribe to the environment any essential role in the developmental process. Critical developmental transitions and the attainment of developmental landmarks by the child are still attributed to biogenic mechanisms, to a natural maturational sequence. While Rousseau articulated predeterminism in its philosophic form, educators and developmentalists have revived the position in varying forms. Thus the essence of predeterminism—i.e., the concept that development in the final analysis is biologically predetermined—seems implicit in such propositions as child-centered early education (Froebel, 1826), "internal ripening" (Gesell, 1948), and the "spontaneous self-regulation" postulated by Piaget.*

What implications does a predeterministic view of development have with respect to the cause, prevention, and treatment of disability? Fundamentally, predeterminism views disability as the outcome of either unfortunate genetic potential or the intrusion of extreme pre- or post-natal influences. Drugs, disease, physical trauma, and severe deprivation may act to warp or preclude developmental potential. These factors, however, are seen not as contributing to the developmental process but merely as obstacles to or distortions of otherwise "natural" development. Environment, from a predeterministic perspective, can arrest or deflect natural developmental progressions; it can do little to add to, compensate for, or interact with inevitable, predetermined constitutional development. You can become less then, but no better than, your predetermined potential.

Until quite recently, concepts of normal intelligence, mental retardation, emotional disturbance, and other ontogenetic disabilities were predominantly predeterministic. Definitions and suggested treatment for "mental retardation" provide good illustrations of the influence of the predeterministic view. Tredgold's definition of mental retardation, widely accepted until recently, emphasized the endogenous, or internal, biologic determination of defective intellect:

> a state of incomplete mental development of such a kind and degree that the individual is incapable of adapting himself to the normal environment of his fellows in such a way as to maintain existence independently of supervision, control or external support [1937, p. 4].

Intelligence, in this view, is genetically based and vulnerable to only negative modification by exogenous (environmental) factors (Tredgold and Soddy, 1956). Indeed, documented cases of children originally diagnosed as mentally retarded who subsequently showed sharp gains in intelligence (see, e.g., Goldfarb, 1945a, 1945b; Schmidt, 1946; Skeels and Dye, 1939; Skeels and Harms, 1948; Shodak and Skeels, 1949) were dismissed as instances of "pseudomental retardation." In essence, the concept of pseudomental retardation asserts that mental retardation cannot be reversed, that any such reversal is really attribu-

---

* Piaget, in several works (1962, 1965, 1968, 1969) appears to present a modified, but nevertheless basically predeterministic conception of development. For detailed discussion of Piaget with respect to this issue, see Vygotsky (1962) and Ausubel and Sullivan (1970).

table to original *wrong* diagnosis. The diagnosis must have been in error, because mental retardation is "essentially incurable."

Similarly, definitions and concepts of emotional disturbance, slow learning, psychosis, and even "criminal personality" have explicitly or implicitly taken a predeterministic stance. Developmental problems are seen as aberrations from a "natural" direction, pattern, and rate of development under the direction of biogenic variables.

Since predeterminism regards organic factors as having a preeminent role in development, the focus of treatment and prevention is biologic. Surgery, drug therapy, and hormone treatment are used in attempts to alter the constitution of the person and, thus, the assumed biologic basis of his problems.

Perhaps the most extreme example of intervention related to a predeterministic premise is the eugenics approach to improving humanity. Eugenics presumes that many if not most "defects" are genetically based, predetermined, and essentially irreversible. Selective mating among individuals with good qualities and sterilization of defective persons are measures proposed to reduce the incidence of disability. While these measures might effect some improvement in our species, several factors operate against the utility of the eugenics approach. First, modern genetics has established that the hereditary component of such complex characteristics as intelligence, temperament, and talent is *polygenic* rather than simple. That is, many genes operating in groups provide the base for complex "traits." The effects of single genes are modified by other genes and most complex human characteristics are due to polygenic networks. (For a discussion of multiple-factor or quantitative genetics, see McClearn, 1970.)

Such networks (not simple gene pairs) provide the hereditary portion for many frequently occurring human defects. Selective mating and sterilization of the "unfit" might be feasible where characteristics have a relatively simple genetic basis; selection is not feasible where the heredity is complex. There are some extreme problems that indeed are due to relatively simple gene action; however, these problems are so rare that mating control or sterilization would not make much difference. Further, in many of these extreme cases, the individuals affected are naturally sterile or do not live to reproduce.

Second, by its preoccupation with heredity, eugenics overlooks the possibilities for improvement through controlled changes in the environment, improvement that can be effected within a generation as opposed to genetic improvement that takes hundreds of generations (Ausubel and Sullivan, 1970).

Finally, many problems among children labeled as "exceptional children" have no apparent hereditary basis, at least in the way conceived of by those who advocate selective mating. As examples, most children diagnosed as "mentally retarded" show no organic defect and have no identifiable history of defective heredity (Allen, 1958; Reese and Lipsitt, 1970; Sarason, 1953; Tredgold and Soddy, 1956). Likewise, the other common problems encountered by special educators—e.g., disturbed behavior, inferior motor control, sensory limitations—cannot with certitude be attributed to heredity and certainly not to simple single gene effects.

In summary, predeterminism regards the environment as an enabling context in which biologically predestined development can take place. The environment is not seen as a cause of development, merely as a place for it. Disability is believed to result basically from native defect or the imposition of extreme environmental deprivations. Since development is seen as biologically determined, intervention is almost exclusively of a biomedical nature.

ENVIRONMENTALISM

Both preformationism and predeterminism represent extreme points of view with almost exclusive emphasis on the biological determination of development. Environmentalism, in its various forms, has had a history of equal extremism in its emphasis on nonbiological—i.e., situational—factors in ontogeny. John Locke (1632–1704) is the philosophical father of what has come to be called the tabula rasa or "blank slate" theory. Originally, Locke suggested that the mind is a blank at birth, i.e., one is born with no storehouse of memories, instinctive thoughts, or cognitive processes. The "blank slate" view, however, has also been associated with even more extreme positions that allow for little or no biological role in development. John Watson (1925) is noted for his statement:

> Give me a dozen healthy infants, well formed, and my own specified world to bring them up in and I'll guarantee to take any one at random and train him to become any type of specialist I might select—doctor, lawyer, artist, merchant, chief, and yes, even beggarman and thief, regardless of his talents, peculiarities, tendencies, abilities, vocations, and race of his ancestors [p. 82].

Itard (1932), Montessori (1912), Seguin (1866), and others championed the position that even extreme developmental problems could be rectified through "sensory training." Humanism in education, behaviorism in psychology, and cultural determinism in sociology and anthropology are more recent, albeit less extreme, examples of environmentalist approaches. Essentially, then, environmentalist concepts of development minimize biological determinants and emphasize situational variables. In the extreme, humans are considered infinitely pliable with no limits on development. The environment, registered through the senses, constitutes the source of variables responsible for the kind, the direction, and the rate of development.

Obviously, one who believes that personal development is almost exclusively the product of environmental forces will speak of intervention in parallel terms. Accordingly, intellectual retardation, disturbed behavior, and various learning problems are not seen as involving significant anatomical or physiological bases; rather, they are problems generated by and treatable through the environment.

Rather than dwell on further details of environmentalism, especially its extreme versions, we shall move to a discussion of the currently most acceptable position on the control of development, *interactionism.*

INTERACTIONISM

This position views development as the outcome of the interplay between biological and environmental determinants. Ontological changes, whether positive or negative, are attributable to the complex interaction of hereditary material with first the intrauterine environment and later the wider physical and social environment. Interactionism takes seriously the fact that no living thing develops *in vacuo* and that heredity and environment are two broad classes of variables that do not exist independently. Rather, heredity and environment are usually separated only for purposes of theoretical discussion. It is, moreover, simplistic and naïve to ascribe development to either heredity *or* environment. Developmental disabilities, therefore, must be seen as a product of heredity *times* environment. The manifest qualities of an individual's development are always the result of hereditary predispositions as they interact with varying environments. In no way can heredity or environment be proclaimed the "real" or "basic" determinant of development; each influences the regulatory role of the other. A person's constitutional attributes and traits— his intelligence, emotionality, interests, talents, and physique—are the cumulative and progressive product of the continuous reciprocity between heredity and environment (Birch, 1968; Gordon, 1971).

The moment of conception, when parental genetic materials unite, is perhaps the only time when heredity operates alone. At that moment, the qualities of the zygote (the organism resulting from union of egg and sperm) are due to parental contributions. From this point on, however, the environment in which the organism survives modifies the expression of the genetic material and actively contributes to the content, rate, and direction of developmental trends.

The notion of interaction is not a simple one, since it involves the constant accumulation of heredity-times-environment *products,* which again interact with the environment. We have chosen the following expressions to summarize (perhaps too simply) the concept of cumulative interactionism.

H = the hereditary influence on development, exclusive at conception

$(H \times E)$ = the composite product of H (hereditary) variables interacting with E (environmental) variables. This product now constitutes the package of determinants that will subsequently influence further interaction and, thus, development

$[(H \times E) \times E]$ = the new product that is available for interaction

$[(H \times E) \times E] \times E, \ldots$ etc. = the continuously accumulating composite that interacts with E from moment to moment

What is at one time an external, environmental influence registers on the existing attributes of an individual and becomes part of the person. The now changed personal characteristics interact with the environment to produce a new (perhaps only slightly changed) composite of characteristics. From this point of view, it is clear that at any moment developmental characteristics are the result of environmental influences interacting with the historical product of infinite previous hereditary-environmental interactions.

Even though heredity and environment interact to generate developmental characteristics, one might ask: What are the relative contributions of each for particular characteristics? From our previous discussions of single-gene and chromosomal defects (see Chapter 3) and the polygenic heredity of most complex traits (mentioned earlier in this chapter), we may make the following generalizations. Traits with a relatively simple genetic base are less variable and less modifiable by variations in the environment. On the other hand, traits that have a complex or polygenic hereditary base are more variable in their expression and more susceptible to environmental influence. Characteristics such as eye color, skin pigmentation, migraine headache, aniridia (a type of blindness), congenital deafness, kerotosis (a skin disorder), and color-blindness have a single, double, or sex-linked gene basis. The environment has little, if any, effect on these characteristics. More continuously distributed characteristics, such as intelligence, temperament, aptitude, and talent, have a multiple or polygenic base and vary considerably in expression over a range of environments.

The implication of these generalizations for special education is noteworthy: with the exception of some rare defects, *most of the problems of exceptional children are developmental in nature, polygenic in heredity, and highly modifiable through appropriate environmental intervention.*

We have provided an overview of three extreme but historically important developmental viewpoints and have concluded this section with a discussion of interactionism, the most scientifically acceptable position on developmental regulation. In light of this interactionist stance, we shall now examine the role of the environment in greater detail and describe several major classes of environmental variables that relate to developmental disabilities.

ENVIRONMENTAL VARIABLES RELATED TO DISABILITIES

RESTRICTED RANGE OF SENSORY STIMULATION

Optimal human development does not take place in a vacuum. The interactionist position emphasizes the interdependence of biological and environmental variables in development. Without question, the availability of sensory stimulation is a most crucial environmental contribution to favorable development. Several landmark studies which involved the removal of retarded children from one environment to another with greater stimulation (Klineberg, 1935; Liahy, 1935; Skeels, 1966; Skeels and Dye, 1939; Skodak and Skeels, 1949) were instrumental in shaking the then predominant view that qualitative differences in early experience had little effect on subsequent development. This view was an outcome of the prevailing predeterministic conception of development, buttressed by numerous early studies that suggested the pre-eminence of heredity and the minimal influence of environment. Frequently, such investigations seemed to add credence to the immutability of "maturation" and predetermined ontogeny. Dennis and Dennis (1940) reported that Hopi Indian children who were bound to cradle boards walked at about the same age as comparable Hopi children whose leg and arm movements were uninhibited. The same investigators also found normal sequences of behavior in twins reared under "restricted practice and minimum social stimulation" (Dennis, 1938). Other research (e.g., Smith, Lecker, Dunlap, and Cureton, 1930) reported great constancy in the age at which children begin to walk despite environmental circumstances.

But these studies and others, when viewed in light of our recent knowledge, merely qualify, rather than dampen, the current view of the importance of early stimulation. Many of the early studies involved subhuman animals, with considerably less complex nervous systems. As similar studies were repeated with higher animals, it became clear that the higher the animal, the more important is early experience in normal development. Today, the study of infancy is considered a most crucial domain of developmental psychology (White, 1971). In fact, it now appears that early experience is not only an important influence on the general development of competence, but the development of the organs and the nervous system themselves depends on adequate early stimulation (Beach and Jaynes, 1954; Harlow, 1961; Harlow and Zimmerman, 1959; Thompson, 1955).

The vagueness of phrases such as "adequate or optimal stimulation" and "poor environment" are beginning to be replaced with more precise definitions of appropriate stimulation. Specifically, the *volume* of stimulation does not seem as crucial as the *range* of stimulation. Stimulation as defined from the standpoint of physics is not equivalent to stimulation from a developmental or psychological perspective. For example, the continuous background noise of traffic is a stimulus that will register on a meter, but its lack of variety reduces its stimulating properties. Therefore, it is not the presence of stimuli alone but their variety that is developmentally important (Friedlander, 1967; Kagan, 1970; Rheingold, 1963). Especially during the first year or so of life, appropriate sensory stimulation seems disproportionally crucial. Infants must have a chance to do much looking and listening. The existence of such opportunities may account for the finding that infants whose movements are restricted, like the Hopi infants bound to cradle boards, but who experience adequate sensory stimulation are not particularly slow in walking.

Finally, stimulation is important not only for activation of the sense organs and the nervous system but also as cues for behavior. Reaching, grasping, pointing, asking—in general, *reacting*—require the presence of specific objects and events that evoke such behavior. *Reacting to and acting on the environment* build a response repertoire of increasing complexity that enables the child to interact with the physical and social environment in progressively more elaborate ways.

FACTORS CONTRIBUTING TO LOW STIMULATION

"Cultural deprivation," "cultural impoverishment," and more recent terms such as "disadvantaged" are all general descriptions of child-rearing environments that presumably are deficient in stimulating optimal development. These terms are typically, although not exclusively, applied to low socio-economic circumstances. Low income, large families, and uneducated management of existing financial resources result in homes with restricted developmental stimulation. Objects are fewer and variety is limited. Accordingly, *there are fewer objects to label, differentiate among, react to, and behave toward.*

Auditory as well as visual stimulation may be less varied and less detailed. Music in the home, for example, is likely to be simple, repetitive, and lacking in range of style, content, and meaning. The language used in a lower socio-

Psychosocial development is frequently restricted by the culture of poverty.

economic environment typically involves fewer words with less elaboration, variability, and nuances of meaning (Bereiter and Engelmann, 1966; Deutsch et al., 1968). Verbal skills play an important part in development; impoverished language usage, particularly by parental and important caretaker models, is of special concern. Limited language, like limited physical objects, provides fewer cues for behavior. Language development, auditory discrimination, and verbal reasoning must suffer retardation in an environment where words have little value beyond use in coping with the dreary daily routine. "Restricted" rather than "elaborate" (Bernstein, 1961; Robinson, 1965, 1968) and "low signal-to-noise ratio" (Deutsch et al., 1968) are terms that have been used to describe the language and other auditory stimulation associated with "high-risk" environments.

Let us now turn attention away from the context in which a child is reared in order to consider the child *himself*. Even if relatively adequate sensory stimulation is provided within the home, the child may come into the world with less than normal sensory capabilities. A blind or deaf child is, of course, an extreme example. But aside from such extremes sensory acuity may vary considerably among neonates. From the moment of birth, the child has been enrolled in a learning program. "Preschool experience" begins at conception and becomes intense at birth. Sensory receptors interact with the environment; visual, auditory, tactile, and olfactory learning begins and becomes developed much earlier than we have heretofore suspected (Piaget, 1952; White, 1968). Some children have a "head start": not only are their environments rich in effective stimulation, but their sensory apparatus is fully intact and develops rapidly. Other children may have slightly higher than normal sensory thresholds: they are handicapped at the outset. Research on the precise measurement of an infant's sensory capabilities is difficult and has received systematic investigation only recently (Reese and Lipsitt, 1970a; White, 1971). It seems clear, however, that early detection of sensory deficits can lead to compensatory intervention to preempt possible developmental retardation. Prosthetic devices attached to the child or to the environment can be employed to boost stimulation and thus offset a sensory handicap. Studies of infancy and early experience suggest the possibilities of assuring children a "sensational" head start in life (see Mussen, 1970, for a review).

LIMITATIONS ON OPPORTUNITIES FOR RESPONSE

The same factors responsible for impoverished sensory stimulation restrict the building and practice of responses. Fewer objects to see and hear are also fewer objects to manipulate. Certainly, again, economic factors play a direct role in this respect. Crowded conditions can obviously limit response opportunities because of excessive sharing of opportunities, the quick wearing out of objects, and the sheer frustrations of living under crowded conditions.

Additionally, children may experience response restrictions for several other reasons. First, adults may not play with, arrange circumstances for, and otherwise interact with children. Instead, children may be left on their own with little to do. They may frequently be isolated and told to "shut up" and "not bother anyone."

Second, exceptional children who undergo long periods of sickness and are confined to a crib, bed, or wheelchair must have response opportunities brought to them to minimize barriers to active involvement.

Third, a great number of exceptional children have response-mode deficiencies. The usual ways to react to the environment are altered or missing because of, for example, a missing limb, paralyzed arms, defective speech mechanisms, or poor locomotor control. Whether the response problem originates from defective genetics, prematurity, a birth defect, or a postnatal injury or illness, it is critical to apply prosthetics, compensatory training, and response substitution (see Chapter 8) to minimize the negative impact of the deficiency. It is important to realize that limitations in walking or finger manipulation, for example, can also cause limitations on intellectual and even emotional development (Morris and Whiting, 1971). Greatly reduced opportunities to examine, use, and act on the environment must inevitably attenuate developmental progress.

Finally, a highly visible body defect can repel many adults and other children. This secondary effect of "being different" can dramatically reduce learning opportunities for exceptional children. Adults who, for a variety of reasons, compel themselves to help children with what they perceive to be repugnant characteristics may behave toward them in a forced, artificial manner. Often, such adults will avoid physical closeness with the child and deny him the affection he might otherwise experience from a more suitable individual. Persons who cannot relate to exceptional children may not be able to respond to them constructively, refusing adequate reinforcement, misusing punishment, or offering unearned rewards. It is to this problem—i.e., inappropriate responses to children's behavior—that we now turn our discussion.

DEFECTIVE REACTIONS TO CHILDREN'S RESPONSES

Behavior is shaped and maintained by its effect on the environment. The wide and impressive literature of behavior modification demonstrates convincingly that changes in children's competencies can be dramatically brought about by relatively simple rearrangements of behavior consequences (National Society for the Study of Education, 1973; O'Leary and O'Leary, 1972; Reese and Lipsitt, 1970b; Tharp and Wetzel, 1969).

Approaches to objects, initiation of social interactions, and attempts to explore and learn can result in varying outcomes. When consequences are reinforcing, a child's activity is strengthened and his repertoire of responses is built. His behavior must have reinforcing effects on the physical or social environment if it is to survive. From the vantage point of what has been discovered about principles of behavior, developmental retardation or distortions may be produced through several unproductive arrangements in the pattern of responses to a child's behavior.

First, *reinforcement for behavior can be "stingy," i.e., too infrequent, too small, or both.* Institutional "care" is frequently characterized by its paucity of reinforcement. A number of investigations of retarded children have noted the devastating results of a prolonged stay in an institution (Braginsky and Braginsky, 1971; Kirk, 1958; Provence and Lipton, 1962; Skeels and Dye, 1939) and the positive shifts in development, especially intelligence, that occur when children are removed to more stimulating and reinforcing situations (Provence and Lipton, 1962; Skeels and Dye, 1939; Shodak and Skeels, 1949). Parents or caretakers may be too busy, may not know how to encourage constructive behavior, may not have reinforcing objects or events to deliver to children, or may not be good at interacting with children. Whatever the reason, the net effect is nonreinforcement or "extinction" of constructive behavior. Extensive scarcity of reinforcement will not only preclude the development of specific behaviors but may produce generalized retardation of intellectual, emotional, and motor functioning (Ullman and Krasner, 1969).

Delay in reinforcement is likewise a defective procedure for building behavior. Some parents may be generally uninvolved with their children but occasionally heap rewards upon them. Reinforcement is usually effective only if it immediately follows behavior. A frustrated, busy, or unalert parent is just not there to provide the smile, the kind word, the hug—the appropriate reaction—when children need it. Delays in reinforcement usually result in strengthening whatever behavior is occurring at the time of reinforcement, rather than the desired behavior. In this fashion, many unwanted behaviors are accidentally built.

Noncontingent reinforcement can have effects similar to nonreinforcement. Developmental progress in children's behavior will not be as likely to evolve rapidly in homes where reinforcement does not depend on children's behavior. When children need not ask, label objects, explain their wants, go to objects, or in other elaborate ways operate on their surroundings, behavioral growth is stunted. Parents who anticipate their children's needs and attendants who deliver potent reinforcers, such as food and attention, on a routine basis independent of the child's behavior are not helping children. Behavior may simply not develop, progress, or be maintained by noncontingent reinforcement. Unfortunately, many parents of exceptional children guarantee minimal progress by incessantly monitoring and placating their children. In this context, Aesop's advice is correct: "Self help is the best help."

Just as adults and siblings can fail to reinforce constructive behavior, they can provide *unwitting reinforcement of undesirable, maladaptive behavior.* Indeed much antisocial, disturbed, and "institutional" behavior results from inadvertent encouragement (Ullman and Krasner, 1969). This is likely to occur because adults, like children, behave in ways that will eliminate or reduce irritations. The child who does not attend to an important task may be offered other, preferred activities: this reinforces withdrawal from learning tasks. Similarly, fussing and tantrums are often followed by much attention and "diversion" to a pleasant activity. Reinforcing undesirable behaviors may work to restrict opportunities for learning. Because "nasty children" are avoided by other children and adults, there is a lessening of the kinds of social, emotional, intellectual, and motor experiences that are guided and encouraged by others. Also, strong maladaptive behaviors may become the characteristic way for children to deal with even minor disappointments, which in turn means a further increase in opportunities for reinforcement of aversive behavior, escalating the problem and further retarding development.

To close our discussion of defective reactions, let us briefly examine *punishment*. As used in the behavioral literature, the term "punishment" refers to any consequence that acts to weaken or suppress behavior. Punishment need not be intentional or exclusively physical. A frown may be as punishing to one child as a slap is to another. Failure to reinforce behavior which has usually been reinforced may also function aversively (Bijou and Baer, 1960; Marquis, 1943).

Repeated, or even a single, severe punishment may act to eliminate, weaken, or suppress behavior. Often, of course, adults deliberately design and employ punishment precisely to get rid of unwanted behavior. And we do not here advocate total abstinence from the use of punishment when it is in the long-range interests of children. There are, however, several outcomes associated with aversive control that contribute to developmental disability.

When punishment is repeatedly delivered by specific persons or within specific settings, those persons and places become paired with or related to the punishment. In other words, children learn not only to avoid those behaviors that produce aversive consequences but also the people and places connected with punishment. Parents, teachers, and attendants begin to acquire aversive properties as they more frequently rely on aversive means to alter children's behavior. It is especially unfortunate when parents or other important models become aversive; this clearly diminishes occasions for positive, educative interaction. If a number of persons employ punishment, generalized avoidance may result, and children may not discriminate threatening from nonthreatening adults but avoid most adult interaction (Bijou and Baer, 1967; Mearham and Wiesen, 1971; Neisworth and Smith, 1973). Fear of adults and intermittent punishment for a variety of behaviors constitute a strong mechanism for the development of not only "emotional disturbance" but also retardation in any skill that involves social learning.

Children inevitably develop any avoidance behavior that reduces the likelihood of punishment. Thus, frequently playing hooky or daydreaming in school suggests that the child may be too frequently and intensely exposed to aversive stimulation. Severe punishment may even produce rather complete avoidance, such as refraining from any speech, especially if talking gets the child into trouble. Being forced to eat, under threat of punishment, may encourage vomiting or other somatic disorders.

Severe or persistent punishment can also generate numerous biological side effects. Loss of bladder and bowel control, gastrointestinal disorders, and other somatic disorders may emerge under conditions of stress (Lachman, 1972). These disorders then further limit the child's effective exchange with the learning environment.

We previously mentioned that punishment may not be intentional. Indeed, the process of punishment may be hidden and go unnoticed by even alert adults. This may be true especially among exceptional children who undergo sometimes painful treatment for reasons of illness or other dysfunctions. Certainly, chronic illness with its pain and immobilization can dampen and distort developmental progress.

But treatment itself may also act to suppress behavior. Repugnant medications, painful apparatus, and forced training procedures can punish behavior. Additionally, as with intentional punishment, generalization across persons and situations may occur. Parents, therapists, and nurses, for example, may frequently choose to deliver medication or treatment when the child is happy or engaging in some pleasant activity. They wish to catch the child in a "good mood," thereby minimizing disputes and turmoil. If treatment is aversive, however, the constructive behavior—because it is followed by aversive stimulation—is actually being punished and will therefore weaken.

IN CLOSING

Caretakers must pay attention to the content, timing, and sequence of events children experience. Rearing and educating normal children is difficult enough. The physical and behavioral deficiencies of exceptional children present special challenges and increase the demand for planning and precision in arranging for and reacting to their behavior. Existing dysfunctions are easily amplified, and one problem can set the stage for another. Studied intervention can preclude and undo even longstanding disorders. Development is a modifiable process controlled by both biological and environmental variables and their complex interaction. Special educators can be instrumental in providing environments that influence the content, direction, and rate of development in order to preempt or reverse disability.

6

EVALUATION OF PSYCHOLOGICAL AND EDUCATIONAL CHARACTERISTICS

STUDY TARGETS

1 List three broad functional dimensions a diagnostician would consider in conducting an educational evaluation of a child's performance.
2 Describe the types of environmental variables a teacher or school psychologist might consider to better understand the possible reasons for a youngster's functioning in certain ways.
3 Give an illustration of a school-related behavior and describe how it might be explained from the following perspectives (a) hypothetical-internal, (b) hypothetical-external, (c) actual-internal, and (d) actual-external.
4 Cite four ways in which each of the following elements can contribute to inaccuracies in the evaluative data or exert influences that lead to biases against the student and erroneous conclusions: (a) the student, (b) the examiner, (c) the setting, and (d) the evaluative devices.
5 List the four major factors that are used in the MEAN Rating System and give a short description of the meaning each has for the special educator.
6 Give one strength and one weakness for each of the three types of criteria that can be used for comparing a child's performance.

7 Diagram the sequence of four stages involved in diagnosing educational disorders.

8 Cite five of the six erroneous conclusions about performance measures and data that could lead to misinterpretation or inappropriate educational programing or both.

9 Name the two major questions a diagnostician should ask before he decides how to use the diagnostic data collected during the evaluative phase of the process.

Some form of evaluation of children is inevitable in education. Influenced by a weighty tradition, teachers and other educators believe that assessment of children is a necessary precondition to instruction and that meaningful evaluation must identify pertinent individual attributes of children if it is to have any educational meaning (Newland, 1971). The data collected on children range from determining a child's chronological age to using very elaborate complex assessment devices that demand the expertise of highly trained, skillful diagnosticians. The alleged reason for evaluation has been to bulwark judgments the teacher makes concerning the child's instructional program, which is presumed to be appropriate. The practice has become an institution among most school systems. Children are tested, cumulative folders are set up, test scores are profiled, "clinical" (usually subjective) reports are made and interpreted in nearly robotlike fashion. The procedure presumably lends respectability to a child's instructional program and places it within a context of scientific legitimacy. Moreover, it is traditionally assumed that the more exceptional a child the greater the need for psychoeducational assessment (Gearheart, 1972; Kirk, 1972). This chapter will review some of the prominent issues surrounding these assumptions and practices and discuss their utility in terms of education for exceptional children.

THE PURPOSE OF EVALUATION

The main reason for evaluation in special education is to make better decisions about the character and direction of each child's instructional program. A very important contemporary belief among special educators is that schools should no longer assume the duty of screening children to decide where within society they can or cannot serve. This certainly has been an orientation of the testing movement in the past (Capobianco, 1964; Waugh and Bush, 1971; Wolfensberger, 1969a). Children were administered some form of an aptitude test and implicit decisions were made about each child's relative value and predicted contributions on the basis of a test score that presumably reflected potential or capacity. On the basis of this sort of data, some children were said to be mentally defective, presumably on a permanent basis, and thrust into programs of instruction which were geared toward "dealing with" youngsters who were poor producers or of low potential. The personal attribute of "low capacity" suggested a terminal condition which was impervious to many, if not most, educational management procedures. Implicit in this conclusion, then, was the belief that society would have to provide arrangements whereby people with low capacity were "cared for." As one traces the genesis of such conclusions the assignment of a psychoeducational label can most properly be identified with the very tenuous predeterministic assumptions that underlie the measurement of human potential. Increasingly, special educators are adopting the position that not only is hypothesizing about one's potential an unnecessary condition for determining provisions for special education, but that it is impossible to identify one's potential to do anything with enough assurance of accuracy to decide how that individual's life might best be controlled (Neisworth, 1969).

These decisions are terminal. They are interpreted to mean that certain groups of children should not be provided with optimum educational experiences. And, in fact, the orientation has encouraged suspension, expulsion, and exclusion of youngsters on the most flimsy of bases (Cronbach and Gleser, 1957). To restrict or disallow education for children using a rationale which is so clearly inferential, unreliable, invalid, and discriminatory has been the subject of lawsuits and court judgments around the country. The position we have taken here and throughout this book is that (1) everyone has some potential; and it is impossible and, indeed, unnecessary to attempt to identify the limits and characteristics of capacity, (2) no individual characteristic is sufficient as a condition for restricting or refusing education to any child, and (3) the focus of all evaluative efforts is most properly placed on those dimensions that are directly related to observable behavior and its change, that is, functional levels of performance.

In earlier chapters we spoke of behavior as being the result of a person's interacting with his environment. Mention has been made of the need for special educators to design and apply various types of prostheses to an individual and to his environment in order to redirect the performance of the individual toward predetermined ends. A child who has trouble reading is placed in a classroom environment that is especially tailored to increase the probability of his achieving success in this area; another youngster with missing fingers is provided a device which will allow her to pick up objects; and still a third child with a serious hearing problem is taught to read lips. The focus of psychological and educational evaluation efforts should be on identifying the characteristics of the person and of his environment that can be easily observed and that are presumably directly related to his performance or behavior in the area of interest (Newland, 1971). From these data, then, the special educator is able to judge where and how to prosthetize the child, his environment, the training procedures, or all three. Evaluation serves the function of directing the instructional program. It should never be an end in itself; it should be continuous; and it should never lead one to question, assume, or conclude that educational programing for any youngster may not be appropriate. There is never an excuse for giving up on a child because he is too disabled, because your available materials are inadequate, or because the diagnostician paints a dismal picture of the child's aptitude.

THE CHILD

One necessary condition for establishing a youngster's instructional program is knowing as much as possible about his performance and style of functioning. We will be much more specific and comprehensive about the techniques for such an assessment later in the chapter, but we want to emphasize now that the problem of describing a child is not extraordinarily difficult. First and foremost the special educator or diagnostician must decide what it is he wishes to assess. Is it reading speed or comprehension? Is it visual acuity or performance in tracking a line of print from left to right? Is it moving about within a room filled with furniture without bumping into objects or writing a line of figures that are presented orally? Is it knowing how to zip and unzip a garment? Not only would one want to know if the child in question can do any of these tasks, but it is important to be able to judge how well, to what extent, and in which of the subskills involved in each of these larger tasks he is unsure or fails. And so, his performance or functional level in those areas about which we are concerned is one of the important dimensions we must measure.

Another purpose of evaluating a child's functioning is to determine the rate at which he performs a task. It is true that we are interested in the student's making acceptable responses to a situation, but in addition we ought to be concerned that he progresses in executing the task toward increasingly more efficient and effective rates. Speed of performance, number of correct responses during an established time interval, and duration of response are all indices of rate. They will help the teacher determine when a child should be moved to another level of instruction or an alternate set of related tasks, or perhaps when he should be switched to a different instructional setting.

A third category of assessment that has direct implications for considering how to begin altering a child's environment, and thus his performance or behavior, is the style or technique the student chooses to employ in dealing with a problem. Does he count on his fingers in a simple addition problem? Does he always add when he sees a column of figures? Is he prone to both sound and spell when attacking words during reading? Does he consistently look at the teacher's mouth for clues when he is asked to respond to spelling words? Is there a certain group of children with whom he consistently associates socially? Does he insist on using the same pencil, chair, or instructional device whatever the subject area?

To comprehend the importance of considering these three areas of functioning in a plan for evaluating an individual, and the meaning each has in the designing of an educational or training program of management, let us consider the following situation:

David is a child who is not only interested in swimming but is currently able to jump into the deep water and swim to some extent. As his swimming mentor you decide that you want him to increase the distance he is now swimming. It is your purpose to train or "educate" him to do this. The first issue with which you must deal is establishing how well he is swimming now—to assess his performance level. You can best do this, obviously, by asking him to swim and by recording his distance on a number of occasions. Secondly, you may be interested in assessing the speed with which he is able to traverse a given distance. Thus, you can establish time over distance, or functional rate. You should be interested in how he swims as well, for it is clear that certain swimming patterns or styles (such as carrying the head out of the water, not kicking the legs, smacking the water with the arms, or treading water while taking a breath of air) will deleteriously affect distance and speed. Knowing which of these (or any other equally inefficient or ineffective behavior) is present will serve to direct the focus of any program of management you might select for David.

You see, by focusing our evaluative efforts on those functional qualities of the child that we can easily observe, we can find the possible remedial or therapeutic approaches more readily than if we deal with hypothetical constructs. Notice, and here we place great emphasis, that no effort was given to attempting to establish the child's potential or capacity for swimming. We believe that even if it were possible to make such a judgment, knowing this information would not add any precision to the kind of management program you might choose to enhance David's swimming prowess. Indeed, knowing that he has the capacity to swim only 100 yards would probably restrict your inclination to spend much time at all with David in a training program.

To sum up this point, one of the central purposes of evaluation is to establish functional levels, rate, and individual techniques of dealing with the environment. These data are considered, along with other information, as the basis for casting the direction the educational program should take.

There is a second cluster of pertinent traits that are important but often ignored or forgotten in the process of evaluating psychological and educational characteristics. We are referring to a child's appearance and the possible impact that it might have on the way in which a teacher or therapist deals with his educational problem. Exceptional children are very often unattractive: their bodies may be misshapen or their faces disfigured; they may have offensive odors or unkempt clothing, and they may be unable to control bodily functions. These factors affect other people's reactions and have a very significant, but virtually unknown, impact on the effectiveness with which teachers and therapists interact with such children. Although this dimension is not usually part of the process of evaluation, there is no question that more attention must be directed toward appearance and toward somehow altering traits that will be repugnant to most teachers. This must be intentionally considered so that a youngster will not receive a poor program because of such traits.

THE ENVIRONMENT

A child's behavior and his level of functioning are shaped by the interaction that occurs between him and his environment. We have mentioned some of the traits of the individual to which we ought to give attention in evaluation. It is of at least equal importance that psychological and educational diagnosticians, as well as special educators, intentionally and systematically evaluate those aspects of the environment that are likely to influence the child's functioning in all of the important dimensions, e.g., communication, social, emotional, motor, academic, and vocational areas of performance. The idea is to make an effort to determine which components of the child's surroundings are related to and either facilitate or restrict increased development of skills on his part. With this information, the special educator is in a better position to begin considering ways in which the environment might be prosthetized to guide the behavior of the child in the desired direction. When we speak of behavior, we mean, of course, the level, rate, and quality of the child's performance in various areas, including deportment.

What kind of information can one collect about a student's environment? A most obvious type is information about the child's physical surroundings. The kinds of chairs he sits on and the general layout of his classroom, the type and strength of illumination, noises and other potentially distracting conditions, the availability of ramps or elevators, types of writing instruments the child must use, and the height of toilets—all illustrate the kinds of physical phenomena that should come under special education's evaluative scrutiny. The child's social and instructional environment are of equal importance. The evaluator should observe factors such as the way the teacher sequences tasks, the correctness with which reinforcers are offered by the teacher when a child responds in certain ways, the manner in which the teacher uses aides during an instructional sequence, the types of children with whom the child is expected to interact during school, and the attitude with which the teacher approaches the task of providing instruction to a child. Of course, the instructional environment is complex and contains many subtle nuances; however, broadly speaking, the evaluative effort of the environment should deal with the curriculum, the instructional methods used, materials and media, preferred placement settings, and factors of social interaction.

There are several other elements in a child's environment that warrant evaluative attention by the diagnostician before a decision is made on an educational plan. One factor that should be given attention is the stability of the youngster's environment from one moment to the next. Does the teacher change his instructional practices with the child with such frequency that the youngster seems to be confused about how to solve a problem in a certain area? For example, are reinforcers given to the youngster for speaking out at one time and then on the next day withheld when he attempts to converse spontaneously? Are changes in the instructional objectives made so often that fundamental skills are never acquired by the youngster? Does the teacher "fish around" within the curriculum without establishing a progressively more difficult instructional sequence? The stability of the child's environment from one moment to the next is an important aspect of the environmental evaluation. You can see how significant it is when one is deciding on issues pertaining to educational management.

The consistence of the child's environment among the various settings within which he functions is also of importance from an evaluative perspective. If one is to determine possible causes of behavior disorders, it is useful to know the extent and type of possible incongruity between the child's home and school, among classrooms, or between teachers. Inconsistencies can range from expectations of behavior by supervising adults to techniques that are used to deal with the child's exceptionalities, from freedom to move about in his environment to the kinds of reinforcement situations available to him, or from the kinds of supervision he has in one setting in contrast to others to the yardsticks that are employed to assess his behavior. There is no question that lack of stability and lack of consistency contribute to the incidence of debilitating exceptionalities if each is not properly identified and managed.

Finally, if we are concerned about knowing how best to facilitate the development of specific skills on the part of a child, we should know something about the kinds of problems he encounters. The types, intensity, and frequency of problems will vary greatly among youngsters. In short, the idea here is to try to determine what is "bugging" each child as data are continuously collected about his environment.

We hope that the reader will appreciate the reasons for the psychological and educational evaluation of the child and his environment in relevant areas and with appropriate techniques. Just as a physician evaluates your body functioning and the environment within which you exist before determining the course of medical management, the diagnostician and special educator systematically collect data which are going to be helpful in establishing the program of educational management. From these data, the teacher might strive to deal with such questions as the following:

1 Broadly viewed, what personal prostheses, environmental prostheses, and special instructional techniques available for use by the child should be considered as a fundamental part of his educational program?

2 Are the curricular skill targets and goals which I have identified for emphasis in the child's program appropriate for him at this time? Have they been properly sequenced?

3 Are the instructional techniques I am using making a difference in the child's performance, and in which areas can they be improved upon?

4 Given children in a class with identified instructional characteristics and needs, how can each youngster be integrated into the various instructional groups so that all parties will profit?

5 What types of instructional devices are available, or can be constructed, to help him increase in his level and rate of skill acquisition, and, at the same time, not be incompatible with the instructional methods that have been selected for use?

6 How can I best confirm my hypotheses about the child's instructional needs in an informal way?

7 What kind of placement setting, of those available, might best provide the youngster with the instructional program which I view as proper?

8 What possible factors outside of school could be contributing to the child's in-school performance? How can I assess the impact that these are making on his achievement level and rate?

9 How effective has my teaching been with this child in contrast to other children, and what might be some reasons for any disparity?

FUNDAMENTALS UNDERLYING EDUCATIONAL EVALUATION

Before we describe procedures, techniques, and devices for assessing exceptional children and their environments, it is most important that you be aware of some of the different points of view that have been expressed about evaluation. Moreover, we want to apprise you of the basic framework we have selected to employ in this discussion and the reasons for our choice. We anticipate that this will make you a more adept evaluator and increase your skill in dealing with the various facets of evaluation.

WHAT TYPES OF DATA HAVE GREATEST UTILITY?

This question is the most fundamental of all, for the way in which it is answered has a direct relationship to your philosophy regarding the proper role of a teacher. The types of evaluative data which you consider to be important reflect your view of a teacher's mission. Moreover, the explanations of behavior you accept influence the kinds of data you will collect.

Think about what this means. If you take the position that a child has problems in paying attention to the teacher, is consistently wrong in carrying when faced with problems containing two columns of addition, and reverses certain letters in reading and spelling because of "cognitive insufficiency," you will need data that allegedly determine the type and magnitude of this insufficiency. On the other hand, you could say he has these problems because he has been brought up in an impoverished social milieu, or because he possesses an inadequate level of certain neural enzymes, or because he has been exposed to a poorly sequenced set of curricular tasks. Each of these various explanations of the child's inadequacies demands the gathering of different types of evaluative data. Since your overriding goal is to arrange an effective program for each child, it is important to decide where to focus your evaluative efforts and what kind of data you want.

Neisworth and Smith (1973) have summarized four of the most prominent types of causal explanations that are used to describe the occurrence of behaviors (Table 6-1).

1 Explanations for behavior that are classified as hypothetical and internal (quadrant 1) cannot be directly measured and are purported to reside inside a person. Thus, a child who is unable to add, such as 1 + 1, could be using ego-defense mechanisms because of a basic conflict he has over resolving the anxiety attendant on his parent's divorce. Although none of these presumed phenomena can be observed in a direct way, specialists who subscribe to this position would be interested in attempting to evaluate the nature, type, and magnitude of the child's ego-defense mechanisms and anxieties in the psychological and educational assessment procedures.

2 In quadrant 2 we have classified those determinants of behavior that are hypothetical and external to the person. Again, these phenomena defy direct observation. The difficulties our youngster has with simple addition problems might be explained from this perspective as the result of his associating with such a permissive classroom that the social pressures were of insufficient magnitude to impress on him the need for acquiring this skill. In spite of the impossibility of directly observing and quantifying one's milieu in terms of permissiveness and the attendant social pressures, a diagnostician who subscribes to this category of explanations for problem behavior is obligated to direct his psychoeducational evaluative efforts in this direction.

3 Behaviors are caused by circumstances that are observable, i.e., actual and internal to the person (quadrant 3). Inattentiveness, reversing letters in

TABLE 6-1 ILLUSTRATIONS OF FOUR APPROACHES TO EXPLAIN CAUSES OF BEHAVIOR

	Objectivity	
Locus	Hypothetical	Actual
Internal	1. a. Psychoanalysis b. Drive theories c. Cognitive theories	3. a. Neurology b. Brain chemistry c. Genetics
External	2. a. Social pressure b. Role expectation c. Group sensitivity	4. a. Psychophysics b. Operant conditioning c. Respondent conditioning

From: Neisworth, J. T., and Smith, R. M. *Modifying Retarded Behavior.* Boston: Houghton Mifflin, 1973. P. 35.

reading and spelling, and even problems in calculating accurately could very well be caused by biochemical and neurological disturbances that can be accurately observed and measured by medical approaches—although sometimes not accurately until after death. Thus, the physician's diagnostic efforts are quite properly directed toward these potential cause and effect relationships. But let us raise a cautionary flag at this point. A bona fide medical observation of brain injury in a child is quite different from the use of psychological instrumentation and data to explain these behaviors as the result of brain injury. The latter explanation is hypothetical and internal.

4 In quadrant 4, behavior is described as resulting from factors that are outside of the person. These phenomena can be directly observed, measured, and manipulated. There is a functional relationship between their presence and the behavioral characteristics of the youngster, and they are within the control of the teacher, the therapist, or the parent. These variables could include room temperature, extraneous noise within the classroom, illumination, the number of problems the child is expected to solve and their level of difficulty, the type of verbal feedback he is given before and after he attempts to respond to a problem, how often he is praised for his efforts, the makeup of the reading group to which he has been assigned, the kind of instructional devices he is given during the spelling period, the method used in teaching him to speak more distinctly, and the degree of specificity with which tasks are presented during periods of individual instruction. All of these dimensions can be described in a way that allows for direct observation by the diagnostician; they can be measured (very often by a simple frequency count if their description is sufficiently clear); and each of them can be shown to have influence over the child's behavior through a process of continuing to collect data as variables change. For example, speed and accuracy in doing certain types of arithmetic may be controlled to a certain extent by the temperature of the room or the teacher's praise of the child for attending to the task. One could confirm this hypothesis by altering each or both of these variables over a period of time, maintaining records on performance during the interval, and in this fashion assessing the impact that they have on the child's level of functioning in this area.

Because observation is possible, we can say with a good deal of assurance that factors classified within quadrants 3 and 4 have direct influence on behavior and performance. We can actually observe them, manipulate them, and tabulate their influence because of their observable qualities. The presumed conditions in quadrants 1 and 2 defy definition and quantification at a satisfactory level of precision and have dubious use for either evaluation or management. They have obvious research interest for many reasons, one of which is to make attempts toward moving them from the hypothetical to the actual.

Historically, special education has focused a great deal of attention on attempting to explain exceptionalities in children from the perspective of quadrants 1, 2, and 3. "Perceptual-motor integration disorders," "weak cognitive structure," "cultural disadvantagedness," and "minimal cerebral dysfunction" are familiar labels and terms in the professional and lay literature, all of which have been used to rationalize certain performances in children. Such rationalizations have led to the development of various formal psychoeducational evaluative devices that purport to assess the presence and degree of various hypothetical conditions. To further complicate the picture, remedial program kits have been developed and published to deal with children who possess one or more of these hypothetical conditions. Let us illustrate the chain of reasoning and the process by which decisions are made on these issues.

1 Suppose that a child has trouble copying materials from the blackboard onto his paper, confuses certain letters in reading, and has some trouble writing within the lines on his spelling paper.

2 The school psychologist or educational diagnostician secures this information from the child's teacher (or teachers) and makes a decision on the types of instruments he might use to evaluate the child and to explain his presumed disabilities. (It is instructive to recognize here that the instruments which the school psychologist or diagnostician selects are likely to be compatible with his attraction toward one of the four categories of explanations for behavior. Each evaluative device is based on a theory—the examiner, then, selects not only the assessment instrument but the theory on which it is developed as well. There are widely used psychoeducational instruments whose theoretical underpinnings are totally hypothetical, whether internal or external.) And so, if the diagnostician's orientation toward causes of behavior is hypothetical-internal, he might suspect that a child with these characteristics has perceptual-integration disorders. Thus, he would probably select an instrument that ostensibly measures for such disorders. (It is worth noting here that if the examiner is wrong in his hunch concerning the reason for the child's strange performance, as well he might be since his explanation deals with hypothetical constructs, he has compounded his error by selecting a device that claims to assess factors that defy direct observation.)

3 The child performs on the evaluative instrument and his performance is interpreted in terms that themselves are illusory, because the theory and the measuring device deal with hypothetical phenomenona. Because the diagnostician chose not to observe behavior directly, his rationalization of any inadequacies in the child's performance on the test can only add to the illusion.

4 The diagnostician explains the problem as being a perceptual-integration disorder which requires immediate remediation. The recommendation is made to use a published perceptual-integration remedial device that is keyed to the evaluative device on which the child's performance has been

assessed. Both are founded on the same tenuous theoretical construct, and the potential errors begin to multiply (see Table 6-2).

We hope that you appreciate the tremendous errors of judgment that can be made by school psychologists, educational diagnosticians, and special education personnel when prominence is given to the use of explanations, instruments, and remedial procedures that do not provide for direct observation. It is virtually impossible to be precise when hypothetical propositions are used. Validity and reliability will be unacceptably low in such cases, and the diagnostician and therapist will observe the problems in children that their preestablished expectations suggest. These kinds of subjective, impressionistic, hunchy, and imprecise speculations have no place in education because of the potential they have for seriously damaging a child's progress and future. Read *Trick or Treatment: How and When Psychotherapy Fails* (Stuart, 1970) for a complete and penetrating analysis of this issue.

The approach that we recommend to the selection of the kinds of evaluative data which will be most helpful to special educators is to focus total attention on the actual dimensions, i.e., quadrants 3 and 4. Generally, the more inferences and assumptions you have to make about causes of behavior—the more unobtrusive and ill defined the concepts and terminology—the less definite and certain you can be about an appropriate remedial or management program. The preceding chapter has described the various procedures

TABLE 6-2 AN ILLUSTRATION OF ACCUMULATION OF ERRORS RESULTING FROM HYPOTHETICAL EXPLANATIONS OF BEHAVIOR

Child is observed to have certain types of performance problems which the examiner chooses to explain using hypothetical constructs that defy direct observation and validation.	Child's performance is assessed on a test that is based on the same hypothetical constructs. If performance decrements are noted, the child is called deficient in the trait that is presumably evaluated by the device.	Child is recommended for a remedial program that is developed from the test and the hypothetical postulates—both of which have unproven reliability and validity. The child's performance is usually profiled and the "appropriate" remediation is recommended on the basis of his "symptoms."
POSSIBLE ERROR #1 Misconstrued reason for performance problems.	POSSIBLE ERROR #2 (plus typical errors of measurement) Selection of test that allegedly evaluates constructs that are hypothetical.	POSSIBLE ERROR #3 Remediation may be off target because it is based on hypothetical constructs, as is the evaluative device, both of which may be in error, i.e., the remedial devices are based on the test and the test is based on the hypothetical postulates of the "theory."

physicians use to collect pertinent actual internal information about a child's physical state and character. These data are of great value because in a number of instances they can lead to precise forms of medical intervention, both preventive and remedial, some of which are described in Chapters 3 and 4. As a special educator, though, you will find it most helpful, practical, precise, reliable, and valid to focus your attention on actual external phenomena in both diagnosis and remediation.

Quay's (1968) model, which will be discussed in Chapter 7, illustrates an actual-external (quadrant 4) orientation toward educational evaluation and remediation. His framework allows for the direct assessment of a youngster's pertinent educational characteristics. Youngsters can have educational problems because of an inability to see, to hear (auditory acuity), or to feel (tactile acuity). Performance in each of these areas of behavior should be assessed in instances where a teacher or another kind of professional suspects that a child may have a problem. Quay suggests that diagnostic attention should be given to other types of input functions, e.g., the extent to which a child responds to each of the three types of stimulus modes (visual, auditory, and tactile), his grasp of the significance or meaning of these stimuli, and how well he can remember what he has seen, felt, or heard. In each instance very definite behaviors can be observed that one can tie to each of the twelve input cells.

The second major cluster of functions in the Quay model pertains to the child's response, whether it be motor or verbal. Dexterity of responses, their appropriateness in various situations, organization of response components, and response delay are the skill areas that are suggested for evaluation on the output side.

Since behavior is shaped by its consequences, it is important to assess the characteristics of the factors that pertain to reinforcement and punishment. Quay believes, for example, that it is of significance to determine whether a child sees, hears, or is able to feel one or more of the various kinds of reinforcers which the teacher or therapist has selected to use. There may be no problem in any of the input functions or in the response areas; the disorder may be environmental—that is, the consequences of the child's responses may be at fault. In addition to acuity, Quay suggests that the evaluator consider the child's orientation to the reinforcer, the capacity of the reinforcer to change the child's performance, the effect of delay of reinforcement on behavior, and the amount and ratio of reinforcement. None of these factors is hypothetical and all can be directly measured and tabulated. The system which Quay recommends is consistent with our position in this book, i.e., that behavior is caused by the person's interaction with his environment. The evaluation, then, must focus on actual phenomena that pertain to the child (Quay's input and response functions) and to his environment (Quay's reinforcement functions). These are the kinds of data he believes are most relevant to evaluating exceptional children and their environments.

Iscoe and Payne (1972) have suggested a model for testing a child in three categories of behaviors, all of which they believe are of importance to educators and other behavior specialists who are concerned with exceptionalities. The domains are as follows:

I Physical domain (PH)
  a visibility (vis)
  b locomotion (loc)
  c communication (com)

II Perceived adjustment domain (AD)
  a peer acceptance (peer)
  b family interaction (fam)
  c self-esteem (self)

III Educational domain (ED)
  a motivation (mot)
  b academic level (aca)
  c educational potential (ptl)

In each of these six subareas the authors have listed seven criteria for rating a child using as contrast "normal children" of the same sex and age. Being rated "1" indicates no trouble in the area, "7" suggests extreme problems. Assuming that the rater's reliability is at a satisfactory level (the authors report a range of .47 to .85) and that the rating statements are similar at each of the seven levels among all nine subareas (that is, a weighting of "4" means the same throughout the categories), the model suggests a way to focus on pertinent variables in diagnosis and remediation. For example, although we haven't described the various rating categories, consider the ratings in Table 6–3.

This profile of ratings indicates that the youngster has a significant problem in appearance (6), experiences great difficulty in getting about (5) and in communication (4), and has serious problems with school performance (5). Her adjustment behaviors are fairly good (3 and 4), her family is facilitating (1), and her motivation within an educational setting is good (2). As you might

TABLE 6–3 HYPOTHETICAL RATING
PROFILE FOR SUSAN

	vis	loc	com
PH	6	5	4
	peer	fam	self
AD	3	1	4
	mot	aca	ptl
ED	2	5	?

Key: 1 = No problem
     7 = Very serious disorder

suspect, we would prefer not to speculate about her intellectual potential (0), although Iscoe and Payne include that dimension in their scheme.

The whole point here is that the approach of Iscoe and Payne in assessing exceptional children and their environments is a functional one. It has the potential for insisting that the educational diagnostician or special educator be specific and focus on pertinent instructional variables (with perhaps the exception of the educational potential subarea). Of course, the value of the procedure will increase dramatically as the specificity, functionality, and reliability of the rating scales increase. This procedure, as well as the one advised by Quay, clearly has potential for providing clear direction for the collection of information about a child and his environment which could lead directly to appropriate programs of education, treatment, and therapy. This is the orientation suggested by quadrant 4.

DEPENDABILITY OF THE DATA

Since we will be making decisions about educational management programs and procedures for preventing disabling conditions from data that are collected on a child and on his environment, it is of utmost importance that all of the information be correct and represent the situation in the most accurate way. All of us exhibit extreme behavior from time to time, and these high and low levels are uncharacteristic of us under most circumstances. We would certainly not want anyone to judge us and design a program for us on the basis of these extreme, atypical exhibitions. And so, there are several important topics about data, their collection, the measurement of performance, and possible sources of errors that must be considered as a function of the extent to which one can depend on data. The most prominent of these issues will be considered in this section.

The student

A youngster can exercise biasing influences over test results to such an extent that the examiner or observer will draw erroneous conclusions concerning what the child needs educationally or therapeutically. It is obviously important to guard against such influences. When the examiner believes the testing conditions are causing the child to respond in ways that are or could be interpreted inaccurately, these conditions should be changed or the evaluation session should be terminated.

Lack of attention and cooperation on the part of the child are among the most frequent conditions that serve to bias the collection of data. The problems may result from the youngster's physical condition, disturbances within the classroom or school, distractions before or during the period of evaluation, the child's fear of the situation, personal problems including being hungry or needing to go to the bathroom, or not knowing what is expected in the situation. Whatever the problem, every effort should be made to allay the child's concerns, to facilitate attentiveness to the task, and to enlist his complete cooperation. The data that are collected under atypical conditions will be inaccurate and usually result in an interpretation that is of disservice to the youngster.

The examiner

Dependence on the data, and whatever interpretations are given, is in large measure associated with the extent to which one can depend on the examiner. He must make a host of critical decisions that clearly reflect his competence as a collector and analyzer of information. Since in so many cases the examiner is a professional or a specialist within the school system and has allegedly had special training in evaluation, there is a natural tendency for most teachers and parents not to question his competence or findings. We believe that validity checks should be built in at every stage of the process of assessment and management, for few standards or procedures have been unanimously agreed upon and should be accepted without question.

The examiner's competence is unquestionably critical. He must be able to enlist the cooperation of the child, maximize the youngster's performance, and minimize errors of measurement. The examiner must determine for himself whether he is competent to administer and interpret data from whatever evaluative device is most appropriate for a given child (Newland, 1971). This decision is directly related to his previous training and whether he has had supervised clinical experience in the use of various evaluative devices. Instruments are developed around many, many assumptions or "givens," one of which is that the examiner knows what he is doing when he chooses, scores, and analyzes the results of a given test.

Attached to the whole issue of the examiner's competence is the ability to select the most appropriate testing devices and procedures (Newland 1971). He has thousands of possible instruments to choose from; some of them are appropriate for assessing a certain constellation of variables but unapplicable to other situations. Still other tests have built-in weaknesses that render them ineffective in any case. It is of inestimable importance that each examiner be fully aware of the strengths and weaknesses of the most prominent test instruments, and of the circumstances that dictate the use of certain procedures instead of others. One important rule of thumb to aid the examiner in this area, whether he be a psychologist or a teacher, is always to select the procedure that allows for a direct and readily observable measure of performance by the child on whatever variables he wishes to assess. A second, related rule is to choose instruments that do not entail making unobservable and unverifiable inferences about performance, about causes of or reasons for a certain performance, or about the most appropriate ways to deal with a child's educational weakness. It is best to strive consistently to use measurement devices that de-emphasize the need to make inferences at any and all levels.

Bias on the part of the examiner about a certain child or about a group of people of which the child is a representative can exert a very deleterious effect at all stages of evaluation and management. If a child smells bad, is poorly clothed, is unappealing, or comes from a social group or is of a race which the examiner even mildly dislikes for some reason, there is every likelihood that such prejudice will result in the examiner's gathering unrepresentative samples of the child's behavior and misinterpreting the findings (Deutsch et al., 1967; Weiner, 1967). On each occasion the examiner should inquire of himself the extent to which he may be intolerant of or opinionated about the child he has been requested to evaluate.

The kind and extent of experience which the examiner has had in using various tests is important, but of equal importance is the experience he has had with various types of children. Experience is especially pertinent in situations in which he must deal with children who have significant exceptionalities, for the measurement of their behavior often involves such unusual problems that their scores do not reflect their typical performance. This occurs because the necessary adaptations have not been made in the testing situation, which, obviously, is the responsibility of every examiner.

There are a host of other issues having to do with the examiner's dependence on the data and his resulting interpretations. For example:

1 What trade-offs have been made, such as selecting a test which is less valid than another in the interest of saving time or money?

2 Have the observations of the examiner or of the teacher been validated, or is there only one assessment of the child without any further documentation of his performance inadequacies?

3 Have the child's responses been properly recorded, his scores been correctly tabulated, and the appropriate tables used in comparing his performance with that of the normative group?

4 Has the examiner given an economical and reasonable interpretation of the child's performance? Are the examiner's recommendations for the child's program of management clearly stated and possible for the teacher to implement? Do both the teacher and the examiner consider the suggestions as hypotheses which require continued reappraisal?

The setting

The accuracy of the data and the extent to which they reflect a true picture of a child's typical level and style of functioning are not to be overlooked at any stage of evaluation. A teacher who has been given recommendations by an examiner should be able to have confidence that the suggestions will work in the child's natural environment, which in this case is usually the classroom. Similarly, parents of exceptional children ought to be able to have faith that a counselor's or a teacher's advice will have enough generalized validity to help them deal with their youngster's problems at home.

If a child is evaluated within an environment that is contrived and completely unrepresentative of his usual surroundings, there is every reason to expect that his performance or behavior will be different from that expected of him in a normal social circumstance. Unfortunately, many psychological and educational diagnostic efforts are conducted outside of the child's typical surroundings by someone who is often a complete stranger to him. If it is true that behavior is a direct function of the child's relationship with his environment, then submitting a child to an examination by an unfamiliar person, away from his familiar classroom setting, and at a time of day that is not customarily identified with formal diagnosis, can only lead to a performance by the child that defies an adequate and accurate characterization. A foreign environment, during evaluation or management, will lead to unpredictable imperfections in the child's performance that could in turn lead to erroneous conclusions and irrelevant recommendations.

We suggest that the evaluation of performance and the diagnosis of educationally related disorders of youngsters take place within the environment for which recommendations are to be made—that is, the child should be observed and his behavior studied within his natural environment so that the same full range of typical conditions prevails during periods of evaluation as during educational management. Obviously, this is not always possible, nor is it al-

This school psychologist not only employs standardized tests in a formal setting but also assesses behavior in the natural environment.

ways desirable, for sometimes data must be obtained in a situation in which the environment is very carefully controlled. For example, a detailed reading analysis, the evaluation of certain types of communication skills, and the measurement of motor performance may very well require the use of an individually administered test under rigorously controlled conditions.

The evaluative devices

The student may be ready, the examiner well trained and experienced, and the setting appropriate, but if there are problems with the measuring device all of these other important issues are inconsequential. Errors of judgment will be made if a given evaluative device is inappropriate for the situation or has internal weaknesses. All who are concerned with the evaluation of performance or behavior, including those who use such data to arrange the instructional environment of children, must pay careful attention to the characteristics of the evaluative devices that are used with children who exhibit exceptionalities. In this section we will review some of the most prominent of these concerns.

Among the most basic of the questions to be answered is the extent to which a given instrument is appropriate for evaluating a certain set of problems. It is vital that the examiner determine what variables he wants to evaluate before he chooses an instrument. A physician selects a measuring device only after making a tentative judgment about which bodily function he wants to analyze. An automobile mechanic decides on the type of tool to use in evaluating your car's problems after having determined what it is he wants to observe. If it is the fuel system, a certain group of instruments is more appropriate than if it is the electrical components. These same principles apply to evaluating problems of exceptional children. Arithmetic, perceptual-motor, social, communication, or any other area of performance ought to be evaluated with measuring devices appropriate to that area. Of course, there are other issues to which one must attend before deciding on a particular instrument; however, the most fundamental question is the extent to which a given device evaluates a specific area of performance in a direct way.

The reliability and validity of the scores associated with the instrument that you have selected to use in a given situation will influence the dependability of the data and your interpretation of the scores. First, reliability refers to how well the device measures what it claims to measure from one time to another (test-retest), in terms of the test's own internal consistency (split-half or odd-even), and in the alternate forms of the test. Second, one must be concerned about validity, or how well a test evaluates what the authors claim for it. Three prominent types of validity are content validity (determined by analysis of the contents of the test, using as a standard of comparison subject matter which the device purports to measure), concurrent validity (assessed by comparison of scores on the test with scores on another measure which evaluates the same characteristics), and construct validity (determined by the degree to which the test measures factors that are contained in relevant psychological theory or pertinent constructs).

Scores which a child obtains on a given test can be expected to vary somewhat on successive administrations of the test. These variations are related to the reliability of the instrument: the higher the reliability, the less the variation, and vice versa. The reliability of each test and subtest will vary from group to group (e.g., inner-city youngsters as opposed to the rural poor). Test manuals usually provide an estimate of the degree of variation in scores one can expect should the test be given to a defined group of youngsters over and over again. This estimate is called the "standard error of measurement."

It is most important to be aware of and account for the peculiar unreliability or error of a test as you interpret the results of a child's scores. Assume that a child scored an IQ of 92 on an individual intelligence test whose error of measurement is 8. If the youngster was evaluated under optimum conditions, 68 percent of his scores would be within one standard error of his "real" score, which, of course, can never be known for certain. In this case, the range of scores would be from 84 to 100. Two standard errors on the same test would broaden the band to between 76 and 108, and we can be 95 percent sure that the child's "true" or "real" score lies within that range.

If one is aware of the error of measurement peculiar to each test, it is no surprise to see some differences in a child's scores on repeated testings. Unfortunately, not enough attention is given to this concept in the professional literature, and dogmatic interpretations are given to mild variations in test scores when such differences can reasonably be expected. With exceptional children, the standard error of measurement must be carefully considered before a plan for instruction is finalized.

The usability of an instrument is a practical consideration that should not be neglected when one is evaluating exceptional children. Some tests are very difficult to administer, they take a long time to give, or they may have very complicated procedures for scoring. Some devices are difficult to interpret and others have simplistic, or almost naïve, procedures for analyzing the meaning of a child's performance. A test may be rejected because it is too costly either to acquire or to administer. All of these issues of usability are important to consider as one approaches the testing situation, whether for an individual or for a group of children. An examiner must decide what he is willing to "trade off" among all of these factors before he makes a final decision regarding how, when, and where evaluation of performance is to take place.

The Center for the Study of Education at the University of California at Los Angeles has developed a procedure for evaluating tests along a number of important lines. Their procedure began with an analysis of the educational objectives of the elementary school program (they have since done the same thing for nursery and kindergarten levels). Standardized tests, and their associated subtests, were then categorized according to their objective or objectives. A test rating system was developed, called the MEAN Rating System after the four major areas to be evaluated: (1) measurement validities, (2) examinee appropriateness, (3) administrative usability, and (4) normed techni-cal excellence. Each test and subtest was rated in twenty-four areas according to specific criteria. The final products, the *CSE Elementary School Test Evalu-ations* and the *CSE-ECRC Preschool/Kindergarten Test Evaluations,* provide a compendium of goals along with an analysis of the tests and subtests that can be used to evaluate a child's performance in each area.

Table 6–4 lists the criteria which were used to judge each of the dimensions of the MEAN Rating System. Figure 6–1 illustrates one analysis from the over 1,600 scales that were evaluated in this effort.

TABLE 6–4   CRITERIA USED IN THE MEAN RATING SYSTEM

Dimensions	Total Possible Points	Criteria or Relevant Questions
1. *Measurement va-lidity*	0 to 15 (total)	
A. Content and construct	0 to 10	Does the test appear to measure the specific educational objective? Examination of instructions and items with psychological (content) insight, and consideration of re-ported construct-validation research resulted in assignment of a rating between 0 and 10.
B. Concurrent and predictive	0 to 5	Is there direct or indirect evidence for predictive or concurrent validity? Examination of technical and ad-ministration manuals for supportive research on the test led to a sub-jective judgment on a scale from 0 to 5 points. No attempt was made to comb the research literature for additional or more recent supportive findings.
2. *Examinee appro-priateness*	0 to 15 (total)	
A. Compre-hension	0 to 4 (in each of two subareas)	Is the comprehension level correct for the age and educational level to which the test is directed? Examina-tion of the instrument that the ex-aminee sees or hears in terms of comprehension, both of items and instructions, led to two subjective judgments of 0 to 4 points each.
B. Format	0 to 2 (in each of two subareas) 0 to 1 (in a third cate-gory)	Is the test printed and organized for ease of the examinees or is taking the test a test in itself? Examination of test-page format in terms of ef-fective usage of gestalt visual prin-ciples resulted in a subjective rating from 0 to 2 points, and appropriate-ness of pacing in a rating from 0 to 1 point.

Source: The material appearing in this table was extracted from: *CSE Elementary School Test Evaluations,* Center for the Study of Evaluation, UCLA Graduate School of Education, 1970, pp. xvii and xviii. It is reproduced here with the permission of the Center.

TABLE 6-4   CONTINUED

Dimensions	Total Possible Points	Criteria or Relevant Questions
C. Recording answers	0 to 2	Is the response recording procedure simple and direct for the examinee?
3. *Administrative usability*	0 to 15 (total)	
A. Administration	0 to 2 (in one subarea) 0 to 1 (in two subareas)	Is the test easily and conveniently administered? Administration of the test from individual situations to small groups to large groups resulted in credit of 0 to 2 points. The need for training of the test administrators was credited 1 point if school staff were sufficient and 0 points if a psychometrist were needed. Tests needing more than 43 minutes were credited 0 points; tests needing less time, 1 point.
B. Scoring	0 to 2	Can the test be easily and reliably scored? Simple, objective scoring that can be done by the administrator or a scoring service received 2 points, while more difficult but objective scoring earned 1 point and subjective scoring received 0 points.
C. Interpretation	0 to 1 (in three categories) 0 to 2 (in one subarea)	Is the score interpretation simple, through use of clear and adequate norms and descriptions? If the norm range is broad, 1 point is credited; if restricted, 0 points. Common and simply interpreted scoring systems receive 1 point, while uncommon or abstruse systems receive 0 points. If conversion from raw to normed scores is clear and simple with graphs or tables, 2 points are credited. Simple, but not well-presented conversions receive 1 point and complicated conversions receive 0 points. One point is credited for national and well-sampled normative groups and 0 points are credited for normative samples that are local, outdated, or poorly sampled.
D. Score interpreter	0 to 1	What qualifications must the score interpreter have? If school staff can interpret the scores accurately, 1 point is earned; if a psychometrist is necessary for accurate interpretation, 0 points are credited.

TABLE 6-4   CONTINUED

Dimensions	Total Possible Points	Criteria or Relevant Questions
E. Can decisions be made?	0 to 3	Can decisions be made or aided on the basis of the scores? Tests with manuals providing tables or charts for educational decision making were credited 3 points. If the claim is made and appears to be reasonable that decisions can be made, 2 points are earned. The possibility or implication of decision aiding earned a test 1 point, while the doubtful nature of a test in decision-making potential earned it 0 points.
4. *Normed technical excellence*	0 to 15 (total)	
A. Stability	0 to 3	Is the test reliable? Three reliability ratings were made; one each for stability (test-retest), internal-consistency (Kuder-Richardson, alpha, split-half, or odd-even), and alternate-form reliabilities. Points were assigned according to the size of the reported reliability coefficients, computed from a specific, limited age group. An appropriate coefficient of .90 or more earned 3 points; .80 to .90 earned 2 points; .70 to .80 earned 1 point; and less than .70 earned 0 points.
B. Internal consistency	0 to 3	Same as "A" above.
C. Alternative forms	0 to 3	Same as "A" above.
D. Replicability	0 to 1	Are normed scores obtained under replicable conditions? If so, 1 point is earned; if not, 0 points are earned.
E. Range of coverage	0 to 3	Does the test have an adequate range of coverage? Test score distributions with more than adequate ranges received 3 points, and distributions with adequate floor and ceiling for the specific group received 2 points. Whenever examinees appeared to have reached the floor or ceiling, or there was evidence of score truncation, 1 point was assigned. If no information was given to make an evaluation, or even to extrapolate one from centile conversion tables, 0 points were assigned.

TABLE 6–4 CONTINUED

Dimensions	Total Possible Points	Criteria or Relevant Questions
F. Scores	0 to 2	Are the scores well-graduated, interindividual comparison scores? Scores that are well graduated but perhaps not easily understood, or poorly graduated but commonly utilized, were credited with 1 point. Scores that are poorly graduated and poorly obtained, or are poorly graduated and difficult to understand were given 0 points.

The efforts of the Center for the Study of Evaluation are of consequence to special education in two primary areas. First, having a digest of the instructional goals of available tests and evaluations is of inestimable value. One does not have to search around for descriptions that tell what kind of instruments are most appropriate for measuring a certain constellation of educational problems. A summary of these data has now been provided and they have been categorized in a system that is educationally relevant. The "trade-offs" about which we spoke earlier can be more accurately assessed since the important dimensions and their individual strengths and weaknesses have been evaluated in the MEAN Rating Scale.

Second, the process suggested by the MEAN Rating Scale is of value to special educators who find it helpful to develop their own informal evaluative devices. The factors included in the scale signal areas of great importance for one to consider as the informal procedures are formulated. This is especially true in instances when an informal device is to be used to assess a student's progress over a period of time.

STANDARD FOR THE COMPARISON OF PERFORMANCE

Sending children to school, whether they are exceptional or not, implies that some form of intentional intervention of an instructional nature will cause youngsters to gain certain skills more quickly and effectively than if they are not involved in a school program. All teachers are continuously faced with hosts of decisions about how best to deal with children individually and collectively. Some of the decisions have long-term implications and require extensive consideration and deliberation. Other judgments are of a more momentary character. In both instances, however, the teacher's behavior is the issue in question: how he elects to arrange the environment of a child to facilitate a higher level and a more rapid rate of skill acquisition. In short, with exceptional children the decisions revolve around which types of individual and environmental prostheses are desirable for each youngster at a given time.

All of these decisions require the collection of appropriate, on-target information about the child and his environment. Even as the data are collected one begins to formulate some opinions about the child or the group of chil-

Rating (circle one number in each row)

Scale headings: 0 (only in name) · 2 (a few) · 4 (some) · 6 (fair job) · 8 (best available) · 10 (hit nail on the head)

Evaluation Criteria

1. Measurement Validities
- a. Content and Construct: 0 (only in name) | 2 (a few) | 4 (some) | 6 (fair job) | 8 (best available) | 10 (hit nail on the head)
- b. Concurrent and Predictive: 0 (none reported) | 1 (very little) | 2 (some) | ③ (not enough) | 4 (considerable) | 5 (exhaustive)

M Total **7** Grade **P**

2. Examinee Appropriateness
- a. Comprehension; content: inappropriate 0 | doubtful 1 | possibly appropriate 2 | probably appropriate ③ | exactly right 4
-    instructions: 0 | 1 | 2 | ③ | 4
- b. Format
  - 1. Visual principles: ⓪ (complicated) | 1 (probably good) | 2 (outstanding aids)
  - 2. Quality of illustrations (print): 0 (not good) | ① (helpful) | 2 (excellent)
  - 3. Time and pacing: 0 (bad) | 1 (standard) | ① (appropriate for broad range)
- c. Recording answers: 0 (complicated) | ① (standard) | 2 (especially easy)

E Total **9** Grade **F**

3. Administrative Usability
- a. Administration
  - 1. Test administration: 0 (individual) | 1 (small groups) | ② (large groups)
  - 2. Training of administrators: 0 (psychometrist) | ① (school staff)
  - 3. Administration: 0 (43 + minutes) | ① (42 minutes or less)
- b. Scoring: 0 (subjective) | 1 (difficult) | ② (simple)
- c. Interpretation
  - 1. Norms
    - a. Norm range: 0 (restricted) | ① (broad)
    - b. Score interpretation: 0 (uncommon, abstruse) | ① (common, simple)
    - c. Score conversion: 0 (complicated) | ① (simple) | 2 (clear, tables)
    - d. Norm groups: ⓪ (local, outdated, or poorly sampled) | 1 (national, well sampled)
  - d. Score Interpreter: 0 (psychometrist) | ① (school staff)
  - e. Can Decisions Be Made: 0 doubtful | 1 possible | ② probable | 3 yes—charts and graphs

A Total **12** Grade **G**

4. Normed Technical Excellence
- a. Stability: not reported or less than .70 / .70 | ① .70 to .80 | .80 to .90 | .90+
- b. Internal Consistency: 0 | ① | 2 | 3
- c. Alternate form: ⓪ | 1 | 2 | 3
- d. Replicability: 0
- e. Range of Coverage: 0 (no information) | 1 (floor or ceiling reached) | ② (adequate) | 3 more than adequate
- f. Scores: 0 (poorly graduated and uncommon) | 1 (poorly graduated or uncommon) | ② (well graduated and standard)

N Total **7** Grade **P**

KEY: "G" (good; 12-15 points). The test meets the criterion very well. Little improvement appears necessary for its immediate utilization. The Center for the Study of Evaluation would endorse such a measure or employ it in its own assessment efforts.

"F" (fair; 8-11 points). The instrument is probably among the better tests available, but it does not meet well the criteria desired. Alterations would probably render the test a candidate for "G" status. If no better qualified measure were available, the CSE would employ an "F" measure, but would interpret results for the "F" criteria more cautiously.

"P" (poor; 0-7 points). The instrument does not meet the criterion; it is clearly unsatisfactory in that specific criterion. Rather than employ such a measure for assessment, CSE would seek a better device or attempt to develop one.

FIGURE 6-1   Evaluation form for the MEAN Rating System. (This evaluation form and the criteria are reproduced from *CSE Elementary School Test Evaluation*, Center for the Study of Evaluation, UCLA Graduate School of Education, 1970, pp. xvi and xvii, by permission of the Center for the Study of Evaluation.)

dren being observed. Every judgment formulated and decision reached requires the measurement of performance or behavior by either formal tests or informal, teacher-made tests. As important as any other factor involved in the process of diagnosis and evaluation is the criterion against which the performance of a child is judged. Every decision that a teacher makes about how to deal with a child requires some form of measurement, whether subjective or objective, and those data are related to some standard before management of the child is begun. At a rather subjective level, one can estimate a child's performance using past experience with other youngsters of the same chronological age or with tables of general developmental stages. These landmark stages, while imprecise and very broad, can be used as a general guide for comparison of a child's achievement prior to a more thorough analysis.

Norms that have been developed on individual tests are most frequently used as a basis for judging how well a child has performed. Most formal evaluative instruments specify the average level of achievement of children at the various age levels for each major section of the instrument. In addition, data are typically given concerning the amount of variation in the test scores for each of the different categories along with the standard error of measurement. With this information, the examiner can compare the child's score on each segment of the instrument with the performance of others of his chronological age. The examiner can then estimate his relative position within this normative group on each subtest. The accuracy of the estimate is closely related to the extent to which the youngster is a bona fide representative of the group of children who served as the normative sample. If the norms were based on the performance of urban children, and the youngster we are evaluating comes from an entirely different type of setting, we would certainly want to be cautious in our interpretation of his performance in relation to the normative data. Fortunately, most well-respected evaluative devices report data on their normative samples for large groups of children and include children of different chronological ages, different intellectual capabilities, various geographic locations and socioeconomic levels, and both sexes and various races, and according to any other variables that may have some influence on the child's performance.

We must be cautious not to use norms or developmental stages as criteria for determining the potential or the capacity of children in the respective areas of performance. It is often tempting to interpret scores that exceed or fall below the norms as a manifestation of overachievement or underachievement. Such an interpretation assumes that the scores of the normative sample are real, true scores for children that age and are reflective of their capacity to perform. It is clearly a misinterpretation of the data to suggest that a person who scores higher than the norms is exceeding his capacity. "A cup and a half of coffee" is simply not possible. This is really a manifestation of underprediction on the part of the test.

Another standard by which a student's performance can be assessed is his own previous achievement in the area under study. Here the youngster is continuously compared with himself. His own previous achievement is the standard against which future performances are judged. Obviously before a measurement of the student's performance can be taken, the examiner must have firmly in mind the exact behavior that he wishes to observe and how the evaluation will take place. The sequence, then, is to decide on the behavior, select an instrument or activity that will allow for direct observation of the child's behavior, administer the evaluative instrument to the child, and record what he did. On future occasions the same kind of evaluative procedure can be used and a direct comparison made between previous and present performances. Between the evaluative periods we would expect that appropriate and direct educational intervention would occur. The basic model is as follows:

1 Decide what behavior you want to evaluate.

↓

2 Decide what evaluative activity you can use to measure the behavior directly.

↓

3 Administer the evaluative device.

↓

4 Record the child's performance level or rate of achievement or both.

↓

5 Intervene with an instructional program in an individually appropriate way.

↓

6 Find out where the child is now by administering the same or a very similar evaluative device.

↓

7 Continue intervening with increased precision as a result of the data that are collected. Alternate with evaluations of performance.

This comparison, which is usually called an "intraindividual evaluation," can be done with great ease and precision. It also has a great deal of meaning if the teacher or evaluator is specific about the task or skill to be evaluated. Let us illustrate this point about specificity. Suppose we have a student who has trouble in addition and we finally determine that his most basic problem at this time is with the simple addition of two-digit figures without carrying. We want to find out how well he does in this area of skills. We present him with perhaps twenty or thirty of the following kinds of arithmetic problems and ask him to complete the group:

$$\begin{array}{ccccccc} 72 & 64 & 12 & 16 & 92 & 76 & 45 \\ +13 & +24 & +80 & +43 & +\ 6 & +22 & +54 \end{array}$$

We could simply record the number of problems he correctly completes by keeping a frequency count over time (Figure 6-2). This count gives a measure

Objective: Addition of two-digit figures without carrying

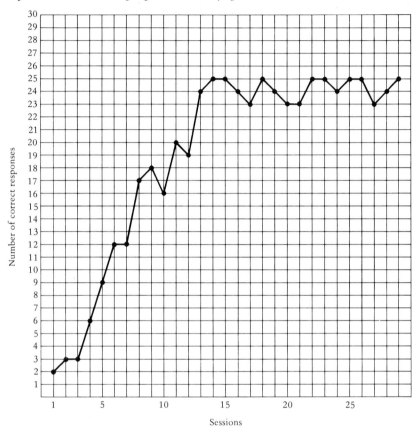

FIGURE 6-2 Frequency record for two-digit addition problems.

of performance level. We could also determine his rate of performance by presenting him with the same number of problems and recording the length of time it takes for him to complete the group with total accuracy. We must know, of course, what kind of instructional environment the child has had between the periods of evaluation.

Table 6-5 summarizes the three prominent types of criteria with which a child's performance can be compared and describes some of the major strengths and weaknesses of each.

Considering all of those who have an interest in the problems of exceptional children, it is impossible to conclude that any one of the standards of comparison that appear in Table 6-5 is better than the others. It depends on one's reasons for desiring the data. Professionals who make decisions about groups of people, who need information about categories of characteristics of various populations, or who must justify expenditures for certain types of exceptional conditions usually employ normative or developmental standards.

TABLE 6-5   STANDARDS FOR PERFORMANCE COMPARISONS

Types of Criteria	Strengths	Weaknesses
1. Normative data on a test obtained from an allegedly representative sample of subjects of whom the child is a representative	1. Facilitates comparison of child's achievement with that of other children with whom he will likely interact and be compared by society. 2. Since this type of criterion is most commonly associated with a formal evaluative device, the diagnostician and teacher can find out about the important characteristics of the test, e.g., validity, reliability, usability, etc.	1. Possibility of misinterpreting the normative data as indicative of what children at the various ages should be able to do, i.e., as a measure of capacity. 2. Norm performance is a function of so many variables (teacher's excellence, materials available, learning history of subjects) and these vary so greatly within and between normative samples that it is impossible to isolate the true character of a child's performance and the prominent influences that were and are related to it.
2. Developmental stages	1. Provides broad, general estimates for various levels of skill development. 2. Usually based on observations of large, diverse groups of children. Validity and reliability of observations are typically high.	1. Skills associated with developmental stages and their sequence are often viewed as essentially inborn, of constitutional origin, and relatively impervious to intervention. 2. Developmental stages are frequently reported or erroneously interpreted as occurring at very specific times instead of during a range of times.
3. Individual's past performance	1. Absolute measures of individual's performance. Progress is therefore defined as improvement over past performance rather than as relative to standards of others. 2. Evaluator can directly assess instructional intervention by monitoring individual increases in competence instead of relating performance to a group of subjects who are judged to be similar to the child in pertinent traits.	1. No measure of relative performance, if needed, can be obtained. 2. One must usually develop evaluating activities and recording procedures as opposed to the standardized activities and format usually associated with formal evaluating devices.

Administrators talk about 70 percent of the children within a given school area as having certain characteristics and then relate this fraction to larger normative groups. Pediatricians speak of a child's being at the sixtieth percentile in his head size; that is, 60 percent of the same sex and age as the child being examined have smaller head sizes.

Most teachers, on the other hand, should not be mainly concerned with how a child is performing with regard to other children the same age. We operate under the assumption that our mission is to provide circumstances that will allow *each* youngster to move from his present level of achievement to progressively higher levels. We do not stop a program of language training because the youngster is performing better than 80 percent of his peers. Likewise, we don't give up on a systematic instructional program because "most severely retarded children *can't* learn to talk," a comment heard so frequently in years past. In short, the standard for comparison is inextricably related to the use one wishes to make of the data.

AN EVALUATIVE SEQUENCE

The assessment of a child's performance and the collection of data for subsequent use in the design of an instructional program should not be done in a haphazard way. There are many real and potential problems involved in administering tests to children without a clear rationale, because the tests happen to be available, or as a result of a particular device's having received special attention in the literature. Deno (1971) has summarized the situation regarding the use and interpretation of tests by numerous school administrators, diagnosticians, and teachers as follows:

> The products of test developers were taken over enthusiastically by the schools, as though essential clues to educational management resided in test-derived data. In many cases enchantment with tests grew to the point that Kaplan's "law of instrument" ("Give a small boy a hammer and he will find that everything he encounters needs pounding" [1964, p. 28]) seems to prevail. The adequacy of a school or a clinic's evaluation system seemed to be judged more by the size of the test battery administered than the amount of action-relevant information provided by the procedures used (p. 359).

Diagnostic "fishing expeditions" are to be avoided at all costs. Indiscriminate testing of children is expensive, and it also increases the likelihood that the evaluation will "find something wrong" with the child. That is what tests are intended to do in spite of the fact that the variance of a youngster's performance from the norm may not be extreme enough to be of any educational consequence. If one looks long and hard enough, even small deviations of performance (whether intra- or inter-individual) appear magnified and become interpreted as having real educational significance. This erroneous conclusion is compounded when one blithely accepts conclusions from the

literature which fail to remind the reader of the inappropriateness in generalizing a conclusion to all children of a certain category—for example, suggesting that mentally retarded children are characteristically weak in automatic-
sequential skills. Many examiners who have faith in the generalizability of
this type of conclusion will exhibit extraordinary persistence in attempting to
locate such a weakness in every mentally retarded child they test, because the
literature says that the difficulty is typical. When he cannot locate the presumed disorder, an extremist will take the position that the instrument or the
testing situation was inadequate for diagnosing this presumed disability—i.e.,
the child really has the problem but it is yet to be located or identified.

It is only too obvious that great care should be taken that these highly
erroneous conclusions not be reached about any child. Clearly the educational
diagnostician, whether basically a psychologist or an educator, must be well
trained in the use and interpretation of evaluative instruments. A rule of
thumb for all who evaluate human performance is to be extremely careful and
intelligent in the selection and administration of tests, in the interpretation of
test data, and in the communication of relevant information to only the appropriate people, such as the child's teacher. Lack of clarity about what should
and should not be done in all aspects of testing and diagnosis will inevitably
result in a large number of errors in the testing, interpretation, and implementation phases of any diagnostic effort.

One of the requirements in the educational and psychological characterization of a child is that the evaluator have a stable plan that will provide clear
direction for collecting diagnostic data. We have already pointed to the need
to avoid indiscriminate and random collection of data; at the same time we
want to avoid the pitfall of not collecting enough information. In short, an
evaluator's concern should be to attempt to refine a series of hypotheses,
which are generated by previous data and which become increasingly specific
as pertinent data are collected. Perhaps an illustration from the field of medicine will serve to clarify this point.

Let us assume that your chest hurts and you seek the advice of a physician.
The first question he asks is, "What's wrong?" (a broad-band screening procedure). Your answer is, "My chest hurts." He asks, "Where?" (another broad-
band query but a bit more specific than the previous inquiry). You point to
your left side. At this point the physician begins to generate some hypotheses
about the reasons for your condition, decides what procedure he can use to
evaluate each of the hypotheses, and considers the kind of data that he will
accept either to verify or to deny each hypothesis. Thus, he advances two
hypotheses to himself after you have indicated that your left side hurts: the
problem pertains in some way (1) to the functioning of your heart or (2) to the
functioning of your lungs. As a means of checking out each proposition he
decides to use a screening instrument—namely, the stethoscope. Mind you,
this same instrument is used to evaluate two kinds of behavior, that of the
heart and of the lung, but the difference is in what he is looking for and the
manner in which the device is used. He *decides* to confirm or deny the hy-

pothesis about the heart *before* he does anything at all with the instrument. (Note that every evaluative procedure should be preceded by a clear specification of what the evaluator wants to observe to validate a hypothesis.) Choosing to deal with the functioning of the heart, the physician places the correct end of the stethoscope in a position that will allow for the direct observation of heart rate and other pertinent characteristics. Using criteria against which he can match your heart's functioning, he decides that sixty beats a minute is "normal" under the existing conditions, and thus he discards the possibility that your pain is the result of heart failure. He then proceeds to the alternative hypothesis, i.e., that your left lung is the genesis of the problem.

Picking up the stethoscope again, he places the instrument in a position on your chest and back that will allow direct observation of the functioning of your lung. The sounds suggest that the left lung is deviant to some extent, and so the physician tentatively confirms the lung hypothesis dependent on more detailed analysis. To that end, he orders a screening X ray, which is also a broad-range evaluative instrument. In due time, as progressively more specific hypotheses are confirmed or rejected, the physician either himself evaluates or has specialists evaluate the various pertinent dimensions of the problem so that a full and detailed description becomes available. The process moves from a wide-spectrum screening analysis to a very detailed and precisely directed evaluation, the latter stages of which often require the services of a specialist.

In addition to coming to a full characterization of the problem, the physician will seek to determine the reasons for your having the condition, including reasons that are associated with your environment. This information will be used not only to explain possible causes for the disorder, but it has clear implications for directing your physician in your future management during and following treatment.

Armed with these data, then, your physician begins to formulate a program for dealing with your lung problem. Among the factors included in his plan are (1) the type of medication required; (2) the setting in which the program of management can best be delivered, monitored, and controlled; (3) the criteria he will use in deciding when to alter the prescription and other management procedures and move you to a less well-monitored setting (e.g., hospital versus nursing home versus home); and (4) the types of environmental restrictions or alterations that should be made in order to facilitate your developing a progressively more healthy lung.

The process of diagnosing educational disorders follows a philosophy that is much like the one presented in the above example. It should not be haphazard and random; it should be planned, sequenced, economical, and focused on those variables that pertain to instructional dimensions, and it should deal with both the person and his environment. The flow of diagnostic activities that illustrates an ordered approach has been suggested by Smith (1974). Figure 6-3 summarizes this sequence.

Figure 6-3 suggests four major stages in the evaluation of educational prob-

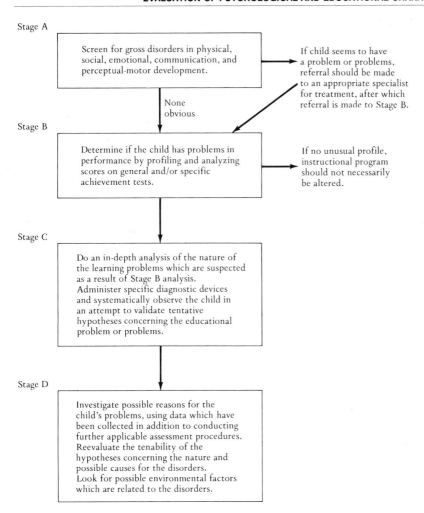

Stage A

Screen for gross disorders in physical, social, emotional, communication, and perceptual-motor development.

If child seems to have a problem or problems, referral should be made to an appropriate specialist for treatment, after which referral is made to Stage B.

None obvious

Stage B

Determine if the child has problems in performance by profiling and analyzing scores on general and/or specific achievement tests.

If no unusual profile, instructional program should not necessarily be altered.

Stage C

Do an in-depth analysis of the nature of the learning problems which are suspected as a result of Stage B analysis. Administer specific diagnostic devices and systematically observe the child in an attempt to validate tentative hypotheses concerning the educational problem or problems.

Stage D

Investigate possible reasons for the child's problems, using data which have been collected in addition to conducting further applicable assessment procedures. Reevaluate the tenability of the hypotheses concerning the nature and possible causes for the disorders. Look for possible environmental factors which are related to the disorders.

FIGURE 6-3 Flowchart describing various levels of diagnosis. (From Smith, R. M., *Clinical Teaching: Methods of Instruction for the Retarded.* (2d ed.) New York: McGraw-Hill, 1974. Reprinted by permission of McGraw-Hill Book Company.

lems. First, like the physician in the previous example, the teacher or therapist uses broad-band observation procedures for identifying disorders of functioning that are blatantly obvious. For example, the following types of behavior are sufficiently unusual to warrant further study: rubbing eyes, drainage of ears, bumping into furniture or difficulty with general mobility, unclear speech patterns, frequent and intense outbursts, not following verbal commands, extreme problems in getting along with others, or confusion in dealing with various types of instructional stimuli. If children seem to have such difficulties, they should be referred to a specialist in the area of concern, e.g., ear disorders to an otologist, audiologist, or otolaryngologist; eye problems to an

ophthalmologist; motor disorders to an orthopedic specialist, physical therapist, or neurologist; speech and language problems to a speech pathologist or
clinician; and so on. Any physical problem attendant on functional disorders
should be considered for complete evaluation and treatment as soon as possible.

At stage B, the evaluator attempts to assess the child's general performance
in the relevant areas, usually making use of a standard achievement test that
taps multiple subject areas and skills. A second procedure that is increasing in
popularity among special educators is to use for evaluation a cluster of tasks
that are related to a given subject area and that have been sequenced according to their levels of difficulty. For example, the materials that have been
developed by the Instructional Objectives Exchange might well be used in lieu
of or in combination with standardized tests for purposes of identifying deficiencies in a child's performance in various subject areas. At this point, most
commonly a profile of the child's scores in various areas is developed so that
the relationship among his scores can be examined. Performance can be profiled in terms of standard scores or grade-level equivalents. In the case of
individual clusters of skills for which there are usually no normative data, we
recommend a simple count of the number of tasks the child was successful in
accomplishing. The percentage of accuracy demonstrated by the child in each
constellation of identical tasks can also be revealing. For example, you could
ask the child to respond to twenty different sound-blending situations which
are progressively more difficult. You can then tabulate the number to which
he correctly responded, his percentage of accuracy, and the level of difficulty
he reached. These tabulations can then be recorded on a profile or chart form
and informally contrasted with his performance in other areas.

There are a number of potentially serious hazards of which you should be
aware when dealing with performance data that have been collected during
this second stage. Unless you are aware of these possible problems, gross
misinterpretation and totally erroneous conclusions can occur. The most
prominent of these issues are the following:

1 The misconception that achievement tests measure all, or even the most
   prominent, skills involved in a subject area

2 The common belief that scores on standardized tests are infallible and provide reliable samples of a child's performance

3 The failure to recognize that a comparison of performances in several subject areas is often inappropriate because the scales used for measuring performance in different subject areas may not be comparable

4 The erroneous conclusion that the subject areas which are evaluated and
   interpreted are independent of each other and share few, if any, common
   characteristics

5 The tendency to misinterpret differences in profiled scores as representing significant weaknesses or strengths in performance, when in fact they may represent normal errors in the achievement measures or variations in performance

6 The false assumption that if one has administered a battery of achievement tests, one has a total picture of the prominent educational characteristics of a child

The entire emphasis at this second level is on obtaining information concerning a child's general performance across areas. If you choose to use broad achievement tests as the basis for conducting this analysis, further evaluation is recommended if the child scores more than about one grade level lower in one subject area in contrast to his performance in other areas. If you use a task-analyzed sequenced hierarchy of skills in various subject areas as the procedure for evaluating achievement, it is difficult to make a fair comparison across subjects. In this instance, you might use the child's chronological age (as well as an evaluation of his general level of achievement) as the standard for deciding on the need for conducting a more penetrating analysis of a child's achievement characteristics.

If, in your opinion, there is enough discrepancy in a youngster's performance in one or more of the major subject areas to warrant special educational attention, a more detailed analysis of functioning in those areas of special weakness will be required. At stage C, the focus is on judging where within a major subject area the child is experiencing difficulty. For example, two children may have the same relatively low score in arithmetic in contrast to their general achievement levels in other subject areas. This discrepancy is discerned at stage B. The emphasis at stage C is on separating each child's performance into segments to whatever degree of specificity is necessary to allow for a precise characterization of his effort. In this illustration one child may exhibit extraordinary weakness in combining fractions and the other youngster in certain components of multiplication or division. The educational focus for each must be different if the remediation efforts are to be effective. At stage C, then, the diagnostic effort begins to narrow in focus, takes on more precision as a result of data which serve to confirm or reject each new hypothesis, and eventually results in a clear statement that describes the character of the child's weaknesses and strengths in the relevant areas of performance.

Stage D involves efforts in obtaining data pertaining to the probable cause of the child's educational or functional disorders. The thrust of activity at this level is directed toward the child's environment; those things that either historically or currently have caused or may be causing the functional deviations that were described in precise terms at stage C. The instructional environment is often to blame for many functional problems of children who are served by special education programs. Poor instructional practices of various types; unsequenced curricula from one grade to the next; frequent changes in teachers and, hence, in educational orientations; inadequate physical facilities to provide for all children; erroneous diagnostic conclusions regarding the proper educational focus for a given child; poor match between instructional materials and instructional strategies; the unwitting results of labeling—all these are examples of inept instructional situations and counterproductive environments that can only serve to restrict a child's performance and exacerbate his problems. We repeat, these are not the child's problems; they are environmental and do as much damage as the child's own physical deviations.

Of course there may be environmental weaknesses in a child's daily situation other than those generated by or at the school. All forms of incompatibility between schools and homes, inconsistency in dealing with behavioral problems, inadequate physical facilities at home, meals that lack the basic nutrients, disease in the home that goes unattended, lack of opportunities to interact with others in ways that will be personally facilitating, and living in a setting in which there is constant threat of censure—all those are illustrations of significant environmental weaknesses that will seriously affect a child's performance and development. As much of an attempt as possible should be made to identify those components of the youngster's school and home surroundings that contribute to performance decrements.

This proposed sequence of diagnostic activities is identical to the general procedures that the physician used in evaluating the characteristics of and possible reasons for the chest pain in the earlier example. The aim of this progressively more refined and focused assessment is to better appreciate which of the multitude of possible goals intervention should be directed toward. As accuracy in the description of the condition increases it allows for much greater precision in making decisions about how best to deal with the problem. The efforts of the educational diagnostician must be systematized so that the focus is on the child's demonstrated performances and the environment within which he functions. To emphasize again, diagnosis should not be haphazard; it should provide for the evaluation of a series of progressively more focused hypotheses about the child, his performance, and the environment within which he functions.

USE OF DIAGNOSTIC DATA

There are two major questions which the diagnostic data collected during the evaluation phases are meant to answer:

1 In what areas of functioning is the child in need of direct instructional help, and what is the priority for intervention in each of the areas?

2 What types of personal or environmental prostheses or both can be provided for the child to enhance his level and quality of functioning in the areas of concern?

If it is impossible to obtain practical responses to each of these questions that will lead to a program of direct instructional intervention, then the diagnostic effort has not been properly focused. Table 6-6 lists concluding statements from various diagnostic procedures. The conclusions on the left are vague, and they do not respond adequately to the two questions that form the basis for diagnosis. The conclusions on the right-hand side are precise and functional and answer the two questions.

In stressing the need for precision, directness, and clarity in the conclusions

TABLE 6-6   ILLUSTRATIONS OF TWO TYPES OF DIAGNOSTIC CONCLUSIONS

Vague and Imprecise	On Target; Can Be Implemented
1. "The child's accommodative flexibility is faulty and indicative of minimal cerebral dysfunction. Remediation should be focused upon information-processing tasks which emphasize visualization skills."	1. "The child can remember the names of various objects (up to six) that are presented to her. She was unable to remember both the names of objects and the sequence of their presentation beyond three. Priority in the instructional program should be given to both of these areas, using the visual and auditory modalities."
2. "This child could learn to read at about the fourth-grade level if he had a more positive attitude toward the task and did not have the obvious learning block and emotional overlay that are restricting his progress in this area. They are the underlying causes for his academic problems and will have to be resolved before academic progress can be expected."	2. "The child has no problems in attacking words. He uses a combination of phonics and visualization in a consistent way and with few errors. The instructional focus should be on providing activities which will allow for expansion of his repertoire of sight words. To this end, he needs more opportunities to read in and out of school and appropriate reinforcers to encourage him to read more. Establish a contract or token system with him as a means for expanding his sight vocabulary."
3. "The fact that the child did not look directly at the examiner during the diagnostic session is indicative of the fact that he desires not to have a direct confrontation with adults or authority figures. These immature patterns of social interaction border on the pathological and warrant immediate attention by a psychiatrist."	3. "Charles exhibits shyness toward adult men and women in most situations by avoiding direct verbal encounters, by not initiating conversations with adults, and by speaking in a very low voice in the presence of adults. With children his own age, his conversations are normal. Priority should be given to increasing the frequency of his interaction with adults. Using other children as models, reinforcing conversing behavior with people who are older than his peers, and providing a specific setting within the school or classroom for informally speaking with adults under conditions of constant reinforcement should be considered as possible approaches for dealing with his functional weaknesses in adult interaction."

a diagnostician reaches following the educational and psychological evaluation of a child, we have circled back to the proposition that was presented in the opening paragraph of this chapter. Again, we believe that meaningful evaluation of the child's pertinent individual attributes and relevant environmental conditions must be determined before appropriate instructional goals can be identified and procedures of intervention initiated that will have any meaning at all. In this chapter we have attempted to identify and discuss the prominent issues that pertain to the evaluation of exceptional children and their environments.

SUGGESTED PROJECTS FOR PART II

1   Visit a medical center, specialty clinic, or diagnostic unit within your community and observe the process used to evaluate the problems of children who are referred to the center. Your local pediatrician or physician will be able to direct you to a clinic which is interdisciplinary, such as a cleft palate, cystic fibrosis, muscular dystrophy, or developmental disability center. Interview the physician after an examination has been conducted so as to understand better the types of data that were being obtained and the kind of response that the physician considered to be normal in each instance. If the opportunity exists, you might also wish to speak briefly and in a general way to parents of the children being examined. Before going to the clinic refer to relevant sections of Part V of this book to become familiar with the characteristics, procedures, and nomenclature of conditions treated by the clinic.

2   After you have had an opportunity to observe a child being examined in a medical or developmental disability center, make a list of the behaviors that you feel are atypical or exceptional for a youngster of his age. Next to each entry in your list describe some possible alternative reasons for the atypical behavior or condition and decide whether each explanation is hypothetical-internal, hypothetical-external, actual-internal, or actual-external. Finally, construct a checklist or scale that you might use in the classroom to observe and record at least two of the behaviors you believe are actual-external. And then go ahead and collect the data for several days or for a week.

3   With four or five fellow students, decide on three behaviors you want to observe in a child. Arrange your schedule so that all of you can observe the youngster at the same time. Each of you should independently review the frequency with which the child exhibits the behaviors during a given span of time, say, for 30 minutes. After you have recorded your data individually, compare your observations of frequency with those tabulated by your colleagues. If there is wide variability, you choice of behaviors may not be specific enough or precisely defined. The ultimate criterion for degree of specificity is: Can it be counted?

4   The following report has been extracted from a child's cumulative folder. Read it over carefully and do the following:

    a   Draw a line through all statements that are hypothetical (either external or internal).

    b   Circle information that has no educational relevance.

    c   Place brackets around statements or data that may have some educational pertinence but that you feel need further confirmation or assessment.

    d   Underline those portions of the report that you believe are on target and can be of obvious and immediate assistance to a teacher in developing a potentially appropriate educational program.

e List the kinds of data a teacher could collect within the classroom in order to check systematically on the child's progress in two specific areas that you feel warrant special instructional attention.

SAMPLE CASE FOR INSTRUCTIONAL PURPOSES ONLY

NAME: Susie Brown   RACE/SEX: White/Female   AGE: 9–4
BIRTHDATE: 5-3-62   DATE OF EXAMINATION: 6-25-70
PARENTS: Mr. and Mrs. Frank Brown
      1104 Skyline
SCHOOL: Smith Elementary   GRADE: EMR
REFERRED BY: Mrs. Jaspers, Teacher
REASON FOR REFERRAL: Disruptive classroom behavior and learning difficulties
SOURCES OF EVALUATION: Wechsler Intelligence Scale for Children
                      Bender Visual-Motor Gestalt Test
                      Wide Range Achievement Test
                      Draw-A-Person Test
                      Stanford-Binet Intelligence Test
                      Illinois Test of Psycholinguistic Abilities
                      Teacher Interview
                      Parent Interview
                      Neurological Evaluation
DIAGNOSTIC TEAM: Staff Psychologist
                  Neurologist

Psychodiagnostic Evaluation
DESCRIPTIVE AND BACKGROUND DATA:
Physical Description:

Susie is an average-sized, 9-year-old, white female, who appeared "bright-looking" at the time of testing. She is described as an attractive girl with blond hair. She was referred for testing approximately 2 weeks after school started because of her disruptive behavior in the classroom, for example, throwing a pair of scissors at another student.

Susie is the only child of the father, age 41, and the mother, age 38. She was adopted at the age of 4 days. The father is employed in a skilled blue-collar position and the mother works part time in an accounting office. The family moved from a large, metropolitan area to a smaller rural community when Susie was beginning the first grade.

The mother has exhibited considerable concern over Susie's progress in school, beginning with the kindergarten experience. The mother would wait at school for Susie because the child would cry often and exhibit emotionally dependent behavior. The mother reported that she is presently working to remove pressure from Susie, feeling that her constant concern with Susie's progress in school was not helpful to Susie or herself. The parents implied that their living conditions, job placements and future plans are determined by what they feel is advantageous for Susie.

Developmental and Health History:

The mother reported that Susie's delivery was delayed approximately 6 weeks, after the doctor attempted to induce labor. Developmental history was reportedly normal, with "first words" before 1 year of age; talking in simple sentences and phrases from 15 to 18 months; crawling at 7 to 8 months; sitting alone at 4 months; walking at 14 months. Tonsils and adenoids were removed at 3 years because of ear trouble; at this time she was found to have many allergies and continues to have allergy problems. In November of 1968, Susie was given radium treatments for her ear.

Classroom Behavior and School History:

When Susie was 5 years of age, the mother reported that her physician recommended that Susie attend kindergarten to be in contact with other children.

Mrs. Rose, Susie's kindergarten teacher, reported that she felt that Susie was an emotional child. She stated that Susie cried often, especially on occasions when her mother, who often waited at the school for Susie, would leave for a short time. Susie would then ask if her mother would return to pick her up.

Mrs. Rose further reported that Susie was a rather slow child. She did feel, however that Susie had made a great deal of progress during her year in kindergarten. She reportedly learned to write her name, was able to count to ten, and learned her colors.

Susie's first year in public school was one of frustration and failure. Her teacher, Mrs. Daisy, reported that she knew Susie before she entered the first grade. The teacher further stated that she felt that Susie trusted and liked her; however, upon entering the classroom, Susie appeared fearful of the teacher. Mrs. Daisy reported that Susie could not relate well to the other children in the classroom. She would laugh about what she had done.

The mother and teacher had numerous conferences during the year, according to Mrs. Daisy. At the beginning of the year, it was hard for the mother to leave Susie. Mrs. Daisy said that Susie was much easier to control while the mother was in the room. The teacher felt that Susie made some progress during the year. She learned to recognize letters and numbers. Mrs. Daisy recommended that Susie be retained; Susie's father insisted that Susie be placed in the second grade; however, before the next school year the family moved to another community and Susie was placed in the first grade.

Susie's second first-grade teacher, Mrs. Jaspers, reported that Susie was able to memorize and retain well. Susie appeared to be able to recognize single words if they were presented over and over again. She developed some sight vocabulary and could recognize all of her numbers from 1 to 100. However, she was not able to link words for meaning or work simple addition facts even with blocks. In the second year of the first grade Susie was reported to have difficulty in relationships with other children. She generally stayed away from other children and they stayed away from her. She often hurt or appeared to try to hurt other children. She also taunted them; however, Susie often asked her teacher "Does so and so like me?"

Recognition or approval by others appeared to require some physical contact. Her teacher stated that she found touching Susie helpful when reinforcing any behavior. Susie's single friend in her class was an affectionate child who like to touch and hold hands. Susie was reported to have attractive handwriting and her work was displayed on the bulletin board. The displaying of her work had little observable influence except when her paper was displayed alone. Susie had tantrums of kicking and screaming in class, expressed fear of the principal, and was unable to find her way home on more than one occasion.

The teacher reported that Susie had good moods and bad. On bad days Susie's appearance was different to the teacher than on good days, her art work was colored outside of lines in inappropriate color (mainly black), and she was more difficult to handle. On good days her art work and behavior conformed more to that of the average girl.

Susie was placed in special education classes during her third year of school, where she failed to show any particular progress. Rather, her behavior deteriorated, with Susie acting more aggressively toward other children and running away from home and school.

Susie's present teacher reported that she is reading at the primer level. She exhibits few word attack skills and uses sight vocabulary. Little comprehension of the material read was indicated to the teacher by the fact that most of Susie's answers were unrelated to the questions concerning the material read. Exercises in oral language indicate that Susie is still having difficulty in understanding the difference between a stated sentence and a question. However, she has on occasion used full sentences in these exercises. Copy work from the board or from a sheet at her desk is generally inaccurate. Portions of the material are omitted. Susie's general work habit was described as "helter-skelter." Susie enjoys art and enjoys working in clay very much.

Susie's relationships with others appear to be changing. At the beginning of the year she had an ongoing feud with Carla. Carla often complained that Susie hit and hurt her. Susie's teacher reported that this relationship is much better and Susie remarks that Carla is pretty. Her hostility toward other members of the class is lessened. Susie's attempts to relate positively with others are better. She continues to ask the teacher "do you love me?" several times a day. The teacher indicates that Susie now appears to have some good days and on occasion tries to please. This, the teacher feels, is progress.

Results of Previous Evaluations:

School testing of hearing and vision revealed adequate functioning. A general physical examination as well as a neurological exam at a neurological clinic in June of 1969 were normal. A skull X-ray done in the hospital was normal. Psychological testing was also done by the staff psychologist, which placed her in the upper mental defective range with a Full Scale WISC IQ of 64 (Verbal IQ 67; Performance IQ 68). She also evidenced a "Marked problem in the area of psychomotor coordination" and graphic skills, based on administration of the Draw-A-Person and Bender Gestalt.

Observed Behavior:

Susie appeared to be a bright-looking child who was generally quite friendly and emotionally responsive. She was quick to respond to social-type questions; however, her response time to most of the verbal test questions was rather long. She was also observed to engage frequently in diversionary tactics particularly during administration of the more difficult items. She would interrupt with statements about her pet dog, comment about a small cut on her finger, or ask questions about items in the rooms. It appears that the items in the room did not attract her attention but rather served as points of conversation to avoid the task at hand.

Findings:

Testing with the Stanford-Binet on October 6, 1970, reveals that Susie is currently functioning within the mentally defective range of intelligence. Her chronological age was 9-4; mental age was 6-4; and IQ 66. The basal age shown on this test was Year 5. In Year 6, Susie was able to correctly complete the following subtests: Vocabulary, Mutilated Pictures, Number concepts and Opposite Analogies. She was unable to complete successfully the subtests that dealt with verbal differences. In Year 7, Susie missed all subtests with the exception of copying diamonds. In Year 8, Susie completed two subtests correctly, the Vocabulary and the story "The Wet Fall." She was unable to complete any subtests in Year 9.

On the Wide Range Achievement Test, Susie achieved a reading grade-level of 2.1, a spelling grade of 1.5, and an arithmetic grade-level of 1.2. Equivalent IQ scores range from 72 to 81, which are somewhat inconsistent and higher than IQ scores attained on the Binet. Performance on the Reading portion suggests inadequate development of phonics concepts. It appeared to the examiner that Susie relied strongly on sight. In Spelling, she reversed "d" for "b" twice. If she did not know the word, it appeared that she was unable to spell any part of it by sound. In arithmetic, she appeared to be able to recognize numbers through 19 but appeared to have no basic addition or subtraction skills.

Susie completed the Bender Visual Motor Gestalt Test within normal time limits. Drawings contained 11 errors, giving her an approximate mental age of 5-4, according to Koppitz' norms. Design errors were in the forms of perseverations, distortion of shape, rotation (90° to 180°), and integration. The Bender mental age of 5-4 is relatively consistent with the WISC mental age of 5-2 (both administered on June 25, 1969).

Administration of the Wepman Auditory Discrimination Test revealed 14 errors, suggesting difficulty with both beginning and ending word sounds.

An analysis of the subtest scores of the WISC administered June 25, 1969, revealed a Full Scale IQ score of 64, with a Verbal IQ of 67 and a Performance IQ of 68. A profile of the subtest scores indicates Verbal scaled scores were uniformly depressed and her responses were generally oversimplifications or concrete to an extreme degree. Her verbal abilities with regard to memory, judgment, comprehension of number concepts, definitions of words, and comprehension of connected discourse were all very significantly affected. Similarly, most tasks involving psychomotor perception and psychomotor coordination were performed in the upper defective range, especially those requiring visual sequencing, formation of abstract designs, assembling a whole from its composite parts, and eye-motor coordination. Generally she demonstrated poor concept development and profited little from trial and error experiences.

Testing on the Illinois Test of Psycholinguistic Abilities reveals that Susie had a composite psycholinguistic age of 6-9, which is consistent with her mental age of 6-4 on the Binet. A profile of the subtest scores indicates relative strengths in the areas of verbal expression, auditory reception, and visual association. The lowest subtest scores reflect weaknesses in

SUSIE BROWN: TEST RESULTS

WECHSLER INTELLIGENCE SCALE FOR CHILDREN

FINDINGS

Verbal Subtests	Scaled Score	Performance Subtests	Scaled Score
Information	4	Picture Completion	9
Comprehension	4	Picture Arrangement	5
Arithmetic	6	Block Design	4
Similarities	6	Object Assembly	5
Vocabulary	4	Coding	4
Digit Span	4		

Verbal IQ Score	67
Performance IQ Score	68
Full Scale IQ Score	69
Intelligence Classification	Mentally Defective
Equivalent Mental Age	5 - 2
Chronological Age	8 - 1
Date Administered	6/29/69

ILLINOIS TEST OF PSYCHOLINGUISTIC ABILITIES

Subtests	Scaled Score	Subtests	Scaled Score
Visual Reception	26	Auditory Reception	31
Visual Memory	16	Auditory Memory	28
Visual Association	29	Auditory Association	29
Visual Closure	29	Grammatic Closure	7
Manual Expression	27	Verbal Expression	30
Chronological Age	9 - 4	*Supplementary*	
PLA	6 - 9	Auditory Closure	22
Test Mean	36	Sound Blending	22
Child's Mean	25		
Date Administered	9/30/70		

WIDE RANGE ACHIEVEMENT TEST

Subtests	Grade Level	St
Reading	2-1	81
Spelling	1-5	75
Arithmetic	1-2	72
Date Administered	10/6/70	

BENDER VISUAL MOTOR GESTALT

		Types of Errors:
Number of Errors	11	Perseveration
Equivalent Mental Age	5-4 (-2 sd.)	Distortion
Completion Time		Rotation (90-180°)
Time Norms		Integration
Date Administered	6/26/69	

WEPMAN AUDITORY DISCRIMINATION TEST

Number of Errors ___14___

Performance Invalid Yes_____ No_X_

12 = x errors, 2 = Y errors

Date Administered ___10/6/70___

Stanford Binet Intelligence Test

Date Administered ___10/6/70___

Types of Errors:

Beginning Word Sounds ___X___

Vowel Sounds _____

Ending Word Sounds ___X___

Chronological Age _9-4_ IQ_ 66_

Mental Age _6-4_

BASIC TEST RESULTS

NAME Susie Brown

CASE

SCHOOL Smith Elementary   D.O.B. 5-3-62   C.A. 9-4   GRADE EMR   DATE 6-25-70

WRAT	WISC		I.T.P.A.
r- 2-1	Verbal IQ – 67	CA: 8-1	CA: 9-4
GE s- 1-2	Performance IQ – 68	MA: 5-2	
	Full Scale IQ – 67		I.T.P.A. Language Age – 6-9

Age + X = 11

TEST	SUBTESTS CATEGORY
	Reading
	Spelling
	Arithmetic
	Information
	Comprehension
	Arithmetic
	Similarities
	Vocabulary
	Digit span (forward-backward)
	Picture completion
	Picture arrangement
	Block design
	Object assembly
	Coding
	Auditory reception
	Visual reception
	Visual sequential memory
	Auditory association
	Auditory sequential memory
	Visual association
	Visual closure
	Verbal expression
	Grammatic closure
	Manual expression
	Auditory closure
	Sound blending
WEPMAN AUDITORY DISCRIMINATION	

the areas of grammatic closure, visual sequential memory, auditory closure, and sound blending.

For a pictorial description of test results, please refer to the graphic analysis of Susie's diagnostic evaluation which is included in this report.

Impression and Summary:

Susie appears to be a youngster who is currently functioning within the upper limits of the Mentally Defective Range. All previous testing suggests that Susie has limited capabilities to use abstract thinking. She functions best on a concrete basis. Her difficulties may be in part due to deficiencies related to her auditory functioning, especially those verbal communications demanding synthesis of or discrimination among discrete auditory cues, as in the auditory closure and sound blending subtests of the ITPA. She was unable to discriminate similar sounds on the Wepman, making fourteen errors, whereas she functioned adequately on the ITPA Auditory Reception Subtests. This suggests that similar, competing sounds are confusing to Susie, but that limited, individually presented, dissimilar auditory clues may be mastered. In the areas of visual functioning, Susie can perform more consistently and has relatively more strength, particularly in tasks demanding visual acuity or "alertness" to visual cues in context. However, she has difficulty when visual sequential memory is required, functioning significantly below her own mean as well as the test mean. Her classroom behavior as well as the test results suggest difficulties in graphic skills, copying or reproducing on paper what is seen by the eye. In addition to these learning difficulties Susie exhibits behavior that is suggestive of considerable immaturity and insecurity, possibly owing to being overly protected and isolated as an only, adopted child.

In summary, the impressions are that Susie displays the following strengths and weaknesses:

1   Difficulty in abstract reasoning
2   Auditory perceptual difficulties related to discrimination of similar sounds
3   Visual perceptual difficulties related to visual sequential memory and eye-hand coordination
4   Considerable immaturity and emotional insecurity
5   Strength in visual acuity or "alertness"
6   More visual strength than auditory, a "visual" learner
7   A pleasant appearance and personality
8   Parents who are concerned and want to help

Prescriptive Recommendations:

School
1   Continued placement in the special education classroom at the EMR level for the present. In view of her relative strength on the Wide Range Achievement Test, she may be capable of performing in a slow-moving regular classroom in the future.

2   Further evaluation of specific visual functioning, that is, her accommodative flexibility and convergence, is suggested. Materials are attached herewith to remediate some of her difficulties in visual sequential memory and eye-hand coordination.

Some of the appropriate activities would include:

Drawing simple outline pictures or geometric forms from memory, then providing feedback.

Presenting geometrical shapes for a brief exposure and having Susie reproduce them in the same order, starting with 3 designs.

Presenting series of letters or numbers on flashcards and having her reproduce them orally and in writing.

Pegboard designs could be introduced when she has mastered this level.

3   Exploration of the auditory functioning related to synthesis and discrimination of cues will be necessary before a specific training program is initiated.

Some possible exercises would include:

Blending consonants, starting with two, such as "s" and "t," then associating these with the word "street." Similar work should be done with vowels and blends.

It would be helpful to begin by having Susie look at the teacher's lips as the sounds are spoken, then having her turn around and repeat the same sounds.

Recordings of exercises might be made by the teacher so that more repetition and drill is possible, or a tutor might be employed.

The area of grammatic correctness will be a matter of "practice" on limited stimuli. The parents will be employed to assist in this area, using positive reinforcement techniques.

Placement in a resource room or MBI classroom for part of the day may be an efficient means of providing Susie with training in visual and auditory perception.

4   Perceptual motor training involving gross and fine motor exercises would be helpful if the school has such a program.

5   In view of Susie's difficulty with arithmetic, and her relative strength in visual functioning, her teacher should utilize as many visual, manipulative materials as possible. Exercises such as sorting, matching, and comparison of sets would be appropriate as beginning steps. See the attached list for recommended methods and materials.

6   Susie's teacher should place her near her desk and continue to use physical contact and as much emotional support as required. However, she should provide strict limits concerning emotional outbursts or abuse of other children. Susie could be rewarded by being allowed to draw or paint when she has obeyed the rules.

7   Conference with Susie's teacher will be made in 30 days to determine the extent of consultative help desired and the need of revision of recommendations. Re-evaluation should be made in one year.

Home

1   A consultation should be held with Susie's parents concerning the possibility of an unfavorable climate in the home relating to her emotional instability. It may be that the family should seek help from a community agency such as Family Service if the parents are receptive. It should be explained to them that parents of children with learning difficulties often need support and encouragement in order to understand and cope with their responsibilities.

2   The home situation would be more conducive to Susie's growth, if the parents encouraged a more responsible attitude and mature behavior on her part. She should be made to feel wanted and loved as a person, despite her learning problems. Self-sufficiency in self-care activities will do much to build her self-confidence. Established routines will also be helpful to her in structuring her environment.

Agency

1   Communication with the agency the family may see would be helpful in providing them with knowledge of the school's activities and prevent duplication of efforts.

2   Request from the agency examining Susie's visual accommodative flexibility should include an inquiry about the exercises which were recommended to the parents and any further help that is needed.

Follow-up

1   Follow-up should be conducted within 60 days to determine case status.

Educational Diagnostician

ANNOTATED RESOURCES FOR PART II

Birch, Herbert G., and Gussow, Joan Dye. *Disadvantaged Children: Health, Nutrition, and School Failure.* New York: Harcourt Brace Jovanovich and Grune & Stratton, 1970. (273 pages and 33 pages of references; author and subject indexes.) This book reviews theories and empirical research concerning the interrelationships among poverty, poor health, and educational failure. Each of the eleven chapters examines a particular facet of these relationships. Chapter 1 examines the general relationship between health and learning failure. Subsequent chapters are devoted to prenatal, birth, postnatal, and growth problems of mothers and children in an environment of poverty. The relationship between nutrition and malnutrition and pregnancy and development of the child is explored; and the effect of illness and deficient medical care on children and their capacity to learn is examined. The book presents principles and findings fundamental to an understanding of child development from an interactional viewpoint.

Hurley, Roger L. *Poverty and Mental Retardation—A Causal Relationship,* New York: Vintage, 1969. (Paperback.) This easily read book not only discusses a wide range of possible contributors to mental retardation but presents them with such boldness that the reader is forced to enter into the world of the poor to see how development can be adversely influenced. The contents include such topics as poverty and organic impairment, the effects of cultural deprivation on intellectual performance, the self-fulfilling prophecy fulfilled, the health crisis of the poor, and welfare: the cycle of dependency. The book is well written and makes a strong case for environmental bases of intellectual deficiency.

White, Burton L. *Human Infants: Experience and Psychological Development.* Englewood Cliffs, N.J.: Prentice-Hall, 1971. (160 pages; bibliography and index.) This is a brief book written in a parsimonious, often terse, fashion. It is well illustrated and well documented and contains an amazing amount of information for its size. The author does not hide his biases. The book opens with a 9-page introductory chapter that presents a powerful rationale for the boom in infant research. The next four chapters include a digest of the current state of knowledge concerning infant behavior and the role of early experience and emerging knowledge of infant behavior and early experience. Chapter 6 concerns major issues in research; Chapter 7 is composed of a memo to students in developmental psychology and a somewhat direct memo to funding agencies.

III

COMPLICATIONS
OF EXCEPTIONAL
CONDITIONS

Even within a group of people classified as similar, handicaps are not pure, static, or homogeneous. Most often handicapping conditions occur in combinations, overlap, and change in their characteristics and intensity over time. Recently special educators have turned their attention to problems of the multi-handicapped; indeed, the profession has more clearly recognized that few children have problems that can be neatly classified into one category. The problems of mental retardation overlap with problems of emotional disturbance, and both may be related to psychomotor or sensory disorders. Even if pure conditions can be identified, their effect is most certainly not merely additive. Rather, they interact in complex ways to form individual patterns of exceptionality. No longer is it considered fruitful to spend endless numbers of journal pages or endless hours of debate attempting to ascertain whether a child is really mentally retarded or really emotionally disturbed and which condition is primary or secondary.

One might view complications as overlapping across vertical traditional disability groups. Mental retardation, emotional disturbance, and physical disability, for instance, can be viewed as overlapping in various ways. This vertical overlapping makes it difficult, if not impossible, to group children according to any kind of pure handicap. There are, additionally, what might be considered "horizontal" complications: the additional problems that occur because of the visibility of a deviation and the social reaction to it, the negative labeling of a child, and the inept management of his problems. Hypothetically, if we had a youngster with a pure handicap, that is, with no "vertical complications," he would nevertheless be subject to the "horizontal problems," which are socially imposed. Family complications, reactions of others to deviations, the stigma of functional limitations and unattractiveness, and the classification systems used by schools and other institutions serve to exacerbate the basic problems of even the hypothetically pure handicaps. With these social complications always present, it is little wonder that handicaps are not homogeneous and static.

Chapters 7, 8, and 9 present three major sources of and settings for the horizontal complications. Labeling a child and classifying and grouping him on the basis of his defect can have very deleterious consequences both in inviting a generalized negative social reaction and in suggesting a narrow treatment approach that is allegedly label-specific. Likewise, the visibility of cosmetic and functional deviations is a major source of complications for most exceptional children and youth. "Somatopsychological" is the term used to describe such complications. Finally, an early and continuing source and setting of variables that can confound handicaps is the family. Because of the great impact of parental influence on child development, the family can produce a compounding of handicap. Special educators must be more than casually aware of such possibilities and become concerned with parental education and close interaction of the home with the school.

7

PROBLEMS OF LABELING AND CLASSIFICATION IN SPECIAL EDUCATION

STUDY TARGETS

1 Name the several purposes of classification within any science.
2 Write a brief summary of the weaknesses of traditional classification practices within special education.
3 Summarize in your own words the difference between "genotypic" and "phenotypic" language and the implications of each for special education labeling.
4 Describe some of the variables and processes that might account for a child's downward "progress" as a result of the teacher's expectations.
5 Explain why the practice of labeling children often contributes to increasing handicaps.
6 Cite the major advantages of the three suggested models for classifying special education variables, summarizing how they differ from classification based on noneducational or paraeducational variables.

A fundamental assumption of science is that there is order in the universe, that relationships, similarities, and progressions are ordered by natural laws rather than occurring randomly. Partly based on this assumption and partly for pragmatic reasons, a basic activity of all science is a continuing attempt to classify or categorize things and events. "The developmental path from an art to a science is the classification of information" (Griffiths, 1959).

While classification serves various purposes, depending on the science involved, there are several general functions and advantages of systematic classification. Classification aids enormously in (1) arranging what otherwise might appear chaotic; (2) detecting orderly relationships among seemingly separate events; (3) setting the boundaries of the phenomena of concern to a particular science; and (4) discovering "missing pieces" or discrepancies. Once a classification scheme is adopted within a science, communication and research within that science become greatly accelerated. As new items or phenomena are discovered, they may be analyzed in light of existing categories, properly placed, and thus further add to the information and clarity of a particular category. Each entry in a category becomes an instance of the generalization described by the categorical heading; in turn, major categories become modified in description by the instances they subsume. Therefore, it is through a continuing process of induction and deduction that a classification system is built and modified. New instances that do not quite fit into an existing category necessitate the creation of new headings or the modification of existing ones. Likewise, the inclusive nature of categorical headings allows scientists to make general descriptions of and inferences and predictions about the more specific entries in a category and to discover commonalities and differences among the entries.

While we have touched on only some of the basic characteristics of classification, you can see what a valuable tool a well-designed classification system can be and what an enormous amount of information can be contained and systematized.

For example, the system originally devised by Linnaeus for the classification of living things acts as the foundation for communication, description, and research in biology. You are all probably familiar with this system; it is a classic illustration of a comprehensive and scientifically productive classification scheme. The system involves dividing all life into kingdoms; each kingdom is then subdivided into phyla. Each phylum is divided into classes; each class into orders; each order into families; each family into genera; each genus into species. For example:

Category	Dog	Category	Dog
Kingdom	Animal	Family	Canidae
Phylum	Chordata	Genus	Canis
Class	Mammalia	Species	Familiaris
Order	Carnivora		

Similarly effective systems have been developed in chemistry, astronomy, geology, meteorology, and many other sciences. Generally, such classification schemes serve to impose order, detect relationships, enhance communication, and promote research.

Obviously, the degree to which a system fulfills the purposes of classification is a measure of its quality. That is, a science does not merely classify for classification's sake, but rather to meet the needs for information, communication, and research of that science. There are good and bad ways to classify. For example, the Dewey classification system in use by libraries involves cataloging by author, title, and topic and admirably serves the purposes of librarians. Books could, however, be classified by thickness, weight, or color, or on the basis of other arbitrary criteria. While such a system might be "orderly," it would not be effective or practical for most purposes and it certainly would not meet the particular needs of library science. So it is with any classification system; we must ask the questions: (1) does the system meet the general criteria of acceptable classification? and (2) does it serve the specific needs of the science?

We shall now move from a general consideration of classification systems to a specific discussion of the purposes and qualities of classification schemes employed in special education.

The classification, categorization, and labeling of children are much more than a dry, academic topic. Why and how we group and label children has far-reaching implications. Indeed, this is a philosophical and practical issue at the heart of many other issues in special education (see, for example, Missouri Conference on the Categorical/Non-categorical Issue in Special Education, March, 1971 or the Florida State University–Special Study Institute Report, 1972).

One hundred years ago, there was not much of a problem in subdividing children who had problems in the regular school: such children were simply excluded from school. Although there were some activity and provisions for special education in several large cities at the turn of the century, it was not until 1917 that New Jersey developed the first codified curriculum and method of teaching for "dull children" (Doll, 1917). By 1927, there were only fifteen states with educational provisions for children with retarded development; there were virtually no special arrangements for other children who could not adequately function in standard public school circumstances. Thus substantial difficulties in communication, social interaction, deportment, and locomotion resulted in exclusion from the schools. Preparation of teachers, school materials, curriculum goals, and physical arrangements of the schools precluded any productive education for what we now call exceptional children. Early twentieth-century education for the common man was just that—there was no room for the uncommon, the exceptional. The little red schoolhouse or its equivalent could accommodate only the average; substantial deviation in almost any educationally relevant dimension meant exclusion. Thus the little red schoolhouse comfortably fit the middle of the normal curve. The tails of the distribution were not the concern of public schooling. Children of more wealthy, culturally advantaged families went to private academies; exceptional children stayed home or were sent to institutions. Today, our public schools are increasingly directing efforts to enhance the education and development of all children. Children who were once destined to be placed in an institution or a private-care home are now being included in the public school's planning, staffing, and curriculum development. The Pennsylvania Right to Education Law (1971) is a dramatic milestone that clearly commits and legally mandates schools to provide for the education of all children, regardless of the label, "condition," "potential," or other characteristics of a child.

The rapidly evolving concern for the education of children previously designated as "unable to benefit from education" reflects some general trends in our society. Our faith in science to do almost anything, the growth of technology in education, greatly expanded college training programs in special education, changing economic circumstances, and corresponding changes in social philosophies and expectations—all these social dimensions influence our educational philosophies and policies. As many authors have pointed out, our philosophy of public education is a good index of the prevailing society and level of culture (Corwin, 1965; Goodman, 1971; Parsons, 1971; Yamamoto, 1969).

CLASSIFICATION SYSTEMS IN SPECIAL EDUCATION

A number of disciplines and professions outside education have wielded great influence on the nomenclature used to identify and classify children with special educational needs; among these have been medicine and psychiatry, developmental psychology, psychometrics, sociology, and law. All such groups, of course, have their own foundations and interests; accordingly, each views and labels children from its own perspective. "Mental retardation" and its subdivisions, for example, are basically defined in psychometric terms, i.e., by scores or standardized psychological (intelligence) tests. "Psychotic," "schizophrenic," "neurotic," and "emotionally disturbed" are classifications derived from a psychiatric point of view. "Culturally deprived," "delinquent," and "socially maladjusted" are terms with basically sociological or legal implications. "Brain-injured," "minimal cerebral dysfunction," "neurological impairment," and "perceptual disturbance" obviously suggest a biomedical stance.

Basic labels have been further subdivided by various professions to suit their own needs, and the literature abounds in a multitude of names for children. The resulting terminological confusion has generated much fruitless controversy and debate. The following is a partial list of labels drawn from articles published during the last five years in several special education journals, e.g., *Exceptional Children, Journal of Special Education, American Jour-*

nal of Mental Deficiency, Journal of Learning Disabilities, and Academic Therapy.

1	Academically handicapped	30	Low IQ
2	Acting out	31	Mentally defective
3	Adjunctive	32	Mentally handicapped
4	Aggressive	33	Minimal brain dysfunction
5	Antisocial	34	Neglected
6	Aphasia	35	Neurotic
7	Autistic	36	Overgratified
8	Behavior-disordered	37	Overstimulated
9	Below-average learner	38	Perceptually handicapped
10	Brain-damaged	39	Physically handicapped
11	Cerebral dysfunction	40	Primitive
12	Child with educational problems	41	Psycholinguisticly disabled
13	Child with failure sets	42	Psychopathic
14	Culturally deprived	43	Psychotic
15	Delinquent	44	Retarded development
16	Educable mentally retarded	45	Schizophrenic
17	Educationally disabled	46	Slow learner
18	Ego-development deficiency	47	Socially defective
19	Emotionally disturbed	48	Socially deprived
20	Emotionally handicapped	49	Socially disruptive
21	Emotionally maladjusted	50	Socially handicapped
22	Exceptional	51	Socially impaired
23	Genotypically retarded	52	Socially maladjusted
24	Hyperactive	53	Socially rejected
25	Hyperkinetic	54	Speech or language latency
26	Impulse-ridden	55	Symbiotic disorder
27	Latent development	56	Trainable
28	Learning-disabled	57	Withdrawn
29	Low cognitive capacity		

An examination of the preceding "classificatory" labels strongly suggests that there really is no classification system within special education. What might appear to be a system is, in reality, an unsystematic crazy quilt of labels. The categories and labels do not constitute a scientific classification system. First, there is no common logic, criteria, or order within the scheme. Second, the various classificatory labels come from different disciplines, reflect differing perspectives, and serve no single purpose. The crucial and fundamental inadequacy of current special education classification is simply that the scheme does not serve educational purposes.

The major organizing logic, criteria, and purpose of special educational classification must serve to (1) identify significant *educational* problems of children; (2) order educational problems in ways that detect similarities and relationships; and (3) provide nomenclature that promotes communication and research within education.

It seems clear that a medical rather than an educational posture character-izes current special education classification. The nomenclature is inappropriate and basically nonproductive for educational purposes. Numerous special edu-cators have made this point and have spoken out against the pathological or disease orientation of special education terminology. Reger, Schroeder, and Uschold (1968) bluntly assert that "grouping children on the basis of medi-cally derived disability labels has no practical utility in the schools" (p. 19). Stevens (1962) (whose suggestions for an educationally based classification system will be discussed later) has stressed that "preoccupation with disability was [and is] forcing a kind of classification ill-suited to the training of teach-ers" (p. v). Not only has teachers' training been impeded by the noneducation-al orientation of the terminology, but the legal basis for special education services has centered on medical nomenclature, and thus warped special educational activities into a disability or disease orientation. The pathology orientation has spread to other aspects of special education in addition to classification of children: a child's problem is to be "diagnosed," a "prognosis" is made, concern is directed toward "etiology," and "incidence" and "prev-alence" figures are sought.

We previously pointed out how useless and confusing it would be to have a library classification system based on variables such as the color, size, and weight of books; these factors are unrelated to the purposes of librarians. There appears to be an analogous situation in special education classification. The tasks of special educators include identification of educational problems, selection of learning materials and methods, grouping of children for instruc-tion, and making various other educational decisions. Classification on the basis of medical terminology does not facilitate accomplishment of such tasks. Unfortunately, then, educational decisions have not been based on educa-tional or learning variables but rather on medical, psychiatric (or legal or sociological) variables that are, at best, remotely related to the educational enterprise. Categorizing children as "mentally retarded," "emotionally dis-turbed," or "socially maladjusted" or as "having special health problems" con-veys some information about children; but most of this information is outside the domain of education. Classifying a child as "mentally retarded" or "emo-tionally disturbed," for example, does little to assist in matching educational methods and materials to the child. Such classification is of little help in select-ing a proper reading, arithmetic, writing, or language program, in designing incentive arrangements, or in providing educational consultation for parents.

Teachers must deal with children whose behaviors are varied and have multiple causes but are subject to positive change through educational inter-vention. There are behaviors to be speeded up, slowed down, strengthened, weakened, elaborated, or simplified. There are decisions to be made concern-ing learning materials to use or not to use, seating arrangements, motivational tactics, and prosthetic devices. Such decisions are educational decisions based on educational variables. And making effective educational decisions is not facilitated by classification based on noneducational criteria and perspectives:

> The children are given various labels including deaf, blind, orthopedically handicapped, trainable mentally retarded, educable mentally retarded, autistic, socially maladjusted, perceptually handicapped, brain-injured, emotionally disturbed, disadvantaged, and those with learning disabilities. For the most part the labels are not important. They rarely tell the teacher who can be taught in what way. One could put five or six labels on the same child and still not know what to teach him or how [Becker, Engelmann, Thomas, 1971, pp. 435–436].

We have emphasized that current labels reflect a preoccupation with medical, psychiatric, legal, and sociological perspectives that are, at best, remotely related to educational decision making. But there is another characteristic of current labels that produces a further liability to progress in special education: the dispositional or "underlying cause" nature of labels.

Dispositional or "basic cause" labels again reflect the pervasive influence of the medical approach on special education. In medicine, health problems are usually viewed as "symptoms" of some underlying dysfunction or pathology. The removal of the symptoms is somewhat dependent on treatment of the underlying cause. This underlying-cause–symptom model has been extrapolated to educational and behavioral phenomena for purposes of explanation and intervention. It is consonant with this model to consider a child's frequent fighting, swearing, and resistance to discipline as "symptoms" of an underlying "condition." The "condition" is variously labeled, e.g. as "a character disorder," "emotional disturbance," or "hostile-aggressive impulse," depending on the biases of the person imposing the label. Whatever the specific label, the common denominator is the inference of a general, underlying disposition to behave in certain ways. Stuart (1970) describes this as "genotypic" language, which attempts to explain behavior by reference to alleged subsurface dynamics and to describe what a person *is*. This language is the opposite of "phenotypic" language, which describes what a person *does* (Stuart, pp. 65–66). A behavioral or phenotypic approach focuses on identifying the problems of children, measuring them, and relating them to actual (rather than hypothetical) variables subject to manipulation for purposes of positive intervention. Classifying children with genotypic or dispositional labels diverts attention of educators from what can be done now and directly to help the child. Further, such labels based on inference and elusive hypothetical conditions promote a kind of endless scapegoating that allows the educator to find excuses for failure and blame the "condition" on some "deeper" (hypothetical) problem, historical incident, or poor home life. Thus, Johnny can't read because he has a condition of "low motivation," "perceptual disturbance," and "minimal cerebral dysfunction," because he was exposed to some trauma earlier in development, or has an "insecure home life." As Reger, Schroeder, and Uschold (1968) point out "while the school is chasing down basic causes, the child is no better off than he was. . . . Whenever a specialist from another profession, whether legal, medical, or psychological, says 'This child has such and such a condition,' the school always must ask itself what this means when translated into the educational context" (p. 43).

Dispositional labels, then, tag children with assumed conditions that do not identify relevant and specific educational characteristics that make instructional intervention feasible.

Thus far we have discussed the confusing, unsystematic, and diversionary nature of classification and terminology employed in special education. If the labeling system does not help teachers, it would seem to be of little use or benefit to the children who are labeled. It is to that point, i.e., the impact of labels on children, that we now turn our attention.

THE HANDICAPPING IMPACT OF NEGATIVE LABELING

It is pointed out in the chapter on somatopsychological problems that handicap is a socially imposed burden. Current labels generally function to further debilitate rather than help the child; they can thus be viewed as further handicaps that impede the child's development and amplify the number and intensity of his problems.

In discussing the handicapping influence of special education labels, we shall examine two dimensions of deleterious impact: (1) the "spread" effect of negative labels; and (2) the self-fulfilling trend produced by such labels and the consequent effects on the child's self-esteem.

The generalization of negative labels

An inspection of traditional special education labeling reveals that almost all classificatory labels identify and focus on deficiencies of the child (Iscoe and Payne, 1972; Stevens, 1962). Some labels focus on constitutional inferiority (e.g., "crippled," "cerebral-palsied," "blind," "deaf"), while others specify character or personality disorders (e.g., "emotional disturbance," "mental retardation," "social maladjustment"). Whatever the label, the emphasis has been on real or assumed liability. "Accentuate the negative" seems to have been the theme. While tagging children with such labels may in itself produce a handicap, the handicap would perhaps not prove insurmountable if perceptions of the child's other attributes were not also tainted by the label. Once a label has been imposed there appears to be a spread or generalized influence on others' perceptions of the child. Inferiority or deviancy in other areas of functioning is assumed by virtue of the deficiency in a specified area, even in the absence of supportive observations and, indeed, in the face of contrary evidence (Kugel and Wolfensberger, 1969). A negative halo and general stigma become attached to the child.

Historically, there are dramatic illustrations of the clumping together of "deviates," reflecting the inferred spread of a specific deviancy. Early in America, there is evidence that so-called emotionally disturbed people, epileptics, socially deprived people, prostitutes, alcoholics, and others were grouped together and placed in institutions for "safekeeping" (Deutsch, 1949). Display of one class of disorder seemed sufficient to provide grounds for global "defectiveness" or "degeneracy."

> The chronic insane, the epileptic, the paralytic, the imbecile and idiot of various grades, the moral imbecile, the sexual pervert, the kleptomaniac; many, if not most, of the chronic inebriates; many of the prostitutes, tramps, and minor criminals; many habitual paupers, especially the ignorant and irresponsible mothers of illegitimate children, so common in poor houses; many of the shiftless poor, even on the verge of pauperism and often stepping over into it; some of the blind, some deaf-mutes, some consumptives. All these classes, in varying degree with others not mentioned, are related as being effects of the one cause—which itself is the summing up of many causes—"degeneracy" [Johnson, 1903, p. 246].

Research in semantics (Manis, Houts, and Blake, 1963; Osgood, Suci, and Tannenbaum, 1967; Stuart, 1970) has illustrated that the influence of negative labels is generalized and that one "bad" or devalued trait suggests another. The platonic thesis that truth, beauty, and goodness are all part of the same is a classic illustration of the perceived coherence of otherwise independent characteristics. Something that is viewed as beautiful, then, is also viewed as possessing the virtues of truth and goodness. This semantic clustering and its influence on perception is supported by studies documenting how a teacher's ratings and attitudes of a child's performance are biased by the teacher's view of the physical attractiveness of a child (Fleming and Anttonen, 1971; Kehle, 1973; Hanson, 1974).

Similarly, it has been posited (Wilkins, 1965) that departure from any single characteristic, i.e., truth, beauty, or goodness, may be viewed as evidence for corresponding deviations in the remaining two virtues. Thus, so the speculation goes, those persons who are judged as ugly or of unpleasant appearance are also viewed suspiciously with regard to truth and goodness. For example, it is common practice for governments to picture an enemy as unpleasant or evil in appearance; this strategy is obviously designed to magnify distrust or hate of the enemy and to reinforce the stigma attached to the foe. A handsome enemy wouldn't fill the bill.

As a final instance of the spread of negative labeling, consider how some people behave as if multiple defects exist where evidence for only one is presented (Goffman, 1963). Consider the waitress who, having been told that a patron is blind, shouts at him as it he were also hard of hearing. Additionally, she may oversimplify the menu as if the patron had difficulty in comprehension. Such behavior illustrates the insidious generalized response toward specific deficiencies. Attaching the label of a specific deficiency to a person may condemn him to excessive social discrimination because of the generalized or nonspecific response toward deficiencies.

Self-fulfillment of negative labels

In view of the reaction to labels just discussed, the self-fulfilling potential of labels becomes an even more potent source of handicap. But what is meant by "self-fulfilling labels" and what are the mechanisms that may account for the phenomenon? While we have no definitive answers to either of these questions, there are a number of interesting investigations that shed light on these issues.

Rosenthal and Jacobson (1966) reported a study, "Teachers' Expectancies: Determinants of Pupil IQ Gains," and later presented an extended discussion (Rosenthal and Jacobson, 1968) that stimulated much subsequent research and controversy over the influence of expectancy on behavior. They informed teachers (falsely) that certain students had shown unusual intellectual potential on a test that had been administered to all children in the teachers' several classes.

"Eight months later these 'unusual' children (who had actually been selected at random) showed significantly greater gains in IQ than did the remaining children in the control group" (p. 115). It must be pointed out, however, that several attempts to replicate these results have failed to find similar or as dramatic results (Barber et al., 1969; Claiborn, 1969). Further, critiques of Rosenthal and Jacobson's efforts have raised serious doubts about the generalizability of the expectancy phenomenon (Elashoff and Snow, 1971; Thorndike, 1968). At this time, therefore, we cannot speak with certainty about the impact and mechanics of teachers' expectancies on pupils' performance. It would appear, however, that when a teacher, for whatever reason, *expects* better performance of certain children, he or she may *behave* differentially toward the children. It is possible, for example, that the teacher may act to reinforce and thus shape increased attention, volunteering, persistence, and success of pupils who are expected to be better students. Thus, results of psychological tests (particularly IQ scores), prior grades, rumor, and the reputation of a pupil may serve as cues which influence the behavior of teachers and evaluators toward the student (see Johnson, 1974, for a review of variables influencing special education classification). In turn, a teacher's behavior may so alter a student's behavior that it begins to drift in the predicted or expected direction. The altered behavior of the student then "confirms" and thus reinforces the teacher's behavior. This dynamic interaction may continue until the student's behavior becomes aligned with the teacher's expectancy.

While the foregoing analysis is speculative and will require much research, other related findings strongly point to the impact of expectancy on behavior. For example, several studies (e.g., Irwin, 1953; Jessor and Readie, 1957) have demonstrated that the child with a high expectancy of success performs better on an intellectual task than one whose expectancy of success is low. An interesting report concerning therapy with "disturbed" men in the military shows that treatment consisting of expecting normal role performance from persons displaying disturbed behavior seems to be an effective means for normalizing the deviant behavior (Talbot, 1969). In other words, simply expecting and demanding normal behavior seems to be a powerful therapeutic strategy for eliciting normal behavior. (Obviously, behavioral demands would have to be programmatically gauged and altered in relation to the person's progress.) Perhaps this technique is powerful partly because much of a person's problem may be due to a history of expectations of abnormal or inferior behavior. Expect and accept defective behavior and you will probably get it.

Tizard (1970) points out how professional behavior (e.g., of physicians, psychologists, and teachers) toward an individual is "profoundly influenced by the perspective from which they view the individual in their care" (p. 379). If academic or social problems are viewed as medically based, the professional has a different expectation of improvement of the individual than if some other explanation is used. "Defining such persons [the mentally deranged, alcoholics, drug addicts, the mentally retarded] as 'ill' changes their status in society, the roles they are expected to play, the social institutions which will treat them, and the professional persons who will be responsible for their cure" (Mercer, 1970).

The distorting influence of stigmatizing labels on face-to-face personal interaction has been reported in an interesting series of investigations (e.g., Cohen and Struening, 1964; Farina, Allen and Saul, 1968; Farina and Ring, 1965; Jones, Hester, Farina, and Davis, 1959). Studies such as these demonstrate the impact of negative labels on both the stigmatized person and the individual perceiving him. Essentially, the studies provide two general findings. First, persons who are informed that other persons are negatively labeled behave differently toward them than if the label is not supplied. Generally, the informed person finds more fault with and sees more problems with the stigmatized (labeled) person. Second, persons who believe that others "know their label" attempt to dispel the negative influence of the information carried by the label. This compensatory behavior often creates rejection by others, and thus confirms and strengthens the negative perceptions generated by the label. This effect occurred in studies when the label was arbitrarily attached to a "normal" person. Similarly, Edgerton (1967) discusses the enormous handicap faced by ex-patients of institutions for the retarded. Such persons try to convince others—and themselves—of their adequacy. They constantly strive to create a "cloak of competence" to offset the fact that they have been labeled deficient. Thus, once negatively labeled, a child is in much the same position as the ex-convict: the stigma of the label lives on, even after it is totally unwarranted.

In summary, negative labels, as well as socially visible physical or functional differences, impose a handicapping stigma, so that "an individual who might have been received easily in ordinary social intercourse possesses a trait that can obtrude itself upon attention and turn those of us whom he meets away from him, breaking the claim that his other [positive] attributes have on us" (Goffman, 1963, p. 5). It appears, then, that the language of classification schemes that focus on deficiencies and employ derogative labels greatly stigmatizes and thus imposes surplus handicaps, i.e., a burden beyond the actual physical or functional limitations of a child.

In view of the existing evidence from the fields of psychology, sociology, and education, it appears that labels employed for diagnosis and treatment are actually part of the treatment or mistreatment. What we call a person influences how others act toward him (a multitude of subtle social interactions), how the person acts toward himself (i.e., self-referent behavior), and what roles he will be expected to fill or not fill. Classificatory labeling can handicap or help; it behooves us to be critical and cautious about the terminology we attach to those whom we are dedicated to help.

ALTERNATIVE CLASSIFICATION SYSTEMS

Happily, we see a distinct trend within special education to revamp the traditional categorical schemes or replace them with systems more in keeping with the scientific purposes of classification, i.e., to seek order, detect relationships, enhance communication, promote research, and facilitate the work of the science. In the following pages of this chapter, we summarize classificatory systems proposed by three leading special educators who know well the problems of traditional terminology. None of the three systems that are presented is complete and without problems; each is, in our judgment, however, a giant step in the right direction. The proposed systems have been organized by special educators. Thus, the terminology is not medical, psychological, sociological, legal, or a random mixture of these, but rather is clearly focused on variables of concern to special educators.

THE ISCOE SYSTEM FOR CLASSIFYING SPECIAL EDUCATIONAL VARIABLES

Iscoe and Payne (1972) suggest that children may differ from what is considered "normal" along several basic dimensions: physical, adjustment, and educational status. Each of these central dimensions is further analyzed into three subcomponents that allow for measurement and that suggest special education intervention. Following is an outline of the main entries in the system.

I Physical Status
   A Visibility of physical deviation
   B Locomotion capabilities and limitations
   C Communication capabilities and problems

II Adjustment Status
   A Peer acceptance
   B Family interaction
   C Self-esteem

III Educational Status
    A Motivation
    B Academic achievement
    C Educational potential

It is crucial to note that the system is based on a *functional* analysis of a child's status, rather than on etiology or deviation. The physical dimension, for example, focuses on competence in locomotion and communication and on the social visibility of physical difference. It is educationally important to know how socially visible the child's physical difference is, since it is this difference that may produce a social handicap. Likewise, we can gain educationally relevant information by describing and estimating the locomotor competence of a student. Can he or she walk, manipulate objects, use one or both arms or legs, run or maintain balance? Scales are available for describing in some detail locomotor and psychomotor capabilities. Communication is another salient subdivision of the physical dimension that can be described and measured by various instruments and scales. (See Part V for listings of these evaluative devices.) Sensory capabilities (such as hearing and vision) and delivery capabilities (such as articulation, volume, and other speech dimensions) are important considerations to the educator. Simply labeling a child "cerebral-palsied" does not provide the educator with information for educational decision making. Some cerebral-palsied children can walk, others cannot; some have severe speech problems, some do not; some present striking physical differences that are highly visible, while many others would be judged as presenting "low visibility." The label "cerebral-palsied" may be medically pertinent but, educationally speaking, it is only roughly and inadequately correlated with the visibility, locomotor, and communication considerations crucial to the educational enterprise.

The adjustment dimension again includes subcomponents that cover several facets important from an educational and developmental point of view. Peer acceptance is a good measure (e.g., by sociogram or other rating methods) of one kind of adjustment that has instructional relevance. Family interaction and self-esteem are other areas in which the quality and degree of adjustment can be defined. Note that these perspectives on adjustment are not arbitrary, but are directly related to goals of education, i.e. to promote getting along with others, to build an effective view of oneself, etc.

The third dimension, education, contains components most commonly considered within the domain of education. The motivation of the student is of paramount concern. The teacher must judge what "turns on" the child, prepare and sequence materials in accord with interest level, and employ informal or contrived motivational systems where necessary. Achievement level in various skills and educational potential are indices to every teacher that, when properly assessed and interpreted, are valuable tools in planning instruction.

A child's status in all dimensions may be displayed simply on a chart such as Table 7-1. Entries for each cell may be in the form of ratings, such as low-

TABLE 7-1 STATUS SUMMARY OF MAJOR AREAS OF FUNCTIONING

	Visibility	Locomotion	Communication
Physical status			
	Peer	Family	Self
Adjustment status			
	Motivation	Achievement	Potential
Education status			

medium-high, a rating of 1 to 5, or any other consistent description. More subjective assessments in these dimensions may also be entered.

More than one entry may be made within any one cell. Thus, the achievement cell might include separate values for achievement in reading, arithmetic, and writing. Likewise, motivation could contain interest ratings of 1 to 5 in each separate curriculum area, e.g., a 1 (low interest) for reading, but a 4 (fairly high interest) for arithmetic. Details for the entries can be worked out by each teacher or within groups of teachers. The point is that each of the nine cells deserves consideration in the comprehensive description of a given child's status.

Use of this system in no way involves labeling a child with terms that relate to broad genotypic, etiological, medical, or hypothetical "conditions." Thus, children with the same etiological label, e.g., "brain-injured," might display quite different patterns in the nine dimensions of Iscoe's system. By the same token, children with diverse medical or etiological labels, e.g., "mentally retarded," "cerebral dysfunction," "blind," or "emotionally disturbed," might all have identical or similar values in many of the dimensions. The thrust of the system is to obviate the need for labels for children. Instead, the system provides for profiling each child's status in each of the educationally relevant dimensions.

Let us speculate for a moment on what might happen if the Iscoe system, or a similar one, were widely employed. We might, for example, see the development of teacher-training programs that employ each of the nine cell entries of Iscoe and Payne's model in the preparation of special educators. Teachers might receive training in all nine areas and specialize in one or two. A teacher could, for example, become an expert in motivation. Such an educator would work with all children (regardless of the traditional label) who are in need of motivational engineering, incentive programing, interest surveying, etc. Similarly, a teacher might choose to become an expert in locomotion training. This teacher could work with children who have low vision capability and require mobility lessons, children who have motor impairment and must learn to move about with prosthetic aids such as wheelchairs, crutches, and braces, or children who have no sensory or motor impairment but are just "awkward" or who have trouble remembering their way around.

Teachers with such preparation would clearly be valuable resource personnel within a school and would speed the day when "exceptional children" can be optimally integrated within regular classes. No longer would there be a need for deciding if a child is "really" brain-damaged, emotionally disturbed, socially maladjusted, or mildly retarded. Rather, he would be given the help he needs in each of the educationally pertinent dimensions by teachers prepared to give him that help. Such a division of labor based on educational variables rather than on categorical labels could go far in making special education a potent discipline practiced by experts who make a real difference in the education and development of children.

We have presented extended commentary on what we see as the virtues of Iscoe's system. The next two proposed approaches are somewhat more detailed and will be presented with less commentary since they embody many of the same assets as the Iscoe system.

THE STEVENS SPECIAL EDUCATION TAXONOMY

Stevens's taxonomic model is more extensive than that of Iscoe. It goes beyond the classification of educational variables directly concerned with the child and includes the areas of law, finance, and administration as they relate to special education. Because Stevens's taxonomy is so extensive, we shall present it in outline form with comment where necessary to clarify the terms and their relevance.

The taxonomy includes three basic domains of special education as seen by Stevens: somatopsychological variants, attributes of body disorder, and special education procedures. Each domain contains several subclasses that provide detail and comprehensiveness to the domain. As in Iscoe and Payne's system, the basic entries relate to functions or capabilities rather than to alleged origin or diagnostic labels of children.

Special education taxonomy*

I Somatopsychological variants—constitutional differences and resulting behavioral differences that give rise to problems of educational significance.
   A Handicap—the burden imposed on the child by virtue of the interaction of a constitutional difference with the functional demands of the school setting.
      The principal demands of the school are:
      1 Motility (roughly equivalent to locomotion and psychomotor skills).
      2 Communication (verbal and nonverbal input and output).
      3 Self-concept (sufficiently effective to preclude interference with developmental progress).
      4 Social interaction.
   B Disability—organ dysfunction that, when not compensated for or accom-

---

* Adapted from G. D. Stevens, *Taxonomy in Special Education for Children with Body Disorders: The Problem and a Proposal*, Pittsburgh: The Department of Special Education and Rehabilitation, University of Pittsburgh, 1962.

modated, generates varying handicaps within the school context. Reduction of the following organ functions seems most related and apt to create problems:

1 Motion (flexion, extension of body parts).
2 Sensation (vision, hearing, touch, taste, smell).
3 Intelligence (includes rate and degree of learning, recall, problem solving, and many other factors).
4 Emotion (includes capability for experiencing joy, enthusiasm, sorrow, hostility, etc.).
5 Physiological processes (includes fundamental body processes such as respiration, digestion, metabolism).

C Impairment—defective tissue that may or may not result in significant organ dysfunction, but may nevertheless be germane to school progress. Scar tissue, for example, may not impede bodily functioning but may still be a source of social handicap and, thus, influence development.

II Educationally significant attributes of body disorder—those aspects of disease or pathology that have relevance to educational administration, planning, financing, therapy, etc. Such considerations have less relevance for the individual teacher than domains I or III, but are pertinent to planning within districts and articulation with medical, dental, social, and legal services.

A Nature of the condition—descriptive data that have pertinence for overall planning.
1 Epidemiology (prevalence, sex differences, contagion factors).
2 Temporal factors (age of onset, duration, chronicity, etc.).
3 Symptomology (severity, course, sequence).

B Nature of therapeutic procedures—treatment of disease or illness that may complement or interfere with school participation or educational practice. (For example, it is clear that use of drugs to treat an illness may have far-reaching impact on a child's progress in school and may dictate changes in instructional demands.)
1 Amenability.
2 Prognosis.
3 Treatment factors (e.g., duration of treatment, side effects, needed prosthetics).

C Psychological aspects—consideration of the psychological impact of the condition and its treatment. (The language and strategies discussed in Chapter 8, "Somatopsychological Problems," are related to this area.)

D Social considerations—existing public health laws and social and legal regulations that provide assistance or impose limitations. For example, availability of funding, tax relief, restrictions on voting, licensing, and possible legislation bearing on mandatory birth control would have implications for broad curriculum planning and articulation of services between the school and other personnel.

E   Cultural considerations—the attitudes, beliefs, mores, prejudices, and needed public relations that bear on acceptance or rejection of a child.

III Special educational procedures—the body of educational practices, services, physical arrangements, and administration that essentially is a modification or extension or both of the general educational process.

This domain can be viewed as the taxonomic entry point for factors that should be considered in order to bring about positive changes in or adjustments of the somatopsychological variants listed under domain I and several of the factors entered under domain II.

A   Modification of laws.

B   Finance (e.g., government, private, methods for accounting and reporting).

C   Instructional process.
   1   General and specific objectives.
   2   General and individualized curricula.
   3   Methods.
   4   Materials, equipment.
   5   Instructional organization, e.g., team teaching, open classroom, resource teachers, instructional space.
   6   Evaluation procedures, e.g., formative, summative, continuous; monitoring, reporting of children's progress to other teachers, parents, and other agencies.
   7   Teachers' competencies, i.e., those skills and knowledge central to actualizing objectives for children.

D   Noninstructional services, e.g., considerations including case finding, needed transportation, food services, counseling, and psychological services.

E   Administrative modifications, e.g., staff patterns, use of professional, paraprofessional, and nonprofessional personnel, certification, overall plant facilities, financial allocations, salaries, and merit or other staff incentive systems.

F   Ancillary services, i.e., services that are basically noneducational but impinge on the educational enterprise. It has been emphasized that the role of the school is education, and not the provision of medical, legal, and other social services. Nevertheless, special education must articulate with paraeducational services, e.g., medicine, law, welfare, and business, in order to effect supplemental assistance, continuity, and follow-through for children.

Summary

Stevens presents a rather comprehensive system for classifying an array of factors and concerns pertinent to the education and development of children who need special provisions. While portions of the taxonomy are of direct relevance to the teacher-student dyad, numerous entries, especially in Domain II, pertain to broader administrative concerns. Like the Iscoe system, however, the emphasis of the terminology is on the functions of the educational enterprise and the capabilities of children.

The taxonomy permits meaningful educational diagnoses that make special education intervention feasible, unlike labeling systems based on etiology or on general "conditions" of children.

> The study and assessment of educational deficiency in school children can be done in a systematic and educationally meaningful fashion. The educational diagnostician can follow the logical organization of defining his problem. Using the subclasses he can assess the limitations of a child in terms of the subclasses deemed to be educationally relevant, i.e., limitations in motility; communications; the self-concept; and social interaction. This becomes the basis of a thoughtful and logical organization of the facts leading to a systematic diagnosis of the educational handicap or burden [Stevens, 1962, p. 82].

We shall now move to a presentation and brief discussion of a third and final suggested framework for classifying exceptionality.

THE QUAY SYSTEM FOR CLASSIFYING FACETS OF EDUCATIONAL EXCEPTIONALITY*

In keeping with the tone of this chapter, Herbert Quay (1968) rejects the use of traditional special education labels for educational diagnosis or instructional grouping. Instead, Quay's system focuses on educationally relevant variables which can be directly manipulated in the school situation. "While hypothetical constructs may be of value in the construction of theoretical explanations of learning, these are inferred from stimulus-response relationships and they cannot be directly manipulated. While defective auditory-association may help explain some facet of poor performance in the learning process it is only stimulus, response, and reinforcement variables which can be manipulated to improve 'auditory-association' " (p. 4). Thus this framework, like those previously described, is a promising classificatory device for use in identifying educationally pertinent factors over which educators have a feasible degree of control.

Unlike the previous two systems, however, the Quay system concentrates on learning parameters per se and does not include some of the somatopsychological concerns of the other two systems.

Visibility of deviance or cosmetic factors, for example, are not identified or assessed. We recommend, therefore, that this system be viewed as a good approach for elaborating the instructional dimensions related to teaching and modifying the sensory and expressive skills of children.

Quay identifies three fundamental parameters of learning: stimulus input, response, and reinforcement. (See Figure 7-1.) That is, educators must be

---

* Adapted from H. C. Quay, "The Facets of Educational Exceptionality: A Conceptual Framework for Assessment, Grouping and Instruction." *Exceptional Children*, 1968, **35**, 25–31.

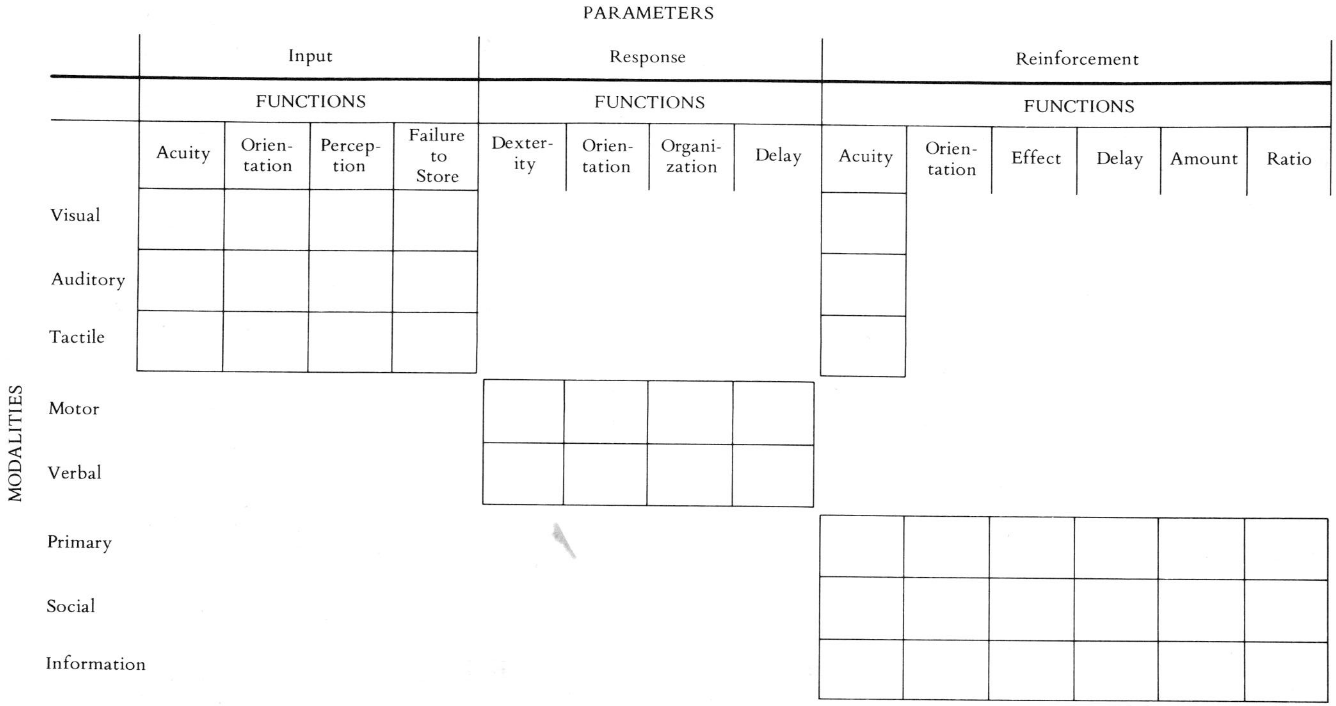

PARAMETERS

Input | Response | Reinforcement

MODALITIES

	Input FUNCTIONS			Response FUNCTIONS					Reinforcement FUNCTIONS			
	Acuity	Orien-tation	Percep-tion	Failure to Store	Dexter-ity	Orien-tation	Organi-zation	Delay	Acuity	Orien-tation	Effect	Delay	Amount	Ratio
Visual														
Auditory														
Tactile														
Motor														
Verbal														
Primary														
Social														
Information														

FIGURE 7-1 The parameters, modalities, and functions of classroom learning. (Reprinted from Quay, H. C., The facets of educational exceptionality: A conceptual framework for assessment, grouping, and instruction. *Exceptional Children*, 1968, **35**, 25–31. By permission of The Council for Exceptional Children.)

concerned with the nature and presentation of instructional stimuli; the type, quality, and possibility of the student's behavior in response to the stimuli; and the consequences (principally reinforcement) of the response. Succinctly stated, educators must engineer the cues and consequences of an instructional attempt in order to attain the response objectives they seek.

For each of the three learning parameters, several facets or functions are identified. Each of these functions is an important consideration that must be assessed and that isolates possible stumbling blocks in the instructional program with a particular student.

Parameters of learning

Stimulus

Input, acuity, orientation, perception, and failure to store are the principal functions listed for the stimulus input parameter. These entries pinpoint four functions or features of stimuli crucial to learning. Instructional stimuli must, of course, be detected or sensed by the student; this relates to stimulus acuity. Obviously, auditory stimuli must be different for a child who has a hearing problem than for a child with normal hearing.

Likewise, orientation to the stimuli is necessary. A stimulus of even optimal acuity is not really a stimulus if it is not within the purview of the child. Thus, a child who stares at the ceiling will not be much influenced by a visual stimulus until the orientation problem is solved: the stimulus must be "aimed" at the selected sense organs. (Headsets, for example, minimize problems of orientation to auditory stimuli.) "Stimulus perception" refers to the discriminability of the relevant dimensions of the stimulus. A child may "see" a flashcard, be oriented toward it, and yet not perceive or discriminate the features on the card. Accordingly, materials must be engineered to increase figure-ground contrast and exaggerate subtle differences in stimuli (e.g., "d" versus "b"), simplify the presentation, or in other ways be modified to optimize delivery of the intended stimuli. Finally, the failure to store or recall a stimulus can be enhanced by repetition, exaggeration, contrast, and other methods (see, e.g., Adams, 1967).

Response

The response parameter includes the functions of dexterity, orientation, organization, and delay. "Dexterity" is the response counterpart of stimulus acuity and refers to the accuracy and ease of response. No matter how well engineered the stimulus input, a child will not learn to eliminate a speech articulation problem if the response apparatus does not allow for the required dexterity. Response orientation, as with stimulus orientation, is concerned with control of direction. The child who stares at the ceiling will not only have a problem orienting to stimulus input but will not respond properly until the response is aimed. Organization of response is concerned with the integration or articulation of response units that make up a complex response. For example, children may have trouble in controlling speech volume simultaneously with proper articulation, or the collateral expression of two or more response modes, e.g., motor and verbal. Delay of response is frequently critical to learning. Abrupt responding to the preliminary aspects of a stimulus can preclude attention and thus learning of the total stimulus complex.

Reinforcement

The reinforcement parameter of learning includes acuity, orientation, effect delay, amount, and ratio. As with stimulus acuity, reinforcement acuity is clearly a prerequisite of reinforcement influence; a reinforcing consequence that is not detected cannot be reinforcing. Similarly, orientation to the reinforcer is required to ensure "consumption" of the reinforcer. "Reinforcer effect" refers to the potency of an intended reinforcer and varies with the status of the child, amount of deprivation, and availability of other competing reinforcers. The social class of a child, for example, generally relates to the effectiveness of feedback as a reinforcer. Likewise, the age and socialization level of the child are associated with the power of social (especially verbal) reinforcement. "Different strokes for different folks" summarizes the effect function of reinforcement; choice of reinforcers must be individualized for maximum effect. Delay of reinforcement is yet another aspect that must be considered in the optimal use of reinforcers. A number of correlates such as age, intelligence level, repertoire sophistication, and reinforcement history are associated with the potency of delayed reinforcement. One developmental objective for children is to increase the delay between behavior and back-up reinforcement. "Delay of gratification" has long been recognized as a mark of maturity and, indeed, is necessary for continued development. Various tactics are available for teaching increased toleration for delay of reward. Finally, amount and ratio of reinforcement are two dimensions of reinforcement that deserve attention if this parameter is to be optimally employed to facilitate learning. Some children require large amounts of reinforcement for learning; the amount will depend, again, on degree of deprivation, accessibility to other (uncontrolled) reinforcers, reinforcer history, and the difficulty of the task. Clearly, some behavior changes require larger doses of reinforcement than others—even for the same child. Whatever the case, an educational objective for some children is to reduce the absolute amount of reinforcement required for a particular behavior yield. Similarly with ratio of reinforcement, the scheduling of reinforcement is to be considered in effecting learning. A great deal of evidence is available that provides the following two generalizations. First, when one is attempting to initiate or establish a behavior, reinforcement should usually be frequent. That is, the ratio of behavior to payoff should be small. Often it is necessary to reinforce every instance of a new or developing behavior. As learning of the behavior proceeds, the ratio of behavior to reinforcement may be stretched to a leaner schedule. Indeed, such a leaner schedule has definitely been found to result in greater stability or endurance of the behavior. Thus, the second generalization with respect to reinforcement ratios is: After a behavior is established, use of an intermittent or random schedule of reinforcement will result in much greater persistence of the behavior.

Modalities
Sensory
In discussing the functions of stimulus input, it becomes clear that the quality of the various sense organs interacts with the stimulus input to determine the impact of the stimulus. The best of visual stimuli are of little consequence with a blind child. Thus, the design of instructional stimuli must consider the sensory status of the child. The principal sensory modes of relevance in the classroom are the visual, the auditory, and the tactile. Any significant limitation in one or more of the sensory modes requires compensatory design of the stimulus input or dependence on a remaining intact sense or both. Accordingly, a child who has a hearing limitation must be provided with auditory input designed to make use of residual hearing and with special visual input to capitalize on satisfactory vision and to compensate for the auditory deficiency.

In addition to interaction with instructional stimulus arrangements, the sensory modalities also conjoin with reinforcement acuity. (See the three cells under reinforcement acuity in Figure 7-1). Just as with instructional stimuli, reinforcing stimuli may be seen, heard, or felt. (Other senses, of course, can be involved, such as taste and smell, but limitations in these senses are not as frequent or consequential in learning.) Thus, reinforcer delivery must be adjusted and suited to the sensory apparatus.

Response
Motor and verbal response are the principal modes that interact with the response functions. The eight-cell matrix under the response parameter in Figure 7-1 identifies possible facets for educational assessment and focus related to a child's performance. The response dimensions of dexterity, orientation, organization, and delay have been detailed in our discussion of the response parameter. Each of these functions or dimensions must be considered for both the motor and the verbal response modes. For example, a child with cleft palate would most probably display a deficiency in the dexterity function of the verbal response mode, whereas a "hyperactive" child might frequently display deficiency in the delay function of the motor response mode. Of course, the traditional label of a child does not in itself pinpoint capabilities and deficiencies. It remains for the special educator to assess capabilities in each of the cells of the framework and to design educational materials and tactics in accordance with this assessment.

Reinforcement
Primary-sensory, social, and informational constitute the modes of reinforcement. The six dimensions of the reinforcement parameter are applicable to each of the three modes. Thus, the effect, delay, amount, and ratio functions

of social reinforcement may be quite different than the same functions of informational (feedback) reinforcement. We cannot assume that the required delay, amount, and ratio of primary-sensory reinforcement (e.g., food, toy, preferred activity) also hold for social reinforcement. In order to have the same reinforcement value as a tangible reward, for example, praise may have to be provided at a much different delay, amount, and ratio.

The frequent misuse of programed instructional materials provides a glaring example of the faulty assumption that informational or feedback reinforcement is sufficient to promote learning for any child. Some children's learning behavior is little influenced by knowledge of being right or wrong. When this is true, the feedback feature of programed materials must be supplemented with social or primary reinforcement.

This concludes, then, the presentation of Quay's formulation for identifying and relating educational variables. We close this chapter with a summary of the assets of the three proposals, especially in contradistinction to the traditional schemes of special education classification.

SUMMARY OF PROPOSED SYSTEMS

We have discussed in some detail the disorder, educational irrelevance, and handicapping impact of special education classification labels based on a real or assumed etiology of disorder. The preoccupation with classification according to the origin or "cause" of educational and developmental problems has provided little help to educators in making decisions regarding objectives, grouping, and instructional tactics. There is copious evidence that current labeling practices not only fail to be educationally constructive, but, indeed, tend to be developmentally destructive to children in terms of depressing expectancies for progress, lowering self-esteem, and generalizing negative perceptions.

Several alternative approaches to special education classification have been offered that avoid the problems of current labels and that provide promise for systems of identification, assessment, grouping, and instructional practice based on educational variables.

The proposed alternatives have the following characteristics in common:

1 Language systems based on a common foundation—education—as opposed to terminology coming from various disciplinary perspectives that reflect noneducational or paraeducational concerns
2 Avoidance of labels for children based on pathology or abnormality
3 Categories based on educational variables that facilitate the pinpointing of educational objectives and that suggest guidelines for feasible educational grouping and intervention
4 Basic frameworks that assist in formulating the competencies needed by special education teachers

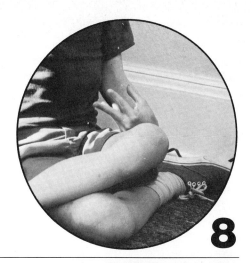

8

SOMATO-PSYCHOLOGICAL PROBLEMS

STUDY TARGETS

1 Define and differentiate between "somatopsychological" and "psychosomatic" problems.
2 Provide illustrations of (a) deviation that is related to disability that, in turn, relates to handicap; (b) deviation that relates to handicap without an intervening disability.
3 Suggest an environmental arrangement that might turn one of your own currently irrelevant deviations into a handicap.
4 List and describe the intervention strategies for (a) reducing the functional deficit of deviation; and (b) reducing the visibility of deviation.
5 State what is meant by "enhancing stimulus and response opportunities."
6 List three ways in which the social reaction to deviation might be positively modified.

It is likely that you know some people who are considered "handicapped." Perhaps even you or a member of your family is so labeled. What does it mean to be disabled or handicapped? Do all persons with the same physical deviation suffer the same handicap? What can special educators do to reduce handicaps?

SOMATOPSYCHOLOGY

In order to consider the above and other questions, it is first necessary to discuss several basic definitions and concepts of "somatopsychology," the study of the impact of bodily deviation on behavior. Terms such as "disability" and "handicap" are used loosely by most people; most frequently, they are used interchangeably. However, special educators and others involved in education, treatment, and rehabilitation must differentiate between such terms since they carry with them implications for education and therapy (Hamilton, 1950; Stevens, 1962).

"Disability" can be described as (1) a deviation in body or functioning (2) that results in a functional inadequacy (3) in view of environmental demands. "Handicap" may be used to refer to the problems, disadvantages, social censure (i.e., the various degrees of punishment or loss of reward) that are generated by a disability (Stevens, 1962).

Figure 8-1 depicts the relationships between disability and handicap. The following discussion will elaborate and clarify these relationships.

First, "disability" relates to some actual, objectively measurable deviation in physique or functioning. Of course, as discussed previously, we all differ or deviate from "average" in a multitude of ways. Deviations in hundreds of characteristics of an individual may be slight or great and still never even be called "deviations." Individual differences in hair color, food preferences, length of neck, rate of eye blinking, size of eyelids, or amount of saliva produced usually go unnoticed or unlabeled as "deviations." Except for extreme variations of such characteristics, these personal differences are of little consequence in our culture. There are, then, *differences that make no difference.* But take note that whether or not a difference "makes a difference" depends on another crucial consideration: the environmental or cultural demands. Among certain African tribes, for example, length of neck is a very important difference. Variations in skin color, which would seem to have little or no objective importance, unfortunately have been of great significance in our culture.

The same individual differences manifested in different environments,

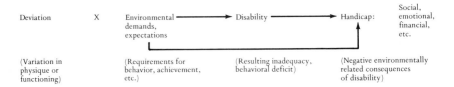

FIGURE 8-1 Relationship between environment, disability, and handicaps.

then, produce different consequences for the person. "Variation" or "deviation" is *relative to the context.* Within our culture, certain deviations are rewarded, some are punished, and some receive no effective consequence. In another culture, the consequences of the same deviations may be reversed (Freedman, 1968; Goffman, 1963; Klapp, 1962; Rubington and Weinberg, 1968).

A "disability" then, is an objectively defined deviation in physique or functioning that, through interaction with a specified environment, results in behavioral inadequacies or restrictions for the person. Disabilities do not exist with the person himself; disability is not exclusively a personal characteristic. It is the product of the interaction of an individual difference with an environment. It follows, therefore, that the term "disabled person" is inappropriate since the term overlooks the role of the environment and implies that the defect lies within the person. Perhaps a better, but not ideal, alternative would be to refer to persons "with a disability"; that is, persons whose appearance or functioning in an environment (or both) places them at a disadvantage. The disadvantage subsequently results in loss of reward, in more difficulty in attaining reward, or in exposure to punishment. The various and accumulated negative consequences comprise the handicap.

A blind adolescent American girl (blindness constituting a deviation in physique) may encounter difficulty in school and work and may suffer from social punishment and loss of reward. In this culture, therefore, the girl is the one with the disability and handicap. The deviation interacts with the environment to produce significant disadvantages for the girl. The blind condition is a "deviation" that can be termed a "disability" in view of the girl's environment. The disadvantages that result, in the social and emotional consequences, make up the handicap. "Handicap," then, refers to the burden imposed upon the individual by the unfortunate product of deviation and environment.

As another illustration, consider a man with paralyzed legs who is confined to a wheelchair. Generally speaking, in this and most other cultures this deviation in physique constitutes a disability with subsequent multiple handicaps. But there may be certain environments in which such a deviation does not produce disability. Consider, for example, an employment situation in which workers must sit all day at an assembly line and inspect products that pass by on a conveyor belt. Since our man with paralyzed legs must sit all day anyway, this employment situation does not put him at a disadvantage. In fact, since sitting for long periods of time is something he is used to, the man's condition may very well constitute an advantage in this situation. This illustration may be stretching the point, but it does again emphasize that handicap depends not only on the deviation but also on the environmental context (Rubington and Weinberg, 1968).

Thus far, the discussion has proceeded in a way that suggests that deviation (given a mismatch in the environment) leads to disability, which in turn may yield a handicap. There are many instances, however, in which deviation may not interact with the environment to produce a disability, but may, nonetheless, result in a handicap. Remember that disability involves a deviation-environment mismatch that results in a physical or functional *inadequacy*. Numerous combinations of deviations and environments do not generate any objective inadequacy or behavioral defect but, because of cultural or other environmental standards, do produce a disadvantage for the person (thus, the lower arrow in Figure 8-1 connecting deviation and environment directly with handicap). Within limits, such diverse things as height, weight, skin color, sex, age, length of hair, religious or political beliefs, ethnic background, and breast size may in no way produce a behavioral or functional inadequacy but may, nevertheless, produce a handicap.

Consider a man whose hair length deviates from the norm of the environment in which he interacts. Unless the hair is so long that it actually constitutes a hazard for the person, it is difficult to imagine that the deviation should actually be termed a disability, i.e., an actual behavioral inadequacy or defect. The deviation, in the *absence* of disability, may nevertheless put the person at a distinct disadvantage. In other words, a handicap may arise from the interaction of deviation and environment without an intervening disability. As a deviation within a "white culture," dark skin results in numerous handicaps (e.g., difficulty in access to rewards, higher frequency of social punishment). Obviously, however, dark skin is not a deviation that interacts with the environment to produce any real behavioral inadequacy. As we shall see later, many exceptional children struggle against severe socially imposed handicaps even where disability does not exist. Chapter 7 discussed extensively the handicapping impact of labeling children with categorical descriptions such as "retarded," "disturbed," "crippled," and so on. It is unfortunate but perhaps true that social punishment for deviation or even suspected deviation can be more handicapping than actual functional inadequacies.

It is, therefore, a twofold struggle that the exceptional child must wage: first, to achieve some success in the usual environment in spite of some deficit, and second, to keep trying in spite of social expectation of failure.

PSYCHOSOMATICS

Yet another dimension of debilitating forces acts on the exceptional child: psychosomatic involvement. Note here that we refer to *psychosomatic* in addition to somatopsychological problems. You will recall that the chapter opened by describing "somatopsychology" as the study of the impact of bodily deviation on behavior; i.e. "body on behavior." "Psychosomatics," on the other hand, refers to the study of the impact of the environment and a person's self-referent behavior on bodily functioning; i.e., "behavior on body." (See Lachman, 1972, for a discussion of psychosomatics.)

Traditionally, "psychosomatic" has referred to one's "state of mind" or "psychological state" and how it influences bodily processes. A familiar example is the worried, frustrated executive whose "psychological state" results in gastric distress, high blood pressure, loss of sleep, muscle tenseness, and eventually ulcers. Instead of referring to "psychological state," we have chosen to describe psychosomatic problems in terms of environmental events and self-referent behavior, that is, *the things a person says to himself about himself* and the various learned responses to the environment that eventuate in bodily impairment or dysfunction.

Perhaps a classroom example will serve to clarify this discussion. Consider the child who is having difficulties in learning. If these failures or difficulties are minimized, not focused on, and do not constitute a deviation by which the child becomes labeled, psychosomatic problems may not arise. If, on the other hand, the child's learning rate becomes a central feature which is emphasized, labeled, and used to "peg" him, the child may quickly learn to refer to himself as "slow," "retarded," or "learning-disabled." When a child begins to refer to himself in such negative ways (commonly referred to as "poor self-concept"), it becomes increasingly difficult for him to pull out of a downward trend. Prolonged stress may produce physiological changes, avoidance behavior, and emotional side effects. These deviations may, in turn, generate their own problems in the environment.

COMPOUNDING OF SOMATOPSYCHOLOGICAL AND PSYCHOSOMATIC FACTORS

In the relationship between somatopsychological and psychosomatic mechanisms, a vicious circle may begin to operate to "keep the child down." This process can be summarized in the following steps:

1 A child has some deviation in physique or functioning, for example, a hearing loss.
2 The environment, especially the academic environment, includes demands or expectations that make success less probable and punishment more probable.
3 The hearing loss, which may not be a crucial problem in other settings, becomes a disability in the standard academic environment.
4 As a result of the disability, a social, emotional, and academic burden, i.e., handicap, is imposed on the child.
5 The handicap becomes extreme, thus focusing attention on the deviation (i.e., hearing loss). With the focus on the deviation, this particular characteristic of the person becomes a cue or stimulus that influences the behavior of the teacher and others.
6 The altered behavior of the teacher and the other students, frequently providing lowered expectations, pity, restricted learning opportunities, minimized access to reward, and various stresses, feeds back to the child.
7 Eventually, the child begins to refer to himself as less perfect, less valuable,

and less competent. The lowered self-referent behavior of the child becomes a continuing personal cue for even less success, for even lower levels of functioning.

8 Finally, the continued negative self-referent behavior, the increasing disabilities, and subsequently increasing handicap may produce not only an aggravation of the original deviation, but additional deviations in body or functioning. The child, in all probability, will develop a variety of emotional behaviors, social withdrawal, aggressiveness, fears, or decline in various constructive behaviors, or all of these. These new problems or deviations then become the source for a whole new series of interactions with the environment that produce more disability and subsequently great handicap.

Thus, somatopsychological problems may generate psychosomatic problems, which, in turn, produce further somatopsychological involvement.

Figure 8-2 diagrams the suggested sequence and relationships between somatopsychological and psychosomatic factors.

In summary, somatopsychology is the study of the impact of bodily deviation on behavior, whereas psychosomatics is primarily concerned with the impact of behavior on the body. Somatopsychological and psychosomatic factors can become reciprocal and constitute a self-feeding vicious circle. Deviation can be assessed in terms of differences in physique from established or expected norms. Disability accrues from a deviation's interacting with an environment to produce a functional deficit. The handicap is the cumulative burden imposed on a person with a disability.

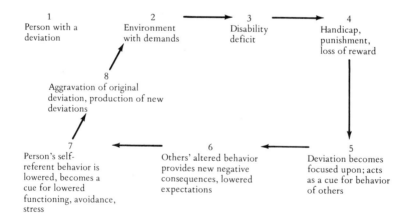

FIGURE 8–2 Suggested relationships between somatopsychological and psychosomatic factors.

IMPLICATIONS FOR INTERVENTION

Now that we have discussed the broad dimensions of somatopsychology and at least one facet of psychosomatics, we are now at a point where we may consider what educators and therapists can do to minimize the problems faced by persons with critical deviations. Since other portions of this book deal with educational strategies, here we will only summarize categories of intervention.

There are two broad domains of possible intervention. Since disability and subsequent handicap are the product of personal deviation with an environment, we may attempt to (1) change the deviation, (2) change the environment, or (3) both. An appreciable change in either will alter and short-circuit the usual resultant chain of problems.

CHANGING THE DEVIATION

Within this domain of possible intervention, there are several generic strategies worth consideration: reducing the deviation itself, and reducing the visibility of the deviation.

Reduction of the deviation

Special education has been philosophically committed to minimizing negative deviations. Developing intelligence, modifying social behavior, improving vision and hearing, developing psychomotor coordination, and raising competence in reading, writing, and arithmetic are all attempts to move a deviation, if not towards normality, at least in the direction of fewer problems for the child.

These attempts may be categorized into at least three dimensions of psychoeducational effort: extra practice, compensatory learning, and prosthetics.

Extra practice

Textbooks in special education and education in general discuss a variety of methods and materials that emphasize extended practice with and continued repetition of tasks that are problems for children. The strengthening of weak muscles through graduated exercise is a clear example of the strategy of repeated practice. Writing the same letter over and over, repeating words correctly, drilling on numbers tables, being frequently required to display socially acceptable behavior and conventions (e.g., "thank you," "please"), repeating left-to-right eye movement, using workbooks that involve repetition of skills, and using introductions and summaries that repeat important material—all are instances of the principle of extra practice. Indeed, most educators emphasize "overlearning" as important for establishing and maintaining skills for children with educational problems. Such overlearning can frequently reduce a social, intellectual, or physical deviation to a point where it does not draw attention and is not viewed as a deficiency.

Substitutive learning

Often when a deviation is extreme, and especially when it is biologically based, various strategies are needed to teach skills "around" the deficiency. That is, it is frequently possible to teach certain skills that functionally compensate for a deviation.

If a child's right hand is paralyzed or otherwise functionally impaired, it may be possible to teach him to write and manipulate with his left hand. Where persons do not have the use of either hand, they often can become quite skillful with their feet in painting, manipulating objects, etc. Special educators should be alert to possibilities that will enhance the capability of the person.

Other examples of substitutive learning available through special education are noteworthy. Children with substantial hearing loss may be taught to lipread. In addition, such persons can learn "sign language" or manual language to substitute for oral communication. Persons with significant visual deviations may learn to become specially skilled in the use of other senses, e.g., smell, touch, and hearing. Braille reading is an obvious substitute for reading the printed word. Likewise, teaching children to listen expertly and to use talking books and other auditory materials is teaching skills to compensate for visual loss.

Notice that in all the above examples, the objective is to teach the same functional skill, but through other avenues. "There's more than one way to skin a cat," and special educators must become experts in teaching children other ways.

Functional prosthetics

"Prosthesis" refers to a replacement through use of an artificial substitute. Most frequently the term "prosthetic" has been used in reference to artificial body parts, especially limbs, hands, and eyes. However, the concept of prosthesis is much broader. As used here, the term includes any device or agent that replaces or improves some personal function. In this broader sense, then, there are a myriad of prostheses employed by almost everybody.

A notebook or written memos may be used to improve memory, eyeglasses to improve vision, hearing aids to improve hearing, special diets to minimize certain metabolic disorders, and insulin injections to substitute for the natural enzymes that control sugar metabolism.

There are numerous other examples of functional prostheses specially developed for persons with troublesome deviations. Chapter 11, "Special Education Prostheses," presents a variety of such devices.

The development and use of functional prosthetics is an exciting enterprise with great potential for special educators and therapists. Anyone with some interest and basic know-how in mechanical or electrical devices can become involved in developing many do-it-yourself prosthetics. Chapter 11 presents a wide array of prosthetic devices that are available; perhaps in reading the chapter you will be stimulated to see other possibilities for simple devices that can make a big difference for a child. We urge educators to conceptualize the enterprise of "education" to include the design and use of prosthetics. Often relatively simple devices can dramatically minimize disability and make other facets of teaching-learning more successful.

Reduction of the visibility of the deviation.

Although "you can't tell a book by its cover," most people, even children, do make inferences about others and behave differentially toward them on the basis of appearance (Hanson, 1974). People constantly judge others in many dimensions. Frequently, knowledge, skill, or interests are inferred on the basis of totally irrelevant characteristics. Hair length, for example, need not be related to any other important personal characteristics. Yet some people may decide that a man with extremely long hair is lazy, unhealthy, addicted to drugs, impolite, and unclean. Likewise, other people view a man with a crew cut as stubborn, crude, reactionary, and stupid.

Since small deviations in appearance can generate burdensome prejudice, consider the social liability imposed on the person with more significant deviations. It becomes important to minimize the obviousness or visibility of the deviation in order to reduce the potential handicap. To do this, at least two strategies are possible: cosmetic prosthetics and compensatory cosmetic learning.

Cosmetic prosthetics

"Cosmetics," as everyone knows, refers to the improvement of appearance. Thus, "cosmetic prosthetics" refers to the use of cosmetics to reduce the social visibility of deviations in physique.

Examples of cosmetic prosthetics employed by relatively normal persons include such things as makeup, girdles, toupees and hair coloring, elevator shoes, false eyelashes, synthetic fingernails, and beards and hair styles worn to hide some facial scar. It is, of course, unfortunate that many of us feel impelled to hide what should be irrelevant characteristics; however, unless social reactions can be modified, there frequently is a personal payoff for "covering up."

Because of social reactions it is no wonder that persons with a disability often develop multiple social handicaps. It is, therefore, often strategic to alter the visibility or appearance of a deviation in order to preclude or reduce social stigma. Increasingly, an array of materials for replacing or camouflaging a part of the physique are becoming available. Artificial ears, eyes, noses, and so on have little functional advantage but can provide enormous cosmetic improvement. Orthodontics, plastic surgery, and other corrective surgery techniques can result in astounding changes in appearance. Removal of scars, closing of clefts, repairing of congenital malformations, and numerous other cosmetic (and functional) improvements can be effected through surgical intervention.

Frequently, as an alternative to hiding a deviation directly, it is possible to highlight some other personal feature that detracts attention from the deviation. Thus, certain hair styles, kinds of clothing, eyeglass frames, and use of jewelry can call attention away from various "defects."

Many of the functional prosthetics already mentioned also perform a cosmetic purpose. The artificial hand (rather than a hook) and the artificial leg (rather than a peg leg) serve the user by enhancing appearance as well as function.

Whatever specific procedure, material, or device is chosen, the objective of cosmetic prosthetics is to reduce the cueing effect of a deviation, and thus the socially imposed handicap.

Compensatory learning

Just as persons can be taught certain skills to make up for functional deficits, they can also learn behavior that reduces the visibility of a characteristic that calls attention to them. Children who fit much of the stereotype of the retarded label can be taught "normal" posture control and movement, pleasant facial expressions, and certain basic social behavior that will lower social visibility. Likewise, blind children and others who have developed rocking behavior (often occurring in children who have been institutionalized) can learn to refrain from rocking. Children with severe hearing loss can learn to behave in ways that do not produce annoying loud noises. In summary, the objective of cosmetic compensatory learning is to reduce mannerisms that call attention to and fit stereotypes that "peg" children as peculiar.

CHANGING THE ENVIRONMENT

We have emphasized that disability and the resulting handicap grow out of the interaction of personal deviation with an environment. Accordingly, not only may we work in altering the deviation, but we can change the environment and, thus, the deficiency. When we focus on environment, we can consider both physical and social dimensions for possible change.

Alteration of the physical environment

Prosthetic devices that are attached to the person have been discussed in the preceding section, "Changing the Deviation." The only real difference between changing the deviation and changing the environment concerns the locus of prosthetic intervention. In this section, environmental attachments that improve reception of and response to stimuli are considered.

Improving responses

In many ways we deliberately design our environment to make life easier. We install optimally graded steps, escalators, and elevators so that getting from one level to another is as convenient and stress-free as feasible. We use photoelectric cells or weight-sensitive doormats to operate doors, put rubber mats in the bathtub to prevent slipping, install automatic garage-door openers, and even buy remote controls to operate our color television sets.

The principle of changing the environment to remove difficulties and create conveniences can be extended to accommodate persons with even severe deviations. That is, *we can dramatically reduce disability by providing a nondisabling environment.* Through a variety of electromechanical assists, adaptive designs, and novel materials, we can prosthetize the environment. Doors and faucets can have special handles to ease the problem of weak or crippled arms and hands. Ramps can be installed to allow greater mobility for persons confined to wheelchairs. Dishes, cups, and eating utensils can be specially designed to permit no-slip handling. Buttons, zippers, and snaps can be modified to promote easy use. There are, indeed, hundreds of ways the environment can be modified to make manipulation of and movement within the environment easier, i.e., to improve responses.

Improving stimuli

Often, disabilities result from an environment that is not so much deficient in providing for response possibilities as it is deficient in improving stimulus or sensory input. Frequently, children have great difficulty in seeing, hearing, smelling, tasting, or feeling the environment in ways that permit optimal functioning. It makes sense, therefore, to consider "prosthetic stimuli" to enhance sensation. Digital clocks can replace the standard clock face for those who have difficulty in reading the time. Tinted glass or other special surfaces will reduce glare for extrasensitive eyes. Timer bells can be provided as reminders to start or stop an activity (prosthetic memory cues). Children with hyperactive behavior can be provided with attenuated visual and auditory stimuli to reduce distraction and activity. Conversely, the underactive, sluggish child may be helped by an "amplified environment." For many years, educators have employed heightened and multisensory input to accelerate and consolidate learning. Montessori materials that make special use of several senses to teach certain skills have been available for over half a century (Fisher, 1913; Montessori, 1912, 1917). Similarly, the Fernald method requires the multisensory involvement of children in learning letter discriminations and basic reading (Fernald, 1943). There are many other instances of the intensification, multiplication, or repetition of stimuli that have proved educationally useful; many special education materials and methods are based on the principle of compensatory or prosthetic stimulation.

Behavior modification is a rapidly developing technology receiving increased application by special educators. Among other things, behavior modification involves the use of prosthetic motivation systems that effectively stimulate learning. Token economies, contingency contracting, and premack sequencing are among the tactics available for engineering a motivational environment. Fundamentally, all these strategies are based on the simple principle that behavior is altered by its consequences; that is, "interest" or "motivation" can be arranged by the provision of reinforcement or proven rewards for learning. Whenever possible, once target behaviors are set in motion, the arranged incentives are attenuated and gradually replaced with normal or usual stimuli. If needed, contrived prosthetic motivational stimuli can be employed permanently.

Alteration of the social environment

We have discussed the possibilities of reducing deviations and their visibility. Obviously the social stigma of deviation could be minimized or even eliminated if people did not react negatively. There would be no need to hide deviations if they did not function as detrimental cues. Consequently, it is clear that special educators can assist in reducing handicaps by working to change people's reactions to atypical physique. Public relations efforts of this sort can be attempted through public media, especially television.

On a local level, the educator can work with the fellow students of exceptional children. Through verbal explanation, films, reinforcement of acceptance, and informal desensitization procedures, children can learn to integrate with exceptional children and to stop reacting negatively to many deviations (Hanson, 1974).

Finally, it is clear that the social handicap of deviation can be delayed or mitigated by the avoidance of social contact with those who would react negatively. Thus, some people feel more comfortable, i.e., experience less social punishment, when they associate only with persons of similar deviations. Clubs for the blind or the deaf, for example, provide refuge and some degree of social acceptance. Such segregation, however, is not without its problems. Severe social restrictions, a limited world of interaction, inferior status, and a resentment of those not so isolated are some of the effects of segregation. Although there are arguments both for and against segregation, the weight of psychological and educational evidence seems to support integration rather than the grouping together of "birds of a feather." Perhaps segregation is appropriate, however, when social coping is just too taxing. We must face the fact that, in the long run, some people are happier by themselves or with similar persons.

9

FAMILY PROBLEMS *

STUDY TARGETS

1 Summarize what is referred to as the "discrepancy between expectancy and reality." What implications does this have for the parents of an exceptional child?
2 Cite two major types of defensive behavior often exhibited by parents of a "defective" child. Summarize some of the negative consequences these have on the child and on family organization.
3 Write a brief account of several kinds of disruptions that frequently result in the family that fails to face the realities of having an exceptional child as a family member.
4 Employing the principle of reinforcement, explain overprotective behavior of parents, especially the mother.
5 Attempt to construct a diagram, matrix, or other device that illustrates the reciprocity of behavior between parent and child.

* By Alan O. Ross, Ph.D., Professor of Psychology, State University of New York at Stony Brook.

6 Discuss the possible "fixation" at a particular stage during the family life cycle that frequently results when a handicapped child is in the family. How can this be avoided?

7 Explain the "Rumpelstiltskin fixation" and its implications for special education services to exceptional children.

8 List several guiding principles that the special educator should bear in mind when counseling the parents of an exceptional child.

In this chapter we shall consider the various reactions of a family toward an exceptional child, the family's influence on the child's development, and the youngster's influence on them during critical developmental periods. In order to discuss the complex interactions between members of a family within the confines of one chapter it is well to organize the presentation around some basic premises that deal with the nature of human beings and their behavior.

The first of these premises is that human beings perceive the present with reference to both remembered past and anticipated future. The second premise is that human beings—as the result of their experiences—seek explanations for their perceptions in terms of cause and effect. The third premise is that all human acts are modified by their consequences; or, in other words, that behavior is a function of its consequences. This will be recognized as the basic statement of the operant or Skinnerian view about learning (Skinner, 1953). The fourth and last premise is that all of people's interpersonal relations are of a reciprocal nature; that no action that passes between two or more people is ever without a reaction. Let us now take each of these premises and see what they suggest about the relationship between the exceptional child and his or her family.

MEMORIES AND ANTICIPATIONS

The capacity of human beings to anticipate the future in terms of expectations that reflect the past permits a pregnant woman and her spouse to develop an image of the child yet to be born. This image is an amalgam of perceptions of the self and of significant persons in the couple's past, such as mother, father, siblings, and previous children. Included in these expectations is the cultural stereotype of the "ideal child," the child with the attributes of perfection which will enable him or her to compete successfully and to assume the roles society assigns to its members. The expectations further include the achievements the child's parents develop in their fantasy. The cartoonist's stereotype of the father who buys a catcher's mitt for his newborn son represents only a mild exaggeration. While family values will differ, from baseball playing to composing symphonies, parental expectations, at least in our society, invariably include that the child will be able to surpass, or at least attain, the parents' level of sociocultural accomplishment.

These expectations come to be cruelly contradicted by reality when the child turns out to have a defect or deficiency. Whether this be at the time of birth, when obvious physical defects become apparent, or later when perform-ance deficiencies are recognized, the discrepancy between expectation and reality represents a major challenge to the parents' coping abilities. The mother, in particular, will have to come to terms with the dissonance. Her more immediate biological role in the birth process probably endows the dis-crepancy between expectation and reality with greater psychological meaning for her than for her husband. It is the mother who "produces" the infant, it is she who "gives" it birth. If the "product" turns out to be defective, the mother is likely to perceive this as a defect in something she has labored to produce.

THE MEANINGS OF A BABY

In order to understand the mother's response to the discrepancy between the expectation for a perfect baby and the reality of the defective child, we must explore the variety of meanings the birth of a child might have for a mother.* At the same time we recognize the fact that the child is as much the husband's as it is the wife's and that in the stress created by the birth of a defective child the soundness of the marital relationship encounters a crucial test.

The child may be viewed quite literally as a "product of labor," as some-thing the mother has made; a personal achievement. A child with a defect can thus be seen as a reflection on the mother's personal adequacy. The feeling of achievement that might be expressed in the words, "Look what I produced!", when countered by the reality of a defective baby becomes instead, "I have failed" or "I am no good."

In addition to, or instead of, a product of labor, the baby may also be viewed as a gift, a present the mother has prepared for her own mother or for her husband. It is not infrequent that a young woman, upon getting married and moving out of her parental home, feels that she owes something to her mother whom she has thus "deserted." To make up for this, she may wish to present her mother with her own baby, and in many families it is indeed the grandmother who, under the guise of helpfulness, takes over the early care of the infant. If this infant has something wrong with him, the value of this gift is reduced, if not destroyed. We are taught that one does not give an imperfect present, that the present is unacceptable if it has a fault, and under the cir-cumstances here outlined, the mother's sense of worthlessness is likely to be increased.

Where the intended recipient of the baby is the husband, the situation is not much different. While the child is obviously the joint product of both marriage partners, some women view the baby as something a woman pro-duces for her husband, whom she thus makes a father. The new mother, not infrequently, awaits with trepidation her husband's verdict upon first seeing

* This issue has been detailed in Ross (1964), from which some of the following has been adapted. (Ross, A. O. *The Exceptional Child in the Family.* New York: Grune and Stratton, 1964. Pp. 57–60. By permission.)

the infant. If the baby is defective, she may perceive the husband's disappointment as disappointment in her. Unless the marriage is based on a mature and strong bond, the real or fancied blame and recrimination that ensue place a tremendous strain on the husband-wife relationship.

At times, plans for having a child may include explicit or implicit hopes of salvaging an unstable marriage in the expectation that having a child will bring husband and wife closer together. In other, immature marriages the arrival of the first child is symbolic of consummation of the relationship, explicit proof that the marriage exists and that both partners are adults and capable of producing a child. Having a child is seen as a sign of maturity, of manhood for the husband and womanhood for the wife. Every one of these needs and hopes is frustrated when the child turns out to be defective in either the intellectual or the physical sense of this term. The wife's unverbalized exclamation that she would address to her husband, "Look what I made for you!" becomes a hollow mockery when what she has made has something wrong with it.

There is yet another meaning that can be attributed to giving birth to a child: the baby may be seen as a divine gift, a sign of grace. Here again, the expectation is for a perfect baby, and if the child turns out to be defective, the discrepancy may be viewed as a sign of disgrace, a punishment for sins, an indication of unworthiness in the eyes of the deity. A mother who is prone to react to failure with feelings of unworthiness may see the defective child as concrete proof of her own shortcomings. At the same time, a staunch faith may, of course, serve as support in this time of crisis, for the defective child may come to be viewed as a sign of special grace because only the most worthy of mothers would be entrusted with the care of a handicapped child. Those for whom religious faith functions in this manner thus have an answer to their search for meaning, the topic to which we shall wish to turn in the next section.

Expectations for a child are obviously not limited to the period before she or he is born. At each stage of development, parents anticipate the next and make their plans accordingly. The Ivy League father who enrolls his newborn son in his alma mater is, again, only a caricature of reality. With more or less positive anticipation, we all look forward to the child's first tooth, first word, first birthday party. We look ahead to our child's entry into school, graduation, first job, and marriage, and to our own first grandchild. Most of these benchmarks of life are rewarding experiences once they are reached, and knowing roughly when they will arrive and what they will be like permits us to order our lives and to plan our own future. When the child enters school, the mother knows that she will have more time for other activities; when a son gets his first job, the father knows that he will have some money to spare; and there are still many families in this country whose old-age security is tied up with children who will return an investment by supporting their parents in their declining years. These are the rewards of parenthood , the joys anticipated as the child grows up. These are the anticipations which are made uncertain, limited, or totally impossible when the child is, in one way or another, defective or deficient. For such a child, the benchmarks of life are not clearly charted and well known on the basis of the normal child's normal course of development. There are no books in which one can look up when the first word might be expected; there are no neighbors with older children whom one can ask what it is like to go to elementary school; television serials about newlyweds are irrelevant; and one's own memories are no guide when one's child is an exception to all these rules—when one's child is "exceptional." Instead of being able to look forward to an idealized old age, surrounded by grandchildren and supported by successful sons and daughters, the parents of an exceptional child often look forward with extreme uncertainty to the days when they can no longer give their child the necessary care, and the child's future, after the parents' death, is frequently a source of utter dread.

CAUSAL EXPLANATIONS

If one accepts the premise that it is an attribute of humankind to seek explanations for their experiences in terms of cause and effect, it is not surprising that parents whose expectations are disappointed, who are uncertain and filled with apprehension as a result of having an exceptional child, will sooner or later come to ask, "Why?" Why did this happen to us? What did we do to deserve this? What is the cause of this child's condition? Here, instead of looking to the future, the parents look to the past in search of antecedents that might explain present perceptions.

This search is greatly complicated by the fact that for many of the conditions we term "exceptional" causes are unknown or, what may be worse from the point of view of the parents, subject to controversy among presumed experts. For some forms of mental subnormality we have come to know the genetic or metabolic cause; in the case of early infantile autism we have two or three equally plausible causal hypotheses; while for learning disabilities we have the pseudoexplanation of minimal brain dysfunction, which may reduce the ambiguity for some professionals but begs the question as far as the parents are concerned.

SOURCES OF ANXIETY

In the absence of available answers to the causal question, parents are often led to search for solutions in their own past. It occurs to them that it is something they have done or failed to do that resulted in the child's condition. They assume that the damaged child is the consequence of or the punishment for an act of omission or commission, an act that in their fantasies is often related to circumstances surrounding conception and pregnancy, hence, having to do with sexual practices, alcoholic intake, or the use of drugs. In present-day society each of these is associated with the illicit, the illegal, or the ill-advised and is thus likely to elicit the emotions of anxiety and guilt.

Another source of strong emotions is the frustration that parents encounter when they are faced with a deficient or defective child. It is a well-substantiated observation that emotional arousal occurs when anticipated reinforcement is not forthcoming. Parents anticipate the rewards of parenthood, the joys of a responsive baby, the pride in a successful child. These expectations are thwarted in the case of the exceptional child and the parents' resulting emotional arousal is often identified as anxiety or guilt.

DEFENSES AGAINST ANXIETY AND GUILT

Anxiety and guilt are powerful aversive states which nearly always lead to behavior that serves to reduce them. This reduction in discomfort then reinforces and thus maintains such behavior, which is sometimes called a "defense mechanism." Defensive behavior often distorts perceptions of reality and thus complicates the search after a causal explanation. In that sense defensive behavior is paradoxical and self-defeating. What is more, it interferes with the relationship between the parents and their exceptional child.

One of the most primitive of the defense mechanisms is *denial.* Here, the recognition of the discrepancy between the expected healthy baby and the reality of the damaged child is simply held untrue, leading the parents to live the myth that there is nothing wrong with the child. Since this self-deception serves to reduce anxiety, it is maintained at all costs. Refusing to recognize the realistic limitations of their child, such parents may insist that he or she can do all things other children are capable of doing, thus placing the child in situations of unnecessary stress and unavoidable frustration.

It is unfortunately true that the parents' denial is at times supported by professional people with whom they come in contact. Through identification with the parents and overinvolvement in their situation, the professionals may experience anxiety of their own, which they, in turn, minimize by belittling the severity of the condition, holding out unrealistic hopes, or promising unlikely cures. The professional, whether teacher, physician, or psychologist, can do no greater disservice to parents than to support their denial in this manner. The only truly helpful approach is an honest presentation of reality, even though this reality may be extremely painful and threatening. One task of helping parents of exceptional children is to facilitate a realistic perception of conditions as they are, and the first principle of such help must be absolute honesty.

The defense of denial is relatively easy to maintain as long as the child is young and can be kept from situations where comparison with other children might make the reality of the condition too obvious. As the child grows and enters school, however, the reality may intrude so forcefully that maintenance of denial becomes increasingly difficult. At this point parents often engage in complex psychological maneuvers that serve to maintain their self-deception. In order to prove the normality of their child they may keep him or her out of competitive situations in which the condition might become glaringly obvious, often keeping the child from developing capacities in areas in which the actual deficiency would not interfere. Conversely, the need to deny the fact of impairment may lead parents to exert undue pressures for achievement on the child, for if there is nothing wrong with the child why should she or he not be able to succeed?

EXPECTATIONS AND REALITY

Setting and maintaining realistic expectations for the performance and accomplishment of an exceptional child are among the most difficult aspects with which parents must cope. Implicit norms for expectations, which in the case of unimpaired children are derived from a composite made up of the parents' own childhood memories, ambitions, and accomplishments, comparisons with other children in the family or neighborhood, and society's general notion of what a child of a certain age should be able to do, may all be inapplicable in the case of the child with a significant deviation.

Where expectations for achievement are greater than the child's capacity for accomplishment, the pressure which may be exerted on the child and the frustrations both he and his parents experience when he is unable to meet these expectations, may result in irritability, excessive aggression, and a sense of failure and inadequacy. Expecting more than the child can accomplish is, however, only one extreme of unrealistic parental attitudes. The other extreme is represented by overprotection resulting from unrealistically low expectations of what the child can do. Here, instead of helping the child do as much as possible for himself and by himself, the parent anticipates his needs and helps him with tasks which the child should be able to carry out himself.

The psychosocial development of all children involves a gradual move from the total dependence of the very young infant to the independence of the late adolescent. The handicapped child may have an increased need of physical dependence and this need may extend over a long period of time. The parents must therefore be helped to learn to differentiate between realistic physical dependency and the developmentally stunting dependency of a child. In the healthy psychological development of the normal child the emancipation from physical dependency is paralleled by increasing social independence or by a shifting from primary attachment to parents to involvement with others. This parallel achievement of independence in both the physical and the social realms is disrupted where the child's handicap requires continued physical dependence. This makes it doubly important for the parents to be able to permit the child to develop social independence by demonstrating increasing respect for his judgment and ability to make his own decisions. The parents must learn that merely because they have to help their child in certain physical activities this does not mean that they must also make his decisions and manage his affairs.

The ideal balance between unrealistically high expectations on the one hand and overprotection on the other lies, of course, in helping the child to maximize his capacities in areas where he is handicapped and to compensate for his inabilities in some areas by achievement in others. Thus the physically handicapped child can be guided to find accomplishment and success in the intellectual area just as the intellectually deficient child may be able to experience accomplishment in some area of physical activity. Needless to say, the prerequisite for helping a child to become competent in an area not affected by his handicap is a thorough understanding of his capacities and deficiencies in all areas. Only added pain and frustration result if one tries to help a child with an obvious motor deficiency excel in the intellectual area when that domain of his capacities is also limited. Careful assessment, often requiring the collaboration of a variety of professional specialists and repeated at intervals as the child grows older, is, of course, essential. The results of such assessment must be sensitively and honesty interpreted to the parents since this is the only way in which one can hope to avoid the unfortunate consequences of unrealistic demands and expectations. All but the most severely impaired children have some area in which they can succeed in reaching a realistically set goal and achieving a sense of competence.

Related to expectations and demands is the question of discipline and punishment, which troubles many parents of handicapped children. Largely because of such understandable but inappropriate reactions as guilt and pity, parents frequently feel constrained in enforcing limits as they would with an unimpaired child. As a result, the child may become more difficult to handle, the parents' reaction may grow more and more irrational, and eventually the parent-child relationship can become completely disrupted. Just like his unimpaired sibling, the handicapped child must have reasonable limits which are consistently enforced by appropriate and realistic manipulation of consequences. Obviously the child should not be punished for actions or omissions that are the direct result of his handicap. This must be stressed because the parents' unacknowledged anger at the handicapped child may at times manifest itself in irrationally punitive behavior.

In cases in which denial is not used or in which it has broken down as a result of increasingly obvious evidence of the true state of the child's condition, related defensive behavior may be manifested. One such defense is often shown in the derogation of the professional who tries to point out the reality of the child's condition. Most would-be helpers in the professions have had the experience of being called poorly trained, inexperienced, or lacking intelligence. They have heard at one time or other that they lack understanding, interest, or skill with respect to their work with exceptional children. In effect, the parents are saying, "It is not we who can't see the truth, but you," "It is not our child and, thus, we who have something wrong with us, but you." This is, of course, behavior associated with what has been termed "projection." In line with this defense, parents often begin a long and desperate search for a professional or a school that will agree with their version of what the child is "really" like. This, unfortunately, at times leads them into the hands of the unscrupulous quack who promises a "cure."

It will have become obvious that having asked the "why" question about their child's condition, parents will, in the absence of an acceptable answer, experience anxiety and guilt. These reactions, in turn, lead to defensive behavior which distorts their relationship to the child without leading any closer to the answer to their original question. We shall ultimately conclude that there is little gained by asking the causal question in the first place, but first we shall explore some further implications that flow from the remaining two organizing premises.

BEHAVIOR IS A FUNCTION OF ITS CONSEQUENCES

Behaviorally oriented psychologists find Skinner's operant formulations heuristically sound and pragmatically useful. They would thus view all of the parental behaviors just discussed as maintained by their consequences. As indicated, the self-deceiving denial of reality, the blame-projecting accusations of others, the overindulgence or overprotection of the child, all have the consequences of reducing the unpleasant state of emotional arousal people identify as anxiety or guilt. It is the reduction of this arousal which maintains the defensive behavior.

When parents have an exceptional child, the usual rewards of parenthood are often severely limited. Other consequences then come to play a major role in maintaining parental behavior. The excessive care-giving of the overprotective mother and her exclusive devotion to the needs of her child are often reinforced by the admiration and sympathy others tend to bestow on the "martyr mother." The parent who refuses to institutionalize a severely handicapped child, who still carries him around when his weight makes this a tremendous physical hardship; the mother who sleeps sitting next to his bed, who gives up all of her own needs and interests for the sake of her child—these are all-too-familiar figures, and their behavior can be understood in terms of the admiration it elicits from others or of the avoidance of tasks and emotions that are even more noxious.

Recognition of the principle of reinforcement not only permits an explanation of puzzling behavior; it also leads to steps for helping the parents. As long as we cannot prevent the child's exceptional condition, we should at least be able to reduce the parents' unconstructive and often detrimental reactive behavior. We must attempt to provide them with alternative sources of reinforcement, and their positive steps toward constructive help for the child must be accorded the positive regard they deserve. Professionals who reward overly meticulous care-taking, who support denial, or who join the parent in a phantasmic search for a causal factor do nothing to help the parent and often contribute to harming the child. Anxiety about the child and his future can be reduced more constructively than by avoidance and escape responses. We can seek to reduce uncertainty by helping parents make concrete and definite plans. We can make sure that parents need not worry about their own future security by providing needed financial support or alternate resources, and we can give them as much information as we ourselves have available about what they can expect in terms of their child's achievement.

Having a handicapped or deficient child represents a major stress on any parent's capacity to adapt, yet many succeed in coping with this stress in a constructive fashion. They accept the reality of their child's true state and deal with the resulting challenges in a manner that is helpful to the child. The exceptional child can only be helped if the adults around him are able to accept his condition on the basis of a realistic recognition of his assets and liabilities. Neither the exaggeration of a handicap nor its disavowal are helpful in furthering constructive social development or educational progress. This leads us to the fourth of the premises which serve to organize this chapter.

THE RECIPROCAL NATURE OF INTERPERSONAL RELATIONS

In the oversimplification that is forced upon us by the linear nature of our language, it sometimes seems as if one person does something to another and the other reacts. We say that a mother rewards her child and that the child consequently learns the rewarded behavior. When behavior is broken down into stimulus-response formulations, this unidirectional perception of human relations tends to receive undue stress. Students of human behavior are clearly not as naïve as their formulations might lead one to suspect. They know that any human dyad stands in a complex bilateral transaction; that the child influences the mother, the mother the child, and the child, in turn, again the mother; and that all of this happens at almost the same moment. Add the father and siblings to this and you have need for three-dimensional, moving models in order to describe what is going on; verbal language is no longer sufficient. To overcome this block to communication, you should attempt to visualize such a transactional system as we, of necessity, resort to linear language to formulate some hypotheses about the family and the exceptional child.

In its pendulumlike swings from extreme hereditarianism to extreme environmentalism, psychology is once again coming to entertain the possibility that the newborn child brings with him into the world certain basic behavioral styles, such as activity level (Thomas, Chess, and Birch, 1968), and a limited set of innate cues that have the capacity of eliciting in the mother a set of response patterns which carry survival value for her child. The infant's cry, his cuddling, and his smile all seem to have demand characteristics that lead any normally receptive adult to engage in care-giving behavior. This is reinforced by the infant's response, and, at the same time, the mothering person's ministrations reinforce the infant's signal-emitting behavior.

If this speculation is at all correct, it might serve to explain some of the complications in parent-child interaction that we observe in certain conditions that fall under the broad rubric of exceptional children. Could it be, for example, that in cases identified as "early infantile autism," the infant either fails to emit the signals that elicit mothering behavior or emits these in a distorted fashion so that the mother's responses are inappropriate? The moment this happened, the child's reaction would, in turn, be atypical, leading to a complex cycle of distorted interactions that culminates in the puzzling behavior of the autistic child. Zaslow and Breger (1969) have recently offered a hypothesis along these lines according to which the child requires a form of care giving that is not ordinarily in the mother's repertoire. What would be required, in fact, is to do the opposite of "what would come naturally," such as holding tightly a child who is exceedingly resistive to being held and who struggles to get free. Any "normal" mother would "know" that the baby ought to be put down, but an exceptional child requires exceptional mothering. Eventually we may know enough to teach such mothers just what is required in order to make an appropriate response to the distorted signals sent by some children. It should be unnecessary to point out that the ethological formulation just outlined makes totally irrelevant any question of blame. Just as it is irrational to "blame" the newborn for sending out the wrong signals, it makes no sense to blame the mother for not responding correctly. If nothing else, this formulation has the salutary effect of lifting from the mothers of autistic children the blame and guilt some other theories have perniciously heaped upon them.

If you see some merit in this transactional hypothesis, you should consider the confounded reciprocity of relations in the case of the blind child of seeing parents, the deaf child of hearing parents, or the mentally subnormal child of parents of average or above-average intelligence. Most, if not all, of an adult's communications to a child are based on the adult's attempts to identify with the child and to see the world through his eyes. We usually attempt this identification on the basis of our own vague memories of childhood and the cultural stereotypes, communicated in folklore, art, and literature, of what it is like to be a child. In cases in which the child diverges from this stereotype or these recollections, inadequate as they are at best, we find ourselves at a total loss as to what will and what will not convey meaning to the child. Considering this difficulty, it is not surprising that blind, deaf, and mentally subnormal children often exhibit autistic characteristics; they all share the problem of a communications gap with the adult world. Occasionally and inexplicably, we find a man or a woman who has the reputation of having a "knack" for dealing with severely disturbed, autistic children. Are these people who, for some reason or other, are able to "read" the child's signals and to respond to them appropriately? A detailed study of such "born therapists" should go a long way in helping us decode the distorted messages of these children and to respond to them in a way that communicates to them.

The topic of the reciprocal nature of human relations leads us next to a look at the effect of the exceptional child on the life of his family. Farber (1959) has pointed out that the family, not unlike its individual member, develops through a life cycle with various stages. The family life cycle begins at the point a couple undertakes marriage. The next step in the cycle opens with the birth of the first child and continues as long as the youngest child is of preschool age. Next comes the stage in which the youngest child is preadolescent, followed by the stage that is characterized by the youngest child's being an adolescent. The cycle continues into the stage when all children are adults and closes when all of them are married. If your own family life cycle is at any one of these stages, you will recognize the difference in your style of life, in your major concerns, and in the sources of your anxieties, when you compare your present state with the one just preceding. Parents, it has been said, develop along with their children and woe be to the adolescent whose parents are still in the preschool stage!

This concept of the family life cycle is relevant to a discussion of exceptional children, for such children almost invariably contribute to an arrest in their family's life cycle. With respect to a retarded child, for example, parental roles change only to a point, for regardless of this child's position in the birth order, he ultimately assumes the status of the youngest child, the child at the preadolescent stage, and as long as he is in the home, his family does not emerge from the preadolescent stage of its life cycle. While the mother's role of nurturance and protection never ceases, the father's role of planning and providing for the future is severely curtailed. With this, marital relations undergo a severe strain since the partners may resort to different and incompatible ways of coping with their role displacements.

When, regardless of his chronological age, one child in a family perpetually remains the youngest and has to be treated as such, the impact on the lives of his siblings is considerable. Often expected to care for the retarded sibling and exhorted to plan their own futures with him in mind, they find their own life cycles affected and may respond to this with anger and a variety of ways of coping with this anger. On the basis of his extensive study of families with retarded children, Farber concluded that, especially after the age of nine, a retarded boy is likely to have a disruptive effect on the parent's marital relations, that one can anticipate personality problems for a sister who is given many responsibilities for the child, and that the helplessness of a retarded child is likely to affect the personality development of the siblings in an adverse direction.

While Farber's generalizations are based on his study of families with retarded children, they can easily be extended to any family with a severely impaired child who demands more than the ordinary care and attention from his parents and siblings.

CONCLUSIONS

What then are we to conclude from all this? We have pointed out that parents build up expectations in preparation for having a child and that these expectations are frustrated when the child is other than normal. We have stated that attempts to explain the discrepancy between expectation and reality often lead to blame, guilt, and anxiety and to various defensive maneuvers for coping with these noxious emotions. We have tried to point out that maternal behavior, vis-à-vis an exceptional child, can be explained in terms of the rewarding consequences of such behavior, and we have emphasized the reciprocal nature of all human interactions, raising the possibility that a disruption of this reciprocity may be one of the bases of the problems faced by parents of exceptional children.

If some, or most, or all of this is correct, the premises we advanced at the beginning of this chapter can be drawn upon to answer the question as to what we can now conclude.

HUMANKIND'S ABILITY TO ANTICIPATE THE FUTURE

From this one can conclude that to help parents and their exceptional child, one must help them relate the present to the past and to the future in a factual and realistic manner. While we can learn from the past and particularly from past mistakes, it is preferable not to dwell on the past excessively but to plan and work for the future. The questions to be asked are not "What caused his problem?" or "How did he get this way?" but "Where are we now?" "Where do we go from here?" and "How do we get there?"

HUMAN BEINGS SEEK CAUSAL EXPLANATIONS

From this one can conclude that the causal explanations to be offered must be explanations that point to constructive action, not explanations that merely satisfy one's intellectual curiosity or philosophical bent. Etiological questions are relevant to preventive endeavors; from the point of view of an individual child in need of help they are almost always irrelevant. A "Rumpelstiltskin fixation" (Ross, 1968) characterizes the preoccupation of some psychologists with whether a given child who manifests a learning disability is or is not brain-damaged. That question and related questions of etiology and classification often dominate psychological evaluations and staff conferences as if everything depended on that one answer. In a well-known fairy tale the chance for the princess to live her life happily ever after depends on her discovering the name of an ill-tempered dwarf. As a result she goes to great lengths to learn his name, and upon doing so, earns her salvation. Many clinicians and educators seem to engage in similar fairy-tale behavior. They act as if, could they but give the condition a name, the child would be saved. It is time that psychology and education lead the way in calling a halt to this labeling so that, sooner or later, parents may follow. We must rid ourselves at long last of the mistaken notion that one of our tasks is diagnosis, "identifying a disease from its signs and symptoms." We should instead get on with the job of training, teaching, and rehabilitating the children who have a limited behavioral repertoire and who thus cannot cope successfully with aspects of their environment. The complex reasons they come to have this limited repertoire need not be our concern.

If we know that a 6-year-old child can't dress himself, does not use the toilet, speaks in monosyllables, hits out at other children, and will not remain in his seat, we know the areas in which he needs help, and we should get on without wasting time trying to "explain" his condition by calling him a brain-injured, moderately retarded, aggressive child with an IQ of 42. Not only is such a label no explanation; like all other labels used to date, it tells us nothing about the steps we must take to help him learn bowel control and the other behavior he needs in order to gain better adaptation to his environment and reduce the burden carried by his parents.

BEHAVIOR IS A FUNCTION OF ITS CONSEQUENCES

How to proceed in this job of training, teaching, and rehabilitating happens to be answered by our third premise: Behavior is a function of its consequences. By looking at the child's *current* behavior and the conditions under which this behavior *now* occurs, we can obtain approximations of an answer to the question "How do we get to where we want to go?" For if behavior is a function of its consequences and since we are usually able to modify these consequences, we are able to modify the behavior within the limits of the child's physical capacity and our ability to control his environment. A demonstration of the applicability of these principles of learning can be found in the work of Bailey and Meyerson (1969), who studied a 7-year-old boy who "was blind, at least partially deaf, had no speech or language, was not toilet trained, could not feed himself, and could not walk" (p. 135). From this description it is difficult to believe that this profoundly retarded child could learn anything, yet the investigators succeeded in teaching him a simple motor response that might well be considered "a first approximation to enlarging a child's repertoire to include more complex and useful forms of behavior" (p. 137).

It is by now well known that operant behavior modification techniques have been applied with retarded children to establish toilet training, such self-help skills as feeding and dressing, social skills, classroom behavior, and the learning of academic subject matter. What is more, the applicability of these techniques has been shown regardless of whether a child is labeled "brain-damaged," "culturally deprived," "schizophrenic," "emotionally disturbed," or—for that matter—"normal" (Ross, 1974). In terms of our present focus, it should be pointed out that the basic principles involved are so readily communicated that parents can learn to use them at home with their own children, thus relieving overcrowded facilities and placing growth and development where it belongs: in the family.

THE RECIPROCAL NATURE OF HUMAN BEHAVIOR

We have thus arrived at the fourth of our premises, the one concerning the reciprocal nature of human transactions. This should remind us that anything we do with, for, or to the child in terms of treatment, training, or teaching and anything we do with, for, or to his family in terms of advice, counseling, or support must always be in recognition of the fact that a family is a mutually interacting system of human beings so that what affects one of them will immediately affect every other one as well. We can never take a child and remove him from the family or change him in some way or other as if he were an isolated entity. We can never sit down with the mother and discuss her child's future with her as if her husband, the child's father, did not exist. School interviews, medical consultation, or psychological counseling cannot focus on one or the other member of the family; all must take the entire family into consideration, for the problems involving an exceptional child are invariably also family problems.

SUGGESTED PROJECTS FOR PART III

1   Either by yourself or, preferably, with several fellow students, visit a school that has special education classrooms or the services of a resource teacher or teachers. (a) Observe one or two exceptional children throughout the day; (b) interview the resource teacher or teachers; and (c) rate the children on the several dimensions included in Iscoe and Payne's model.

   You may wish to construct a matrix, similar to the one presented in Chapter 7, as a way of summarizing your observations and knowledge of the children.

2   Conduct an interview with a special educator with respect to a particular child. Ask questions relating to the presumed cause of the child's problems, his current educational and developmental status, and the teacher's estimate of the child's probable progress.

   During the interview, note the following:

   a   Does the teacher employ "phenotypic" language to "explain" the child's problems? How educationally relevant are the terms used?

   b   Does the teacher cite objective measures and data to summarize the child's current level of functioning?

   c   Does the teacher exhibit poor expectancies for the child? How might this influence the child's progress or lack of it?

3   In a local public or private elementary or nursery school or day-care center, obtain the permission of the teacher and parents to conduct the following experiment. Select two children, adjudged to be "normal" and comparable with respect to age, size, and school performance. Obtain two or four observers. During an orientation session, inform half of the observers that the children are "brain-damaged" and "mildly retarded." Read to them the alleged characteristics of such children, drawing on the information provided in Part V of this book. Then ask them to observe the children for about two hours, telling them they may make notes. Inform them that they will be asked at the end of their observations to rate the children on several characteristics, namely: (a) attention span; (b) persistence at tasks; (c) gross motor activity; (d) impulsiveness (i.e., abrupt shifting of activities); (e) social maturity; and (f) apparent intellectual development.

   Explain to the observers that they should use a rating scale of 1 to 5, 1 being "low" or "poor," and 5 being "high" or "good." They should rate on the basis of comparison with what they believe to be normal for a child of the same age.

   Ask the other half of the observers to rate the children similarly, but in this case *do not imply any defect.* Tell them that they are to observe normal children chosen at random.

   Request that *all* observers perform *independent* observations and ratings. Have all observers see the children at the same time, so that comparable activities and events will occur.

When completed, compare the ratings of the two groups of observers. Determine if labeling the children as contrasted to no labeling produced any differences in what the observers "saw" and inferred.

This will not be a well-controlled, flawless study. Nevertheless, this project may reveal the stigmatizing influence of negative labels. In addition, conducting this experiment will further acquaint you with children, with the educational context, and with procedures for research.

4 Visit the home of a child who is acknowledged to have significant sensory, motor, emotional, or intellectual limitations. Talk with the family members to gain a view of how this family manages the problems (as discussed in Chapter 9) of having an exceptional child. Be sensitive, of course, and avoid asking embarrassing or guilt-producing questions. Try to determine the roles of the mother, the father, and the siblings with respect to the exceptional child, evidence of "defensive" behavior, and the future plans and expectations of the family. Finally, look for instances in which the child's progress is encouraged or discouraged by the family. Are prosthetic arrangements and interpersonal relationships provided in the home to assist the child in becoming functionally more independent, or is the child catered to, thus prolonging and consolidating his dependence?

5 The following brief article, "Teachers Don't Want to Be Labeled," by Harry W. Forgan, has been included because of its direct relevance to the discussion of the complications of labeling and classifying children presented in this part. Further, the article summarizes how the stigmatizing influence of labels can influence even competent, nondisabled adults. Forgan's demonstration of the labeling effect is simply accomplished and sufficiently dramatic so that you may wish to replicate his study with an available group of adults. After reading the article, determine if you can secure the cooperation of a college instructor whose class might be an appropriate one for the lesson taught by the project. Of course, the participants must be unfamiliar with the article and be willing to take part.

Teachers Don't Want to Be Labeled*

by Harry W. Forgan

When teaching a course on tests and measurement at Kent State University recently, I decided to administer an adult group intelligence test to the class. I wanted the students to "feel" what it was like to take such a test and realize what items we use to measure intelligence. I also thought they might be more aware of the short time it takes to obtain a number which is regarded as very important by many educators.

The students were told not to write their names on the test papers, but rather to use a code such as their house number, physical measurements, or

---

* From *Phi Delta Kappan*, September 1973. Reprinted with permission.

any less obvious symbol. I explained that I really didn't have faith in IQ scores; therefore, I didn't want to know their IQs.

The administration of the test required only 50 minutes. The students seemed to enjoy taking it and chuckled at some of the tasks they were expected to perform. I had to laugh myself when I saw some of them looking at their hands and feet when responding to items concerning right and left.

Upon scoring the test I found that the lowest IQ was 87 and the highest 143. The mean IQ for the 48 students was 117. I was not astonished by the 87, even though all of the students had successfully completed the general education courses and student teaching at Kent State and were ready to graduate by the end of the term. After all, IQ tests have many limitations.

Then I got an idea. I decided to prepare a report for each student, writing his code on the outside and "IQ 87" on the inside of each. I folded and stapled each paper—after all, an IQ is confidential information!

At the next class period I arranged all of the folded papers on a table at the front of the room. I wrote the range and the average IQ on the chalkboard. Many students snickered at the thought of somebody getting an 87. The students were eager and afraid as I began by explaining the procedures for picking up their papers. I made a point of telling them not to tell others their IQ score, because this would make the other person feel as if he too had to divulge this "total endowment." The students were then directed to come up to the table, row by row, to find their coded paper. I stood sheepishly—ready to laugh out loud as I watched the students carefully open their papers and see "IQ 87." Many opened their mouths with astonishment and then smiled at their friends to indicate they were extremely happy with their scores.

There was dead silence when I began to discuss the implications of the IQ scores. I explained that in some states a person who scores below 90 on an IQ test is classified as a slow learner. The fact that group intelligence tests should not be used to make such a classification was stressed. I also emphasized the fact that *someone* in this class could have been classified as a slow learner and placed in a special class on the basis of this test.

I told how many guidance counselors would discourage a child with an 87 IQ from attending college. Again I emphasized the fact that one person in this room was ready to graduate from college having passed several courses in history, biology, English, and many other areas.

I then went on to explain that the majority of elementary and secondary school teachers believe in ability grouping. This is usually done on the basis of intelligence tests, so I explained that I would like to try ability grouping with this class—again to see "how it feels." Some students objected right away, saying that "I did not want to know their IQ scores." I calmed them by saying it would be a worthwhile learning experience and assured them that I really didn't believe in IQ scores.

I told the students not to move at this time, but I would like all of those with an IQ below 90 to come to the front so they could sit nearer to me for individual help. I told the students who had an average IQ (between 90–109) to go to the back of the room and then take the seats in the middle of the class. The students with an above average IQ were asked to go to the side of the room and take the seats in the back because they really didn't need much extra help.

"O.K., all those who got an IQ below 90 come to the front of the room." The students looked around to find those who scored below 90. I said that I knew there was an 87 and maybe a couple of 89's. Again, there was dead silence.

"O.K., all those students whose IQ is between 90–109 go to the back of the room." Immediately, to my amazement, 8 or 10 students picked up their books and headed for the back of the room. Before they could get there I said, "Wait a minute! Sit down! I don't want to embarrass you, but you would lie and cheat—the same way we make our students lie and cheat—because you don't want to be classified as 'slow.' I wrote 'IQ 87' on every paper!"

The class erupted. It was in an uproar for about five minutes. Some of the women cried. Some indicated that they needed to use the restroom. All agreed it was a horrifying and yet valuable experience.

I asked them to do one thing for me: Please don't label kids. Because we are all "gifted," "average," and "slow," depending on the task at hand. They promised.

ANNOTATED RESOURCES FOR PART III

Edgerton, Robert B. *The Cloak of Competence: Stigma in the Lives of the Mentally Retarded,* Berkeley and Los Angeles: University of California Press, 1967. (219 pages, bibliography and index; foreword by Walter Goldschmidt.) Presented as a research study of numerous portraits describing the lives of adult "retardates" living outside an institution. The study describes the everyday lives of mildly retarded adults, former patients of a state institution, most of whom had been confined for more than ten years and many since childhood. Detailed case studies provide insights into post-hospitalization problems of making a living, managing sex, marriage, and reproduction; utilizing leisure time; and coping with loneliness and alienation. Edgerton describes through the eyes of the patients themselves the stigma of being labeled "retarded," the need to deny the reality of mental deficiency, the frustration of attempting to "pass" as normal, and the necessity of depending on benefactors, while maintaining self-esteem through a "cloak of competence."

Lockman, Sheldan J. *Psychosomatic Disorders: A Behavioral Interpretation,* New York: Wiley, 1972. (184 pages; bibliography; author and subject indices; paperback.) The text concerns the interaction of emotions and human physiology and provides a conceptual framework for understanding the development of psychosomatic disorders in addition to presenting empirical research findings. The first five chapters examine basis psychosomatic concepts, biological foundations and emotional behavior, and the learning and psychosomatic theories upon which the book is based. Chapters 6 to 14 are devoted to discussion of various psychosomatic disorders affecting the following systems: cardiovascular, gastrointestinal, respiratory, skin, genitourinary, musculoskeletal, endocrine, and sensory. Associated case histories are included. Chapter 15 examines the effects of psychotherapy on psychosomatic disorders. The final chapter is a summary discussion.

McDaniel, James W. *Physical Disability and Human Behavior,* New York: Pergamon, 1969. (224 pages and subject index; foreword by Beatrix Cobb.) Written as a text or source book for college students and researchers in rehabilitation counseling to provide a comprehensive and concise survey of pertinent theories and research approaches in the area of physical disability. There is a bibliography of relevant references following each chapter. The chapter titles themselves present a logical progression from theoretical foundation to research studies providing attitudinal information and implications for treatment and comprehensive rehabilitation: (1) Theoretical Foundations. (2) Attitudes and Disability. (3) Emotional Factors in Illness. (4) Sensory and Perceptual Processes in Disability. (5) Motivation—The Organization and Direction of Behavior. (6) Regulation and Control of Behavior: Learning and Skilled Performance. (7) Summary and Theoretical Considerations. The book emphasizes the somatopsychological problems involved with physical disability.

Ross, Alan O. *The Exceptional Child in the Family: Helping Parents of Exceptional Children.* New York: Grune & Stratton, 1964. (206 pages and annotated bibliography, references, and indexes.) Written for advanced students and practitioners in special education, counseling, social work, psychology, and the medical professions, the book is best described as a guide for better understanding of family interaction around an exceptional child. There is an annotated bibliography for parents and an extensive list of references. Ross describes the general dynamics of family interaction, parental reactions to a child with a "defect," the counseling of such parents, and then the particular dynamics for families with mentally retarded, sensory-handicapped or physically handicapped, emotionally disturbed or mentally ill, gifted, or adopted children. He concludes with an in-depth case history.

Wolfensberger, Wolf. *The Principle of Normalization in Human Services.* Toronto: National Institute on Mental Retardation, York University Campus, 4700 Keele St., 1972. (238 pages and references and index; foreword by G. Allan Rocher.) Written as a proposal to human service personnel, the book is divided into three parts: (1) Defining the "normalization principle" and its major implications. (2) Application of normalization principles to specific problem and program areas. (3) Special implementive strategies and mechanisms. The book is intended to explain, clarify, and elaborate the principle of normalization as a system of human management. Wolfensberger stresses the point that human service personnel need to acknowledge the control they exert on the lives of those they propose to help and recognize the positive and negative consequences of such control. The book provides a potent rationale for the urgency of implementing the normalization principle on a broad social scale.

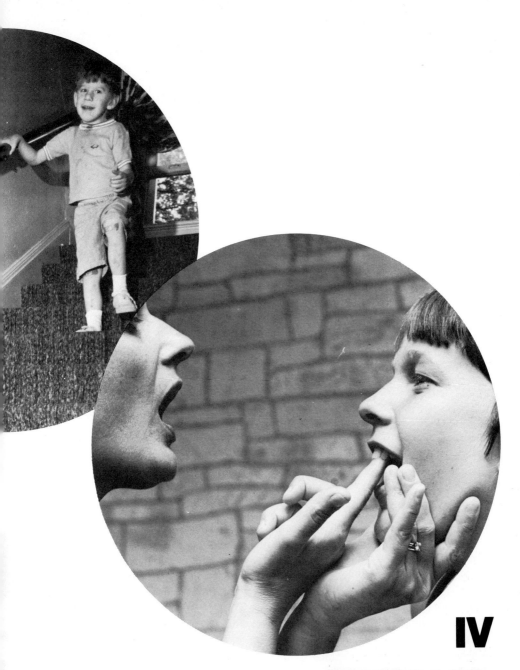

IV
SPECIAL
EDUCATION
INTERVENTION

The special educator's primary function is to intervene, to change in a positive way the content and direction of a child's development. This means manipulating those educational variables within the jurisdiction of the special educator with the ultimate goal of raising each child's competencies to a level approximating normality. To realize this goal, the educator must become skilled in implementing principles of learning and in adopting a scientific methodology in designing and evaluating instructional problems, objectives, and procedures. Beginning in the early 1960s, there has been a rapid and highly successful expansion of attempts to apply principles of learning and motivation discovered in the laboratory. It is only recently, then, that special education has found a firm and substantial foundation in more basic scientific disciplines, such as psychology and biology, that will enable special education to become more of an applied science than an art.

Instructional procedures and materials available to special educators now form a cohesive body of knowledge that can be effectively applied to a wide range of handicapping conditions. Further, just as scientific technology has augmented and accelerated work in other areas of applied science (as in engineering, medicine, and agriculture), its potential to do so in special education is beginning to be evidenced. While prosthetic devices and arrangements currently employed in special education are relatively primitive, there is clearly a growing interest among educators, physicians, specialists in rehabilitation, and scientists in applying technology to the problems of special education.

The special educator has traditionally been confined to a special class or school. It is only recently that this conception of the setting for special education has been broadened. Most of the contemporary positions on placement involve a series of teaching environments that progressively move from highly contrived to more natural, normal arrangements. Exceptional children, then, by design can progress from one setting to another according to their individual level of performance and instructional requirements. The ultimate goal is to move children as far into the mainstream of regular education as possible.

Increasingly, not only does special education programming take place in more varied settings, but resources for intervention come from a wider context. The most basic and ultimately influential resource is community support. Local, regional, and national commitment to research and services for citizens with handicaps is directly related to the financial support, cooperation, and prestige afforded to special education. Our country has lagged behind several other less affluent nations in this respect. Fortunately, however, special education and rehabilitation is now receiving greater attention and concern, and special educators may expect a broader base of support and respect for their efforts. "Right to education" laws, child advocacy, career ladders in special education, increased articulation among agencies, better public relations, and the growing proportion of citizens who are themselves handicapped all bring special education into a more visible and prominent place. Contemporary special educators see not only the school but the community as a ready resource. They may enlist the help of volunteers, paraprofessionals, civic and religious organizations, and university personnel to work directly with children and to assist in the continuing education of each other.

10

FUNDAMENTAL INSTRUCTIONAL PRACTICES

STUDY TARGETS

1   Describe current procedures for identifying competencies required of the special educator.
2   Summarize the four major aspects of the instructional environment that the special educator must design and manipulate.
3   Cite three examples of specific learning objectives for exceptional children that probably have low "external validity."
4   Develop a list, diagram, acronym, or some other device for summarizing the fifteen major recommendations for the special educator in practice.
5   Identify the eight considerations involved in efficient classroom layout.
6   Review the twenty-six criteria for evaluating instructional materials. Design a checklist of these criteria that could be used by a teacher as an instrument for making decisions concerning materials selection.
7   State the differences between summative, normative assessment and formative, competency-based assessment.
8   Describe two examples of performance that can be measured most appro-

priately by the use of (a) frequency; (b) duration; (c) rating; and (d) checklist data.

9 Outline the major aspects of a good curriculum plan.

10 Cite one example for each of the five techniques for managing consequences of student behavior.

11 Identify several characteristics common to effective instructional approaches.

Although children possess individually unique characteristics, it is patently clear that all youngsters—even those with significant exceptionalities—have a great deal in common. Aside from the usual attitudes and interests of children of like ages, exceptional children are often similar in terms of the causes of their problems, the functional manifestations of various disorders, and the kinds of social consequences that so often attend exceptional conditions. You have already learned about many of these likenesses.

This chapter will present and discuss another cluster of likenesses that pertain to children, and especially to those with significant exceptionalities. We will be describing a number of instructional considerations relevant to the special education of children who exhibit various types and degrees of disorders. These considerations have logical, empirical, and pragmatic validity, and their proper application will serve to move effectiveness in teaching from being primarily an art to more of a science. Before we present and illustrate these basic propositions for making instruction more effective, it will be instructive to discuss briefly some notions about the training of special educators that have implications for the skills necessary for effective performance in special education.

THE SPECIAL EDUCATOR IN PREPARATION

Most of the concepts in this book have a strong logical and philosophical rationale and are buttressed by sufficient empirical documentation. Causes and diagnosis of conditions, the adverse consequences of environmental deprivation, the prevention of handicapping conditions, the psychological and social impact of deviation, the value of prostheses, and the efficacy of various possible special education settings are all issues that have been explored from various angles by behavioral, social, and medical scientists. Procedures and practices related to these areas are kept under constant surveillance and are frequently reevaluated. Unfortunately and ironically, this is not true of training programs for special educators. To be sure, numerous articles have been written by advocates of various training approaches. Footnotes have been written back and forth among authors and university training programs have undergone numerous changes in direction and focus according to the prestige of the particular advocate—but training programs have been devised virtually on hunch.

As heretical as it may sound, the fact of the matter is that we still do not have a definitive and clear notion of what it takes to be an effective special educator. Most of us feel that we could identify some central traits that separate good from poor teachers—but again most, if not all, of these traits are subjectively determined and are difficult to justify empirically.

From approximately 1968, the push from state and federal government has been toward a competency approach. Certification, degrees, merit raises, and promotions have become increasingly tied to various competencies. Special education has become caught in this quasi-empirical web. We should know what skills it takes for one to function as a special educator; after all, we expect physicians, attorneys, and pharmacists to have demonstrated a certain array of performance skills before they have the privilege of serving the public. Equally basic is the way in which the competencies are identified. In special education they are most often generated as a result of "round table brainstorming" by academicians, administrators, teachers, or all of these. Following the generation of a multitude of skill statements, some form of categorizing occurs, a sequence is identified so that the teacher-training curriculum is respectably ordered, and the die is quickly cast. No theory is used as the foundation for the generation of these competencies, principles of behavior are often avoided, and there is usually no systematic procedure for evaluating each skill adjudged to be important for special educators. The upshot of this situation is that special educators collect lists upon lists of competencies, share them among colleges and universities in a most indiscriminate way, and we still do not really know for certain what is required to be an effective special educator.

What is the answer to this training problem? Certainly not teaching a prospective teacher of exceptional children to employ every approach the teacher trainer can get his or her hands on in hopes that one or a combination of the procedures will work with a child. For one thing, it is doubtful that a fledgling teacher will have enough mature professional judgment to know which of these approaches to use for the educational problem at hand. And for another, this "shotgun" approach to training teachers is obviously wasteful—there is simply not enough time to teach prospective teachers the vast number of instructional approaches that are currently available. The literature certainly does not make clear which program or methodology to use with which child under what circumstance.

The issue is not whether training programs based on competencies are appropriate—it is clear that we should move in this direction. The real issue is how we choose to select the competencies. As we have noted, they are now selected on intuition, expert opinion, or casual observation. We have stressed that empirical bases should be used in selecting the skills teachers need. Research in this area is critically needed and must serve as the basis for defining and refining the range of teacher competencies in special education. Until such systematic research is conducted, we must be satisfied with something second best, i.e., with competencies drawn by logical inference from proven principles of learning, management, and counseling.

SOME UNDERLYING PROPOSITIONS

Fundamentally, teachers are responsible for manipulating the environment of children in such a way that the likelihood of certain specified behavior is increased. This is true no matter what kind of behavior or child we are talking about. If the child of any age or intellectual level exhibits motor problems, attention disorders, a high frequency of articulation errors, arithmetic reversals, the educator is still faced with the problem of how to arrange the instructional setting to reduce the unwanted behavior and increase wanted behavior.

There are four aspects of the environment to which the special educator's attention should be directed in an effort to provide an optimum instructional setting. The first component of the environment is the curriculum, goals, or target behaviors. Teachers need to decide what curricular goals are appropriate for each youngster who possesses a particular constellation of behaviors. Within a very broad range, there are hierarchies of skills in which certain behaviors are dependent on the prior acquisition of other more elementary skills. Special educators must be aware of this ordering of skills, for the consequences of placing a child in a program in which the tasks are too difficult can be devastating for the youngster, his parents, and the schools.

The second aspect of the environment to which the teacher must give attention is the methodology or procedures to be employed in the instructional setting. This aspect is of secondary importance to the goals—one must have a firm grip on where he would like the youngsters to go (or what he would like them to accomplish) before he makes a decision about how the environment is to be arranged to effect accomplishment of the targets). Methodology is a complex area and contains many components, some of which are: mode of presentation of a stimulus (e.g., visual, auditory, or both); procedures for observing and collecting information on performance; types of responses required of students; appropriate use of positive or aversive consequences; establishing an appropriate criterion for performance; knowing when and how to cue the student; properly fading stimuli to maintain a correct response; using lecture, discussion, and demonstration correctly; and knowing when to place children in one or more of various possible competitive situations. Each of these subareas, and the others contained under the category of methodology, is more complex than most teachers realize and can be used successfully with certain instructional problems but not with others. This second aspect is a very important element in the educational environment for exceptional children.

A third component of the youngsters' educational setting is the kind of instructional materials the special educator chooses to use, with certain methods, to encourage progress. Materials are facilitators; they augment and enhance the methodology so that the appropriate preset objectives can be more nearly achieved. A poor choice of materials can easily neutralize and perhaps even stifle the methodological procedures a teacher uses even if the methods are correctly selected and used. For example, one would not select a primarily visual device or instructional material for auditory instruction. And one would not use a game that punishes a child for a certain response when the method used rewards the very same or approximately the same behavior. Methods and materials should go hand in glove, irrespective of the objectives for individual children or their unique syndrome of behaviors or presumed etiology.

The fourth principal factor in a child's educational environment is the setting or place in which the unique combination of curriculum, methods, and materials can most efficiently and effectively be delivered. Since we will discuss in a subsequent chapter the major ramifications involved in selecting a setting, we will simply emphasize at this point how important this aspect of the child's environment is for maximizing performance. The place of delivery and the skills of the teacher in that place have a direct relationship with how well each child acquires the desired skills.

This unique mix of curricula, methods, materials, and settings is the essence of special education. If each is chosen appropriately and properly orchestrated, with frequent evaluative checks built into the system, it is very reasonable to expect continued progress from exceptional children. The consideration of these four environmental aspects leads us to a second cluster of fundamental propositions that have direct pertinence to the child's environment, that is, the teacher's competence and, indirectly, the whole issue of the preparation of special educators. The concepts to which we refer are summarized in Table 10-1.

Quadrants I and II suggest that special educators should be trained to demonstrate effectively the selection of appropriate diagnostic and management procedures before applying the approaches. They should be able to evaluate a child properly and efficiently, along with his environment, in terms of educational relevance and with due consideration to the host of possible approaches available for dealing with the situation. They should know the advantages and disadvantages of possible approaches.

Second, once chosen, an approach or approaches must be correctly applied to the situation if the maximum benefit is to be realized (quadrants III and IV).

TABLE 10-1   CLASSIFICATION OF MAJOR PROFESSIONAL COMPETENCIES

	Diagnosis of Relevant Educational Problems	Instructional Management of the Problems
Technical skills in analyzing and selecting appropriate procedures	I	II
Proper application of the procedures selected for use	III	IV

It is one thing to have a full awareness of all of the technical nuances of various procedures, but it is an entirely different matter to be able to apply techniques skillfully and properly. Thus, it is clearly necessary that special educators be schooled not only to *know about,* but to be able demonstrably to deliver (or apply) appropriate environmental management procedures. In all probability, the true test of a teacher-training program is how well the special educators who are its products can perform the diagnostic and educational management skills that underlie the selection and application of procedures. These are fundamental propositions in the preparation of special educators.

THE NEED FOR PRACTICAL, SUPERVISED EXPERIENCE

Effective special educators cannot be trained *in vacuo;* just as pathologists need cadavers, paratroopers require jumping towers, and mechanics need cars, prospective teachers of exceptional children must have many and early opportunities to be around and work with youngsters. Few other propositions have received as widespread acceptance among academicians as the belief in extensive field involvement (Blumberg, 1970; Hensley and Patterson, 1970; Kendall, 1970; Schwartz et al., 1972). Universities and colleges differ dramatically over the manner in which these practical experiences ought to occur. Some have very comprehensive on-campus demonstration schools, others make extensive use of local school systems and districts, and still other programs provide simulated classroom experiences during the early years of training followed by a heavy dose of practicum during the junior or senior year.

Whatever the arrangement, there is clear wisdom in intentionally and intensively monitoring and supervising students in training. Immediate feedback is necessary so that prospective special educators do not practice mistakes. Indeed, some supervisors have used a "bug in the ear" approach in which the student teacher carries a small radio receiver to which an ear phone is attached. The supervisor observes the fledgling teacher interacting with students and speaks into a microphone, and the signal is transmitted immediately to the student's receiver. In this way the student is trained to apply appropriate procedures correctly within an actual classroom setting, adjust the procedures while under direct observation by an experienced mentor, and continue with the adjusted approach. Gradually, as the student gains experience and skill in all of the four quadrants in Table 10-1, supervisory attention is withdrawn and the major source for monitoring is the children's achievement on preestablished behavior objectives.

RESOURCES FOR TRAINING MODELS

Numerous models have been proposed in the literature as efficacious in training professional personnel in special education. Dunn's clinical educator procedures (1968), Schwartz's clinical teaching model (1967), and Peter's prescriptive teaching system (1967) all suggest that the preparation of special educators must focus on training in diagnostic and management procedures.

Lilly (1970) has presented a procedure for training supportive personnel to work with children with most forms of disability, and Garwin (1970) has discussed a plan for training consulting teachers. Wiegerink (1972, 1973) has detailed the major dimensions of Project In-Step (Interrelated Special Training of Education Personnel), in which the major thrust was directed toward an *in situ* (within the actual classroom) procedure based on competencies. All these approaches have some commonalities and differences, and they are well worth studying in detail for those students with a particular interest in this area.

THE SPECIAL EDUCATOR IN PRACTICE

The teacher of exceptional children must take a wise view of educational objectives and the context within which education takes place. While the teacher may be a most influential part of the child's educational environment, it would be most unfortunate to overlook components of the environment such as the arrangement of the classroom, the potential influence of other components of the school and its resources, the community's demands regarding what is expected of children and adults, the community's assets, and, of course, the characteristics of the home setting. Both the objectives and the mechanisms for the children reside not only in the classroom but within the broader environments in each of these areas. For example, teaching a child to make change properly becomes more than an isolated classroom objective and activity when the youngster finds himself faced with a situation in the community in which those skills are required. Paralleling this, the child's family can further enhance the student's skills in this general area by not making change for him when the opportunity exists. And so, there are "many teachers" and numerous situations outside of the classroom walls that will either facilitate or inhibit the achievement of children.

A second example of the role of a teacher within this broad social system lies in the general area of language development. Language objectives and procedures for their accomplishment must be derived with an eye toward the requirements and capabilities of the total educational environment. It would be foolish to teach a youngster certain vocabulary words that have little use in the real world. Such learning would have little validity outside the classroom. Words, terms, and phrases should be focused upon according to their practical utility for the child in his natural surroundings. Further, attention should be given to how well the child's family and peers will (or will not) provide conditions that are conducive to the child's language progress. After all, the parents may well have goals in language performance that are quite incompatible with or even contradictory to those of the teacher. Thus, the identification of objectives for children and the means for achieving them must be constructed in harmony with the various components of each child's individual environment.

This concept has parallels with issues pertaining to environmental ecology. An industry, like a school, should be concerned not only with what goes on within its facility but with what happens to its product, like the student, when it interacts with wider social and physical systems. For instance, a medicine may well meet objectives in the laboratory but be devastating in the environment because of misuse. Thalidomide is an example of this point.

The real issue here is generalization in terms of providing appropriate instructional environments for the child as well as having him demonstrate skills at a satisfactory level within ever-widening social and physical contexts. Performance of a skill within a classroom is no guarantee that the child will demonstrate and be able to apply the same skills in a broader social and physical setting. To enhance the external validity of the curriculum, the world the child will experience must be brought into the classroom or the child taken to the world, or both. And the world of the student includes not only the teacher but other students, classroom aides and assistants, other school personnel, the parents and siblings, neighborhood acquaintances, members of the community, and so on. From a physical standpoint, the child's world of experience occurs in the classroom, the school, the home, and the town or city. To be sure, "special education" is not an island unto itself.

The remainder of this chapter will center on specific practical recommendations to make the special educator more effective.

ACCEPT THE CHILD AS HE COMES TO YOU

Many children special educators work with come from lower socioeconomic circumstances, are neglected by their parents, and have learned a host of inappropriate behaviors. They often look odd, smell bad, speak offensively, have socially inept habits, and are personally distasteful. That is the way it is, and it is your responsibility to assess your own feeling about and reactions toward youngsters with these characteristics. Frequently these characteristics set the stage for the teacher either to avoid or somehow to punish the student. Guard against the formation and operation of a negative halo that may cause your personal feelings about a student to interfere with your functioning as a real educator. As a prospective special educator, you should be aware of these potentially biasing phenomena before you make a final decision about your career.

The potential consequences of being unable to overlook these negative attributes in children are (1) less progress by the children in those areas for which the school has concern; (2) increased hostility and alienation between the teacher and the students; and (3) a relatively poorer instructional experience throughout the students' schooling. An aide or assistant can be used to monitor a teacher's behavior toward individual children to detect instances of continued unfairness, favoritism, an "unequal-opportunity classroom," or even personal vendettas. The important consideration is to be monitored by someone else, because these problems in interpersonal relationships occur in very subtle ways and without recognition or awareness until the situation gets out of hand.

REALIZE THAT EVERY CHILD CAN DO BETTER

Historically, special educators have tended to underestimate the progress exceptional children can make. Too often, psychometric information, medical reports, school records, diagnostic labels, and first impressions are translated into limited expectations of development. Lowered expectations will inevitably result in decreased effort by the teacher and, thus, in lowered performance by the child.

Remember that a child's progress is a function of his interaction with an environment. How far he will succeed will depend not only upon his characteristics as they now exist, but upon the quality of the environment you provide. When the child is not improving do not assume that he will never be able to improve. Instead, adjust your instructional practices until you observe improvement. Developmental potential does not reside within the child but is a product of the interaction of child and environment. As a teacher, your attitudes toward the child and the instructional setting you provide are important components of his environment that will ultimately influence his progress and "potential."

SURVEY YOUR RESOURCES

In line with the proposition that the instructional situation is larger than either the teacher or the classroom, consider facilities and personnel both in and out of school to assist in the accomplishment of instructional objectives. More specifically, the potential school resources include (1) audiovisual equipment available, (2) instructional materials, (3) availability of specialized consultants, and (4) other special educators or remedial specialists. One should not overlook the potential offered by programs in industrial arts, home economics, physical education, music, and vocational education.

Recognize the wide range of help your community can offer. Professional clubs, social and civic organizations, local colleges, parent groups, local businesses, churches, regional centers that provide special education instructional materials, community recreational facilities, and local professionals who are interested in exceptional children should be assessed for the contributions they may be able to make as part of the children's instructional environment. For example, the Lions Club has a history of providing aids and braille apparatus to the blind and those with very poor vision in local communities, certain dentists specialize in providing dental care to handicapped children, and certain corporations have chosen to employ handicapped persons where feasible. Possibilities for field trips, special events, and donations ought to be investigated.

Be sure to inquire of other teachers about the resources they have found useful. Mobilize the efforts of parents and other special educators to get a more coordinated effort in the efficient use of these community assets.

RESPECT THE OPINIONS OF OTHER PROFESSIONALS

Special education teachers are usually inundated with various points of view from co-workers on how best to deal with difficult instructional and deportment problems. This is especially true when certain children are particularly resistant or when the teacher is fairly new on the job. If the teacher is a recent graduate or has had some additional university training, it is likely that she or he will have acquired skills and knowledge that are contemporary. Older colleagues, in contrast, may be a bit outdated in their understanding of new instructional procedures but may have a broader, more practical perspective on educational practices. The new teacher will want to take advantage of the wisdom and maturity of the more experienced staff without compromising on the more contemporary philosophy and teaching approaches to which he or she subscribes. And so, be alert for the recommendations and suggestions of others; you may wish to consider building them into the philosophical framework that you have chosen to adopt.

The time will come when you will be confronted with a well-credentialed professional, like a school psychologist, whose pronouncements and admonitions are foreign or contradictory to your beliefs and instructional approach. Now, what do you do? We suggest that you give the person a full hearing, accept the information he or she provides, and then request that the recommendations be translated into practical classroom procedures. You, then, can judge the utility of those suggestions and tell the consultant, in a courteous way, your view of the relevance of the report's recommendations. By all means, avoid being abrasive and so dogmatic in your behavior that you alienate those whose intentions are to help.

If you accept the perspective expressed in this text, you, as a teacher, would undoubtedly have some concern over a school psychologist who reported that Billy "has an IQ of 54 with minimal cerebral dysfunction and can't be expected to do well in school," "has dyslexia and has a poor prognosis for achievement in reading," "has undifferentiated perceptual integration problems that require patterning therapy," or "has identification problems." Upon receipt of these kinds of reports, your task will be to inquire as to the educational implications for you—that is, what do these numbers and labels offer with respect to instructional strategy? If the response to your inquiry is simply more jargon and numbers, it would probably be wise to lay aside such reports in favor of more accurate and meaningful ones. It may be better for you simply to operate on your own by systematically collecting performance data on children in an informal way (Smith, 1969). In sum, be gracious and open, respond in a professional manner, use whatever information passes the test of pragmatism, and maintain your own records on the children's achievement.

Remember, too, that you no doubt have skills that can be of help to others, including those whose instructional responsibilities may not be with exceptional children. Do not be shy about sharing the information and techniques you have acquired in your training, but there is no need to hit them over the head with your newfound competencies. One of the best ways to be of assistance is by example; if you have a well-managed and effective classroom the word soon gets around. Other teachers will eventually seek your advice—but play it cool and don't be a know-it-all.

DETERMINE THE ROLE AND PREPARATION OF YOUR ASSISTANTS

Some teachers may be fortunate enough to have the services of a part-time or even full-time aide. Increasingly, teacher's aides and other paraprofessionals are receiving training that enables them to provide a valuable helping hand in the educational enterprise. While paraprofessional training programs vary considerably in their length and content, teacher's aides often become acquainted with many of the practical problems encountered in the classroom, such as establishing rapport with children, student deportment, assistance with seat work, operation of audiovisual equipment, and odds and ends like helping children with their coats and boots, seeing that youngsters get on the correct school bus, and preparing snacks.

Regardless of the preparation of the aide or his previous experience with children, the teacher must provide an orientation to the aide and an explicit description of the division of labor between teacher and aide. In every instance the teacher must be the final authority. Some teachers prefer that the aide function in a "servantlike" role; whereas other teachers use the aide in a quasi-teaching role.

In situations in which the aide is used in a teacherlike role, absolute consistency must exist with the teacher in the approach selected in working with the children. In all cases the teacher's aide must support the teacher so that the children do not play one against the other. This often happens in families in which one parent is more lenient or more protective than the other. Inconsistency can lead to mismanagement of the students and conflict between the teacher and the aide.

Perhaps the best recommendation for the preparation of an effective teacher's aide and the establishment of a positive working relationship is at first to assign to the aide relatively simple duties that do not require extensive interaction with the children. This will provide the aide with an opportunity to observe the teacher, to understand his or her style better, and to follow the model provided by the teacher. It is important at this point, even in the execution of routine activities with the children, that the aide's approach be consistent with the teacher's. For example, if the teacher has established the rule that crying, whining, and fussing will be ignored, it would be wrong for the teacher's aide to attend to that kind of behavior while removing boots, distributing materials, or cleaning up after lunch. If the aide does so, the goals of the instructional program will be weakened.

Gradually and progressively, as the teacher's aide becomes skilled in routine activities and understands the teacher's methodology, the role of the aide can be expanded to include instructional activities. We recommend that the teacher develop behavioral objectives for the aide. For example, you may require that your aide be able to:

Thread a 16-millimeter projector
Demonstrate to children how to put on their coats
Conduct snack time
Prepare dittos that provide for practice of skills
Tutor children in cursive writing

It is important to evaluate systematically how well the aide is performing and to provide feedback. Look for how well the objectives are being accomplished by using a check-off sheet, rating system, self-report, or weekly conferences with the aide. While this may seem inordinately time-consuming, it is a vital part of your total program because it will preempt a host of possible problems among the aide, teacher, children, and parents.

Like aides, volunteers can be very helpful, but only if adequate preparation and role descriptions have been developed by the teacher. If a teacher is unable or unwilling to consider these details prior to the involvement of assistants in the classroom, it would probably be best to do without such help.

INVOLVE PARENTS REALISTICALLY

Some parents of exceptional children have the knowledge, time, and patience to augment the school's program in the home—but most parents do not. A substantial number of parents of exceptional children are from lower socioeconomic circumstances, do not have the educational background to deal with difficult educational problems, have been reared in an environment in which education is not valued, spend most of their time preoccupied with problems of coping with daily needs, and usually deal with discipline problems in an inconsistent and primitive fashion. "Slow learners" and "mildly mentally retarded children" frequently have parents with these attributes. There are, of course, parents who are able to carry through in an effective way a home program that is compatible with the class program.

Since exceptional children come from all social classes, teachers must be prepared to relate to parents from middle and upper socioeconomic levels as well as from the lower levels. Sometimes parents are too eager to help; they unwittingly destroy the impact of the classroom program (1) by uncritically accepting "therapies" or "cures" that they have heard about but that have little scientific credibility; (2) by being so eager to help their child that their haste leads to the inaccurate and detrimental application of suggestions made by the teacher; (3) by forcing their child to practice at home beyond a constructive point and thus tainting the teacher's efforts; (4) by entering their child into competition with others instead of looking at individual progress; and (5) by being unwilling to accept that their child is indeed in need of special education.

In order to involve parents realistically and effectively, we recommend the following policy:

1 Schedule periodic conferences with parents.

2 As a result of the conference, and any other information you have available, estimate the parents' competence in working with you. Are they naïve, misinformed, pushy, prone to compare the child with siblings, apparently incapable of following a supplementary program of any complexity, or too demanding of the child?

3 Avoid discussion of possible causes of the child's problems, the history of the situation, and hunches as to prognosis.

4 As the parents become cooperative and informed, progressively involve them in home-school programing for their child. Initially, you may request that the parent simply be with the child for a portion of the evening in any type of simple exchange. Later, the parent may assist the child in completing take-home exercises. Eventually you might recommend that the parents tutor the youngster, develop in-home behavioral objectives, and establish a management program for use at home. This will require careful preparation by the parents and monitoring by you.

5 Depending on the child's problems and the parents' capabilities, you may wish to recommend a variety of sources to the parents, including manuals, seminars, and continuing education programs in child development and special education. You may also want to recommend that a parent become a teaching assistant if time permits.

6 Whenever possible you should encourage parents to keep records on their child's behavior at home so that their reports on how the child is doing will not be filled with unreliable impressions. Again, you may wish to recommend a number of sources to the parents for keeping such records.

7 Be realistic about the extent to which parents can contribute to the education of their own child. There will be a tendency on the part of most parents of exceptional children to overestimate the amount of time and energy they have available for working with their child. Do not blame them if the child is not progressing in your classroom. To be sure, their collaboration will facilitate the child's progress but do not depend on their participation.

PLAN THE LAYOUT OF YOUR CLASSROOM

Classrooms are organized for different purposes. Some teachers arrange the physical environment with aesthetics in mind; that is, their major concern is how pleasing to the eye their classroom is. Their focus is on a public relations dimension. For example, bulletin boards are lavish and not to be touched by the children—they are designed more for adult appeal than for the instruction of the children. Furniture is selected and arranged to suit the taste of the teacher and not primarily for purpose or utility.

Another rationale for the organization of the classroom is administrative convenience. In this case the teacher is principally concerned about minimizing his or her own efforts—making life easier at the possible expense of restricting instructional effectiveness. In this type of classroom, materials and supplies are stored so that children do not have access to them. Children are seated alphabetically so that records are more easily maintained. Provision for individual learning areas is at a minimum, and the teacher's desk is usually isolated from the pupils' activities.

There are, of course, other personal and noninstructional criteria for organization of the classroom. Indeed, some teachers "organize" the classroom in a most haphazard way, changing the layout on the basis of whim or temporary expediency.

What is lacking in all the preceding bases for organization of the classroom is a *consistent instructional rationale* based on therapy. The classroom is an environment for learning; all other considerations must be subordinate.

In arriving at an effective physical arrangement, it is important for you to see what modern learning theory has to offer. One clear conclusion is that learning efficiency and effectiveness are influenced by the characteristics of the physical context. That is, either because of accidental or intentional prior arrangement, activities come to be associated with, and thus influenced by, certain stimuli. For example, if you are accustomed to napping in your favorite easy chair, the chair becomes a cue for napping. Reading becomes difficult in that setting since the napping competes with the reading. Or if you frequently eat while you watch television, the television becomes a cue for eating. As a result you may search around for a snack when the TV is on even though you have eaten quite recently.

Within a school setting it is not surprising if schoolchildren are messy at their lunch table if this is the same table on which they are encouraged to smear paint during the art period. Such settings are technically called "discriminative stimuli," and they set the occasion for certain behaviors that occur in a specific setting and that are reinforced in that environment. Successful teachers have found that children are more likely to be quiet, attentive, and persistent in activities such as reading or arithmetic in a corner or area that has been specifically set aside for that activity and in which behaviors incompatible with these activities do not occur. This principle, that is, the control of behavior by cues, can be expanded to include not only location in the room but any other stimulus that can be used to set the occasion for desired behavior. To illustrate, the teacher may set a timer during which the children are expected, and reinforced, to engage in quiet seat work. Color cues can also be used in various ways, e.g., a blue card held up by the teacher signals the fact that quiet talking is permissible. The characteristics of the physical setting, therefore, are important components of the instructional enterprise.

In your planning of your classroom layout, the following factors are pertinent:

1 Decide what major student competencies you desire to see exhibited and where they are to be demonstrated within the classroom. You might list certain activities such as reading, spelling, or writing, arts and crafts, or group conversations and select specific areas where these activities are encouraged.

2 Determine which activities require that the students be able to see or hear certain stimuli or both. The Distar Program, for example, requires instruction in small groups because the children need to see small visual presentations and be within reaching distance of the teacher.

3 Assess where within the classroom the target activity can most easily be achieved by the children. It would be unwise, for example, to have two activities occurring side by side, one of which requires concentration while the other involves group discussion.

4 Arrange the setting so that you can actively interact with the students. This means that your desk and resources should not be isolated from the learning environment. Your position should be part of, not apart from, the children's environment.

5 Consider whether group or individual materials are required and arrange the classroom accordingly.

6 Be sure to consider the importance of making traffic patterns in the classroom efficient and nondisruptive. During transitions between tasks children should move into the adjacent areas and not crisscross throughout the room.

7 It is important to identify the characteristics of the environment outside the classroom in which the skills you are teaching will, hopefully, be practiced. For example, if you wish children to practice reading at home, a simulated living-room setting in the classroom where reading is taught may facilitate the transfer of this activity to the home.

BE CAUTIOUS AND DELIBERATE IN YOUR SELECTION
OF INSTRUCTIONAL MATERIALS

Teachers are often rushed to select instructional materials at either the beginning or the end of the school year. In haste, teachers will order materials on the basis of whatever catalogue is available, whatever salesmen are handy, or whatever they may happen to hear from other teachers. A combination of the salesmen's ability to mesmerize and the number of materials available leaves most teachers in a quandary over how to make the best selection.

We probably need not emphasize the importance of instructional materials;

they, along with the instructional strategies, are the essence of teaching. To help you select the most appropriate instructional devices and materials, you may wish to consider the following guidelines, which have been derived from learning theory and research. We have attempted to provide a rather comprehensive array of considerations because of the crucial role materials play in the instructional program.

1 Do the materials specify objectives for performance in explicit behavioral terms that allow for reliable measurement to assess students' achievement?

2 Is the material organized in such a way that one can teach and test for unit mastery, i.e., achievement of groups of skills arranged in a progressively more difficult sequence?

3 Is success probable at each step in the sequence? The steps should be small enough so that students can succeed and not be frustrated because of inordinately large gaps between skill objectives.

4 Are there explicit criteria for success at each step? What will the student have to demonstrate to be considered competent at each step?

5 Are pretests available, and are evaluative checks for progress built into the materials? These provide not only checks for the child but feedback for the teacher who must be alert for the need to adjust instruction and to establish the child's proper location within the system.

6 Are opportunities for positive reinforcement integral to the materials? Reinforcement should be available following the successful accomplishment of an objective and should be either provided by the teacher or intrinsic to the materials. For example, the use of humor or relatively easier materials should follow more difficult materials in the total sequence, providing built-in rewards for persistence.

7 Is any punishment, even of a subtle variety, involved in the materials? For example, poor sequencing may punish the student because of frustration in not being able to accomplish successive objectives.

8 Do the materials allow for the use of standardized signals or cues for responses by students? This is especially important in materials that involve interaction between student and teacher where students are expected to answer or repeat during the lesson. In the Distar Reading Program, for example, the teacher must learn certain hand signals to cue the students concerning when and how to respond. This avoids confusion, situations in which the same child always is first to respond, and other forms of instructional inefficiency.

9 Does the material encompass a wide range of accomplishments, or is it restricted to a range of skills? In the former instance, every student can use

the materials at a level appropriate to his current status. Materials with a restricted range are usually more intensive and detailed in their steps and sequence and often more useful in remedial situations.

10 Can the students become actively involved with the materials? Active participation, which requires frequent responding in the selection of answers and production of correct behavior, is much preferred over materials in which the child is a passive agent. Programed workbooks, which require student responses of various forms throughout the material, are generally superior to materials that solicit answers at the end of the lesson.

11 Do the materials provide for frequent and varied repetition of correct behavior? Repetition has been demonstrated to be one of the most crucial factors in learning. Repetition should not be boring formal drill but rather should require the review of previously achieved skills.

12 Do the materials promise to hold the interest of children at different ages and levels of socialization?

13 Do the materials incorporate remedial provisions that will return a child who has failed at a certain level to a prescribed level for correction?

14 Can the student use the material or device independently? Can a teacher's aide or another child work with the student in using the materials? Or must a teacher be involved for some or all portions of activity with the material?

15 Is multisensory involvement possible? Generally speaking, learning is enhanced when several senses are involved, such as in materials that present a concept visually, auditorily, and perhaps tactually. However, children who don't have use of certain senses should not be penalized by the materials.

16 Can the materials be used with groups as well as with the individuals? If so, how large a group is feasible?

17 Is cheating possible? Certain programed texts, for example, include answers, so that students can peek at the answers, fill in the blanks, and claim to have completed the assignment.

18 If you are considering purchasing a mechanical instructional device, do the available materials for use with the machine meet the aforementioned programing criteria? Some machines are marvelous, but the programs for software are instructionally inferior.

19 Can the teacher make up his or her own programs or extend existing ones for use with the teaching machine or material?

20 Is at-home involvement possible for the pupil? Some materials contain take-home exercises and projects in which students can practice skills alone or with their parents.

This independent learner is mastering size, shape, and color concepts with a simple teaching machine.

21 Does the material or device fit in with other parts of the daily program? Such materials should be of high priority for purchase as opposed to programs that have specialized and relatively little routine use.

22 Are research data available on the effectiveness of the materials? What is the source of these data—the publisher, the author, or relatively unbiased sources?

23 Does the use of the material require extensive teacher training? If so, this should be considered before purchase of the materials. For example, the Distar series assumes teachers' participation in an intensive workshop.

Children are eager to learn with teaching machines that reward them and never lose patience.

24 Can and do teachers become excited about using the materials? No matter how good the materials are with students, if the teacher does not enjoy them or is irritated when using them, the materials may end up in storage.

25 Are the materials easily transportable? Can they be borrowed? Can students take them home? Do they have to be located in a special place?

26 What is the initial cost? How frequent and how costly are repairs or replacements? Are the materials durable and reusable?

Few materials will meet all the foregoing criteria. Nevertheless, materials should be selected that meet as many of them as possible.

DECIDE ON THE BASIC KINDS OF AND PROCEDURES FOR COLLECTING DATA

Reliable, valid, and systematic measurement is an essential activity of any science, basic or applied. Like the civil engineer, physician, or other technical professional, the educator must employ procedures and instruments of measurement that provide sufficiently precise information to permit accomplishment of professional goals. The educator's goals, of course, center around bringing about progressive and positive changes in students' competence. "Teaching" or "educating" must be assessed by its intended result: learning. A teacher has not taught when children have not learned. Measurement, then, is crucial not only for gauging the student's status and progress but also for guiding the teacher's behavior.

Unfortunately, measurement in education has been predominantly *normative* and *summative*. Children have most frequently been compared with *other* children in terms of performance, rather than with *their own* past performance. Age norms and grade norms are examples of measures of average attainment with which children are compared. These normative measures are usually administered in the schools at the beginning or the end of the school year. Summative evaluation, infrequent and only after large blocks of time and effort, is generally unsatisfactory for at least two reasons. End-of-year achievement tests, for example, do not provide enough detail to enable the teacher to pinpoint the specific learning problem or steps that may be responsible for lack of progress. Second, year-end testing is just too late. Teachers "discover" after the school year is over that certain children show marked incompetence in areas where they could have been helped.

The fundamental solution to the problems of normative and summative testing is not to do away with these kinds of evaluation, since they do have value, but to employ an ongoing program of *formative evaluation based on competencies.* Briefly, this involves the identification of specific objectives or competencies and frequent evaluation or checks on progress to provide the feedback that makes possible continual adjustments in methods and materials.

In addition to deciding on evaluative procedures (formative or summative, based on competency or norms), you must determine the major content areas and priorities for measurement. Not everything can be measured in the same detail; you will have to make decisions about *what* is more important to evaluate, *when* certain skills should be assessed, and *how* or to what extent they must be measured. Making these decisions will certainly depend upon a number of factors, and no two teachers may pursue exactly the same program of evaluation. However, the following recommendations may assist in at least focusing attention on the issues or concerns involved before you become preoccupied with the day-to-day problems of the classroom.

1 Regard achievement, intelligence, and aptitude tests as global measures of the student's current status. Examine the results to provide suggestions for curriculum emphasis.

2 Supplement the formal achievement tests with your own informal assessments of each child's competence in each major subject area, i.e., reading, language, writing, and arithmetic. Complete the initial formal and informal assessment *before* you begin regular systematic instruction toward specific

objectives. Indeed, the objectives for your instructional programs are derived from the initial assessments.

3 Identify and measure social behavior critical to the smooth functioning of the educational program. Initial estimates of punctuality, honesty, cooperativeness, politeness, acceptance of disappointment, and other socioemotional behavior may be difficult to obtain. It is difficult to define such terms clearly enough to permit reliable measurement. However, it is worth the effort because the socioemotional behavior of children often makes or breaks their careers in the classroom.

4 Decide on how on-task, formative evaluation will be accomplished. Some teachers make daily checks of progress on what is ostensibly being taught. It is not possible, nor required, to check on every child in every learning area every day. Rather, many teachers reserve 5 minutes at the end of each instructional session to find out quickly which children can and cannot demonstrate the skills emphasized in the lesson. Some teachers systematically select, for example, five children each day for more comprehensive checks. In this fashion not every child is checked daily, not too much time elapses between checks, and the burden on the teacher is not as great.

5 Consider the various options for collecting data. You may want to observe and record the behavior of just one or two children all day, especially if they are your only major problems. Usually, however, it is more feasible to collect *samples* of performance. You may decide to record a particular behavior at a particular time for all or some of the children; for example, volunteering to answer or to accept tasks could be counted and recorded just during cleanup time. Similarly, you can set aside 5 minutes sometime during the morning and afternoon periods of seat work to scan the room to see who is attending to their work.

Not only should the time and place for measurement be considered, but the type of data. You should consider the use of frequency and duration data, checklists, and rating scales. Sometimes simply counting the frequency of a behavior is the easiest and best measure. The number of times a pupil gets out of his seat during an hour, the number of words he reads during a 10-minute session, and the frequency with which he says "please" and "thank you" during the day are instances of frequency data. Duration is sometimes the most practical measure of a behavior, especially when children seem to take too much time to do a particular assignment. Objective checklists, on which attainment of specified skills can be marked off and dated, are helpful in providing a record of a student's progress. Often, you will want to rate or judge a skill, rather than count it, especially if it deals with social characteristics that are difficult to define as precisely as would be required to permit frequency counts. "Tolerance to criticisms," "initiative during free play," and "cooperativeness on the playground" are examples of behavior that can be rated. After this behavior has been somewhat objectified, measures of greater precision than ratings can be employed.

6 Finally, review the possibilities for help in conducting evaluations of students. Sometimes students can test themselves, especially if you use self-instructional, programed materials. A teacher's aide can be quite valuable as an assistant in this respect. Also, do not overlook the possibility of having one student check on another.

Evaluation can be comprehensive and frequent, and it need not be confusing or burdensome if the teacher takes advantage of possible shortcuts and assistance. Perhaps the best admonition is "a little at a time and a little every day"—systematic, routine checking of the progress of a few children in a few dimensions each day will supply the necessary information for a comprehensive assessment of each student's progress so that teaching strategies and materials can be monitored and modified.

PLAN A WORKABLE, PRACTICAL CURRICULUM

There are many published curricula in special education that can be drawn upon as resources for content, sequence, and activities (Bereiter and Englemann, 1966; Goldstein, 1969; Meyen, 1972; Stephens, 1970; EMR Curriculum, 1970). Each has its own philosophical rationale, range of content, degree of specificity, and practical relevance. There are strengths and weaknesses in all of them, and you should not feel wedded to any single approach because of its current popularity. As you analyze these curricula and decide for yourself the kind of instructional focus you believe to be appropriate, consider the following:

1 After you have determined the major subject areas to be included in the curriculum, progressively differentiate each curricular topic into subunits and sequence according to their dependence on each other.

2 Make sure that your program of studies stretches far enough to include the lower and upper boundaries of skills likely to be exhibited by the children. Use these boundaries to establish a list of skills to be acquired by the entire group. As each child demonstrates each skill he can be checked off and proceed to the next skill in the sequence.

3 Keep in mind the range of learning objectives that will predictably be required of each child as he moves toward independent living. Your curriculum should be relevant to the child's future. In addition to the usual tool subjects, the teacher should cite objectives that focus on social, vocational, personal, and family dimensions. Sex education, respect for authority, proper grooming and personal hygiene, and prevocational skills should be as important as, and not incidental to, the skills in tool subjects.

4 At the beginning of each school year, the teacher should focus immediately on social, personal, and attitudinal competencies that are fundamental to further instruction. For example, many children need to be taught how to pay attention, follow instructions, take turns, volunteer, and avoid being disruptive toward other children. The teacher should definitely decide on the ground rules for operation of the classroom before the students arrive. These are the "dos" and "don'ts" of the classroom, and they should be clearly posted and discussed with the children almost daily initially and as frequently thereafter as necessary. Start out with only a few rules. Academic skills should be introduced gradually as social and personal skills are shaped.

5 Break down curricular goals into explicit and specific performance objectives. This breakdown will require the development of lists of behavioral objectives which permit measurement of their attainment. Such objectives become the content for your lesson plans. This process is often called "task analysis."

Not all these suggestions can be accomplished before the children arrive in your classroom, but the overall curriculum plan, the determination of the subunits, and initial sets of behavioral objectives for the first few weeks of the school year should be developed. This degree of organization will minimize confusion and frustration during those trying first few weeks.

BE PRACTICAL IN YOUR PLANS FOR GROUPING CHILDREN

While it is true that individualized, personalized instruction is desirable in many instances, such an arrangement simply is not possible within most classrooms. Instruction in small groups can possess many of the advantages of individualized instruction and, in fact, be more efficient. Do not be too fastidious about the similarity of children in a group. Obviously, we recommend that you group by achievement from your analysis of each child's performance on checks of progress. You will have to compromise—not all children will be at the same level: some will be slightly behind and others will be slightly ahead. Some children will be placed in a less than optimum grouping situation just to be manageable. As a general rule of thumb, try not to have more than three groups operating at any one time.

CONSIDER HOW CONSEQUENCES AFFECT BEHAVIOR

It is well established that the kinds of events that occur immediately after a behavior exert great influence on the future of that behavior. Behaviors that are ignored are likely to be weakened, whereas behaviors that are followed by rewarding outcomes will subsequently occur with greater frequency, intensity, and duration. Consequently, the teacher should study the advantages in controlling consequences as a means of accomplishing curricular objectives. The techniques involved in the effective management of consequences in the classroom include the following, each of which individual teachers will need to assess for possible implementation in the classroom:

1 *Task-imbedded positive reinforcement.* The teacher should select or design lessons that have built into them high interest and pleasant consequences for children's participation in the lesson. Humor, improbable events, current activities, and use of the actual names of children within the group can be woven into a lesson to maintain their involvement.

2 *Premacking.* The probability that a child will engage in low-preference activities is increased when they are followed by high-preference activities. Activities that children do not find exciting should be followed by high-interest activities if performance in the low-preference activities has been at a satisfactory level. Don't cluster music, art, recess, and snack time together at the beginning of the day (if they seem to be high-preference activities), only to be followed by what are frequently lower-preference activities such as reading, arithmetic, spelling, and writing. Tasks should be appropriately alternated. What is a high-preference activity for one child may not be for another. Assess the situation carefully and sequence the activities somewhat individually, as is practical.

3 *Social reinforcement.* Attention, praise, and approval from an adult are powerful reinforcers for a child's behavior. While it is difficult, teachers must learn to refrain from paying attention to incorrect or inappropriate behavior during lessons and at other times. Be sure to demonstrate immediate approval of even small instances of progress on the part of children. Your approval can take the form of verbal praise, a pat on the back, a smile, or a shake of the child's hand. "Positive ear-shotting," i.e., saying something positive about a youngster's behavior within his hearing, may help to increase a behavior.

4 *Charting progress.* When the teacher or child keeps track of individual accomplishments, the mere charting of such progress often serves as a reinforcement. In a sense, it is like charting your own weight loss while on a diet.

5 *Material rewards.* Much has been written about the efficacy of using prizes to reward certain progressive behaviors. Trinkets, candy, games, and various other forms of material goods can serve as primary reinforcers. Token economies have been widely used in special education settings. Poker chips, stamps, check marks, or holes punched in a card can be accumulated by a student and be exchanged for privileges and tangible rewards. A system of this sort enables a teacher to "credit" a child quickly and thus reinforce his performance, without disrupting the classroom routine by immediately providing a material reward. Usually children "cash in" their tokens at a convenient time during the day.

All of these approaches to management of consequences can be employed to boost and maintain motivation and persistence in the classroom. Frequently parents can be trained in using these same approaches in the home in order to effect transfer from one setting to the other. One of the important goals in using these systems is to move children from dependence on material rewards to social rewards and, eventually, to the rewards associated with achievement of the task itself. This movement varies from child to child and situation to situation. A youngster may generally be motivated by achievement of a task but still require extrinsic motivation for attempting new and more difficult tasks.

STUDY CONTEMPORARY INSTRUCTIONAL TECHNIQUES

Instructional approaches have been presented in the literature of special education, and specific teaching strategies have been developed that are held to be effective with various categories of instructional problems. For example, there are numerous approaches for responding to perceptual-motor disorders—each of which has its own idiosyncracies. The greatest diversity of approaches occurs in the treatment of behavior disorders. Many of the people espousing these approaches disagree among themselves; many of the approaches are promoted with evangelistic fervor; and many approaches have little empirical validity. We do not mean to imply that these techniques are without merit. There are, however, at least two issues that must be clarified before one can have confidence in using the techniques.

First, most of the approaches that have been developed are supposed to have specific and differential utility for children within a specific category of disability. Certain perceptual-motor approaches are presumed to be applicable to children with "learning disabilities" and not to youngsters with "mental retardation." There are reading techniques for the "disturbed," others for the "retarded," and still others for "slow learners." But this "category-specificity" of instructional techniques is undocumented and unparsimonious.

Second, portions of each instructional approach are undoubtedly effective; however, the segments contained in each have not been separately analyzed. One is usually faced with the choice of adopting a whole approach or selecting segments from various programs that have face validity.

There are some common characteristics in almost all of the prominent instructional approaches that have been developed for dealing with exceptional children. Many of these features come from learning theory, and the probable effectiveness of these various instructional approaches relates to the extent to which they incorporate the major principles of learning. In the following list we have identified a number of the most prominent of these principles which have applicability for effective instruction across traditional disability categories and instructional situations.

1 *Identify the targets for teaching.* In an earlier section we discussed the great

importance of specifying clear instructional objectives. This is an important first step in whatever approach you select.

2 *Provide for motivation.* A fundamental of any teaching-learning situation is that students be excited, interested, attentive, and eager to participate. A major component of the teaching task is to arrange for motivation rather than taking for granted that it will occur spontaneously. Management of consequences, especially the role of positive reinforcement and incentive programing, has been discussed as a primary means for motivational control. Do not lose sight of the fact that continued reinforcement can be attenuated or gradually withdrawn as appropriate behavior becomes established.

3 *Arrange for repetition and practice.* There is no question that repeated presentation of instructional stimuli is crucial to good teaching. Repetition can be multisensory, that is, stimuli can be presented visually, auditorily, or tactually. Generally speaking, multisensory repetition will enhance learning.

Likewise, children should be given numerous opportunities to practice making responses. As we want multisensory repetition in the presentation of the teacher, multiresponse practice by students will help to consolidate learning. Children should practice correct responses by writing, speaking, and even demonstrating. A related consideration is to have the newly learned skill practiced in a variety of contexts. Keep in mind the need for the child to be able to generalize his responses to different situations. Make sure to provide opportunities for youngsters to repeat and apply the skills, once they are learned, in subsequent portions of your curriculum throughout the year. In summary, practice of correct responses should occur in three dimensions: (1) in various response modes, (2) in different situations, and (3) during intermittent periods throughout the school year. Since repetition is a vital part of instructional techniques, do not allow repetition of errors to occur.

4 *Use shaping procedures.* A common characteristic of most instructional approaches is the incorporation of a sequence from easy to hard. To assure the smooth progress of students, learning objectives and tasks should be ordered in terms of increasing difficulty. Students should be rewarded as they approximate achievement of each objective. Do not expect Rome to be built in a day. Be patient but persistent; reinforce any sign of progress no matter how slight.

5 *Be consistent.* Perhaps one of the most devastating errors teachers and parents can make is to be inconsistent in their approach to children. Use consistent and standard stimulus cues for behavior you wish to establish and encourage. There are standard hand cues that can be used to signal the children to pay attention or to speak out, certain activities can be scheduled for consistent times of the day, routines should be established at the outset

of the school year, and verbal instructions must be the same from one time to the next to minimize confusion. Consider the possible ambiguity in the directions as perceived by a child in the following typical activity. Teachers may want a child to add 2 + 2 and use the following inconsistent phrasings at different times:

2 and 2 are 4
2 plus 2 is 4
2 added to 2 is 4
the sum of 2 and 2 is 4

This is obviously perplexing to children who haven't learned the identity and meaning of the various terms. Therefore, choose one consistent phrasing at the outset until the skill is learned and then begin to introduce synonyms or variations.

A major dimension that demands consistency is the way the teacher reacts to behaviors. The same behavior should not at different times be rewarded, ignored, and punished depending on the mood of the teacher. Establishing new learning requires the consistent use of positive reinforcement. Only after the behavior is well established should you consider using reinforcement on a variable basis. Likewise, behaviors that you choose to punish should be punished in every instance. Do not let the youngster get away with unwanted behavior without your reacting in an appropriate and consistent fashion. Finally, if the decision has been reached to ignore certain behaviors, technically termed "extinction," it would be a big mistake to attend to the behaviors from time to time.

6 *Reduce the child's dependence on you.* One of your primary goals as a special educator is to develop independence in the learner. At the beginning of an instructional sequence use consistent cues. For example, you may ask each child to "put your finger on the little hand; it tells you what time it is." "What time is it?" Gradually you must fade out the initial prompting so that eventually the youngster will state the correct time with the usual cue, "What time is it?" In helping children put on their coats, help them through most of the sequence and let them do the last step themselves. Gradually complete less of the task, letting the children do more and more of the activity. Similarly, children should become independent of you as the primary source for reinforcement. Associate tangible rewards with social incentives and gradually shift from contrived to more natural reinforcers. It is just as wrong to "crutch-trap" a child as to deny him the crutch in the first place. Finally, consider the advantages in having children work independently or with other children without your immediate presence. Your teacher's aide can be used in this regard as well. This will serve to increase the probability that the child will continue to progress with other adults and not only when you are available to him.

7 *Continuously evaluate.* We have already stressed the central role of evaluations of progress. It cannot be separated from proper instructional techniques.

AVOID DEAD TIME

Like a good play or television production, every minute of instructional time is important. Unplanned time will lead students to be restless and teachers to be haphazard. With exceptional children particularly, thorough organization is critical because greater focus must be given to intentional instruction. In short, you cannot leave skill acquisition to chance.

Often times dead time results from teachers' not having previously organized the classroom. For example, decisions should be reached before school begins on the location of materials, the things that will be in the students' desks or on a library table, and the placement of routine school supplies.

STRUCTURE FORMATS FOR CONFERENCES WITH PARENTS
AND REPORTS ON STUDENTS

Decide how frequently and where you wish to meet with the parents of your students. Careful consideration must be given to the nature and format of your reports to them. The material must be meaningful, simply stated, and without educational jargon. Avoid discussing your view of the origin of the child's problem and giving definitive prognoses that may generate false hope or despair. You can be sure that many parents of exceptional children will "read into" your statements and mannerisms support for their own biases or hunches. Stick to discussing the educational objectives for the child, his progress toward achieving those objectives, the procedures you are using to help him achieve them, and suggestions as to how the parents can help. Conferences with parents will be time-consuming; you should decide on a realistic commitment to these activities.

MAINTAIN YOUR OWN MOTIVATION

Being a teacher of exceptional children is not an easy job. It is an exacting profession and requires time and particular expertise. To be sure, it is rewarding to help exceptional children achieve competence and dignity. Do not depend on these altruistic motivations, however, to maintain your persistence during periods of frustration and discouragement. Consider using some of the learning principles we have mentioned to maintain your own professional activity. Many teachers, for example, find it useful to "premack" or otherwise "reinforce" getting their own class preparation done with a personal contract. You may decide to "earn the privilege" of going shopping, eating out, or going on a coffee break only after having completed a certain facet of your preparation. You cannot be faulted for "practicing what you preach."

The following abbreviated lesson plan illustrates the care and planning necessary to implement more fully several of the teaching principles previously discussed.

SAMPLE LESSON PLAN*

Lesson plans must be developed to focus on the development of specific student competencies. This presumes that the teacher, prior to designing the lesson plan, has assessed the child's major strengths and weaknesses to "zero-in on" a relatively specific instructional target.

MAJOR STEPS
1 State the instructional target.
2 Perform a task analysis.
3 State the target in terms of a specific behavior objective.
4 Prepare a criterion test to use in assessing the acquisition of the target behavior.
5 Determine stimuli to bring about that behavior.
6 Determine a method to teach the behavior (response signal), including appropriate consequences.
7 Administer the criterion test.
8 Determine various ways to practice the behavior to enhance generalization and maintenance of the behavior.

LESSON PLAN
1 Have a general goal. The students will properly use periods or question marks at ends of sentences when writing independently.
2 Make a task analysis.
   a Students will recognize the end of a sentence.
   b Students will properly identify and discriminate between periods and question marks (will touch the proper written mark when given the verbal label).
   c Students will properly label periods and question marks when presented with written punctuation marks.
   d Students will answer verbally that a period comes after a "telling" statement.
   e Students will answer verbally that a question mark comes after an "asking" statement.
   f Students will correctly identify a telling statement when presented with telling and asking statements.
   g Students will correctly identify asking statements when presented with telling and asking statements.
3 State specific objectives. When randomly shown periods and question marks, the student will verbally label them correctly 100 percent of the time.
4 Prepare a criterion test for the behavior objective. Each student is presented with a shuffled deck of cards containing four question marks and four

* We are indebted to S. J. Forsberg for providing this sample lesson plan and for discussing with us those instructional variables that contribute to her outstanding educational planning for exceptional children.

periods. The student draws cards one at a time and is requested to answer, "Which punctuation mark is this?"

5 Create stimuli to bring about the behavior. The teacher will ask (pointing), "Which punctuation mark is this?" (Instructional materials are also considered.)

6 Use a method to teach the behavior. The "fading of cues" method may be employed: e.g., visual stimulus (?) is presented with the verbal statement, "This is a question mark." "Which punctuation mark is this?" The words "This is a question mark" are faded. Administer reinforcers during learning, and reward final achievement.

7 Administer the criterion test and remediate if necessary by refining objective, methods, and materials.

8 Other ways to practice the behavior:

  a Children who have passed the criterion test may have a contest in which each child gets a page of a newspaper and circles as many question marks as he can see. The one with the greatest number is the winner.

  b Children are periodically asked, "What punctuation mark is this?" when reading in groups.

11

SPECIAL
EDUCATION
PROSTHESES *

STUDY TARGETS

1 Name and briefly describe three general prosthetic strategies.
2 Study the types and descriptions of motor and sensory disorders summarized
   in Part V of this book. Then, reviewing the devices described in this chapter,
   try to match a specific disorder with an appropriate prosthetic device. Do this
   for about ten types of problems. Examples:
      Blindness—braille writer
      Conductive hearing loss—bone conductor receiver
3 Write a short paragraph that summarizes your understanding of "environmental barriers." Include those general aspects of public environments that
   are most critical.
4 List several prosthetic devices that persons considered "normal" routinely
   use. Think about devices attached to the person or environment that make
   personal functioning easier, more efficient, or more effective. (Hint: automatically opening doors in supermarkets make exits with shopping carts more
   manageable.)

* Permission has been granted for reproduction of many of the illustrations contained in this chapter by the
ICTA Information Centre, FACK, S-161 03, Brooma 3, Sweden. Some drawings originally appeared in the
glossary of *Information System on Adaptive Equipment Used in Schools for Physically Handicapped Children*, U.S.O.E. Bureau of Education for the Handicapped, Division of Research, Washington, D.C.

Earlier we discussed the implications of viewing behavior as the result of a person's interaction with his environment. We emphasized that behavior will be faulty or lacking in those situations in which the person or his environment or both are significantly deviant. This is a distinct philosophical and theoretical departure from the historical tradition in special education of viewing only the person as disabled or handicapped. The position we advanced, then, is that modifications must be made in the child, in his environment, or in both as a means of shaping his behavior in desired directions. Prostheses are applied to the person, to his environment, or to both to maximize interaction between person and environment and, thus, to facilitate behavioral development.

It is important to recognize that whether prosthetic intervention should take place with the person or with his environment must be given considerable thought. To illustrate, assume that a child is born with both hands missing. All the doors in a school could be designed in such a way that the child could simply bump them with his elbow. This expensive, but effective, type of prosthetizing may be appropriate to certain restricted settings but will not help the child in outside settings. We could choose to fit the child with artificial hands that would allow him to open a standard door. This solution would require specific training but have wider generalizability. We could, finally, train the child to grasp a doorknob with both elbows and thus open doors without benefit of either an individual or an environmental prosthesis.

It is clear that the type of prosthetic program that is appropriate is an individual matter. To prosthetize the environment will require little training for the disabled person, but a great deal of environmental technology and physical modification; and it will usually have little generalizability. For children who will be institutionalized for long periods, this may be the best option. Attaching a prosthesis to a person, in contrast, requires individual training and has potential psychological implications because it increases the visibility of the deficiency (unless, of course, it is a cosmetic prosthesis); but it is generalizable outside a protected environment such as a special class or school. Compensatory training, such as using the elbows to open the door, involves teaching alternative ways to deal with a problem and is less expensive from a technological point of view; but it may require much more training than the other two options. If at all possible, a combination of these options should be provided. Situations occur in which one would need to open a door quickly and may not have time to strap on the prosthetic appliance. In such a case the individual should have been trained to use compensatory back-up procedures.

In this chapter we will present a sample of the technology that is available for minimizing handicaps. Obviously, we cannot explore in detail all of the many types of advances that have been made within even the past few years. Our purpose is to whet your appetite and encourage you to study the detailed material that has been suggested at the end of Part IV. We have arranged the presentation of prosthetic devices into several broad classes of function: locomotion, life support, personal grooming and hygiene, communication, and household aids. Further, there is a brief section on advanced technology in which more elaborate and sophisticated apparatus is discussed. A final section discusses environmental barriers characteristic of public facilities that produce or amplify handicaps.

LOCOMOTION

CRUTCHES

Crutches (Figure 11-1) are used by relatively normal children during periods of temporary disability, such as after an operation on part of the lower extremities or when the child has broken a leg or sprained an ankle. When the disability is permanent or of long duration, however, crutches and canes have to be comfortably designed to reduce the weight the legs must bear and to provide stability and support. Numerous considerations enter into the design of such prostheses, because many times people who require crutches and canes have other types of disabling conditions. Articulation and strength of shoulders, elbows, and wrists must be considered in the design along with equilibrium, head balance, and involuntary motion of various body parts.

No opportunity should be lost for maximizing the utility of crutches, not only as regards their primary functions (balance, locomotion, and reducing weight on the lower extremities); it is also important to consider other possible purposes which all prosthetic devices can serve. Although crutches aid movement of the lower extremities, they may reduce the amount and range of functioning of the arms. It is difficult to carry items when one uses crutches.

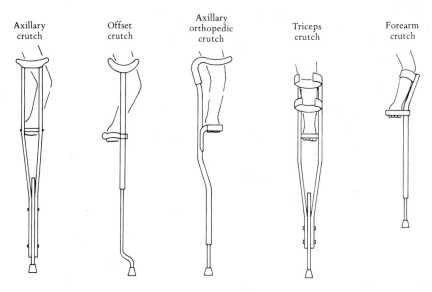

| Axillary crutch | Offset crutch | Axillary orthopedic crutch | Triceps crutch | Forearm crutch |

FIGURE 11-1 Crutches.

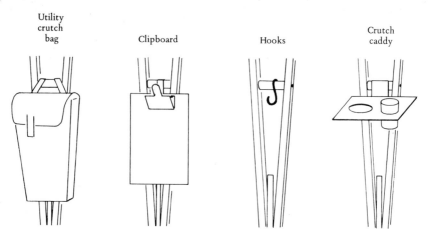

FIGURE 11-2   Attachments for crutches.

Therefore, to offset these liabilities, attachments can be designed with the aim of maximizing the independence of the person (Figure 11-2).

One must consider the surface on which the person with a crutch will be functioning. If it is slippery, then rubber-tipped ends, spiked ends, or tripod legs should be provided. Other surfaces will not require these attachments.

WALKERS

These constitute another category of upright devices to assist support and movement. They can be modified in various ways according to an individual's unique needs. Some have casters, wheels, seats, handlebars, and various types of grips. We have selected for illustration a stair-climbing walker and a more complex apparatus for individuals with problems of involuntary motion during ambulation. Trays, bags, and baskets can be attached to the walker as needed or desired.

Stair-climbing walker

This apparatus (Figure 11-3) makes stair climbing possible by providing excellent support and stability. It is most useful for persons who have excellent control of upper extremities.

Multiple walker

This device (Figure 11-4) is specifically functional for persons with involuntary movements, as in some forms of cerebral palsy. The features provide restraint to spastic movements and support the trunk of the body. Skids can be placed over the rear wheels to slow the movement.

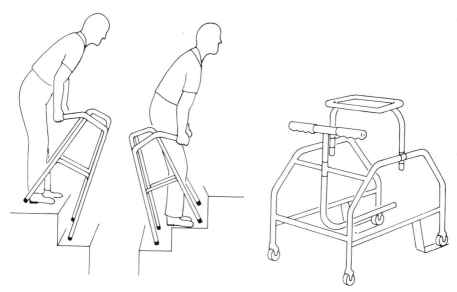

FIGURE 11-3   Stair-climbing walker.   FIGURE 11-4   Multiple walker.

WHEELCHAIRS

Wheelchairs are available in an amazing range of variations and models. They can be motorized with front-wheel drive, recline in various directions, have different types of seats including commodes, be adapted for stair climbing and curb hopping, be collapsible, and be equipped with numerous types of attachments, including straps, supports, cushions, grips, safety devices, and convenience adaptations.

Motorized wheelchair

This battery-operated wheelchair (Figure 11-5) is moved by the control of a

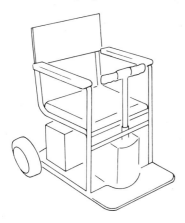

FIGURE 11-5   Motorized wheelchair.

knob placed in the most appropriate position for the handicapped individual. It is a means of independent transportation for people who cannot use a standard wheelchair because of significant motor disability or disability of arms or hands.

Stair-climbing wheelchair

This ingenious wheelchair (Figure 11-6) is equipped with caterpillar treads, much like a tank, and, like a tank, it is able to traverse "rough territory," even climb steps. The seat tilts to maintain an upright position during climbing. During level transit, the treads clear the ground. Everything is operated by battery-powered push-button controls.

Stand-up wheelchair

By locking the main wheel brakes and releasing the seat from its attachments, the individual can lean forward and swing into an upright position. Adjustments can be made according to an individual's weight and 10% from vertical positioning can be effected. It is useful to individuals with a range of physical disorders, but most especially to paraplegics. (See Figure 11-7.)

Adaptations for wheelchairs

Some of the ancillary adaptations that can be made on wheelchairs include those shown in Figure 11-8.

FIGURE 11-6 Stair-climbing wheelchair.   FIGURE 11-7 Stand-up wheelchair.

Gloves

Devices for carrying

Commode attachment

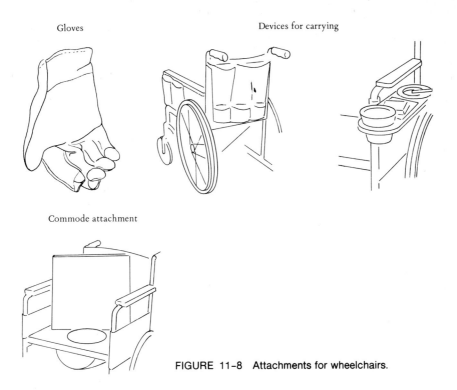

FIGURE 11-8 Attachments for wheelchairs.

RECLINERS

People with certain types of disabilities must remain in a reclining position. Devices have been developed to provide for self-propulsion or assisted propulsion while in this position. These range from a simple creeper to elaborate hydraulic stretchers. (See Figure 11-9.)

Again, Figure 11-10 emphasizes how a prosthetic device that enhances one function (locomotion) need not limit possibilities in other areas (e.g., reading).

Creeper

Wheeled stretcher

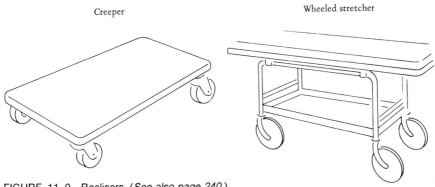

FIGURE 11-9 Recliners. (*See also page 240.*)

Hydraulic stretcher

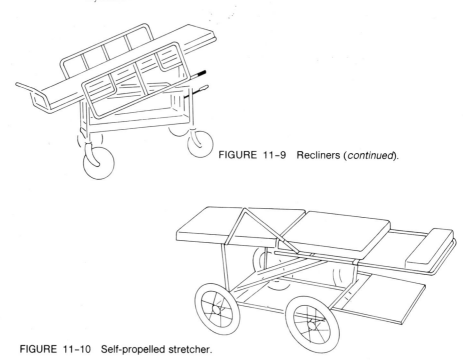

FIGURE 11-9   Recliners (*continued*).

FIGURE 11-10   Self-propelled stretcher.

VERTICAL LIFTS

These devices provide assistance to the individual for movement from one location to another, e.g., from a bed to a wheelchair or to a toilet. The ramp is the simplest of the various transfer devices, whereas other types of lifts are much more complex. (Figure 11-11.)

AUTOMOBILE PROSTHESES

(See Figure 11-12.)

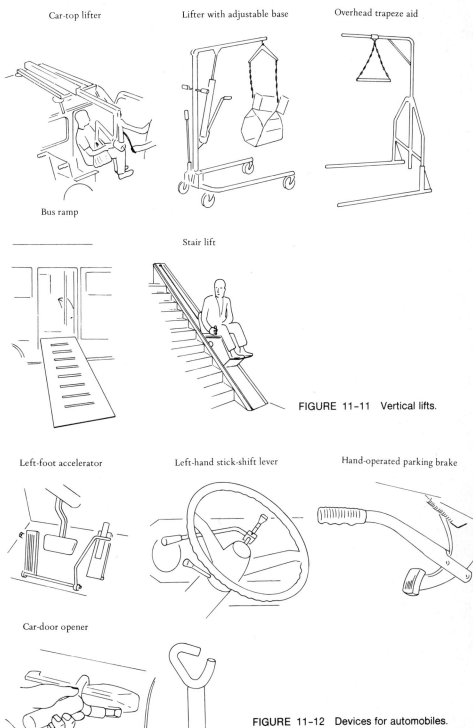

Car-top lifter

Lifter with adjustable base

Overhead trapeze aid

Bus ramp

Stair lift

FIGURE 11-11   Vertical lifts.

Left-foot accelerator

Left-hand stick-shift lever

Hand-operated parking brake

Car-door opener

FIGURE 11-12   Devices for automobiles.

LIFE-SUPPORT AIDS

The prosthetic aids that are presented in this section are amazingly similar to those that have been developed to help astronauts function in a weightless environment. There is an amazing range of variation in the types of adaptations found in life-support aids. Friction, counterbalance, suction, leverage, manipulation of weight, pressure, and rotation are all used as principles in the development of aids to enhance a person's level of functioning.

EATING AND DRINKING

The adaptive equipment used for eating and drinking should foster independence, provide for ease in the act of eating, and be as normal in appearance and function as possible. In most instances some form of specialized training will be required for the child to gain competence in the use of the aids. Illustrations of devices are given in three major functional areas: containing solids and liquids, holding and manipulating food, and delivering food to the mouth. (Figures 11-13 to 11-21.)

FIGURE 11-13 Suction cup. This cup will work only on surfaces that are flat and nonporous and thus permit the formation of a suction.

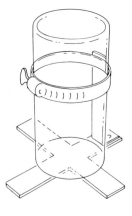

FIGURE 11-14 Glass holder—a stable base for a cup or glass that prevents spilling. This is an alternative to the suction cup.

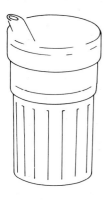

FIGURE 11-15 Vacuum cup. This container allows one to drink while lying down; because it requires sucking, it controls spills.

FIGURE 11-16 Cup with detachable handle. (The handle can be adapted for any grasp.)

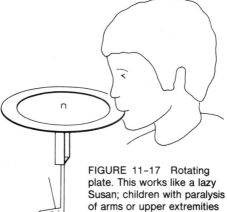

FIGURE 11-17 Rotating plate. This works like a lazy Susan; children with paralysis of arms or upper extremities can rotate the plate with the mouth. The food is arranged along the edge of the plate so that the child can choose.

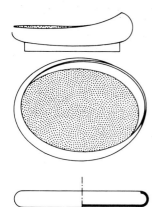

FIGURE 11-18 "Easy-scoop" dish. The rim is rounded and turned upward so that one can find a spoon or fork without spilling the food. A suction cup or high-friction base can be placed on the bottom to control slipping.

Palm-grip utensils   Swivel handle   Side-cutter fork

Rocking knife   Sandwich holder   Extension handle

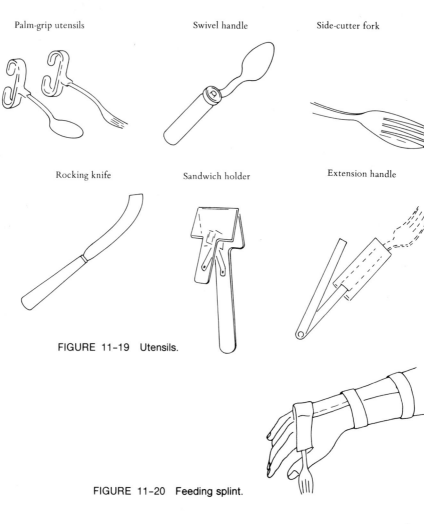

FIGURE 11-19   Utensils.

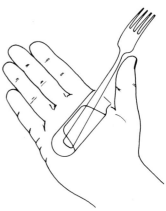

FIGURE 11-20   **Feeding splint.**

FIGURE 11-21   **Utensil holder.**

ELIMINATION

For many handicapped persons the bathroom is not only inconvenient but a potential hazard. The prosthetic devices shown in Figures 11-22 to 11-26 illustrate the range of possible adaptations, from improvisations of existing fixtures to totally new apparatus.

FIGURE 11-22 Portable safety frame.

FIGURE 11-23 Portable commode and skewer chair.

FIGURE 11-24 Cleansing apparatus (bidet).

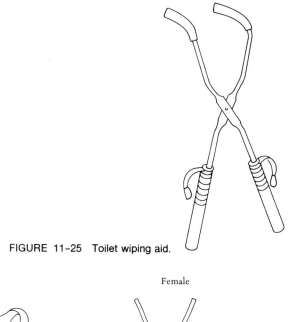

FIGURE 11-25   Toilet wiping aid.

Male   Female

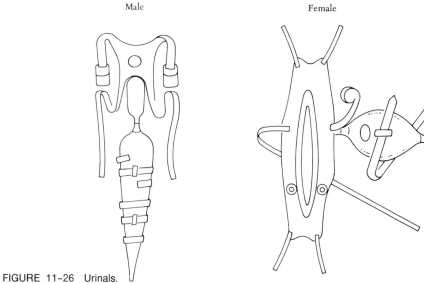

FIGURE 11-26   Urinals.

PERSONAL GROOMING

Being well groomed reduces the potential somatopsychological complications of disability. Unpleasant odors, dirty appearance, and untidy clothes all act to alienate the disabled from others. Every attempt should be made to reduce the stereotype that the handicapped cannot take care of personal grooming needs and do not care about their appearance. The aids shown in Figures 11-27 to 11-36 illustrate some approaches that have been used to make grooming a more independent and likely behavior.

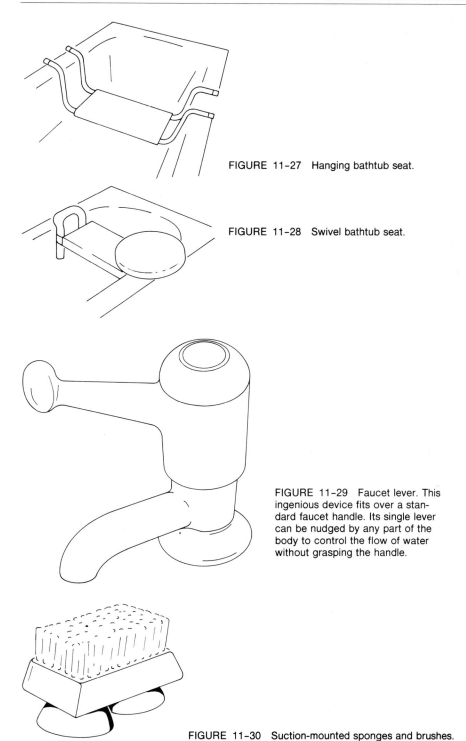

FIGURE 11-27   Hanging bathtub seat.

FIGURE 11-28   Swivel bathtub seat.

FIGURE 11-29   Faucet lever. This ingenious device fits over a standard faucet handle. Its single lever can be nudged by any part of the body to control the flow of water without grasping the handle.

FIGURE 11-30   Suction-mounted sponges and brushes.

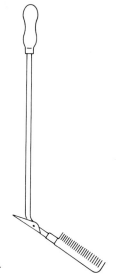

FIGURE 11-31 Comb on extended handle.

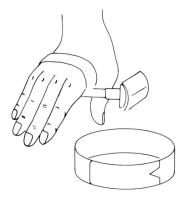

FIGURE 11-32 Razor handle.

FIGURE 11-33 Oral-hygiene device. Toothpaste is applied to the rubber mouthpiece, which is inserted into the mouth; a simple chewing motion cleans the teeth and stimulates the gums.

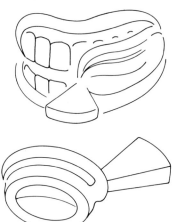

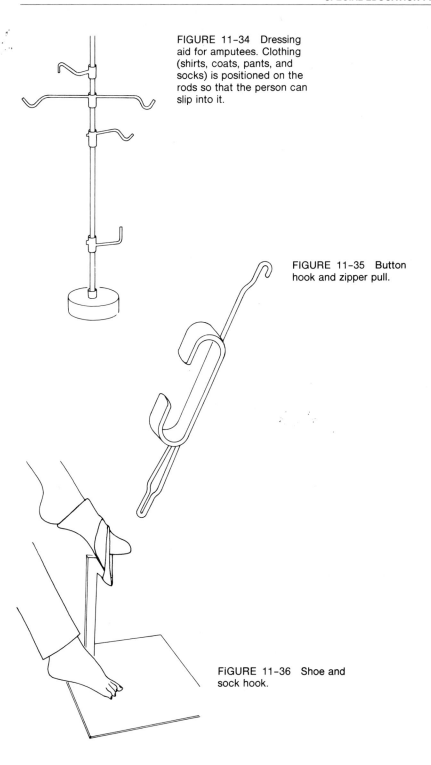

FIGURE 11-34 Dressing aid for amputees. Clothing (shirts, coats, pants, and socks) is positioned on the rods so that the person can slip into it.

FIGURE 11-35 Button hook and zipper pull.

FiGURE 11-36 Shoe and sock hook.

CLOTHING ADAPTATIONS

In addition to using various types of instructional procedures for dealing with the task of dressing and undressing, it is most helpful to have clothing adapted in whatever way is necessary, especially during early stages of teaching dressing skills. Some examples of alterations that might be made include the following:

1 Openings (Figure 11-37) should be wide enough to allow ease of entry and exit.
2 Fastenings must be made in such a way that they can be easily manipulated (e.g., velcro-type fastening and zippers such as those shown in Figure 11-38).
3 Garment material should be considered to minimize snagging, wrinkling, pulling, tearing, and soiling.

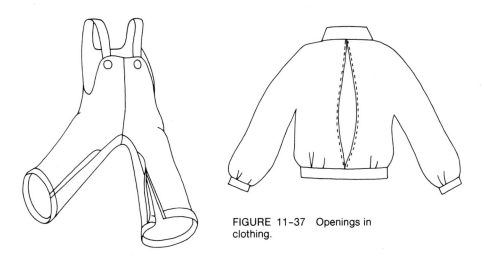

FIGURE 11-37 Openings in clothing.

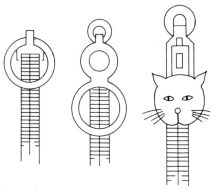

FIGURE 11-38 Zippers.

COMMUNICATION

This area focuses on devices that improve reception and expression of information. Amplification and magnification of stimuli, whether coming in or going out, are important considerations in designing prosthetic communication devices; however, there are conditions for which increasing the stimulus level alone is not enough. There are fewer areas of a technical nature which have received more attention and support than those involving communication. We have tried to identify some examples of the range of possible aids in this important area (Figures 11-39 to 11-50).

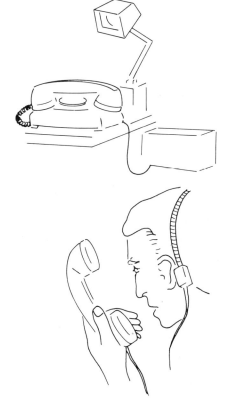

FIGURE 11–39 Telephone signal control. A lamp of some sort is plugged into the telephone and lights up when the telephone rings. This device can be used in other situations, as with a doorbell.

FIGURE 11–40 Bone conductor receiver. A sound vibrator is connected to the telephone receiver, allowing a person with a conductive hearing loss to hear.

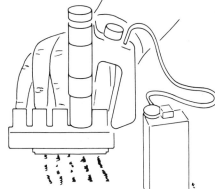

FIGURE 11–41 Sound-tactile reading machine. This device, which requires special instruction, converts written letters into separate tones or unique tactile sensations as it passes over a line of type.

FIGURE 11-42 Larynx transmitter, an apparatus for people whose voice-box is inoperative or has been removed. The transmitter is held against the throat, speech is mouthed, and the device amplifies and transmits the natural vocal vibrations.

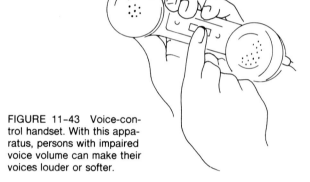

FIGURE 11-43 Voice-control handset. With this apparatus, persons with impaired voice volume can make their voices louder or softer.

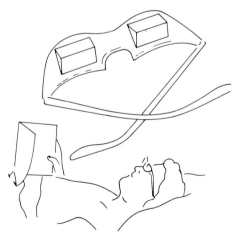

FIGURE 11-44 Prism glasses. These can be adjusted to any angle and worn over ordinary eyeglasses. They allow people with limited head movement to read while lying down.

FIGURE 11-45 Braille typewriter. This conventional electric typewriter, which can be used by both the blind and the sighted, has a standard keyboard but transcribes into braille.

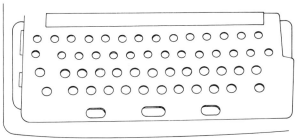

FIGURE 11-46 Typewriter keyboard shield, a metal or plastic plate that fits over the standard electric keyboard and prevents the user from striking two keys or the wrong key. It can also be used, without the typewriter, as a means of pointing communication.

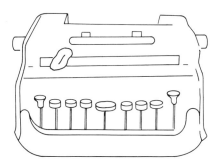

FIGURE 11-47 Braillewriter, for blind persons who want to make single copies of braille. It has six keys that are used in combination to emboss forty possible braille cells. (A slate and stylus can serve as an alternative.)

FIGURE 11-48 Braille receiver. By means of this device, a deaf-blind person who understands braille can communicate through tactile sensations. A standard alphabet keyboard is used. The deaf-blind person receives the braille configurations by holding his finger over the receiver button at the back of the machine.

FIGURE 11–49 Pointer. A pointer attached to the head is a communication device for children without speech and with impaired upper-extremity functioning. Along with a typewriter keyboard shield (see Figure 11–46), it can be used to operate an electric typewriter.

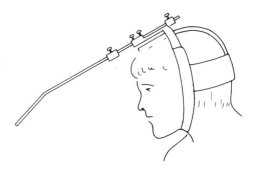

FIGURE 11–50 Page turner, a suction device which turns a page in either direction. It is operated by a remote-control device that can be triggered according to the disabled person's needs.

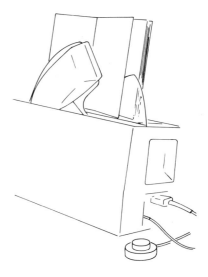

HOUSEHOLD AIDS

(See Figures 11–51 to 11–54.)

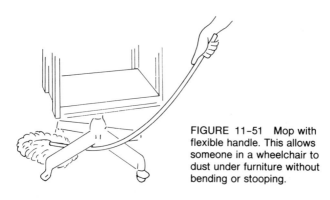

FIGURE 11–51 Mop with flexible handle. This allows someone in a wheelchair to dust under furniture without bending or stooping.

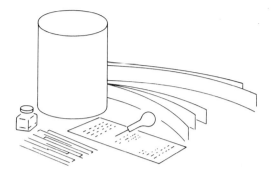

FIGURE 11-52 Marker kit. Plastic labels embossed either in braille or in ordinary letters can be used to identify shelves, canned goods, cleaning materials, etc.

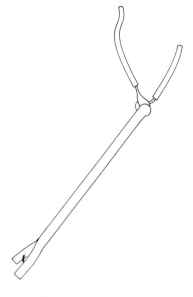

FIGURE 11-53 Squeeze-handle retriever. This reacher has two curved fingers and a squeeze handle; it allows the user to reach items within 30 to 40 inches.

FIGURE 11-54 Keyless lock, to replace a conventional door or ignition lock. It is a pushbutton combination lock that can be operated with a reacher or mouth stick and thus makes using a key unnecessary.

ADVANCED TECHNOLOGY

Research and development in many of the nation's scientific programs, especially in the aerospace effort, have resulted in heretofore unimagined technological advances. This advanced technology has drawn upon numerous disciplines, and the application of the principles and discoveries that have come from these research and development activities have considerable pertinence to the practical problems encountered in handicapping conditions. Control mechanisms, unique sensory devices, alarm systems, new materials, powered apparatus, portable equipment, stimulus detectors, unique processes of fabrication, implantable devices, sensitive measurement techniques, economical recording and playback mechanisms, and ingenious training procedures represent broad categories of technology which are applicable to habilitation and rehabilitation. Many of the prostheses that have resulted from these discoveries are still in developmental stages and have not been widely advertised or discussed. It is our purpose in the section to alert you to examples of some unique technological accomplishments. We will present them in no particular order.

The *Optacon,* which is about the size of a college textbook and weighs 4 pounds, is a unique reading aid for the blind. A miniature camera, mounted on rollers, is moved across a line of print. Connected by a small cable to the main chassis, the camera picks up an image and transmits the signal to an electronic section in which conversion of the visual image to a tactile image is accomplished. Each of 144 rods, vibrating independently according to the received pattern, protrudes through a plastic cover and touches the blind person's finger in the same configuration as the stimulus received by the camera. Differences in type size are handled by a zoom lens on the camera.

The *Laser Cane* is an electronic apparatus to assist in mobility for totally blind persons. The device has the appearance of a normal cane, but it emits pulses of infrared light. Pulses reflected from an object in front of it are detected by a receiving mechanism which, in turn, warns the traveler. The cane emits three beams simultaneously. The downward beam warns the traveler, by a low-pitched tone, of a drop from the cane tip to any distance larger than 9 inches. A second beam focuses straight ahead, approximately 2 feet high and 10 feet in front of the cane tip. Any obstacle detected within this range will actuate an index-finger stimulator. The third beam focuses upward from the cane top and activates a high-pitched tone when detecting objects at head height.

Sonic glasses utilize an ultrasonic transmitter that scans an angle of 55 degrees and receives bounce-back signals from two receivers that are embedded within the spectacle frames. These signals are converted to an audible frequency level and are conveyed to the user through earphones. The power supply is located in a shirt pocket.

The *sight switch* is a control device operated by eye movements. It was developed by NASA for astronauts. Designed to be worn on standard spectacles, the device activates electrical control mechanisms by sensing variations in light reflected from the white portion of the eye. The light source for this reflection is a low-intensity beam. As the eye is moved in different directions, the control device is activated. The mechanism can be used to control battery-powered wheelchairs, turn pages, position and reposition beds, answer telephones, activate self-feeding devices, control fans or heaters, and, in general, give paralyzed persons greater control over their environment.

The *nasal airflow meter* offers an impressively accurate measuring system for assessing inappropriate nasal emission in children with clefts of the palate. Heretofore, it has been virtually impossible to evaluate accurately the nasal airflow in such children because all of the available procedures altered normal nasal emission. This NASA-built device makes use of heated thermometers that rest beneath the person's nostrils. The temperature of the thermometers is changed as a result of the person's nasal airflow, and thus allows for inexpensive but effective evaluation. By attaching meters to each of the thermometers, the individual can observe the degree of nasal emission as various sounds are made and thus seek to reduce the airflow through successive practice sessions.

Although cosmetic prostheses have been constructed for centuries, it has been only since World War II that major advances have been made in materials and fabrication. Indeed, only in the last decade have prosthetists learned how to handle effectively the new vinyls, acrylics, and silicone rubber in a way that allows for naturalness in the appearance of face, hand, or body prostheses. Realistic face and body restoration in plastics is truly an art in spite of the amazing array of new materials. The construction of a hand, an eyelid, a breast, an ear, a nose, or a limb equalizer requires enormous artistic skill, time, patience, and experience on the part of the prosthetist.

A wide range of powered limb protheses has been developed. Elaborate control mechanisms of various forms have been designed to allow an amputee to perform a very complex series of tasks ranging from those that necessitate the greatest degree of delicacy to activities that require the operation of heavy and complex machines and tools. People who have been unable to function in such ways now have the potential for controlling many aspects of their surroundings in ways they never would have considered possible.

MINIMIZING ACCESS BARRIERS

We have repeatedly made the point that a handicap does not reside in the individual, but rather is the result of the interaction of the person with the environment. This consideration is most crucial when we are discussing the nature of public architecture, transportation, and other aspects of community design. Characteristics of public facilities can be so handicapping that no amount of education, training, or therapy can surmount the obstacles. In other words, handicaps cannot be minimized simply by focus on the handicapped

TABLE 11-1   PROVIDING AN ENVIRONMENT WITHOUT BARRIERS

Barriers to Movement	Recommendations
Doors	Sufficient depth between inner and outer doors to prevent wheelchair from being trapped
	Adequate clear opening for all doors
	Light pressure to open
	Easily gripped and well-placed handles
	Protected windows in all swinging doors
Passageways	Sufficient width (minimum of 5 feet)
	Minimum slope
	Nonslip surface
	No steps, or at least one pathway without steps connecting vital facilities
	Adequate lighting
Stairways	Low risers, without projecting nosings
	Nonslip treads
	Well-placed handrails on both sides
	Landings of contrasting color and texture
	Adequate lighting
Elevators	Controls accessible from sitting position
	Cab size to accommodate wheelchair
	Elevator and building floors meet exactly at stops
	Doors equipped with sensor to prevent premature closing

Barriers to Use of Facilities	Recommendations
Drinking fountains	Location and height for easy use
	Controls located at front
Telephones	Location and height to accommodate wheelchairs
Vending machines	Convenient controls, easy operating tension
Toilets	At least one conveniently accessible for each major area or floor
	At least one stall large enough for a wheelchair, with doors opening out
	Grab bars on both walls of stall
Sinks	Unobstructed space below, to permit room for legs
	Faucets easy to operate
Floor, room identification	Raised symbols conveniently located for use by visually limited
Miscellaneous	Convenient placement of light switches
	Warning signals should be both auditory and visual
	Special parking facilities nearby

person; in addition, we must prosthetize critical aspects of the public environment. What good is vocational training if the person cannot get to work? Of what consequence are programs for incentive and motivation for building strong and worthwhile personal goals if the individual is thwarted at every attempt to achieve some measure of independence in an environment that is oblivious to anyone but the "average," ablebodied person? Teachers, rehabilitation counselors, physicians, and therapists may all do an excellent job, but their efforts can be frustrated by community barriers—in architecture, in transportation, and elsewhere—that restrict or preclude access by millions of individuals to opportunities for a fuller life.

Imagine, for a moment, the problems you would face in going to work, getting on the subway or bus, visiting the library, or just going to the shopping center if you required the use of a wheelchair. In the absence of a ramp or an elevator, even one step can bring your attempts to a dead end. Doorways are too narrow; public restrooms will not accommodate your wheelchair; you cannot get into the telephone booth; taking a bus is almost impossible; water fountains are inaccessible—there is little reinforcement, but much punishment, for your attempts to function independently. Such barriers to independence do not operate exclusively against the wheelchair-bound citizen. The dim lighting, lack of shelters at bus stops, and long flights of stairs prevalent in public settings produce enormous impediments for the aging, the sensorily limited, persons with heart conditions, and millions of people with temporary limitations.

The environmental defects that produce handicaps are manifested most dramatically in the area of employment. Seventy-one percent of the nondisabled population (between the ages of 17 to 64) are employed, compared with only 36 percent of the disabled population (U.S. Department of Transportation, 1970, p. 19). Fortunately, something can and is beginning to be done about the grossly unequal opportunities perpetuated by our handicapping public facilities. In 1959, architects, businessmen, community leaders, and legislators organized a sectional committee of the American Standards Association (ASA) devoted to the study of the restrictive effects of public facilities. The efforts of this committee resulted in the approval and publication of the "American National Standard Specifications for Making Buildings and Facilities Accessible to, and Usable by, the Physically Handicapped, A117.1-1961" (American National Standards Institute, Inc., 1961).

The standards of this report, along with other recommendations, have been incorporated and detailed in the more recent report of the USA Standards Institute (summarized by Hilleary, 1970).

A summary of the recommendations for a "barrier-free" environment is provided in Table 11-1.

CONCLUSION

The examples of technical aids that we have presented in this chapter are but a very small sample of a large number of prostheses that are currently available or under development. As mentioned earlier, the rate, type, and volume of improvement in this field have increased during the last decade to an unprecedented level. Most of the devices we have illustrated and described have been developed after extended research. Some have appeared as a result of an immediate need, were developed on the basis of a local prototype, and eventually found their way into the commercial market. Our desire has not been to overwhelm you with the fruits of great technical and scientific achievements. Rather, you should be aware of these achievements while not losing sight of some of the practical, more common and ordinary devices that you can use within a special education setting to facilitate self-sufficiency and higher levels of accomplishment on the part of exceptional children. For example, teachers should intentionally look for opportunities to make use of technical devices such as low-vision aids, tape-recording and playback systems, overhead projectors, teaching machines, slide projectors, talking books, and other forms of instructional systems.

As a final comment on the content of this chapter, we emphasize the importance in not losing sight of the need to fade out prostheses or technical aids or both whenever feasible and to as great an extent as possible. With the exception of those protheses that are cosmetic, other devices will tend to call the attention of others to the disability and to the individual's functional inadequacies. Walkers, for example, are a stimulus or signal to others that the person is "disabled." When possible, the concept of fading can be implemented here by slowly altering the characteristics of walkers so that the individual is less and less dependent on the apparatus. Gradually, the person may be shifted to crutches, then to canes, and eventually relinquish dependence on these forms of aid. The same general principle of fading by successive approximations to a normal environment should be viewed as a primary goal for special educators whatever the type of prosthesis used.

12

SETTINGS FOR SPECIAL EDUCATION

STUDY TARGETS

1 In a short paragraph, summarize the principal components of the concept of "normalization."

2 Provide at least two illustrations of fading contrived, "special" arrangements, and shifting to more normal arrangements. Consider concomitant alterations in personal and environmental prostheses or arrangements.

3 State the arguments for social integration of the handicapped with the non-handicapped community.

4 Develop a chart, list, or other means to organize the series of reasons related to the emphasis away from special, segregated classes and toward integration within normal classrooms for exceptional children.

5 Outline and describe the major levels of the "special education service cascade system."

6 Compare and contrast a resource-room program with a special-school program with respect to benefits and disadvantages of each for children of varying characteristics.

7 List the factors to be considered in designing or remodeling a physical facility for use by exceptional children and related staff.

The environment within which the special education program is delivered is of utmost importance. Subsequent to the identification of the relevant educational characteristics of the child and the kind of instructional setting that will predictably lead the child to gain the skills considered to be appropriate, a decision must be made as to where, within existing instructional resources, the child should be assigned. A match is needed between what the child needs instructionally and what programs are available. Deciding on the needed types of personal and environmental arrangements for a child to allow him to function within a more normal context is at the heart of the placement issue in special education and rehabilitation. This chapter will consider three issues that impinge on the assignment of children to special education settings: (1) the concept of normalization as it pertains to placement; (2) the variety of placement alternatives and the advantages and disadvantages of each; and (3) the kinds of prosthetic designs characteristic of various physical facilities used by exceptional individuals.

MAXIMIZING NORMALIZATION

We have suggested that special educators have responsibility for providing appropriate and necessary arrangements for the child and his environment in order to enhance the child's level of functioning. Essentially this means building progressively more normal behavior. But we want to emphasize that the issue of maximizing normalization is more involved than simply focusing on how normal a child's performance or behavior is at any moment. To illustrate the complexity of the situation, for example, Wolfensberger defines the principle of normalization as "utilization of means which are as culturally normative as possible, in order to establish and/or maintain personal behaviors and characteristics which are as culturally normative as possible" (1972, p. 28).

Considering this definition within the context of the philosophy expressed in this text concerning exceptional children and the assumptions we have made about educational programing, Figure 12-1 serves to interrelate many of the central concepts. The model shown in Figure 12-1 has two clusters of factors. At level I we have simply restated the proposition that a person interacting with his environments (here called "antecedent factors") results in some response (labeled "behavior"), which subsequently results in reinforcement of some variety. Of course, we would anticipate an increase or decrease in the future behavior depending on whether the consequences were reinforcing or aversive and whether they were added or removed. We have further suggested that it is possible to discern broadly qualitative and quantitative differences among responses. These will be illustrated shortly.

Level II attempts to reflect the degree of usualness from extremely atypical (labeled "A") to very typical, natural, or normal (labeled "G"). These degrees, we believe, are pertinent in each of the major dimensions listed in level I. Each person has different requirements for special arrangements, prostheses, and so on, according to the extent and degree of deviation. Herb, who needs glasses,

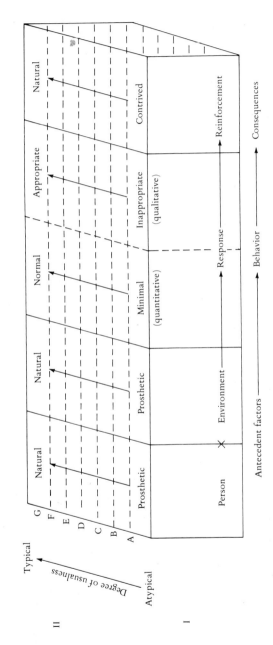

FIGURE 12-1 The interrelationship of factors related to normalization.

an artificial arm and leg, and a hearing aid, has unusual prosthetic needs in contrast to other individuals. His extreme needs might result in his being classified at the "B" degree of usualness. Less severe prosthetic needs would be assigned to one of the categories closer to the typical or more natural circumstances. This same perspective can be related to the environmental category. We have already discussed the notion of prosthetizing the environment to varying degrees according to an individual child's instructional requirements. A highly prosthetic environment might be illustrated by a special classroom for blind children in which numerous alterations have to be made to promote progressively more appropriate behavior.

We believe that it is possible to discern two characteristics of responses, i.e., quantitative and qualitative. In the first instance (quantitative), it is suggested that one's response might range from minimal to normal. To the question, "How are you today?" a child might respond, "Okay," or at the other extreme, "Fine, thank you; how are you?" Both are appropriate responses; one is minimal, and the other is quite normal. To the same question, another child might answer, "Mashed potatoes," an obviously inappropriate response. The response "Fine, thank you; how are you?" is qualitatively as well as quantitatively appropriate.

Finally, in terms of the diagram, we have suggested that differences exist in the degree of usualness of the reinforcer, or consequences of a behavior, that is used. At the lower end, there are a host of contrived, relatively unnatural reinforcers that are used with persons as a way of strengthening or decreasing behavior. Candies, trinkets, tokens, gold stars, and other types of tangible objects might fit into the "contrived" category if the setting within which they are used and the dispensing procedures fall outside of the usual classroom routines. At the other end of this continuum are the host of "natural" reinforcers one uses to control behavior—a simple touch, a kind word, and a frown fall into this category if they are used in a natural, intermittent way.

Now that you have been introduced to this model, we will discuss the implications it has for the concept of normalization. First and foremost, we want every exceptional person (whatever his type and level of disability or handicap) to respond to his environment (i.e., behave) in a fashion that approximates normal and appropriate behavior within his cultural context. As the child learns to behave in a progressively more normal and appropriate fashion, it may well be necessary to provide him with certain types of prostheses, to prosthetize his instructional environment to facilitate more typical behavior, and to provide reinforcers that are to some extent unnatural or contrived. In short, we should be willing to provide whatever prostheses and unnatural consequences are necessary to maximize the youngster's repertoire in the direction of normality.

As an example, suppose we were interested in helping Gloria learn to follow directions that are given orally but that require movement on her part. Assume that she has some motor problems and a significant visual defect. Our goal for her is that she follow directions that increasingly approach what is broadly viewed in the schools as normal and appropriate. To aid her in achieving this normal level of functioning we may find it necessary to get glasses for her and perhaps some type of apparatus to aid her in getting about. These are illustrations of personal prostheses. It may also be essential for us to create an environment that will help Gloria toward more normal and appropriate behavior in following directions. A special ramp, carpets on the floor, a room with much open space and with desks and equipment that are secured to the floor, or frosted window glass might be used to minimize the negative consequences of her environment and foster the acquisition of more normal and appropriate behavior. And finally, we may have to begin our instructional program with Gloria by providing prosthetic motivational arrangements, e.g., immediate, continuous, and tangible reinforcers as she begins to develop skills in the target area. Later, as the tasks are accomplished, we may be able to restructure the type and delivery of the reinforcers. Helen, another girl with the same group of problems, may need a more intensively prosthetic environment than Gloria but fewer personal prostheses in order to acquire the same group of competencies.

We are saying, then, that the primary factor in fostering normalization is concern for the individual. We must do all that is necessary to encourage normal and appropriate behavior within the child's cultural context. Do not lose sight of the fact that as behaviors change and situations vary, you will need to reconsider the types of alterations required to maintain and upgrade the skills that have been established.

Notice, however, that although Wolfensberger's definition of normalization speaks about fostering behavior that is as normal as possible within a given cultural setting, the first part of his definition stresses that the means that are used to establish and encourage this behavior should be as culturally normal as possible. This issue is highly relevant to special education, although often overlooked. To normalize certainly means to focus on behavior, but you must also consider the implications of the atypical procedures that you must use in trying to normalize behavior. In most cultures it is unnatural and not normal for a person to have certain types of obvious prostheses, to operate within a somewhat artificial environment, or to be constantly reinforced with tangible objects following a behavior. These abnormalities, individually and collectively, can call attention to the exceptional person, result in a negative attitude toward him on the part of others, and ultimately cause drops in his performance, lowered self-esteem, or abnormal behavior. And so, normalization ultimately means that special educators and other professional workers must strive to reduce the atypical character of the visible prostheses (both on the person and in his environment) by slowly and meticulously moving in the direction of a natural and normal situation *without appreciably compromising their goals or allowing regression to earlier levels of performance to take place.* Further, the concept of normalization also suggests that the reinforcement program (types and procedures of delivery) must gradually, but systematically, move toward a natural, more typical situation. The more contrived and prosthetic, the less normal the situation will be.

We believe that it is safe to conclude that in most cases normalization of exceptional children will not occur spontaneously or without planned programing. Also, we advance the proposition that from every point of view one cannot help but subscribe to the notion that providing normal experiences and fostering normal and appropriate behavior by exceptional children are primary objectives for special education, for other professional specialities, and for the whole of society. Given this statement of purpose, among our earliest considerations is how best to foster normalization among those with prominent and debilitating exceptionalities. We have spoken in generalities here and in previous sections of this book about some possible ways of dealing with this problem; now, what specific suggestions can be advanced to move in the direction of satisfying this goal? Of course, we must assume that the organization and the person responsible for the program of intervention or management are committed to the propositions we have advanced; this is fundamental. Normalization, in every sense of the word, can be accomplished to the greatest extent by the complete physical and social integration of the exceptional individual into the normal environment. Although you cannot legislate complete integration, because physical integration of exceptional children does not necessarily mean an acceptable level of social integration with normal youngsters, integration is probably the single most important factor in increasing the probability of complete normalization. Ultimately, integration can be said to have occurred when an exceptional individual lives with members of his cultural group in a normal domicile within the community, when he has access to all of the privileges and services that are available to others, when he has the respect of his fellow citizens, and when he is accepted unreservedly by his peers and other persons in his culture. In order for this to occur, physical integration is a necessary, but certainly not sufficient condition.

Wolfensberger (1972) has suggested four factors in the physical integration of a facility and, ultimately, of an exceptional person into the community:

1 The services needed by an exceptional person should be located in the community, so that the individual can be provided for within a normal and natural context. Isolation is to be avoided in every instance.
2 The services to be provided should fit into the appropriate area, i.e., halfway houses ought to be in residential areas and sheltered workshops should be in industrial settings.
3 Transportation should be readily available between all of the components of the system.
4 The exceptional persons in a community should be organized and provided for in such a way that they can become amalgamated or absorbed into the total fabric of the community. Normalization will not occur if exceptional individuals tend to cluster, group, or become congregated. This principle

strongly suggests the wisdom in diversifying services throughout the community, supporting the use of small residential centers as opposed to large institutions, and providing services to all members of the community within the same facility.

The social integration of the exceptional person into the community depends on a number of factors, two of which have already been mentioned: (1) the attitudes of the members of the community concerning the value of all human beings and their rightful place in society, and the attitudes of the members of the community toward integration of the handicapped into the

Children's attitudes toward school can be improved by the provision of after-school recreational activities within the educational facilities.

community; and (2) the extent to which physical integration of services has been realized according to these attitudes. Again, Wolfensberger (1972) has indicated a number of steps that can be taken to maximize the likelihood of social integration. These relate directly to the whole issue of special education settings and the assignment or placement of exceptional children.

How a program or service is labeled will in a large way dictate how the consumers of the services are viewed and accepted by all facets of the community. If a school, workshop, residence, school bus, or recreation center is identified, even in the most subtle way, as a facility for the retarded, handicapped, atypical, or deviant, you can be sure that the community will not allow social integration of the exceptional individuals to take place. People will simply perceive the consumers, and the place, as deviant and to be avoided. The building should not be "set apart," by either location or architecture. You can also avoid social isolation by programing services for exceptional individuals within the context of services provided for all citizens within the community. Educational programs for exceptional children, for the good of all, should be located within the usual school facility with ample opportunities provided for personal interaction among all who use the facility.

When the physical and social integration of exceptional children into the community is made possible, when appropriate prostheses are provided for the person and for his environment, and when the process of integration is continually monitored and revised, numerous benefits related to normalization can be expected to accrue. The most prominent of such benefits include:

1 Members of the community begin to learn tolerance for those with deviations, they relate to exceptional individuals with increased frequency and commitment, they learn of the important contributions that each person can make to the advantage of all, and they become more willing to participate in the various aspects of community life. Respect for all is encouraged.

2 Interaction with the normal public provides the exceptional person with opportunities to:
   a learn acceptable behavior within a natural social context;
   b practice making responses to actual problems and issues within a meaningful social context;
   c learn to tolerate differences in performance, attitudes, appearance, interest, and aptitudes of others;
   d learn to accept themselves when they see that others accept them.

3 Integration promotes equal treatment and services for all citizens whenever needed.

4 It minimizes the possibility that the exceptional person will be placed in an atypical environment and managed by deviant individuals who frequently serve to exacerbate the exceptionalities of all parties, i.e., the consumer, the worker, and the institution.

5 Integration is prophylactic because of the important function it serves in

preventing, and sometimes reversing, exceptionalities that are the result of physical and social isolation from the community.

6 It reduces the possibility that the exceptional person will be blamed for his deviant performance by correctly placing the responsibility for enhancing the functional level of all citizens on the citizens themselves. Individual scapegoating is minimized.

7 Integration is completely compatible with the entire philosophy of habilitation and rehabilitation. Neither can be realized without physical and social integration.

8 It signals the end of an era when the community felt obliged to provide separate services to separate groups who were classified according to artificial criteria. With an integrated system, it would no longer be logical, or compatible with the philosophy of the approach, to have separate community counseling programs, medical services, or fund-raising drives for each of the many types of exceptionalities represented in the community (including the gifted or normal).

9 Integration is not only functionally efficient, but has multiple advantages from a cost-benefit point of view.

10 It suggests that the fundamental principles involved in identifying, understanding, and effectively managing the problems of humans (as well as the principles underlying the provision of human services) are appropriate for all types of people and their problems and needs.

ALTERNATIVES IN EDUCATIONAL PLACEMENT

Only since the late 1960s have educators become especially concerned about normalization in their assignment of exceptional children for special education. Before then special educators seemed to be more concerned about providing an instructional setting that would serve to maximize the academic performances of children with educational problems and that at the same time would be reasonably economical for school systems through the coordination and centralization of services. To these ends, then, during the post-World War II era most special education programs were developed with the belief that special schools and special education classes within regular schools could best serve both the children and the schools. Additionally, the belief prevailed, although without adequate theoretical or empirical support, that placing exceptional children apart from other youngsters would promote more rapid acquisition of skills, satisfy parents of exceptional children that the schools were providing an appropriate program of instruction for their children, and provide an environment in which instruction could be delivered efficiently by a teacher who allegedly possessed special skills and special understanding of the educational needs of exceptional children—and all of this at no apparent expense to the children in the regular classes or their teachers.

This organizational plan for the delivery of education to exceptional children quickly became instituted throughout the country and was supported by practitioners, academicians, school administrators, parents, psychologists, national organizations, and various funding agencies. This plan became tradition, the deficiencies were virtually overlooked or ignored, and a relative sense of satisfaction and accomplishment became evident among special educators. Regular educators felt good about it too, because many of their nagging and most recalcitrant instructional problems were ostensibly being taken care of. The schools were now providing for children who could "profit" from special educational programing. Presumably, those who were not enrolled in either special schools or special classes could not be helped through this unique instructional intervention and, thus, should be excluded. Further, it was argued in certain quarters that public education did not have the responsibility to "train" or to "educate" the "uneducable." This belief resulted in systematic exclusion, suspension, and excusing of children on bases that were arbitrary, and many public institutions for the mentally retarded and mentally ill chose not to provide educational programs because their "patients" were viewed as being "uneducable."

Sporadically, questions were raised about the wisdom of cloistering children in educational facilities away from their normal peers very early in the development of this practice. However, the issue received special attention when it was revealed that children who were adjudged mentally retarded did no better academically when placed in special classes than if left in a regular class program (Cassidy and Stanton, 1959; Mullen and Itkin, 1961; Thurstone, 1960). Immediately the ardent separatists took exception to the conclusions of these studies by noting the potential weaknesses in the design of this research, emphasizing that one should not look at academic progress alone in conducting such an assessment, and that wide discrepancies between the performance of exceptional children and normal children could only lead to rejection and further academic and psychosocial difficulties for the exceptional children who were not placed in special classes (Engel, 1969; Harvey, 1969; Kidd, 1970).

Attempts were subsequently made to conduct efficacy studies, which used control groups to eliminate the potential contaminating influences not considered in the earlier research, on the programing of special versus regular classes for the mildly mentally retarded (Goldstein, Moss, and Jordan, 1965). Basically the findings suggested that at the end of their fourth year of schooling the groups did not differ in measures of intellectual performance, academic achievement, and social knowledge. The validity of the conclusions that were reached in this study was itself called into question (Guskin and Spicker, 1968), and the arguments for and against placement in special classes versus regular classes go on and on (Blatt, 1960; Christoplos and Renz, 1969; Heber and Dever, 1970; Dunn, 1968; Johnson, 1962; Jones, 1971; Kolstoe, 1972; Mac-Millan, 1972; Meyerowitz, 1962; Sparks and Younie, 1969).

During the latter period of the debates over the efficacy of placement of exceptional children in special classes, a number of events caused a relatively rapid reassessment of the philosophical bases for special education. Along with the uncertainty about the value of school systems that offered only special schools or special classes or only regular class instruction, other reasons for the self-appraisal (especially as it pertained to the delivery of special education services) included:

1 Realization that isolation from any or all components of society (and other forms of management which are contrary to the fundamental principles of normalization) not only is legally wrong but restricts the development of a person in many areas.

2 Concern about the unreliable and questionable bases on which children were identified as exceptional and were subsequently placed in special schools or classrooms without adequate justification or documentation.

3 Proof that many exceptionalities can be prevented, that their consequences can be minimized and managed without special equipment or unique settings, and that many of the methods which had been viewed as confined to the domain of specially trained teachers could be fully implemented with equal effectiveness by teachers of regular classes.

4 Belief that the community not only is required to provide instruction for the exceptional child, but that its members should understand and interact with exceptional children, i.e., learn about them. It was thought that this type of reciprocity should extend to all levels of society and that special education should be linked with all phases of the regular education systems.

5 Increased concern about and pressure by parents whose children were excluded from school, for reasons which in many cases were arbitrary and in spite of the clear suggestions in the literature that children with similar disorders could be helped.

6 A switch in emphasis by educators from organic manifestations, etiological patterns, and unique syndromes to observable and measurable problems which are responsive to instructional intervention.

7 Demands by funding agencies for documented reports of results from recipients of funds for special education.

8 Dissatisfaction with the segmentation of services (in both organization and delivery), with the lack of articulation and the loss of effectiveness because of this segmentation, and with the tremendous waste of resources that attends programs that lack comprehensiveness.

9 Belief that all children should be provided a free public school education and have equal access to a full range of resources.

10 Realization that the educational system can and should support more than the simple alternatives of special or regular classes, and that a continuum of education programing should be provided and children assigned at any moment in time according to the degree to which they require special arrangements.

11 Cognizance that special education classes differ, that it is a distortion of reality to assume that special classes and regular classes can be fairly compared because of the multiple variables on which each differs within

its separate category, that the behavior of the special education teacher within the classroom is of more fundamental significance than the administrative organization, and that the field has not yet identified or agreed upon what skills are required in a competent teacher of exceptional children.

DENO'S MODEL FOR SPECIAL EDUCATION SERVICES

Deno (1970, 1971) and her colleague Reynolds (1971) have suggested a realistic educational framework in which instructional services for exceptional children might be efficiently and effectively organized, administered, and delivered. Dunn (1973) has elaborated on Deno's basic model. Fundamentally, Deno's model for special education services suggests a continuum of settings within which specific instructional programing is emphasized at each level. Presumably, there is more commonality within each level of this continuum than among the various levels. As Figure 12-2 indicates, the degree to which the environment is structured differs among the levels, with the greatest degree of special prostheses at level 7 and a decrease in the number, types, and complexity of special environmental arrangements as one moves toward level 1. Moreover, in complete agreement with our concept of normalization and the desirability of reducing unusualness in all phases of the behavior process, as described in Figure 12-2 the Deno model clearly emphasizes (1) that relatively fewer youngsters will be found at each succeeding level as one progresses from level 1 to level 7; (2) that children should not be moved downward in the system unless it is absolutely necessary and clear documentation is available to warrant such a move; and (3) that each child should be moved upward in the system as far and as quickly as possible. In the following sections we very briefly highlight the unique characteristics of each of the levels in the system.

Level 1—regular class assignment

At this most integrated level, children attend the regular classes with other youngsters of the same age. Because they may have functional disorders of various types and degrees, the children may require adjustments in their environment that exceed the usual demands of their peers. An extra-large desk, more space, a ramp into the classroom, a stairway elevator, an amplification system, unique instructional materials, a braille writer, low-vision aids, a special type of chair, modifications in curricular targets, and slight alterations in instructional procedures all illustrate the kinds of supportive services that will most often be found in the level 1 classes. In addition, however, regular class teachers may have need to consult with someone within or outside the schools in an effort to gain some insight into a special problem pertaining to a child. Consultation with an educational diagnostician, special resource teacher, supervisor, reading consultant, or school psychologist should take place with whatever frequency is necessary to secure information which will lead to a more advantageous instructional environment for the child in question.

The key to success for an exceptional child located in a regular classroom is, of course, the teacher. Among the attributes of the teacher which will help to guarantee that a child placed in the regular classroom will have a pleasant and successful experience are:

1 The teacher's judgment of the child's capacity for progress, the teacher's attitude toward having exceptional children in the classroom with other students, and the way in which he or she acts and reacts toward the child.
2 The procedures the teacher uses in forecasting and dealing with the inevitable problems of peer acceptance that will occur between the exceptional child and other youngsters.
3 The efforts of the teacher to maintain as reasonable and normal an environ-

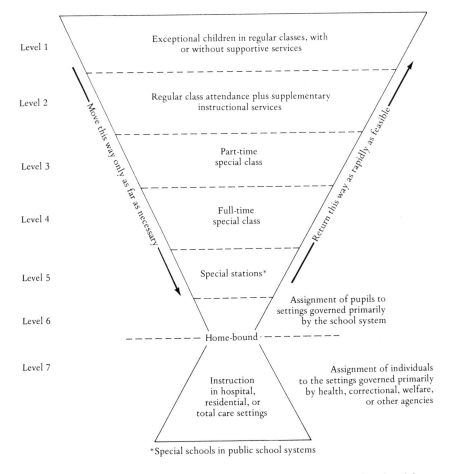

FIGURE 12-2 The "cascade" system of special education service. Reprinted from Deno, E. Special education as developmental capital. *Exceptional Children*, 1970, **37**, 229–237. By permission of The Council for Exceptional Children.

ment for the exceptional student while providing the necessary circumstances to facilitate increased levels of functioning on the child's part.

4 The skill with which the teacher is able to deal with the emotional behavior and problems of the exceptional child as a result of his not being able to compete with other youngsters in certain areas he considers to be important. In like manner, the teacher will need to be aware of and skillful in handling the jealousy of other students when the teacher must give special attention to the exceptional youngster.

You can see that the regular class teacher has a very awesome responsibility when his or her classroom contains an exceptional child. In addition to the teaching of routine academic skills, the teacher has to confront a very difficult social situation that has a host of ramifications. She or he must deal with the issues forthrightly, seek to maintain a mentally and socially healthy environment, and be alert to potential problems that could serve to undermine the entire program and ruin the school year. In preparation for the inevitable return of certain exceptional children to regular classrooms, teachers in service and students in training to become regular classroom teachers are enrolling in special education courses and methods workshops to become better prepared and experienced in how to deal effectively with this range of responsibilities. It is clearly important to recognize that not every teacher can or should be expected to accept an exceptional child in a regular class. Teachers who do not believe exceptional children can profit from the experience or feel that their efforts in behalf of the exceptional child will be fruitless will get what they expect. The child will be penalized, and reassignment of the youngster to another classroom is definitely indicated.

Level 2—regular class assignment with supplementary instructional services

This program option has become quite popular in the United States as a way of dealing with the instructional needs of children who exhibit mild disorders in functioning. The children have their homeroom in a regular class and they remain in that class for most of the day, but certain portions of their instruction are provided in a resource room, which is usually located within the same school building. A trained specialist or resource-room teacher delivers pertinent instructional programing to each child or to groups of children. As soon as the lesson has been completed, the child returns to the regular classroom. The specialties of the resource-room teacher may vary according to the instructional needs of the children within a given school. To a lesser degree than a resource-room teacher who is located in a specific school, reading specialists, speech therapists, or counselors could be viewed as itinerant resource-room specialists or consultants.

Whatever the programing configuration a school decides upon, the whole idea behind this plan is to allow exceptional children to receive as much instruction in the regular program as possible but to provide effectively for their individual educational needs in those areas of major deviation without calling undue attention to the discrepancy. Note that assignment to instruction by the resource-room specialist is based on performance discrepancies and not on IQ, which was used so often in the past. Thus, at any moment during a school day, children with a wide range of disabilities or disorders may well be receiving instruction at the same time, and in an identical way, if their functional level and instructional needs are the same.

Since most resource-room teachers are trained as specialists in the assessment and remediation of recalcitrant instructional difficulties of various forms, the regular class teachers in the school will frequently find it helpful to seek their counsel regarding possible alternative approaches for use in dealing with the functional deviations that occur from time to time. At the very least the resource-room and regular class teachers should share ideas and approaches that pertain to the children for whom they have mutual responsibility. In every instance, agreement should be reached by all parties involved in providing instruction to a child before and continuously throughout the program. Accurate data on performance should be maintained in all settings, the consequences of the child's performing should be coordinated among the various teachers and instructional settings, and alterations in the goals or procedures or both should be discussed and agreed upon by all. Do not assume that adequate coordination will occur spontaneously—the resource-room teacher should usually take the leadership in effecting productive relationships between himself or herself and other teachers.

Level 3—part-time special class

There are certain children in every school system whose educational problems require an instructional setting that is highly prosthetized. When this need is evident for a youngster across several major subject areas, when the complexity of the problem exceeds the expertise of the regular instructional staff, when the magnitude of the instructional need exceeds the normal capabilities of the resource room, or when all three of these circumstances exist, the child may be a likely candidate for, at the very least, a part-time special class. The remaining portion of the school day might be spent in either the regular class or in a resource room.

The characteristics of a part-time special class will differ dramatically among school districts, and even within a given school system from one moment to the next, according to the unique population of children and their needs. It is certainly hazardous for an administrator to plan for a certain number of part-time special classes (and whatever unique orientation each might have) without knowing a great deal about which children might best be served in this type of setting. Moreover, and we say this with the greatest of emphasis, special education classes (and other types of classes as well) are widely disparate and are certainly not comparable because of the great differences that exist among teachers in their philosophy, talents, orientation, approach, attitudes, cooperativeness, and so on. In practice, then, not only must a special education administrator be skilled in assigning children to the setting in which maximum benefits will accrue, but it is essential that teachers be matched to settings according to their unique skills and interests. This is best exemplified in a part-time special class program in which one teacher might specialize in language arts, another specialize in social and occupational instruction, and still another teacher focus on the development of motor and mobility skills. Large school systems can usually afford specialization of this sort. From year to year the character of the part-time special classes will change according to the children's needs and the teacher's skills.

Level 4—full-time special class

School personnel are justifiably hesitant to assign children arbitrarily to full-time special education classrooms because of the possible serious consequences. Some of these have been alluded to in earlier sections of this book; the most obvious is that in many school systems children who are assigned to special classes are left there without ever being considered for an alternate placement. Then, of course, there is the problem that special classes do not provide an adequate level of integration with other segments of the school and community to foster normalization. It is difficult to conceive of a child's being able to function appropriately in an environment that is totally different from his environment during periods of training. This is one of the major hazards of a full-time special education class.

Yet, there are certain groups of children who are so disabled or handicapped that a very comprehensive prosthetic environment must be provided in order to increase their functional level in certain areas and decrease the frequency of undesirable behavior. Often these youngsters have significant multiple disorders with associated maladaptive social and emotional behavior that further exacerbates the problems. They may have school-related problems that are developmental as well as remedial.

Teachers in full-time special education classes must be highly skilled professional people. They deal with the most stubborn and resistant types of educational problems; even under the most propitious circumstances they can expect to encounter frustrations, minimal progress by the children, resistance from other teachers, questioning glances from parents, and only token support by school administrators. Too frequently children placed in full-time special classes are at the "court of last resort." In this case, the teacher becomes the child's advocate as well as his mentor. Teachers frequently find themselves in a situation of having to justify not only their program but the child's existence in school. And then, teachers are faced with providing a modicum of integration with other phases of the school program to foster as much of a normal experience for the children as possible. You can see, then, that full-time special education teachers are, or at least should be, among the most capable and effective professionals in the schools.

Level 5—special stations or special schools

There are a number of possibilities that could be included under level 5 in this system. Some school districts have special day schools for children with moderate, severe, or profound deviations. In certain districts the special school is used to parallel the full-time special class setting, with, for example, all trainable retarded children being placed in the special school and the mildly retarded assigned to special classes. Obviously this type of arbitrary assignment is unjustifiable: not only does it militate against normalization, but every child should be assigned according to his functional level and the most appropriate prosthetic situation. Assignment by clinical syndrome, IQ level, or degree of cosmetic excellence are all inappropriate criteria in deciding on the best educational setting for a child.

It is most unfortunate to observe large school systems, county programs, or intermediate units that years ago decided to deliver special education services for *all* exceptional children through special schools. There are numerous programs of this variety in the United States, and they are very efficient in terms of centralizing services, but they are also very isolated and provide an extraordinarily abnormal, unnatural, and biased instructional environment for children who are and will continue to be members of the community. Some school directors, following World War II and into the 1950s, decided to pool their capital resources and develop a network of special schools, which, quite naturally, are here to stay. The result has been a continuation of the special school plan in those school districts: because the buildings exist, it is most difficult to change the programs regardless of the prevailing mood of the school personnel or the state of contemporary thought or research on the matter.

At the same time, it should be emphasized that special schools for certain types of functional disorders are usually highly appropriate for specific children. For example, the City of Baltimore has an outstanding school for children with serious orthopedic disorders. Comprehensive therapy, as well as educational programs, is offered by a neighboring regular school program. Youngsters are usually assigned to the special school on a temporary basis and they are reassessed periodically from medical, social, psychological, and educational perspectives. At the appropriate time the children are moved into other, more normal types of instructional settings.

The Pittsburgh Schools have a special station within a psychiatric center for children who need intensive therapy at particular stages in their school career. A team of medical, behavioral, and educational specialists work with each child and the family in a form of crisis intervention. The youngsters attend the center until the therapists believe return to a more normal setting is appropriate.

As mentioned earlier, the prosthetic character of a special station or special school is especially important. The teachers who are involved in the programs in these settings must learn to deal with extremely deviant behavior and very difficult problems. To that end, they are usually trained to employ powerful methods of behavior management, and most of them have had years of experience dealing with children who have multiple disorders. The teachers must be patient and tolerant of slow rates of behavioral change in their students, must not become upset by regression, and must approach their duties optimistically.

Level 6—homebound instruction

To an increasing degree, schools are legally required to provide free public education to all children, whatever their types of deviations or levels of functioning. This means that children who are unable to attend school and who are not residents of an institution or a residential center, but who stay at home, must have a school program brought to them. This is a very expensive type of instruction because of the relatively few children that a single teacher can adequately handle, the logistics involved in traveling from house to house, and the expensive equipment that each teacher of the homebound must have available.

There is often a problem with the caliber of instruction that is provided in the homebound program. Especially with older children whose level of performance in various subject areas is fairly mature, the child may know more about a subject than the teacher. This is somewhat restricting for the youngster and certainly a source of anxiety for the teacher. The problem becomes quite complex and significant when the teacher has children of various ages, levels of functioning, and diffuse interests, and who possess a variety of disorders. This is a clear reality, for there is a definite trend toward providing more homebound instruction for children with severe exceptionalities, youngsters who either had been excluded from public school programing or were institutionalized and not provided for educationally.

Level 7—institutional or residential assignment

The courts in many states have decreed that all children of school age must be provided with a free public school education. This means that schools have the mandate to plan and deliver educational programs to children who live in residential centers within the schools' community. Hence, departments of public welfare, which previously were responsible for providing special education to institutional residents, have been relieved of this duty, and the job of providing pertinent instructional programs became the job of departments of education. This change, naturally, caused some measure of trepidation (1) among institutional administrators because an outside agency was given responsibility for a service that had been within the institution's sphere of influence for decades; (2) among directors of education and training in institutions because they would now have to coordinate services with other clusters of professionals; (3) among teachers within institutions because the entire diagnosis of their students required by law would reveal how uninfluential their program of education and training had been over the years; and (4) among teachers in the community because they would now be responsible for educating groups of children about whom they had little knowledge and few of the skills required to formulate and deliver an effective instructional program.

You can see from the diagram of Deno's cascade system that this final level in the continuum of possible special education assignments is most segregated. The drawbacks are even more pronounced if the residential center is isolated from the major segments of the community, as is true of many institutions for the mentally retarded. The Swedish and Danish residential centers for exceptional individuals are exemplary models of the manner in which articulation can take place with all facets of the community. And once again, you see, we return to the thrust of the important theme that opened this chapter: the crucial need to promote normalization for all at every level.

The provision of these various levels of administrative programing is not the complete story for the establishment of a successful system. The exceptional children who are supported by a configuration such as has been suggested by Deno will be successful only according to (1) the administrators' ability to identify what kind of specific instructional focus can be delivered within each type of setting (and, indeed, each classroom within each category of placement); (2) the individual instructional strengths and interests of each teacher on the staff and the assignment of each to the kind of classroom which can be of greatest benefit to each child; (3) the accuracy with which each youngster's instructional needs have been assessed and his assignment to the appropriate level and classroom in the cascade system; and (4) the extent to which there is flexibility within the system and coordination among the various levels.

On the first issue, it is obvious that school systems will vary in the characteristics of the educational program and instructional procedures at each of the levels. A part-time special class will be different in its focus, in the skill of the teachers, and in the types of educational problems it can serve from one school system to the next. The administrator must be cognizant of such differences and decide what each class at every level can do best and which children will be most beneficially served.

Of course, as the second proviso above points out, the abilities, attitudes, and inclinations of each teacher should be appropriately matched with the setting. For example, resource-room teachers must first believe in the concept in order for it to work, but beyond that, these teachers must have keen diagnostic skills, must be competent in various forms of remedial education in almost all the basic subject areas, and must be capable of working with regular class teachers in a consultative role. Full-time special class instructors may not have to be highly skilled in educational measurement and diagnosis; one of their greatest attributes may be attitudinal, such as high tolerance for children who progress very slowly. In short, a matching of a teacher's attributes with the setting that will be mutually facilitating and lead to optimum progress of the student is vital to the success of a cascadelike approach.

We have devoted a great deal of attention to the need for accuracy, parsimony, and appropriateness in the evaluation of a child's educational performance and in his assignment to the most pertinent setting within those facilities that exist in a school system. This kind of match is as essential as that between a teacher's strengths and the type of classroom. Let us, then, move on the last issue: the need for flexibility in the levels of the cascade.

One of the unfortunate facts about special education has been that once a child is assigned to a special class, he tends to remain there throughout his school career. Often, the child and his parents have no recourse and no chance for due process. A cornerstone of the philosophy we have presented is that all children can do better than their present level suggests, that the main mission of education is to arrange the environment so that they do better, and that children should be moved intelligently through the various levels and stages. We have already indicated that normalization implies the fading out of contrived, special arrangements and the movement of a child toward more normal circumstances without compromise or regression of his behavior. A special school is more contrived (and abnormal) than a special class, a special class is more contrived than a part-time special class, and so on up the ladder. Remember, we must keep in mind the urgent need to move children to more normal environments as the situation allows.

To that end, we strongly support the belief that general entrance and exit criteria be developed by a school district for each of the different classrooms and among the various levels of the cascade system. Everyone should know what it takes to move up, including the child's parents. This issue is so crucial that it should not be left to chance. A physician may tell a patient that he can leave the hospital for placement in a more normal environment as soon as his temperature is normal for three successive days, his scar has healed, and the stitches have been removed, and when someone is around to bring him his meals. Then he moves to his own bedroom; other criteria are established for extending his movement to the whole second floor, and so on. This same plan is needed in order for the cascade system or any other system of pupil placement or ladder assignment to work effectively. The final thought on this issue is that specific criteria for the various levels probably cannot be transferred from one school system to another because of the variations among school systems in students' needs, teachers' characteristics, physical facilities, financial resources, and the number of levels of the cascade system that any one school district can reasonably support.

ARCHITECTURAL CONSIDERATIONS

Wolfensberger (1972) has aptly noted that the characteristics of a building imply certain attitudes and philosophies concerning (1) the role that those who are served by the building are expected to play; (2) the meaning of the building as perceived by outsiders; and (3) the purpose for which the building was designed (e.g., for the convenience of the community, the staff, the clients, or the architects, or as a monument to someone or some group of people). The architecture of any type of physical plant must be well considered. It must be forward-looking, for in most cases it is destined to last for years or even decades and should not be found in later years to be out of phase with contemporary thought. Essentially, many of the large institutions for the mentally retarded throughout the United States have become outdated.

Naturally, it is important that the architectural characteristics of a facility contain those prosthetic arrangements that will be required by the types of clients to be served. At the same time, it is unquestionable that the more a facility stands apart from its environment, the more likely it is that a negative connotation will be assigned to the facility as well as to the clients served. One can strive toward controlling the occurrence of such biasing by (1) not setting the facility apart from other similar forms of service in the community; (2) designing the structure so that it fits into the surroundings in a natural way; (3) not naming the facility for the types of people who are its clients; and (4) encouraging an open-door policy throughout periods of design, construction, and use.

We have stressed that the types and degree of environmental arrangements at each of the different levels of service must vary as do those illustrated by Deno's cascade system. This range of complexity, of course, is inextricably related to the needs of those who are being served. It is clear that the architecture and the types of furnishings that are contained in a facility, center, or classroom may be quite specialized. Therefore, they cannot be excluded from the planning if one desires maximum use and control of the instructional environment. The kind of special arrangements will differ greatly, depending mainly on the kinds of problems exhibited (e.g., blindness, deafness, or motor problems) and the types of behavior to be focused upon within the setting (e.g., social, mobility, speaking, academic, or vocational).

We will not review all of the nuances one must consider in designing a facility; suggestions on this subject have been reviewed in great depth in numerous publications (Abelson and Berenson, 1970; Abelson and Blacklow, 1971; Council for Exceptional Children, 1971; Cruickshank and Quay, 1970; Gordon, 1972; Gunzburg, 1972; Hoffman, 1970; Muller, 1970; Nellist, 1970; Wolf, 1968). Instead, we will simply summarize the areas to which an environmental designer must give attention as he or she seeks to provide an appropriate instructional setting. Again, the extent to which she or he must exhibit concern about any one or any combination of these dimensions is directly related to the prosthetic needs of the clientele and the mission of the facility.

When a new unit is being considered for construction, the following types of issues are relevant:

1 The degree to which the site is accessible to the center of community services and activities.
2 The extent to which the location is free from noise, dust, fumes, thick traffic, and other types of hazards.

3 The adequacy of transportation, natural amenities (e.g., plant life, water, open space), outdoor conveniences, schools, and recreation possibilities.
4 The local codes, ordinances, and zoning regulations that pertain to the construction and anticipated use of the facility.

When a new structure is being planned for construction and in instances in which an existing building, classroom, or residence is undergoing remodeling for use by exceptional children, the following factors (related to our discussion of public facilities in the preceding chapter) should be examined and programed into the unit when and where appropriate. The decisions one makes concerning each of these factors will in large measure be dependent on the kinds of activities that are expected to take place in each area, the number and types of youngsters to be served in the different settings, the kind of general atmosphere desired in the various sections of the unit (e.g., lively, cheerful, active, or sedate), and the flow of activities from one center to the others.

1 What kinds of space will be needed within each of the various subunits of the facility?
2 What kinds of interior surfaces will best serve the children and provide the most effective instructional setting? For example, the hearing-impaired will need a classroom in which the surfaces are soundproofed as much as possible, the visually limited a setting in which glare is minimized, and motor-disordered children a classroom in which surfaces are stable and skidproof.
3 What unique characteristics should be included in the facility to foster greater independence on the part of children? For example, specially constructed toileting areas, ramps and elevators, therapeutic pools, specially controlled areas for humidity and temperature, unique seating arrangements, or rooms which are electronically arranged for dealing with certain hearing and communication problems might need to be included in a unit.
4 To what extent should special lighting, acoustics, and climate control be considered?
5 What furniture and equipment will be required for the facility and to what extent and how will the unit have to be remodeled to accommodate this unique requirement?
6 In what manner will the staff's needs be considered within the context of the unit or facility? What unique requirements do they have in the preparation of materials of instruction?
7 If a food center, health room, professional offices, or community facility is required, in what manner will these needs be provided for and how can these various segments of the program articulate with the others?

These few questions are but a brief sample of the large number of concerns that professionals must consider in the planning, design, and development of a special education environment. To a very large extent, the question of developing a facility really boils down to issues that pertain mainly to its location, physical context, size, access, appearance, and internal design (Wolfensberger, 1972). When each of these major dimensions is considered fully in light of the concept of normalization, we could expect progress toward the serving of the instructional needs of exceptional children.

13

COMMUNITY
SERVICES
AND RESOURCES

STUDY TARGETS

1   Decide if you agree with any or all of the rights of citizens as proposed by the Scandinavian countries.
2   List the major types of agencies and several services provided by each.
3   Of the five conditions that determine service effectiveness, decide which one is of initial and paramount concern.
4   Describe the functions of the suggested coordinating unit for optimizing interagency services.

People with significant physical or functional disorders very often require services beyond the special education programing of the schools in order to progress toward normalization in all of its ramifications. Aside from the exceptional person and his family, few other members of the community recognize this need as much as special education teachers, supervisors, and administrators. In addition to the frequent paucity of needed comprehensive services and resources within reasonable distance of many communities, it is clear that those that exist are often poorly coordinated, are overwhelmed by paperwork problems and bureaucracy, and lack singularity of purpose. In fact, some communities' service agencies seem to operate at cross purposes with each other, duplicate efforts, and at times compete for clients and financial support from the citizenry. To an overwhelming extent, these conditions foster frustration among community leaders, divide the local and state resources in ways that are not conducive to optimum productivity, confuse potential clients and those who serve as referral agents, and generally lead to a diminution of professional effectiveness and community service. There are few who escape the grasp of such frustrations.

It is obvious that our society currently has the scientific, managerial, and fiscal capabilities to design and deliver an excellent program of community services and resources to all who are in need. Other countries, notably Denmark and Sweden, have provided excellent prototypes of the provision, organization, and delivery of various forms of community services. It is instructive, we believe, to recognize the beliefs that underlie the provision of an integrated plan such as those of these Scandinavian countries, since such a plan requires an enormous expenditure of personal resources.

Basically, at the outset Denmark and Sweden affirmed the proposition that "all of the human family, without distinction of any kind, have equal and inalienable rights of human dignity and freedom." The central beliefs that are subsumed under this broad declaration state that people who are considered handicapped have:

1 The same basic rights as other citizens of the same country and same age.
2 The right to proper medical care and physical restoration and to whatever education, training, habilitation, and guidance is needed to enable them to develop their ability and potential to the fullest extent possible, whatever their degree or type of disability. (Moreover, no one should be deprived of services because of the costs involved.)
3 The right to economic security, to a decent standard of living, and to involvement in a productive and meaningful occupation.
4 The right to live with their own families or in foster homes, full participation in all aspects of community life, involvement in appropriate leisure-time activities, and (if residing in an institution) reasonable proximity to normal community opportunities and facilities.
5 The right to have a qualified guardian when necessary to oversee their personal rights and interests.
6 The right to protection from exploitation, abuse, and degrading treatment.
7 The right to be protected by appropriate safeguards, in instances when modification of the preceding rights is necessary or appropriate.

The extent to which community services are provided and organized for all citizens is inextricably related to one's personal beliefs in (1) the worth of each

Community playgrounds with special provisions should be available to all children at an early age.

person, whatever his personal character and station in life, and (2) the priority one gives to each of the many community programs that require expenditure of time and money.

We shall illustrate the problems with a situation in the public schools that will strike a familiar chord. Many high schools in the United States expend a substantial level of human and fiscal resources on their football program. Special coaches are employed, equipment is purchased, stadiums are constructed, parents organize booster clubs to provide various fringe benefits to the participants, football fever strikes the school body and even the community at large every fall, many places of employment release their employees or close down during the times the games are played, students and players are bused to different parts of the state or even out-of-state for special events and games, and so on.

Why do the debating teams or the chess teams in the same high schools not receive the same type and magnitude of support and interest? The answer is plain and simple—we, individually and collectively, support those things that we value, that have personal meaning to us, and that other people whose opinions we value consider to be important. The manner in which several of the Scandinavian countries have provided full community-based and financed services to exceptional children and adults reflects a clear indication of the nature of their individual and social priorities. The point we are attempting to make with this discussion, then, is that effective, adequate, and comprehensive community programing for all citizens cannot be expected to occur without commitment. Scientific expertise, ability to organize and deliver a service program, and financial resources are not in and of themselves enough to make a community program possible or workable. These are necessary conditions, but more fundamental is the need for individual and collective commitment to the concept if it is to work at all. One indicator of the degree of commitment is the amount of financial support a society is willing to allocate for social services. For example, Denmark, with a population of less than 5 million and an area of approximately 17,500 square miles, spends 40 percent of the total national income on public expenditures, the biggest item of which is social services, followed by health, education, and defense, in that order.

As an illustration of the commitment the Danes have made to those in their society who are mentally retarded, for example, Figure 13-1 highlights the organizational model that is used in that country, the large variety of programs that are offered to individuals who are intellectually subnormal, and the type of articulation that can take place among the various segments of the program. This same general format pertains to the provision and organization of habilitative and rehabilitative services in other areas of exceptionality throughout Denmark (Bank-Mikklesen, 1969).

The entire system is governed by a board of directors, and each of twelve regions has an appointed board of control to oversee the manner in which local services are being provided and administered and the extent to which they are effective in meeting the client's needs. Each region is administered by a four-man team, i.e., an administrator, a physician, a director of social work, and a director of education. They are responsible to the board of control for children's and adults' services in their region, from cradle to grave. As Figure 13-1 suggests, all services are integrated and administered at the regional level and include not only the client but his entire family, if necessary.

We will not elaborate on all of the nuances of the Danish system, since it is being used here as only one example of what has been done in other countries. However, there are several additional points we want to make before we proceed with other dimensions of this issue. First, the Danish system is entirely financed by the national government. Second, complete procedures for review and appeal are built into every component and level of the system so that a client is not imposed upon in ways that are contrary to his own desires or those of others with whom responsibility is shared. Third, the training of professional workers in each component of the system is given great emphasis and includes both theoretical and practical aspects (Bank-Mikklesen, 1969; Wolfensberger et al., 1972).

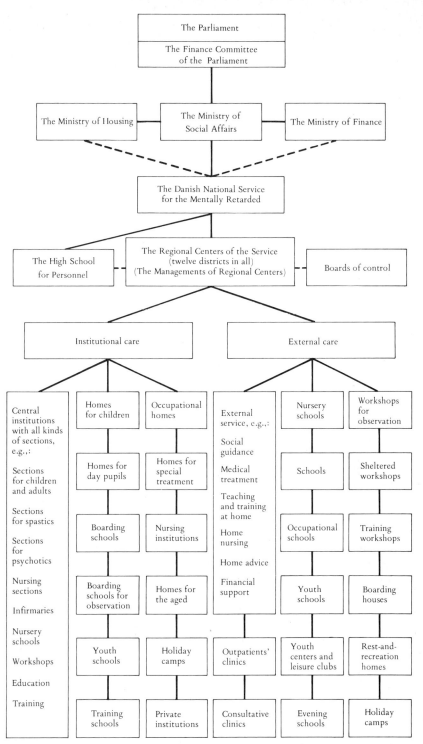

FIGURE 13-1 Organizational model of social services in Denmark. (The Danish National Service for the Mentally Retarded. *General Survey and Brief History of the Development of Service Systems in Denmark.* Society and Home for Cripples in Copenhagen, 1969. P. 41.)

RANGE OF POSSIBLE SERVICES

The variety of services available in a given community will differ a great deal according to a host of conditions. The section following this will consider some of the prominent circumstances that dictate the extent to which a community is able and elects to provide a range of programs. Here we will describe an ideal configuration or a maximum, full range of supporting services without, at this point, considering the various agents that hinder the provision of such services.

There are a number of ways to classify the supporting services that are directed toward exceptional children and adults in the community. In the very broadest sense, one could view a certain constellation of services as being evaluative or diagnostic in focus. Children's diagnostic centers of a multidisciplinary character, certain rehabilitation centers, medical diagnostic facilities, and specific types of programs in vocational evaluation place emphasis on obtaining an accurate characterization of an individual's disability and handicap and the services needed to improve his level of functioning. These agencies rarely, if ever, provide anything other than diagnostic and evaluative services.

A second group of community agencies emphasize the provision of habilitative and rehabilitative services to clients. Their primary role is to work with the exceptional individual—to manage him prosthetically, if necessary, and to provide an appropriate environment so that his functional level will increasingly approximate the normal, or become less deviant. In most instances the program of services will be of a short-term rather than a long-term duration. That is, the agency and the client anticipate the realization of certain habilitative or rehabilitative goals that will allow the person to progress to a higher level of functioning which will be appropriate in a social, personal, and vocational sense. For example, new teeth, speech therapy, auditory training, mobility instruction, or physical therapy illustrate areas of service that are usually of specific duration for a client and not continuous over lengthy periods.

At the same time, however, some of the services of a community have a long-term character. Certain sheltered workshops, community housing arrangements or youth hostels, health insurance programs, outpatient consultation, and adult education opportunities are examples of services that are typically available to clients whatever their type and degree of exceptionality and for whatever duration the services are required. In addition to their concern for habilitating and rehabilitating exceptional clients, community agencies have equal concern for providing programs and services that prevent disabling conditions. Their focus is not only on controlling the occurrence of any primary disorder that might affect an individual and reduce his level of normal functioning, but specialists from these agencies have concern for reducing the probability that an exceptional person will acquire additional or secondary disorders as well. Management, then, includes providing for the person an environment to prevent the initial and subsequent development of deviant conditions as well as remediating existing conditions that deleteriously affect the individual's performance.

Another way to classify community agencies and services is according to whether the emphasis is mainly physical, social, vocational, or of a general support character. These are arbitrary classifications, for in reality many agencies provide combinations of these services. Generally, though, the following list summarizes the main focus of each of the most prominent types or agencies.

I Physical
  A Medical
  B Dental, including oral-facial repairs
  C Nursing
  D Physical therapy
  E Occupational therapy

II Social-Personal
  A Speech and hearing therapy
  B Braille reading and writing
  C Mobility instruction
  D Special education
  E Psychiatric-psychological counseling
  F Occupational therapy
  G Rehabilitation counseling
  H Therapeutic recreation
  I Social casework
  J Home care and homemaker assistance
  K Social welfare programs (e.g., insurance, workmen's compensation, and disability programs)

III Vocational
  A Sheltered workshops
  B Work-study programs
  C Vocational rehabilitation and training
  D Employment placement, counseling, and evaluation
  E Occupational therapy

CONDITIONS DICTATING THE EFFECTIVENESS OF A SERVICE

Numerous factors impinge on the extent to which community services of the number and type mentioned above find their way into the fabric of a community. Likewise, these same conditions determine whether the people who really need the various services will receive them when they are available. It is a community asset to have such programs and services available, but it is quite another thing to realize the optimum delivery needed by members of the community. Obviously, progressive citizens and communities will desire to provide community services to the level required. It is, therefore, vital that community leaders be aware of all the considerations pertinent to the development and provision of the needed services. The most prominent of these will be pointed out and briefly elaborated upon in this section.

1 The most central consideration in the provision of community services and the support of agencies is the attitude of the citizens toward exceptional individuals and the perception of their individual and collective responsibilities toward those in their locale with special needs. The old adage "Out of sight, out of mind" has enormous implications. History is full of instances in which deviant people were cast into institutions and other forms of residential centers far from major population centers—only to be forgotten except during the annual review of the budget. And then it was (and still is) only too easy to reduce the fiscal requests of those agencies that are "not around" or not within view day to day.

   Services will be supported and provided in direct relationship to the attitude of the people. Do they consider it socially, politically, and personally appropriate to have the services available and to support them at an acceptable level? In order to answer this key question we must ask two others. First, are the citizens willing to spend whatever it takes to initiate and maintain the community agencies beyond the point to which the agencies can provide their own support? Second, would the people in the community from whom financial and spiritual support is requested be willing themselves to use the services should the need arise? The answers to these two questions indicate the community's attitude toward providing for the needs of exceptional people. If their responses to these questions are more neutral or negative than positive, the first mission of those who desire to initiate supportive community services will be to deal with the attitudinal problems.

2 The needs of communities differ extensively. Moreover, the type and range of agencies and services provided within a given community will change from time to time as the prospective clientele changes. It is incumbent on planners to have a fairly accurate indication of demand for the different services that might be provided by a community before a program to initiate community support is mounted. This information will serve to bulwark the arguments used in mobilizing community support. It is a key step in the process.

3 Closely allied to the second point above is the need to determine available and prospective resources within the community that might be called upon for support. After a tentative decision has been made regarding the nature of community needs, a status assessment should be conducted in three primary areas. First, the existing community agencies should be carefully analyzed, including a study of their service functions and modes of deliv-

ery, the types and numbers of clients they currently serve, their interest in participating in a coordinated service approach, the attitude of their leaders concerning the provision of services to persons who are currently not served, their financial policies, and the kinds of professionals available.

Second, some attention should be given to the human resources available in the community. Manpower will be needed to plan, provide, and maintain services in the community. Part-time and full-time workers will have to be mobilized on a continuous basis, and it is important to gain some appreciation for the size and commitment of this group of citizens before an expansion and coordination of services takes place.

Third, the financial resources in a community must be evaluated before any plans are solidified. There is no question that the local districts will have to provide some funds to support a program of services. Federal and state funds are often available to supplement certain segments of most community service plans; however, one should not assume that the entire program could be funded by such resources. An adequate system of services should involve diversified sources of fiscal support, including state and national resources, public and private. The magnitude and availability of such funds should be determined before plans are established.

4   Another important factor that will influence the extent to which the needed services in a community will become maximally effective is the general organization of the community. This includes the political bases of power and influence as well as the physical layout. In addition, of course, one must consider such factors as the cultural characteristics of the community, the predominant religious beliefs, the major socioeconomic levels represented, ethnic characteristics, political persuasions and inclinations, and labor-management issues that might influence the establishment and functioning of service agencies.

5   A final consideration not to be overlooked is the need to gain some estimate of the political inclinations of each segment of a community's program. It is natural for well-established groups, agencies, or individuals to be hesitant to turn over any control, power, influence, responsibilities, or funding sources to others who are less well established. Doing so often results in relinquishing control over their own destiny. This is a difficult problem, but it is one that must be faced by the established units and the emerging ones. Before "war breaks out" and "territories" are established, it is important to evaluate the degree to which boundaries have been established around agencies and what they consider to be their responsibility and base of operation. Launching into the development of a program before making such an assessment will simply delay the establishment of a coordinated effort, cause hard feelings among potential contributors, and serve to make more rigid the lines of communication, which should be open for maximum effectiveness.

THE COST-BENEFIT MODEL FOR HUMAN SERVICES

Wolfensberger (1969) has presented a broad outline for the provision and delivery of services to the handicapped on a relatively fair and equitable basis. His proposition takes cognizance of two overriding realities: (1) There is an increasing need for all types of human services; but there is a shortage of such services, and those that exist are provided in an unsystematic, unplanned, undocumented, and sometimes arbitrary way in many communities. (2) The financial resources available for human services are limited; this means that new ways must be discovered to provide an appropriate level of support for all citizens who require services.

Wolfensberger suggests that society should establish eligibility rules or criteria for the use of all publicly funded services and that each prospective client be evaluated according to his needs and in terms of which services are and are not to be made available to him. The client, in turn, has the privilege of selecting from those services that are available, as determined by cost-effectiveness criteria. If the client or his agent selects a service alternative that is not among the options that society is willing to provide with public funds, he could then secure the services he desires at his own expense.

The implementation of Wolfensberger's concept requires a significant reorientation of the present procedures that are practiced by agencies. A most important component of the plan is the establishment of a coordinating agency under whose aegis decisions concerning criteria for eligibility and the articulation of services among existing agencies would fall. This means that individual and relatively independent agencies would relinquish their responsibility and authority in these areas to this coordinating unit. There are gigantic political ramifications in either socially pressuring or legally mandating that a given agency cooperate with a coordinating group and relinquish some power and prestige in the process.

The coordinating center would serve as a depository of information and an agent of communication among all service agents within a given geographic area. Each agency would maintain communication with other agencies through the center, providing each other with data regarding clients, problems of implementation, plans for reducing, increasing, or supplementing existing services, and any new methodologies that have proved effective. A second function of the center would be to act as the agent of first contact for the client. The center would have the responsibility of interviewing the client, evaluating him diagnostically, and determining which options, from all of those that are available, will be offered on the basis of the staff's cost-benefit analysis of the client's situation. A third key responsibility of the center would be to provide continuous evaluation of its own practices, of the clients it directs, and of the effectiveness of the member agencies. Evaluation is most important, because it is only through evaluation that society can determine weaknesses in the system, the long-term impact of the program, and the appropriateness of the cost-benefit criteria that are the bases for providing options to clients.

It is Wolfensberger's contention that the plan he has proposed will marry effectiveness with efficiency at every level of programing. His implicit assumption is that agencies will be able to provide services at a satisfactory and satisfying level in spite of the need to relinquish a measure of independence to a coordinating authority. In fact, he believes that the decision-coordinating center will release the individual agencies from many of the time-consuming, wearisome tasks of administration that plague every service agency. A most important consequence of this proposed system is that it will reduce clients' shopping among agencies. And finally, the system is fully compatible with the concept of a continuum of service options (Deno, 1970) that is becoming a reality in special education programing throughout the United States.

SUGGESTED PROJECTS FOR PART IV

1 Prepare and give a talk on alternative models for the training of special education teachers. You may use one or more of the models discussed in Chapter 7 to suggest areas of training. Give some consideration, also, to the sequence of training and the use and timing of practice. Further, suggest ways to evaluate competence, i.e., assessment methods that would become useful in "certifying" a special educator.

2 Assuming you will be or are a special educator, write a job description for your aide or some other paraprofessional with whom you would work. You must decide on which areas will be your exclusive responsibility, which ones to share, and which ones to turn over to the paraprofessional. In your job description, include a summary of what training or orientation, if any, you would require or provide. Consider, also, the possible shift in paraprofessional responsibilities as training and experience occur.

3 Obtain from the special education department of a university, a materials center, or a local school two sets of instructional materials designed for the same purpose—for example, two reading, language, arithmetic, or social skills programs. Assess both of them in order to determine which one, if any, you might employ. Design a "materials assessment checksheet," using the criteria discussed in Chapter 10. You may find it useful to question teachers and children who have used the materials, as well as inspecting them yourself.

4 Secure a curriculum plan from a nearby special education program. Review it with other students and discuss its shortcomings and strengths in view of the recommendations provided in this book.

5 Determine if any professional or other student is conducting any educational or therapy programs with children that involve the use of behavioral or learning principles, or "behavior modification." If possible, ask to observe the sessions, help to collect data, and find out what you can about the objectives, procedures, and results.

6 Make a list of specific tasks or activities *you* would like to accomplish within a week. Then, design a premack, token, contract, or other motivational system to help you accomplish your targets.

7 On the basis of the architectural considerations presented in Chapter 11, develop a checklist or some other device for evaluating the presence or absence of barriers to use of a physical facility by persons with disabilities. You might wish to select a building on campus or a public facility. Your objective for this project is to identify, and thus assess, the positive and negative aspects of the facility with respect to its use by persons with sen-

sory, motor, or intellectual difficulties. Also, consider your findings with respect to the normalization principles summarized in Chapter 12.

8 Attempt to simulate a disability in order to spend a day as a "handicapped" person. You might confine yourself to a wheelchair, use a walker or crutches, place patches and dark glasses over your eyes, obstruct your hearing in some safe manner, feign muteness, or in other ways impose upon yourself a temporary limitation. Then, attempt to go about your daily routine. Take note of additional difficulties imposed upon you by the characteristics of the physical environment. Further, if your "disability" has high visibility, note the behavior of others toward you. Try, especially, to detect instances of the presumption by others of a generalized deficiency on your part, i.e., responses that suggest you are limited in more ways than the specific limitation you are feigning.

Of course, do not put yourself into hazardous situations. But do attempt to attain an appreciation of the many physical and social burdens of exceptional individuals. Write up your experiences, perhaps in a diarylike account. Finally, discuss in class or elsewhere what you believe can be done to minimize the hardships you experienced only temporarily.

9 Visit a local school district and talk with someone, preferably a special education coordinator, to discover the numbers and types of exceptionalities as classified in Part V of this book. Schools usually group children according to categories of disabilities and have corresponding census figures. Doing this will give you an idea of the actual local prevalence of traditionally classified disabilities.

10 Survey your community in order to identify the agencies that provide services to exceptional individuals. If possible, visit several agencies. You might also be able to determine what overlap in services exists and what degree of cooperation there is among agencies.

ANNOTATED RESOURCES FOR PART IV

Aids for Children (Technical Aids for Physically Handicapped Children) ICTA Information Centre, FACK, S-16103 Bramma 3, Sweden, 1972. (76 pages and bibliography, list of rehabilitation centers, and list of manufacturers and suppliers of equipment; foreword by Duncan Guthie and Karn Mantan, chairman and director of ICTA, paperback.) Written in catalogue format, this booklet was designed to appeal to parents of physically handicapped as well as to pediatric rehabilitation personnel. Photographs or drawings of equipment are accompanied by descriptive commentary and the manufacturer's name. The contents are divided as follows: (1) Equipment for physiotherapy. (2) Equipment for physical and occupational therapy. (3) Equipment for locomotion transport. (4) School aids. An attempt was made to select functionally uncomplicated equipment relatively inexpensive to purchase or construct. The goal of the catalogue is to make life easier for physically handicapped children by providing public information concerning available technical aids.

Lance, Wayne D. *Instructional Media and the Handicapped,* Stanford, Calif.: Eric Clearinghouse on Media and Technology, December 1973. (20 pages and references; paperback.) This booklet serves as a summary of instructional technology and curricular applications for handicapped learners. It is written in a concise manner and is an excellent source for further work in media. The first few pages provide a general introduction, followed by an examination of particular instructional adaptations for those with hearing and oral communication disorders, visual disabilities, moderate and severe general learning disabilities, crippling conditions and health disorders, behavioral and specific learning disabilities. The use of various media (videotapes, films, transparencies, programed and computer instruction) is reviewed, and such media are evaluated. Training of teachers in the utilization of media is discussed and a description of existing delivery services is given.

Meyen, Edward L. *Developing Units of Instruction for the Mentally Retarded and Other Children with Learning Problems,* Dubuque, Iowa: Brown, 1972. (235 pages; appendix and index; paperback.) Designed as a supplemental text to be used in methods courses for general and special education, this book is also applicable to workshops, short courses, and independent study. Each chapter can be read as an individual entity followed by a summary, bibliography, or list of additional selected references; the sequence of chapters is meaningful, however. Each page is perforated to allow convenient removal from the book when necessary. The focus is on a model which stresses a systematic approach to effective unit teaching as a method of instruction particularly suitable for educational programing with the retarded. The eclectic nature of such a method is examined and various skills (i.e., questioning ability, sensitivity to personal needs of pupils, knowledge of sequential aspects of curriculum, familiarity with subject matter and ability to modify materials to needs of the group) are defined and explored. Developmental steps for writing experience units, educational techniques, and numerous examples of appropriate class and seatwork provide important models.

Neisworth, John T., and Smith, Robert M. *Modifying Retarded Behavior,* Boston: Houghton Mifflin, 1973. (213 pages; index; foreword by Samuel A. Kirk.) Written in straightforward but not oversimplified language, the book is intended for use by students, teachers, parents, and paraprofessionals. It is divided into two parts—"Principles" and "Practice." Each part consists of four chapters, preceded by study targets which are also useful as summarizing exercises to test one's grasp of the material. The first four chapters describe and illustrate behavioral principles and the tenets of behavior modification with respect to retarded behavior. "Normality" and criteria defining "exceptionality" are discussed. The last four chapters deal with the application of behavior modification to improving social, personal, and academic problems of children exhibiting retarded behavior. The book provides a comprehensive but concise treatment of the philosophy, principles, and practice of a behavioral approach to retarded behavior and is particularly useful an an introductory text in the area of behavior modification in special education.

Sarason, Irwin G., and Sarason, Barbara R. *Constructive Classroom Behavior: A Teacher's Guide to Modeling & Role Playing Techniques,* New York: Behavioral Publications, 1974. (49 pages and glossary, selected bibliography, references; paperback.) This manual, printed in pamphlet form, is intended for teachers, teachers in training, counselors, and administrators to help them use modeling and role playing in productive ways. Modeling and role playing are defined as learning processes applicable to classroom settings. A summary of the literature is followed by a discussion of modeling with delinquents, modeling by teachers, and modeling for vocational training. The pamphlet concludes with a review of modeling principles and practices.

Skinner, B. F. *The Technology of Teaching,* New York: Appleton-Century-Crofts, Educational Division Meddith Corp., 1968. (260 pages and references and index; paperback.) This book is a compilation of previously published articles, lectures, and additional writings, each presented as an individual chapter relevant to the teaching profession. A list of chapter titles serves as a spectrum of the book's contents: (1) The Etymology of Teaching. (2) The Science of Learning and the Art of Teaching. (3) Teaching Machines. (4) The Technology of Teaching. (5) Why Teachers Fail. (6) Teaching Thinking. (7) The Motivation of the Student. (8) The Creative Student. (9) Discipline, Ethical Behavior, and Self-Control. (10) A Review of Teaching. (11) The Behavior of the Establishment. Skinner presents constructive alternatives as he criticizes what have become dysfunctional teaching patterns in American public schools. The text is easy to read and provides a good orientation to behaviorism in education.

Smith, Robert M. *Clinical Teaching: Methods of Instruction for the Retarded.* (2nd edition) New York: McGraw-Hill, 1974. (352 pages, and appendix of names and addresses of publishers of testing materials, and index.) This new edition of *Clinical Teaching* updates the research on mental retardation and appropriate instructional programs. The text is aimed primarily at teachers and provides a concise overview of current concepts and techniques in the field for parents, administrators and psychologists as well. The first three chapters establish the general philosophy of educational programing for the retarded, followed by instructions for developing specific skills necessary for functioning in society (ie., perceptual-motor, communication, reading, arithmetic, personal, social employment skills). The philosophy reflected in the contents is that appropriate education for the mentally retarded must be founded on: (1) accurate evaluations of individual performance and environmental influence; (2) establishing specific behavioral objectives; (3) selecting appropriate materials and instructional procedures; and (4) assigning each child to a setting and individual program most conducive to developmental progress.

Sulzer, Beth, and Mayer, G. Roy. *Behavior Modification Procedures for School Personnel,* Hinsdale, Ill.: Dryden Press, 1972. (286 pages, and glossary; name and subject indexes; foreword by Donald M. Baer, paperback.) Designed as a guidebook and written primarily for elementary and secondary school educators, parents and clinicians, the text is divided into sixteen chapters, each of which is preceded by specific learning objectives and concluded by a summary and list of references. Sulzer and Mayer have made an attempt to apply many of the operant learning principles that govern human behavior to the modification of dysfunctional behavior in the classroom. The introduction provides a basic foundation of theoretical principles and a model for a behavior modification program. The succeeding chapters discuss the application of various procedures designed to: increase existing behaviors, teach and maintain new behavior, reduce certain behavior, and evaluate the outcome of specific programs.

Travel Barriers, Department of Transportation, Office of the Secretary, Washington, D.C., 20590: U.S. Government Printing Office, 1970. (46 pages; introduction by John Wolpe, paperback.) Designed to report in summary the findings of a research study surveying transportation needs, problems, and suggestions for the chronically handicapped, this booklet provides concise information and accompanying guidelines for community transportation improvement programs. The chronically handicapped are identified as those unable to perform one or more actions required by existing transportation systems at a comfortable level of proficiency; they might range from a blind or physically handicapped person to someone burdened with luggage. The kinds of travel barriers encountered by the handicapped are detailed, and suggestions for redesigning modes of travel are provided, along with guidelines for community action to initiate change and institute educational programs for higher-quality mobility training in rehabilation centers.

Vargas, Julie S. *Writing Worthwhile Behavorial Objectives,* New York: Harper & Row, 1972. (172 pages and index; paperback.) This is a self-instructional book to help teachers write worthwhile, behaviorally stated objectives for increasing the value and relevance of their courses. The book is an example of the kind of individualized instruction such objectives make possible. Chapters 1 to 6 teach how to identify and state objectives behaviorally. Chapters 7 to 9 teach how to recognize and write "worthwhile" educational objectives based on Bloom's taxonomy of knowledge-level objectives. The text contains numerous examples and exercises, with pretests preceding each chapter which cover the skills taught, allowing for rapid progression through succeeding stages of skill development.

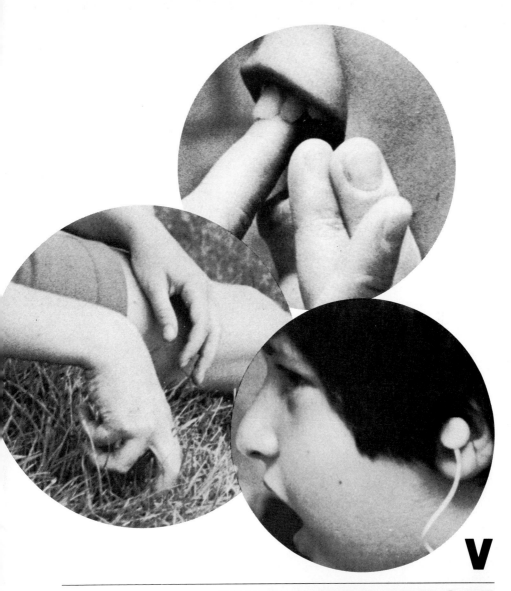

V

INFORMATION
SUMMARIES
OF TRADITIONALLY
CLASSIFIED
EXCEPTIONALITIES

A large portion of this book is concerned with the commonalities that exist among exceptional children in terms of their characteristics, the causes for and ways of preventing disabling conditions, broad social and psychological complications that can result from exceptionalities, and the management procedures that teachers can employ to respond to educational difficulties, whatever the type of disabling condition. However, special educators need as well a repertoire of that basic information which is unique to each general area of exceptionalities. In the past, this information has formed the basis for introductory courses in special education and for beginning textbooks in the field. The current thinking in special education certainly advocates maintaining the fundamental information relevant to each area of disability, and professionals having intimate familiarity with such facts, concepts, and points of view. At the same time, however, there is need to encourage an expansion of the whole special education concept to place at least equal emphasis on the core concepts that were discussed in the preceding sections of this book.

In this section of the book we have attempted to provide a compendium of information about the major traditional areas of disability. The approach we have selected is similar to the outline series that high school and college students have found so helpful in studying for examinations in different subjects. In organizing this important material in an outline form, we have attempted to establish a reasonable compromise between too much distillation and too wordy and elaborate a presentation. This part of the book should be viewed as a reference section to which you can turn for a brief summary of a particular area of concern.

14

LEARNING PROBLEMS

GENERAL LEARNING PROBLEMS

I DEFINITION OF MENTAL RETARDATION (MR).
  A The task has been complicated by several factors.
    1 There is controversy about the nature of intelligence.
    2 Different disciplines have looked at mental retardation from their own individual perspectives.
    3 There is doubt about which abilities to include in the definition.
    4 Intellectual factors and emotional factors are not independent of each other.
  B The definition of the American Association on Mental Deficiency: "Mental retardation refers to subaverage general intellectual functioning which originates during the developmental period and is associated with impairment in adaptive behavior" (Heber, 1961, p. 3). (See Kidd, 1964, for a more precise explanation.)
    1 A diagnosis is a description of present behavior without any mention of potential intelligence.
    2 The definition is developmental, with diagnosis based on samples of behavior appropriate to a subject's own age level.

3 The mental test is still emphasized in evaluations, but only in conjunction with numerous other sources of information.

4 It does not attempt to differentiate mental retardation from other childhood disorders.

5 More emphasis is placed on borderline intellectual retardation, which includes as much as one sixth of the population.

6 The concept of invariability is avoided.

II CHARACTERISTICS OF TYPICAL RETARDED PERFORMANCE.
A Common criteria for identification.
1 Psychomatic performance.
a Hundreds of tests are available to identify various characteristics of the intellectually retarded.
b Mental retardation can be defined in terms of IQ or MA and classified by arbitrary cutoffs based on the normal curve.
c Advantages of clarity and convenience are limited by several factors.
(1) Instrument development (inadequate standardization, behavior samples, etc.).
(2) Error by the tester.
(3) Interpretation (prediction based on status, environment, poor prognostication of social adjustment, etc.).
2 Developmental history.
a Retarded individuals are frequently retarded in all facets of development—physiological, motor, social, etc.
b Knowledge of an individual's growth pattern, and comparison of acquisition of various skills at certain ages (walking, talking, feeding oneself, etc.) to population norms provides valuable supplementary information.
c Interpretation of developmental patterns must be qualified according to degree of environmental opportunity.
3 Learning ability.
a Failure in school: being 2 or 3 years behind in school achievement with no obvious cause is sometimes indicative of mental retardation.
b Specific deficiencies in learning.
(1) Much research has been devoted to determining whether retarded children are more easily distracted, benefit less from transfer of learning, remember what they have learned as well as "normal" children, etc. The results of this type of research have been of minimal value, yielding mostly inconclusive findings. Many methodological problems are present in this research, especially generalization from specific subgroups to MR as a whole.

        (2) It has been demonstrated that learning by the retarded is controlled by the same laws as the behavior of other children.

    c It should be remembered that academic success and social adjustment are not highly correlated.

4 The criterion of social adjustment.

    a The test of social adequacy is the most basic indicator of retarded mental development. If a person is socially and economically self-sufficient, low test scores are relatively meaningless.

    b The frequent concomitance of retardation and emotional problems is probably due to several factors.

        (1) Everyday living is made more difficult by limited problem solving and limited ability to detect and respond to the subtle cues of social interactions.

        (2) The retarded person frequently experiences failure.

        (3) The retarded person is frequently unable to comply with the demands or expectations of peers and society.

B Categorization according to degree of retardation of performance.

1 Educable mentally retarded (EMR).

    a The EMR child does poorly on verbal and nonverbal intelligence tests, scoring most often between IQ 50 and IQ 80. This indicates a rate of development around one half to three fourths that of the average child. More specifically, the child may be slower in conceptual and perceptual abilities.

    b The EMR child is generally not ready for the usual school subjects (reading, writing, and arithmetic) at the age of 6, but, rather, several years later. Progressing at a slower rate than most children, he will probably reach between second- and sixth-grade level.

    c While there are no personal or social traits common to all EMR children, the EMR child's interests correspond more closely to those of children of equal mental ages than to those of chronological peers.

    d The EMR person can do unskilled or semiskilled work at the adult level—approximately 80 percent eventually do.

2 Trainable mentally retarded (TMR).

    a Scoring between 25 and 50 on intelligence tests, the TMR child is expected to develop at the rate of one third to one half that of a normal child.

    b The child is incapable of achieving in ordinary academic subjects, but he can learn self-care tasks, common safety rules, etc.

    c The child can learn social adjustment in everyday situations and is capable of economic usefulness in the home or in sheltered or supervised environments.

3 Profoundly retarded.
  a IQ scores are usually below 25.
  b The child requires total supervision, protection, and care.
  c Some can learn to walk, feed themselves, and speak simple phrases, but many are bedridden.
  d The mortality in childhood among the profoundly retarded is very high.

C Caution in applying labels or categories to children.
  1 The classification systems used are still rough and inadequate. Two children may have identical IQs, and be considered members of the same category, but need totally different educational programs.
  2 We must label and categorize the behavior of the child—not the child himself.
    a There is a danger of "canned" expectations or self-fulfilling prophecies
    b Labels can provide explanatory scapegoats for inefficient teaching.
  3 Assessment must be a never-ending process of formal and informal evaluation at frequent intervals throughout the individual's development until he is successfully adjusted in society.

III PROMINENT POINTS OF VIEW REGARDING RETARDED BEHAVIOR.
Representative positions from the numerous theoretical explanations of mental retardation can be grouped into three basic categories, each of which places relatively greater emphasis on a particular aspect of intellectual development.

A Positions emphasizing genetic contributions.

At the outset, it must be explained that the genetic causation of some MR syndromes is widely accepted. The majority of individuals found among the severely retarded have problems which can be directly traced to specific genetic defects. Whether the problem is caused by a dominant gene, a recessive gene, or chromosomal aberrations, there are clearly identifiable physical signs (Huntington's chorea, Down's Syndrome, etc.). While there is consensus on these severe cases, the theories are differentiated by the positions they take in explaining etiologically the mildly retarded, who are the vast majority of the intellectually handicapped.

  1 Jensen (1968) completed a thorough statistical analysis of intelligence test scores to examine the extent to which genetics accounts for the obtained variance.
    a He held that his results indicate that intelligence is undoubtedly the result of genetic inheritance, not environmental influences.

b The difference of about one standard deviation between mean IQ scores of blacks and whites in America is too large to be explained in terms of environmental differences.

c The logical conclusion was that the failure of disadvantaged children in "Head Start" programs was genetically determined.

2 Psychometric tradition (Guilford, 1956; Terman, 1916).

a The emphasis on future prediction is predicted on the assumption that intelligence is a static dimension and not significantly changed by experience.

b Changes in intellectual functioning during development are largely quantitative in nature.

c Attempts to develop "culture-free" tests are still based on the notion of inherent ability.

B Positions emphasizing the developmental nature of the intellect.

1 Piaget (1950) and Woodward (1963).

a Cognitive growth is seen as the product of a continuous interaction between the individual and his environment. While such interaction determines the rate of development, several qualitatively different stages are seen as following a fixed sequence.

b Active trial-and-error participation by the learner is crucial in the developmental process.

c The central importance given to the process of "equilibration," "assimilation," and "accommodation" necessitates a stimulating environment and an opportunity to interact with it. "The more a child has seen and heard, the more he wants to see and hear," i.e., increased experience in one stage leads to more recognition and familiarity and therefore interest in encounters in the next stage.

d The retarded child proceeds through the same stages as the "normal" individual, but simply at a slower pace. Few reach the levels of "formal operations."

2 Bruner (1964, 1966).

a He bases his theory of cognitive development on the idea of representation.

b There are three different systems for representing reality, and their mastery is critical in intellectual growth.

(1) Action (enactive mode).

(2) Imagery.

(3) Language (symbolic mode).

c These systems serve to "amplify" motor, sensory, and thinking capabilities.

d Different cultures provide varying opportunities for individuals to develop representational competence, especially in the symbolic mode. Intellectual development can be facilitated if such experience highlights the correspondence between the different representational systems.

C Positions emphasizing environmental factors.

1 Hunt (1961).

    a He stresses the critical role of experience in intellectual development.

    b Supported by much research (animal studies, twin studies, etc.), he attacks many traditional beliefs.

        (1) Belief in fixed intelligence.

        (2) Belief in predetermined development.

        (3) Belief in the unimportance of early experience.

    c He stresses the importance of "the problem of the match," i.e., arranging the environment in an optimum manner for an individual to learn. He advocates a certain degree of liberty (Montessori-like) to enable the learner to make the match.

2 Bijou (1966).

    a He advocates a concept of mental retardation based on "observable, objectivity defined stimulus-response relationships" without recourse to hypothetical internal explanations. Retarded behavior is not a symptom of underlying problems.

    b "Psychological development consists of progressive changes in interactions between the individual, as a total functioning biological system, and the environmental events" (Bijou, 1966, p. 2).

    c The environment can be analyzed for those conditions which impede, maintain, or facilitate behavior, and appropriate steps for desired change can be taken. His is an optimistic approach.

3 Mercer (1970).

    a While accepting certain benefits of the pathological model of MR (e.g., study of PKU, Down's Syndrome, etc.), the author attacks its various dangers.

        (1) The condition is seen to exist *in* the person.

        (2) Defining people as "ill" leads to different status and role expectations, creating deviant behaviors. Thus the system perpetuates the behavior it wants to eliminate.

        (3) Prevalence depends on what is culturally "normal," not on universal criteria.

    b Mercer offers a social-system view of MR.

        (1) The focus is on the "definer" instead of the "defined." What are the consequences of the process?

        (2) The preponderance of black and Spanish children in special classes, etc., is noted.

IV PREVALENCE OF MR.
A Problems in determining accurate percentages or estimates.
1 Various definitions are in use, with some (AAMD) including many more borderline cases than others. Different criteria are used in these definitions.
2 MR is relative to cultural situations—what is maladaptive in one population may not be in another; also, the attitude of the society is relevant.
3 Definitive surveys are extremely difficult to conduct with adequate accuracy—many problems are inherent in large-scale national research (e.g., availability of institutional services differs greatly from state to state).
B Current estimates.
1 Great variation—sixty studies report range from .05 to 13 percent of population (Wallin, 1958).
2 The generally accepted figure is roughly 2.5 to 3.5 percent of our population—out of a population of 200 million persons, about 6 million individuals.
3 MR is not normally distributed among the different segments of the population.
a There is a higher incidence of mild retardation in lower SES groups.
b More males than females are retarded.
c The frequency is higher in school-age populations. A sharp drop occurs in late teenage years.
d Racial differences exist (Jensen, 1968).

V PROGNOSIS.
A Of the severely retarded.
1 Generally, the more organically involved, the more limited are the chances for a "normal" existence.
2 Participation in any kind of traditional academic program (reading, writing, arithmetic, etc.) is greatly limited, and often totally precluded.
3 In recent years, progress has been made in training in various skills using behavior modification. This is opening up new horizons in the extent of economic usefulness attainable, the degree of competence in self-care skills, etc.
B Of the mildly retarded.
1 The critical variable is the time of intervention. The earlier optimum environmental arrangements are made, the better the prognosis. The first four years of life are seen as the most important.
2 It is increasingly recognized that most of MR is reversible. Much

attention is being given to those conditions which most facilitate the acquisition of adequate behavioral repertoires. Such an attitude should lead to, and in many cases has led to, methodological approaches which will increasingly lessen the gap between many mildly retarded individuals and the "normal" population.

VI PREVENTION OF MR.

    A Need.

       1 The United States is not a leader in the world in providing comprehensive, nationwide services aimed at preventing MR. The mortality rate, for example, is about 25 per 1,000 live births, making us around fifteenth among industrialized countries.

       2 Considering the relatively minimal effort required for each child, a comprehensive prevention program offers the most hope in dealing with the problems of retardation.

    B Prevention measures which could currently be implemented.

       1 Complete maternal care for all high-risk mothers.

       2 Genetic counseling and comprehensive diagnostic centers for each community.

       3 Research aimed at identifying the various drugs, poisons, and other agents which are harmful to the developing fetus.

       4 Radiation control.

       5 Immediate, comprehensive diagnostic services to newborns, and proper follow-up where necessary.

       6 Study of the nature and causes of childhood accidents, leading to suggestions for control and prevention.

       7 Programs designed to counteract the basic social, economic, and cultural conditions with which MR is associated.

         a Preschool centers.

         b Coordination of public and private agencies.

         c Greater involvement of parents in educational programing.

         d General health care—control of infectious diseases, etc.

       8 Redesigning of institutional programs to prevent problems caused by maternal deprivation or lack of stimulation.

       9 Increased training programs to provide greater numbers of professionals.

VII HABILITATIVE AND REHABILITATIVE PRACTICES.

    A History.

       1 In the seventeenth century, institutions were built for the care and custody of the mentally retarded.

       2 About 1800, Itard worked to disprove the idea of fixed intelligence through efforts with the "Wild Boy of Aveyron."

       3 In the 1840s, Sequin emphasized modern educational methods

with the retarded, including individualized teaching, working with the whole child, and motor and sensory education.

4   Montessori, in the early 1900s, worked with disadvantaged pre-schoolers and had great success in teaching "retarded" children to read and write.

5   Since the 1930s, educators have been increasingly aware of the special needs of the retarded child. Parents became increasingly more vocal leading to their formally organizing in 1950 (NARC).

6   During the 1960s, public responsibility for the education of the mildly retarded became widely recognized.

7   By 1967, more than $400 million a year was appropriated by the federal government for programs for the retarded. Twice this amount was added by individual states, private organizations, etc.

8   In 1971, Pennsylvania's Right to Education court order mandated that the public schools assume the responsibility of educating all retarded children.

B   Educational and training programs for the retarded.

1   Objectives (basically the same for both the mildly and the severely retarded).

a   Maximization of potential skills, social behavior, etc.

b   Normalization—that is, creating the greatest attainable degree of independence, etc.

c   Other. (Objectives can be specified only on an individual basis with the strengths and weaknesses of the child clearly in mind.)

d   Curriculum objectives for the mildly retarded.

(1)   Basic readiness and practical academic development.

(2)   Communication, oral language, and cognitive development.

(3)   Socialization, family living, self-care, recreational and personality development.

(4)   Prevocational and vocational development, including housekeeping (Dunn, 1973).

e   For the severely retarded, educational efforts are focused on basically the same general goals, but at a much more concrete level: i.e., there is more emphasis on self-care, communication, etc., and much less academic content.

2   Methods used.

a   Great variations exist among school systems and individual teachers because of different teacher-training experiences, philosophies, etc.

b   A number of successful methods are currently being used.

(1)   Programed instruction involving carefully sequenced presentations of material to the learner allows relatively errorless learning and prevents frustration.

    (2) Behavior modification is used with great success in nearly all areas of social and academic learning.

    (3) Teaching machines allow the child to proceed at his own pace and provide a good supplement to the teacher's efforts.

    (4) Multisensory approaches are also in use.

  c Methodology and curriculum are carefully selected.

    (1) Data are obtained from various sources, in formal and informal ways.

    (2) The techniques each child seems to use successfully when processing information are carefully inspected.

    (3) Agents which increase or decrease the occurrence of child's behavior are identified and controlled.

    (4) Continual feedback leads to program revisions when needed.

3 Placement options.

  a Residential institutions.

    (1) Only small proportions of the retarded are actually placed there (nearly all of whom are severely retarded).

    (2) They allow for multidisciplinary care: medical, psychological, educational, etc.

    (3) They have been criticized for detrimental effects (Blatt and Kaplan, 1967; Skeels, 1966).

      (a) Because of isolation from normal life and depersonalized character.

      (b) Because of lack of stimulation.

      (c) Because of poor conditions due to overcrowding, underpaid staff, etc.

    (4) Currently, emphasis is on decentralization (Wolfensberger, 1972).

      (a) Increased use of halfway homes, community-based centers, etc.—all which would increase chances for normalization.

  b Special classes: a very controversial subject.

    (1) Arguments in favor of special classes.

      (a) Greater opportunity for individualized instruction.

      (b) Protection from academic failure and social rejection.

      (c) Special training of teacher, which allegedly makes a difference.

      (d) Prevention of slowing down of "normal" students in regular classes.

    (2) Arguments against special classes.

      (a) Evidence indicates limited value to the child placed in special classes.

(b) Labels result in lowered self-concept.

(c) The training of a regular class teacher should equal that of a "special" teacher.

(d) There are weaknesses and invalidities in noneducational classification systems.

(e) Protection is a poor preparation for the social reality students will face later on.

(3) Resource rooms.

(a) They are designed to provide needed specialized help in specific areas to individual children, while at the same time permitting them to function for the most part in the regular classroom. This could prevent many of the problems associated with the self-contained special class.

(b) Problems include frequently unrealistic demands on resource teacher, heavy case load, etc.

(4) Helping teacher.

(a) The more mildly retarded children can be kept in regular class on a full-time basis, avoiding the problems noted above.

(b) The teacher can thoroughly coordinate the special and the regular education programs.

SPECIFIC LEARNING PROBLEMS

I INTRODUCTION TO LEARNING DISABILITIES (LD).

  A The notion that certain behaviors are characteristic of "brain damage" is not new.

    1 Morgan (1896), an English doctor, coined the term "congenital word blindness" to describe a 14-year-old boy who appeared to be intelligent but could not read.

  B The concept has gained wide acceptance in the last decade.

    1 In 1965, the National Association for Children with Learning Disabilities was formed by parents.

    2 In 1968, the *Journal of Learning Disabilities* was begun.

    3 In 1969, "Children with Learning Disability" Act (HR 13310) was passed, providing $36 million over 3 years (1971–1973) for related research, teacher training, etc.

  C Scope of the problem.

    1 Incidence rates vary greatly, depending on the definition used.

      a The U.S. Office of Education estimates prevalence at or near 1 percent of school-age population.

      b Newbrough and Kelly (1962) indicated that 14 percent of the school-age population was performing 2 years below grade level.

II DEFINITION OF "LEARNING DISABILITIES."

    A In the past, and even now, a great number of definitions exist. This is reflected in the diverse labels commonly used to describe problems, e.g., dyslexia, specific dyslexia, developmental dyslexia, specific reading disability, strephozymbolia, developmental alexia, gestalt blindness, congenital word blindness, minimal brain damage, etc.

    B Despite lack of consensus, Myers and Hammill (1969) indicate that Bateman's definition (1965) is in basic agreement with many. It states: "Children who have learning disorders are those who manifest an educationally significant discrepancy between their estimated intellectual potential and actual level of performance related to basic disorders in the learning processes, which may or may not be accompanied by demonstrable central nervous system dysfunction, and which are not secondary to generalized mental retardation, educational or cultural deprivation, severe emotional disturbance, or sensory loss" (p. 220).

III CHARACTERISTICS OF FUNCTIONAL PROBLEMS DUE TO LEARNING DISABILITIES.

    A There are many lists of symptoms or behaviors which purportedly indicate learning disabilities. Together, various professionals in the field have listed almost 100 specific behaviors (Telford and Sawrey, 1972). Of these, according to McCarthy and McCarthy (1969), the most frequently cited are:

       1 Hyperactivity.
       2 Perceptual-motor defects.
       3 Emotional liability.
       4 General orientation and laterality defects.
       5 Disorders of attention.
       6 Impulsivity.
       7 Disorders of memory and conceptual thinking.
       8 Specific learning defects, especially in language.

    B While any one or a combination of the above problems can be reflected in almost any academic subject, including oral language, spelling, handwriting, and arithmetic, they are by far most frequently evidenced in reading.

    C Every child classified as LD need not manifest all of the above symptoms or behaviors.

    D The listed characteristics are not independent. Which are primary and which are secondary is entirely debatable.

    E While LD children often manifest some or many of the above characteristics, it cannot be assumed that they learn differently from the neurologically unimpaired (Barnett, Ellis and Pryor, 1960).

IV THEORETICAL EXPLANATIONS OF LD.

  A A vast amount of research and theorizing has been done. Eichenwald (1967) claims that in the last 70 years over 20,000 books, articles, and papers have been published on the subject. Most have attempted to find behavior patterns which are common to all dyslexic children, thus providing clear-cut evidence of a neurological etiology. This attempt has produced innumerable conflicting theories.

     1 Hinshelwood (1917): word blindness stems from problems in the visual centers of the brain.

     2 Orton (1937): LD is caused by lack of cerebral dominance.

     3 Strauss and Lehtinen (1947): LD is caused by minimal brain damage.

     4 Smith and Carrigan (1959): LD is caused by endocrine disturbance and chemical imbalance.

     5 Kephart (1960): LD is a result of underdeveloped perceptual motor skills.

     6 Delacato (1966): LD stems from poor neurological organization.

  B Nonneurological explanations.

     1 While, by far, most effort has been spent in seeking the organic causes of LD, lack of consensus and concrete findings is increasing efforts to examine the environment, not the child. Learning disabilities can also be considered the result of other factors.

       a Poor teaching.

       b Poorly sequenced or improperly chosen curricula.

       c Lack of motivation.

       d Lack of degree of structure necessary in educational program.

     2 This perspective yields several important results.

       a It focuses responsibility for failure on the educator, not the child.

       b It deals with observable factors whose effectiveness can be proved or disproved.

       c It leads to more effective communication among professionals, it is more efficient, and it leads to productive research.

V IDENTIFICATION.

  A Difficulties.

     1 The definition most commonly used requires the elimination of other causes of the learning problem, e.g., mental retardation, cultural deprivation, poor teaching, or emotional disturbance. This is nearly impossible.

       a We do not know exactly what these factors involve; e.g., what is a "culturally adequate home"?

       b We cannot tell whether emotional and motivational problems are primary causes of the learning problem or secondary to them.

   c Sometimes it is even difficult to determine the existence or non-existence of "gross neurological defects."

2 Lack of theoretical consensus, i.e., each theory focuses on different aspects of the problems.

3 A great variety of characteristics are cited as indicative of LD. A great proportion of the school population would probably, at some time or other, manifest any one or several of these "symptoms."

B Traditional diagnostic approach.

  1 Interdisciplinary team approach.

    a The team usually consists of a number of professionals, including neurologist, psychologist, speech therapist, teacher, etc.

    b The approach basically has had a traditional medical orientation which has been of little value for most classrooms.

    c This strategy is inappropriate for three main reasons.

      (1) It is very costly.

      (2) Educational decisions are not made by educators.

      (3) The emphasis is on specifying the weaknesses or their causes, which are hypothetical and unverified.

  2 School psychologist.

    a This approach has same disadvantages as above, except relatively less costly.

    b Psychologists' reports have been of limited value.

      (1) The validity of the tests used is questioned.

      (2) The relevance to the classroom situation minimal.

      (3) There are inherent dangers in the use of a single evaluation session from which educational decisions are made.

C Current trends.

  1 Informal assessment by the teacher.

    a Task analysis.

    b Continuous feedback to teacher.

    c Increased flexibility and individualization of educational strategies.

  2 Adoption of an actual external perspective on how best to manage the educational environment.

    a The focus shifts from defects in the child to defects in the environment.

    b An educationally oriented diagnosis that focuses on practicality is emphasized.

    c Vague, nebulous terms are avoided.

    d Medical-neurological assessment is still clearly valuable, but only in cases in which such problems are demonstrable, e.g., hearing loss, physical defects correctable by surgery, control of seizures through medication, etc.

VI PREVENTION APPROACHES ARE MUCH THE SAME AS WITH MR, BUT WITH VARIOUS SPECIAL EMPHASES.

   A The provision of better conditions during birth, leading to the establishment of better controls over several factors.

      1 Physical trauma.

      2 Drugs taken by the mother during pregnancy.

      3 Malnutrition of the mother during pregnancy.

      4 Prenatal damage to the central nervous system from anoxia.

      5 Brain injury during delivery caused by instruments.

   B Extra care for premature infants. This group includes a disproportionate number of learning-disabled children. (The incidence of minimal brain damage may be increasing in our culture owing to medical advances and our increased ability to save large numbers of premature infants who earlier would have perished.)

   C Study of better control over childhood diseases and accidents leading to brain injury.

   D Early diagnosis of learning problems, resulting in an increase in the chances for effective educational programs and prevention of a host of secondary problems.

      1 Emotional overlay engendered by frustration in learning.

      2 The development of numerous incorrect learning habits.

      3 Lowered self-concept resulting in diminished motivation.

      4 Unfair judgment by others (e.g., that a child is lazy or stupid).

   E Counseling of parents is effective in preventing unrealistic feelings toward the child and in helping parents to accept findings, prescribed education program, etc.

VII EDUCATIONAL PROGRAMS FOR LD CHILDREN.

   A The theoretical uncertainty previously mentioned has also produced an abundance of unique, and often unsupported, methods and procedures for remediation.

      1 Orton (1937) called for dominance training.

      2 Fernald (1943) devised a method of word tracing that emphasizes the multisensory aspects of learning to read.

      3 Cruickshank (1961) emphasized a structured program with limited environmental stimuli.

      4 Frostig (1961) stressed the importance of readiness training in visual-perception skills (e.g., eye-hand motor coordination, figure general perception, and spatial relationships.

      5 Kephart (1960) focused on perceptual-motor skills, and advocated the use of various devices, such as the balance beam, to develop them.

      6 Delacato (1966) advocated "patterning," a difficult and expensive procedure of imposed muscular movements for the child which

are designed to complete stages missing in his neurological development.

B   While some of these represent educational contributions, many of them are unfortunately promoted as panaceas for LD children. Some of these theories and suggested remedial procedures, such as those of Delacato, are based on insufficient and poorly controlled research (Robbins, 1966). Therefore, other approaches must be used.

   1   Careful selection of educational strategy based on the individual child's constellation of strengths and weaknesses. While some of the activities prescribed above may be appropriate, such remedial programs in their entirety would only by chance meet a given child's needs. Most of them talk in terms of the individual, not the LD population.

   2   Ongoing, frequent evaluations of child's progress within a particular education program will allow for quick adjustments of programing.

   3   Counseling of parents makes them aware of the types of problems children have and what can be done.

C   Placement options are basically the same as those for EMR children.

   1   Residential schools (limited to extreme cases).

   2   Placement in special classes.

      a   Before 1960, this meant placement in EMR class. Now there are classes designed especially for brain-injured or learning-disabled children.

      b   The effectiveness of these classes is debated, and they are attacked for many of the same reasons EMR and ED classes have been traditionally questioned.

   3   Resource room.

   4   Helping teacher.

15

ADJUSTMENT PROBLEMS

I   NORMAL STAGES OF SOCIAL-EMOTIONAL DEVELOPMENT.
   A   From birth to 1 year.
       1   At birth, the child is helpless and dependent.
       2   Important relationships exist between the physical and psycholog-
           ical needs of the infant and the mother or caretaker.
           a   Cuddling and fondling supply stimulation which aids the infant
               in developing appropriate respiration patterns.
           b   The infant's babbling increases when it prompts a response
               from another person.
           c   The infant's crying signals the caretaker to attend to the child.
           d   The sucking reflex serves several important functions.
               (1)   Through this contact, the infant receives predictable, stable
                     nurturance and pleasure.
               (2)   By the second month, sucking becomes related to seeing
                     and hearing.
               (3)   The feeding posture, which involves holding the child with
                     its face directed toward the person holding it, enhances in-
                     terpersonal relationships.

    e Smiling usually appears at around 8 weeks and is typically directed toward the caretaker.

    f The infant's sense of position in space is established by vocal sounds and by physical motions of the mother.

3 The infant responds to the caretaker showing attachment because the caretaker has been paired with pleasant events and relief of distress.

4 Attachment to the caretaker is important for a number of reasons.

    a It generalizes to other persons and leads to increased socialization.

    b When the infant responds, the caretaker is reinforced for providing attention and care.

    c The infant begins developing expectations about the environment (especially the mother) and becomes distressed when exposed to unfamiliar aspects of the environment.

5 By the end of the first year, the child has achieved a degree of physical independence from the caretaker and has developed a number of other characteristics.

    a An awareness of outside world.

    b Communication with others by making sounds.

    c Locomotor capabilities, which include the first steps in walking.

B From 1 to 3 years.

1 This is a period of intense curiosity and exploration.

    a The child has acquired new skills in locomotion and manipulation.

    b The child moves about more freely.

    c The child is able to change situations and solve problems.

    d It is important during this time to encourage rather than restrict movement and exploration.

2 The child has simple elements of speech and is able to communicate with others.

3 Aggressive behaviors are often manifested.

4 This time is critical for the development of self-realization and ego, according to some theorists.

    a Realization of the self is expressed in language.

    b Security given by the mother or the caretaker facilitates the realization of self.

    c Curiosity about the body results in awareness of its oneness.

5 Fear and anxiety are common responses to strange or unexpected events.

6 This period is critical for the development of autonomy, self-reliance, and competence (Erikson, 1963).

7 The role of the mother or caretaker changes from supportive to teaching in areas where the child is expected to acquire increasing independence.

8 The socialization training of culturally defined appropriate behaviors is intensified, most focused on inhibiting or controlling certain behaviors.

   a Elimination or toilet training is one of the first restraints of the child.

   b Training in cleanliness is begun.

   c Limitations are placed on tantrums and destructive activities.

   d Exploration is restricted when it becomes annoying, hazardous, or destructive.

C From 3 to 6 years.

  1 Communication expands rapidly to include a wide array of nonverbal and verbal skills.

  2 Peer relations become increasingly active.

   a The social world becomes more extensive; the child is often sent to nursery school.

   b Close relationships are extended to a new group outside the family.

   c Child becomes more dependent upon peers.

  3 Play shifts from solitary to cooperative activities.

   a Play is used as a means of motor expression and use of muscles.

   b Play is used to imitate the self and others.

   c Most children are aware that play fantasies are "make believe."

  4 Aggressive behavior usually develops, especially in the American culture.

   a The degree of aggression is dependent upon available models and the payoff for aggressive behavior.

   b Boys are more likely to receive reinforcement for aggression than girls.

  5 Achievement-oriented behavior develops, depending upon the prompts and reinforcement received.

  6 Identification with and imitation of models is responsible for rapid social development.

   a Sex typing is learned, i.e., appropriate behaviors for one's sex as determined by culture are acquired through modeling and reinforcements.

   b Morality is a critical aspect of development during this time.

     (1) Moral development involves learning a set of acceptable standards of behavior, living by them, and experiencing guilt if they are not obeyed or upheld.

     (2) Parents are usually the models for values and standards.

     (3) The parents' model is more likely to be followed if they are loving and nurturant than if they are rejecting.

  7 The child may assert his power and vest power in the father or the mother, e.g., the child says "My father is strongest" or "I am the best," especially if such statements receive social support.

D From 6 to 13 years.

   1 This is the period extending from the beginning of formal schooling to the onset of puberty.

   2 Beginning school is important because new knowledge is acquired and social life is broadened.

   3 The child participates in a variety of activities evolving from schoolwork and social play; clubs or informal groups are formed.

   4 The influence of the parents on the child is still important, especially with regard to the formation of the child's self-esteem.

   5 Traditional sex roles become increasingly defined, although social dissent on rigid sex typing may produce less clear sex roles.

   6 Moral development continues; the child no longer holds rigid notions of right and wrong based on adult expectations; instead, he becomes more equalitarian, basing judgments on cooperation and group needs (Piaget, 1932).

   7 Identification with ethnic, racial, and religious groups becomes somewhat fixed during this period.

   8 Children associate primarily with peers of the same sex.

   9 The child continues the trend toward conforming more to the attitudes and values of the peer group.

E From 13 to 18 years: adolescence.

   1 Changes in physical appearance may affect social-emotional adjustment, e.g., an adolescent who is larger than the average may be viewed as an adult and expected to be as emotionally mature as an adult.

   2 Many demands are made on adolescents in our culture, i.e., preparation for a vocation, becoming independent, developing a sense of identity. Consequently this may be a time when social-emotional problems are precipitated.

   3 The major adjustment is establishing independence, i.e., freeing oneself from parental control and influence.

   4 Sexual capabilities and expectations are intensified, which may create tensions and problems, especially since our culture places restrictions on overt sexual activity.

   5 The nature of peer group changes from "gangs" and "clubs" to male and female interactions and heterosexual cliques.

II GENERAL CHARACTERISTICS OF SOCIAL-EMOTIONAL PROBLEMS OR BEHAVIOR DISORDERS.

  A Definition.

    1 "Deviation from age-appropriate behavior which significantly interferes with (1) the child's own growth and development and/or (2) the lives of others" (Kirk, 1972).

    2 Behavior disorders are described in terms of deviance from cultural norms, which are variable, thus making precise definition difficult.

What may be labeled a behavior disorder in one setting may not be in another.

3 The demarcation between "abnormal" and "normal" behavior is not clear and requires a complex consideration of many criteria.

B Incidence of behavior disorders.

1 Incidence figures are unclear because of the inconsistency of labeling and criteria for behavior disorders.

2 Estimates vary from 1 to 12 percent of the child population.

3 Survey data on admissions and releases from clinics (Rosen, Bahn, and Kramer, 1964).

    a The release rate from clinics for children with mental disorders was 212 per 100,000.

    b The rate for boys was almost twice the rate for girls.

    c Usage of clinics was at a peak during two age periods.

        (1) Boys: 9 and 14 years.

        (2) Girls: 10 and 15 years.

    d Rates for nonwhites were lower in childhood than for whites.

    e Transient situational personality disorder was the most common diagnosis.

4 U. S. Office of Education estimates the incidence of emotionally disturbed children to be about 2 percent of the school-age population (Bureau of Education for the Handicapped, 1969, 1970).

III CLASSIFICATION OF BEHAVIOR DISORDERS.

Because behavior disorders have not been specifically defined, a classification system serves only to group behavior disorders and does not represent mutually exclusive categories. No children possess all the behaviors grouped in these categories; rather, children possess some of these behaviors to different degrees. Classification is based on characteristics of the problem regardless of the real or assumed etiology of the disorder.

A Problems of conduct or social maladjustment.

1 These create disruptions for others.

    a These behaviors are unaccepted by society and usually violate cultural norms.

    b The disruptive behavior may be sanctioned by a small peer group, but violates general home, school, and family standards.

2 They are characterized by aggressive behaviors.

    a Disobedience.

    b Disruptiveness.

    c Defiance.

    d Uncooperativeness.

3 The term "juvenile delinquent" is frequently used to identify children who have disobeyed laws and have possibly been arrested or otherwise referred to a court.

B Personality problems or emotional disturbances.
1 These result in suffering for the child, i.e., inner tensions and anxieties.
2 These are characterized by anxious or withdrawal behaviors.
  a Shyness.
  b Self-consciousness.
  c Fearfulness.
  d Hypersensitivity.
3 The American Psychiatric Association (1952) has classified emotional disturbances.
  a Psychotic disorders (functional psychosis).
    (1) This is the most severe type of mental disorder.
    (2) The person is disoriented in time, space, or person or all three.
    (3) Schizophrenia is the most prominent syndrome in this category.
    (4) Professional care is always required with probable hospitalization.
  b Psychoneurotic disorders (neurosis).
    (1) Anxiety is usually the primary problem.
    (2) These problems are far less serious and more responsive to treatment than psychotic disorders.
    (3) Children with these problems may be placed in a special class for the emotionally disturbed or may be phased into normal classes.
  c Transient situational personality disorders.
    (1) Symptoms differ greatly from disorder to disorder.
    (2) Such a disorder is caused by a traumatic event in a child's life, according to some theorists.
    (3) Whether or not special help is needed depends upon the severity and the age when the traumatic event occurred.
  d Psychosomatic disorders.
    (1) These are caused by repression of emotions, reinforcement of organ dysfunction, vulnerability of "target organs" under stress, or other factors, depending on the theory used to explain psychosomatic disorders.
    (2) They are classified according to the part of the body affected.
    (3) Frequent psychosomatic disorders are backache, ulcers, eczema, and headache.
  e Organic brain disorders.
    (1) These may be responsible for some behavior disorders.
    (2) Treatment depends upon the individual needs of the child.
    (3) Frequently the diagnosis "brain damage" has no medical basis, but is an inference based on behavior only.

  f Mental deficiency or mental retardation.

4 Telford and Sawrey (1967) classify emotional disturbance on the basis of anxiety, withdrawal, and hostile aggression.

  a Anxiety is defined as "fear with a future reference" and may be of several types.

   (1) Chronic anxiety.

    (a) This appears to be unrelated to any specific cause.

    (b) The level may be sufficiently high to constitute a serious handicap.

    (c) The symptoms are varied.

     [1] Irritability.

     [2] Fearfulness.

     [3] Problems with sleep and appetite.

     [4] Frequent crying.

     [5] Lack of energy.

   (2) Phobias are defined as "intense, specific fears that have no apparent rational basis" (Telford and Sawrey, 1967).

    (a) Common examples.

     [1] School phobia.

     [2] Death phobia.

   (3) Obsessions and compulsions which are of high frequency; stereotyped acts or thoughts. A compulsion is a repetitive, intense urge to behave in certain ways. An obsession is a preoccupation with the same thought or memory.

    (a) Compulsive and obsessive behaviors seem to reduce anxiety temporarily.

    (b) Examples include excessive compulsive cleanliness and pyromania (compulsive setting of fires).

  b Withdrawal from reality.

   (1) Schizophrenia.

    (a) This is one of the most common forms of functional psychosis.

    (b) It is "characterized by severe withdrawal, disorganization, lack of affect, and distorted emotional reactions" (Telford and Sawrey, 1967).

    (c) Delusions and hallucinations often occur.

    (d) If the onset is before puberty, which is rare, the condition is termed "childhood schizophrenia."

   (2) Early infantile autism.

    (a) Severe withdrawal.

    (b) Impairment in or failure to develop emotional relationships with others.

    (c) Often echolalia, i.e., mechanical repetition of words and phrases others say.

          (d) Rigidity, i.e., the maintenance of sameness, opposition to changes in routine.

          (e) Perseveration, i.e., monotonous repetition of actions and utterances.

      (3) Regression.

          (a) This is a return to less mature behavior or to a response characteristic of an earlier stage of development.

          (b) Examples in children include return to thumb sucking, bed wetting, and baby talk.

          (c) This usually occurs during stress or sudden reduction in reinforcement.

      (4) Daydreaming and fantasy.

          (a) These are considered a disorder when excessive.

          (b) They are considered a disorder when used as a means for withdrawing or escaping.

  c Hostile aggression.

      (1) This is destructive behavior directed toward a person or property.

      (2) It is often a product of frustration.

IV ETIOLOGICAL FACTORS ASSOCIATED WITH BEHAVIOR DISORDERS.

  A Psychological factors, according to various theorists.

    1 Frustration caused by delay of rewards, thwarting, or conflict.

      a "Frustrating events are those which block the individual's goal-seeking behavior, threaten his self-esteem, or deprive him of the opportunity to gratify some salient motive" (Mussen, Conger, and Kagan, 1969).

      b Individuals differ greatly in tolerance of and reaction to frustration.

      c Frustration leads to aggression (Dollard, Doob, Miller, Mower, and Sears, 1939).

      d Aggression is often manifested by destructiveness and hostility.

      e Frustration frequently leads to regression or a return to earlier forms of behavior (Barker, Dembo, and Lewin, 1941).

      f Frustration frequently leads to resignation or lack of motivation and ability to respond to a situation (Maier, 1949).

    2 Childhood bereavement caused by separation from or death of loved one, which may lead to later disorders.

      a Delinquency (Gregory, 1958).

      b Criminality (Brown, 1966).

      c Reactive depression, marital disharmony, occupational maladjustment, and neurosis (Gay and Tonge, 1967).

3 Fixation or regression at an early developmental stage.
    a Oral deprivation in infancy is believed by some to affect oral habits and later personality (Goldman-Eisler, 1951; Levy, 1928; Roberts, 1944).
    b Harsh toilet-training procedures are seen by some as causes of personality disorders (Despert, 1944; MacFarlane, Allen, and Honzik, 1954; Sears, Whiting, Nowlis, and Sears, 1953).
B Environmental factors.
  1 Familiar environments.
    a Family influences are often implicated as a cause of problems of conduct.
      (1) Parental absence.
        (a) As a result of institutionalization and deprivation, children display unsocialized aggression, lack of self-control, and lack of feelings for others (Bowlby, Ainsworth, Boston, and Rosenbluth, 1956; Goldfarb, 1945).
        (b) The effect of the mother's partial absence is uncertain.
        (c) Deviant children come from broken homes more frequently than nondeviant children (Bacon, Child, and Barry, 1963; Glueck and Glueck, 1950).
      (2) Parental characteristics.
        (a) Deviant children more likely to be produced by deviant parents.
        (b) Parents may be models of aggression (Bandura and Walters, 1963; Berkowitz, 1962).
        (c) A criminal father and a cold mother are the most probable combination to produce a delinquent child (McCord and McCord, 1958).
        (d) Marital conflicts are often found in delinquents' parents (Glueck and Glueck, 1950; McCord, McCord, and Gudeman, 1960).
      (3) Certain modes of child management seem to be related to the development of children's problems.
        (a) Maternal punitiveness, overpermissiveness, and inconsistency (Rosenthal, Finkelstein, Ni, and Robertson, 1959).
        (b) Parental punitiveness, neglect, and authoritarian control.
        (c) Parental use of physical punishment and hostility seems to be specifically related to aggressive behavior (Becker, 1964).
        (d) Parental rejection, encouragement of aggression, and hostility (Bandura and Walters, 1959).

(e) Severe parental punishment for aggression is highly correlated with aggression in nondelinquent boys (Sears, Whiting, Nowlis, and Sears, 1953).

(f) Maternal overcontrol is correlated with low aggression in sons, normal control with assertive behavior (McCord, McCord, and Howard, 1961).

(g) Maternal domination and restriction may result in timid, withdrawing children, while excessively permissive mothering seems related to rebellious, disobedient children (Levy, 1943).

(h) Inconsistency in disciplinary practices is more often found in parents of delinquents (Bandura and Walters, 1959; Glueck and Glueck, 1950).

b Family characteristics may contribute to personality disorders.

(1) Parental characteristics.

(a) Neurotic children come from homes with a higher proportion of neurotic parents (Jenkins, 1966; Shields and Slater, 1961).

(b) Neurotic disorders in parents are often associated with marital conflict (Cummings, Bayley, and Rie, 1966).

(2) Parent-child interactions.

(a) Overinhibited children frequently come from restrictive homes (Hewitt and Jenkins, 1946).

(b) Parents with inhibited, neurotic children exhibit more constraint than parents of unsocialized aggressive and socialized aggressive children (Lewis, 1954).

(c) Phobias (e.g., school phobia) in children are associated with overprotective parents (Eisenberg, 1958).

(d) Prolonged separation of the child from the parent is likely to lead to depression and withdrawal reaction (Gay and Tonge, 1967).

(3) Family influences with relation to psychosomatic disorders.

(a) Negative interactions between mother and child involving irritability and competition but little closeness seem to be related to psychosomatic problems of children.

(b) Overprotective mothering may be a causal or maintaining factor in some childhood asthma (Rees, 1964).

c Family illnesses may be associated with the more prevalent behavior disorders in children.

(1) An excessive degree of physical illness in a family may have two results.

        (a) A high rate of delinquency (Glueck and Glueck, 1950).

        (b) Maladjustment of children with behavior disorders (Craig, 1956).

    (2) Association exists between parents with psychiatric disorders and children with behavior disorders (Lewis, 1954).

2 Nonfamiliar factors.

    a The numerous adverse effects of institutionalization include separation from parents, malnutrition, lack of sensory stimulation, and isolation (Bowlby, 1951; Goldfarb, 1945b; Spitz, 1945).

    b The mores of the group, and deviances from these, are different in various classes or segments of society. Acceptable mores and behavior for the "lower class" might be labeled "deviant" by members of the "middle class" (Miller, 1958).

    c The fact that the delinquency areas in Chicago can be divided into different zones shows the great effect of environment with regard to these disorders (Shaw and McKay, 1942).

    d The success of behavior modification and behavior therapy with childhood behavior problems strongly suggests an environmental basis for many of these problems (Franks and Wilson, 1973).

C Physiological factors.

  1 Genetic factors are suspected by some to be possible causes for schizophrenia (Anthony, 1968; Kallmann, 1946, 1953; Rosenthal, 1959).

  2 Constitutional makeup has been considered a cause of disorder.

    a There may be an association of body build to adjustment.

        (1) Ectomorphy is associated with restlessness and anxiety (Davidson, McInnes, and Parnell, 1957).

        (2) Mesomorphy is correlated with aggressiveness and assertiveness (Walker, 1962).

    b The autonomic nervous system may be related to behavior (Wenger, 1947).

        (1) Predominance of the sympathetic system is associated with a more dependent, unstable, insecure child.

        (2) Predominance of the parasympathetic system is associated with an independent, secure, stable child.

    c The relationship of hormonal changes and physical growth to behavior disorders is not yet clear (Tanner, 1947).

    d Original temperamental tendency or activity type (whether one is as hyperactive or inactive) may be related to later behavior disorders (Woolf, 1953).

    3 Reproductive factors.

        a The significance of the prenatal environment is indefinite with respect to later behavior disorders of the child.

        b Behavior disorders are more common in premature children (Drillien, 1961; Shirley, 1939).

    3 Brain damage or dysfunction of the central nervous system.

        a This is believed by many to be a causal factor in behavior disorders (Cruickshank, Bentzen, Rotsburg, and Tannhauser, 1961; Strauss and Lentinen, 1947; numerous others).

        b There is little direct, empirical evidence that brain damage is associated with a specific syndrome of psychopathology (Werry, 1972).

V TREATMENT AND MANAGEMENT OF BEHAVIORAL DISORDERS.

    A Types of treatment procedures.

        1 Individual verbal psychotherapies: those children with communication difficulties are unable to benefit to any great extent from this treatment.

        2 Family (filial) therapy (Guerney, 1969).

            a Group perspective is employed, not exclusive focus on the "problem" individual.

            b This kind of therapy analyzes the communication system within the family.

            c The therapist forms a group within the family and plays an active role.

            d The family becomes the therapeutic instrument.

        3 Group therapy.

            a Emphasis is on the activity of children as individuals in a group (Slavson, 1964).

            b Emphasis is on verbal communications of the group as a whole.

            c Problems in social behavior, cooperation, etc., may be the focus in situation therapy.

        4 Hypnotic therapy.

        5 Behavior therapy.

            a Conditioning procedures are used to establish desirable behavior, such as cooperative behavior (Patterson and Brodsky, 1966) or increased social interaction (Baer and Wolf, 1968), or to eliminate undesirable behavior, such as fears (Jones, 1924) or disruptive classroom behavior (Patterson, 1965).

            b Desensitization is used to eliminate phobias and other abnormal behavior (Wolpe and Lazarus, 1966).

            c Aversion therapy is the use of the escape from and avoidance of shock to increase social interaction in autistic children (Lovaas, Schaeffer, and Simmons, 1965).

        6 Drug therapy for controlling symptoms.

B   Educational approaches to management of behavior disorders (Dunn, 1973; Woody, 1969; Kirk, 1972).
  1   The psychoanalytic-psychodynamic approach.
    a   This is based on Freud's psychoanalytic theory.
    b   Disorder is believed to be the result of intrapsychic conflict.
    c   The treatment is aimed at the removal of the "underlying cause" of behavior deviance.
    d   Problems are thought to result from childhood events.
    e   Essentials of the therapy are the insight of the patient and a positive transference relationship with the therapist (Berkowitz and Rothman, 1960).
    f   There are limitations.
      (1)   Success is questionable (Stewart, 1970).
      (2)   Therapy requires a great length of time.
      (3)   It is expensive.
      (4)   There is a lack of personnel trained in this approach.
  2   Behavior modification.
    a   The position of the advocates is that almost all behavior is learned.
    b   Therapy is concerned with a specific behavior.
    c   There are two types of conditioning models.
      (1)   Respondent conditioning: responses and reflexes that are part of the organism's response repertoire are elicited by specific stimuli in the environment.
      (2)   Operant conditioning: responses emitted by the organism are followed by consequences that increase or decrease the likelihood that those responses will occur again.
    d   Operant conditioning is increasingly used in the classroom to control behavior disorders.
      (1)   Goals for behavior change are determined and established.
      (2)   The child's task is programed or organized in small steps; each step is built on the preceding step, so the child meets with success at each trial.
      (3)   If the child completes a task successfully, he receives reinforcement (social or tangible).
    e   The teacher's role is to structure or "engineer" the educational environment.
    f   Operant conditioning is used in the classroom for children with behavior disorders (O'Leary and Becker, 1967; Quay, 1966; Whelan, 1966).
  3   Developmental (engineered-classroom) strategy (Hewett, 1968).
    a   The behavior modification approach is used with seven educational goals in a developmental sequence.
      (1)   Attention.
      (2)   Response.

    (3) Order.

    (4) Exploration.

    (5) Social approval.

    (6) Mastery.

    (7) Achievement.

  b The essentials of effective teaching (Hewett, 1967) involve a "learning triangle."

    (1) The selection of the task.

    (2) The reward for the accomplishment of the task.

    (3) Structural control by the teacher.

  c The "engineered classroom."

    (1) Mastery center—mastery and achievement area.

    (2) Order center—activities emphasizing participation, the following of directions, and completion of the task.

    (3) Exploratory center—science, art, and communication activities.

  d The child is assigned to a center, given a task, and rewarded for "student" behavior.

4 Learning disabilities strategy.

  a Frequently the discrepancy between the capacity of the child to behave and the requirements of the environment is due to a specific learning disability.

  b Intervention is aimed at a specific disability, e.g., reading, writing, or perceiving (Cruickshank, Bentzen, Ratzburg, and Tannhauser, 1961).

  c Specific strategies and materials have been designed to remediate specific disabilities (Lerner, 1971).

  d There are criticisms regarding the etiology arguments for specific disabilities and the specificity of methods and materials (Neisworth and Greer, 1974).

5 Psychoeducational approach (Fenichel, 1971; Morse, 1971).

  a There are eclectic approaches.

    (1) One is similar to the behavior modification approach in emphasis on what the child does.

    (2) One is similar to the psychodynamic approach in emphasis on why the child behaves as he does.

    (3) One is similar to the learning disability model in dealing with children's specific educational deficiencies.

  b A child possesses innate potentials which, when coupled with experience, determine his ability to cope with situations.

  c If the child is not equipped with skills for succeeding in school, he meets with failure, which produces frustration and anxiety, which in turn lead to maladaptive behavior.

  d If his maladaptive behavior meets with hostility from teachers or peers, more frustration is created for the child and forms a vicious cycle.

e Breaking this cycle is the goal of this approach.

f The aim is to lessen maladaptive behavior and to teach the child to cope with inner needs and stress.

g Emphasis is placed on the importance of the relationship between teacher and pupil; on an educational milieu made up of staff, peers, and school materials; and on the child's motivation for various behaviors.

6 Ecological strategy (Hobbs, 1966).

a "Project Re-ED" for the reeducation of emotionally disturbed children is an example.

b This approach rejects the psychotherapeutic approach; instead it sees the child as a part of a social system which includes family, school, and community.

c This approach uses the home and concurrent programs for education of the family, the school, and the community.

d Principles of this approach.

(1) Life is to be lived now.

(2) Time is an ally.

(3) Trust is essential.

(4) Competence makes a difference.

(5) Symptoms can and should be controlled.

(6) Cognitive control can be taught.

(7) Feelings should be nurtured.

(8) The group is important to children.

(9) Ceremony and ritual give order, stability, and confidence.

(10) The body is the armature of the self.

(11) Communities are important.

(12) Finally, a child should know joy.

C Organization of special services for children with behavior disorders (Kirk, 1972).

1 Regular classroom.

a Regular classroom teacher.

b Regular classroom teacher with consultation.

c Regular classroom teacher and special services from itinerant teacher.

2 Regular class plus resource room.

3 Part-time special class.

4 Full-time special class.

5 Special day-school.

6 Residential school.

7 Psychiatric hospital.

8 Mental health clinics.

9 Residential schools for delinquents.

VI EVALUATION PROCEDURES (SEE TABLE 15-1).

TABLE 15–1

Tests	Specific Age Group	Specific Factors Measured
Nonprojective tests (objective or self-report)		
Behavior Checklist (Rubin, Simson, Betwee, 1966)	Grades K, 1, 2, 3, 5	Seven factors of classroom behavior: 1 Disorientation and maladjustment to environment 2 Antisocial behavior 3 Unassertive, overconforming behavior 4 Neglect 5 Infantile behavior 6 Immature social behavior 7 Irresponsible behavior
Behavior Description Chart (BDC) (Bowman, DeHaan, Kough, and Liddle, 1956)	Grades 4–6	1 Social leadership 2 Withdrawn maladjustment 3 Aggressive maladjustment
Behavior Problem Checklist (Quay and Peterson, 1967)		Differentiated according to: Conduct problem Personality problem Inadequacy-immaturity factor Socialized delinquency
Junior Eysenck Personality Inventory (Eysenck, 1965) Published by Educational and Individual Testing Service	7–16 years	Three scores: Extraversion Intraversion Lie
Minnesota Multiphasic Personality Inventory (MMPI) (Hathaway and McKinley, 1951) Published by Psychological Corporation	16 years and over	Fourteen scores: 1 Hypochondriasis 2 Depression 3 Hysteria 4 Psychopathic deviate 5 Masculinity/femininity 6 Paranoia 7 Psychasthenia 8 Schizophrenia 9 Hypomania 10 Social 11 Question 12 Lie 13 Validity 14 Test-taking attitude

TABLE 15-1 CONTINUED

Tests	Specific Age Group	Specific Factors Measured
Walker Problem Behavior Identification Checklist (WPBIC) (Walker, 1970) Published by Western Psychological Services	Grades 4, 5, and 6	Five factors: 1 Acting out 2 Withdrawal 3 Distractability 4 Disturbed peer relations 5 Immaturity
Sixteen Personality Factor Questionnaire (Cattell, Saunders, and Stice, 1957) Published by Institute for Personality and Ability Testing	16 years and over	1 Reserved vs. outgoing 2 Less intelligence vs. more intelligence 3 Affected by feelings vs. emotionally stable 4 Humble vs. assertive 5 Sober vs. happy-go-lucky 6 Expedient vs. conscientious 7 Shy vs. venturesome 8 Tough-minded vs. tender-minded 9 Trusting vs. suspicious 10 Practical vs. imaginative 11 Forthright vs. shrewd 12 Self-assured vs. apprehensive 13 Conservative vs. experimenting 14 Group-dependent vs. self-sufficient 15 Undisciplined self-conflict vs. controlled 16 Relaxed vs. tense Four second-order factor scores: 1 Introversion vs. extraversion 2 Low anxiety vs. high anxiety 3 Tender-minded emotionality vs. alert poise 4 Subduedness vs. independence
Tennessee Self Concept Scale (Fitts, 1965) Published by Counselor Recordings and Tests	12 years and over	15 scores of self-criticism
Projective tests Children's Apperception Test (Bellak & Bellak, 1949) Published by C.P.S., Inc.	3–10 years	

TABLE 15-1 CONTINUED

Tests	Specific Age Group	Specific Factors Measured
Thematic Apperception Test (TAT) (Murray, 1943) Published by Psychological Corp.	4 years and over	
The Blacky Pictures: A Technique for Exploration of Personality Dynamics (Blum, 1950) Published by Psychological Corp.	5 years and over	
Rorschach (Rorschach, 1951)	3 years and over	(No one method of scoring and interpreting generally accepted)

16
COMMUNICATION PROBLEMS

I NORMAL STAGES IN THE DEVELOPMENT OF VERBAL COMMUNICATION.
  A Reflexive vocalization.
    1 Birth to approximately 3 weeks—crying is undifferentiated regardless of physiological state, i.e., hunger, cold, pain, etc.
    2 Approximately 3 weeks—crying becomes differentiated and depends on specific stimuli, e.g., crying sounds are different when a child is hungry than when he is cold.
  B Babbling or vocal play—6 weeks to 6 months.
    1 The infant reacts to his own sounds.
    2 He produces sounds when physically comfortable and content.
    3 He babbles repeatedly with variations in the types of sounds as he grows older.
  C Lalling—6 to 9 months.
    1 The hearing of sounds and sound production occur in close association.
    2 Self-imitation—the infant hears his own sounds and begins repeating them.

      3 Vocalizations are often used for gaining attention and making demands known to others.

      4 Vocalizations usually involve repetition of consonant-vowel syllables, e.g., "ma-ma."

D Echolalic—9 to 12 months.

      1 The infant imitates sounds made by others.

      2 No meaning is attached to the sounds imitated.

      3 The infant builds a repertoire of sounds and sound combinations according to the uniquenesses of his environment.

E True speech—12 to 18 months.

      1 The child says his first word.

      2 He uses language intentionally and purposefully as a tool for communication.

      3 The first word is usually a single syllable, e.g., "ma," or a duplicated syllable, e.g., "ma-ma."

      4 The first word serves the purpose of a sentence because the meaning can be interpreted from the context in which it was given.

      5 The first words are likely to be nouns since the child usually hears more nouns than other parts of speech.

      6 Verbs are likely to appear next, followed by adjectives and adverbs.

      7 The size of the oral vocabulary is usually 2 to 3 words at 16 to 18 months.

      8 The vocabulary comprehended is always much greater than the child's expressive oral vocabulary.

F From 18 to 24 months.

      1 The oral vocabulary grows to between 3 and 50 words.

      2 The vocabulary comprehended is much larger than the expressive vocabulary.

      3 The child uses new words to generalize, i.e., one word might be used to indicate several different objects.

      4 The child spontaneously modifies the pronunciation of a word to his own established pattern of vocalization, e.g., baby talk or family or sectional characteristics.

      5 The child often leaves off the beginnings and ends of words or phrases.

      6 The child's voice is often unstable and high-pitched or strained at this age.

G At 2 years.

      1 The oral vocabulary is frequently as high as 300 words at 2 years of age.

      2 The child begins using pronouns—"my," "mine," "me," "you," and "I"—and combining nouns and verbs into two-word sentences.

      3 Speech is employed to express needs with increased frequency.

      4 The child continues the spontaneous modification of pronunciations of words to fit his own vocalization pattern.

     5 Repetitions in words and phrases are frequent.

     6 The rhythm of speech is often broken and varied.

     7 The child often repeats sounds, syllables, words, and phrases.

     8 The voice has better control of pitch but is often low and strained.

     9 Beginning consonants are usually pronounced correctly; medial or middle consonants are often slighted.

H At 3 years.

     1 The oral vocabulary usually increases to 1,000 words.

     2 Language is used to express relationships and qualifications.

     3 Echolalia continues.

     4 Conventional syntax and grammar are developed.

        a The child learns to make plural nouns.

        b The child learns to form the past tense of verbs.

     5 Hesitations and repetitions are still frequent although the voice is usually well controlled.

     6 Substitution for /th/ is frequently made.

     7 By three years, the child has mastered vowels, diphthongs, and some consonants: /m/, /l/, /ng/, /p/, /t/, /b/, /d/, /g/, /f/.

I At 4 years.

     1 At 4 years of age, the child's vocabulary increases rapidly and more complicated sentences are used.

        a He uses conjunctions to form compound sentences.

        b He makes complex sentences.

     2 Fundamentals of sentence structure, grammar, vocabulary, and articulation are basically mastered.

     3 Verbal fluency is acquired and repetitions are fewer at this age.

     4 Consonants /k/, /s/, /sh/, /v/, /j/, /r/, and some double and triple consonants, /pl/, /mp/, /mpt/, are usually mastered by this age.

J At 5 years.

     1 Vocabulary has increased and syntax improved.

     2 Sentence structure is characterized by vocal utterances.

        a They average 4.6 words in length.

        b They are grammatically correct.

        c They use compound and complex sentences.

     3 About 90 percent of all sounds are correctly spoken.

     4 Reversal of sounds is typically the most frequent type of error with repetitions rarely present.

K At 6 years and beyond.

     1 A 16,000-word comprehension vocabulary is developed.

     2 A 2,000-word oral vocabulary is used with correctness.

II CRITERIA FOR AND FREQUENCY OF DEFECTIVE SPEECH.

  A Speech is considered defective when it has the following characteristics (Van Riper, 1972).

     1 It interferes with communication.

2 It calls attention to the speaker in negative ways.

3 It causes the speaker to experience socioemotional problems.

B   Estimated incidence of speech disorders (See Table 16-1).

III   TYPES OF SPEECH DISORDERS, THEIR CHARACTERISTICS, CAUSES, AND TREATMENT APPROACHES.

A   Articulation disorders.

1   Characteristics.

a   Defective, inconsistent, or incorrect speech sounds are present.

b   Articulation disorders account for 60 to 80 percent of all diagnosed speech disorders.

c   The sounds most frequently misarticulated are /s/ /r/ /l/ /th/ /sh/.

d   The following are common patterns of articulation disorders.

(1)   Baby talk.

(2)   Lisping.

(3)   Lalling (defective /r/, /l/, /t/, /d/, or /s/ sounds due to inactivity of tongue tip).

2   Categories of types.

a   Omissions (sounds are not produced, e.g., "at" for "cat").

b   Substitutions (person recognizes appropriate sound but uses wrong one, e.g., "yeth" for "yes").

c   Distortions (attempt to approximate correct sound is distorted, e.g., /s/ in "say" articulated like /z/).

d   Additions (improper addition of sound to a word, e.g., "on-un the table").

3   Causes.

a   Functional causes: "dyslalia."

(1)   Poor or inconsistent teaching methods by parents to stimulate speech.

TABLE 16-1   ESTIMATED PERCENT OF SCHOOL-AGE CHILDREN WITH VARIOUS TYPES OF SPEECH PROBLEMS*

Type of Problem	Percent of Children with Serious Problems
Articulation	3.0
Stuttering	0.8
Voice	0.2
Cleft-palate speech	0.1
Cerebral-palsy speech	0.1
Retarded speech development	0.3
Speech problem due to impaired hearing	0.5
Total	5.0

* Adapted from American Speech and Hearing Association and Bureau of Education for the Handicapped data, 1972 estimate.

(2) Poor speech models at home, in the neighborhood, or at school.

(3) Emotional problems.

b Organic causes

(1) Dysarthria (disorders due to brain or nerve damage).

(2) Other factors.

(a) Significant hearing loss.

(b) Oral-facial abnormalities.

(c) Poor coordination of speech musculature.

(d) High and narrow palate that leaves little room for tongue to move.

4 Evaluative procedures for articulation disorders.

a Deep Test of Articulation by E. T. McDonald (consists of items in which each sound to be tested is presented as it is preceded by each of the consonants and vowels and followed by a vowel and as it is followed by each of the consonants and vowels and preceded by a vowel).

b The Templin-Darley Screening and Diagnostic Tests of Articulation by M. Templin and F. Darley (consists of 176 items that test all vowels and diphthongs once, every consonant once in each position in which it occurs, and each of the more frequently occurring consonant blends).

5 Treatment and management of articulation disorders.

a Van Riper's (1972) suggested approach.

(1) Minimize or eliminate causal factors.

(2) Identify both the error and the standard sound to be used.

(3) Ear-train or scan and compare the erroneous sound with the correct sound.

(4) Change the incorrect utterance until the correct sound is produced through a process of successive approximations to the final goal.

(5) Strengthen the new speech sound through practice and reinforcement until it is used automatically in a variety of contexts.

b Methods of teaching new sounds (Van Riper, 1972).

(1) Progressive approximation: reinforcement provided to the child for making successively closer approximations to correct speech sound.

(2) Auditory stimulation: wrong sound is pronounced, identified, excluded, and then followed by correct sound.

(3) Phonetic placement: teacher uses diagrams and applicators to teach the child the correct placement of the lips, tongue, and teeth to make the appropriate speech sound.

(4) Modification of other standard sounds already mastered until desired sound is produced.

(5) Use of key words in which correct sound already appears consistently until sound is produced in other combinations.

B Disorders of rhythm or speech flow.

1 Stuttering.

    a Characteristics.

        (1) Normal flow and rhythm of speech are disturbed by oscillations, fixations, repetitions, or prolongations of sounds, syllables, words, or phrases.

        (2) Stuttering occurs intermittently in the total flow of speech.

        (3) Dysfluency varies with such factors as rhythm, rate, linguistic factors (initial sound, word length, grammatical function, and position in sentence), contingent punishment and reinforcement, skill in producing speech sounds, listener's response, and speaker's attitude (Perkins, 1971).

    b Stages.

        (1) "Primary stuttering" involves more dysfluencies or prolongations and repetitions in the child's speech than are considered normal; the child seems to be aware of these difficulties.

        (2) "Secondary stuttering" occurs when the child labels himself and others as stutterers, leading to frustration and struggle in subsequent speech production.

    c Causes.

        (1) Organic theories.

            (a) Constitutional differences: the stutterer allegedly has a predisposition to stuttering which causes fluency to break down easily under emotional stress (Eisenson, 1958).

            (b) Cerebral dominance: there is a presumed lack of control by either cerebral hemisphere (the belief is that one cerebral hemisphere governs speech flow), which causes stuttering (Travis, 1931).

            (c) Dysphemia: this is a neuromuscular condition characterized by nerve impulses that are poorly timed in coordinating speech musculatures.

            (d) An epileptic type of condition results in a series of small seizures which interrupt speech.

            (e) Poor coordination of the speech apparatus results from brain damage or basic hereditary problems.

    (2) Functional theories.

        (a) Diagnosogenic or semantic theory (Johnson, 1956).

            [1] In normal development of speech, the child has dysfluencies.

            [2] Parents and others react to dysfluencies by labeling them defective and the child a stutterer.

            [3] The child responds with emotional behaviors and tries to eliminate the dysfluencies.

            [4] Competing emotional behaviors result in more speech dysfluencies, which, in turn, produce more competing avoidance behaviors ("vicious circle").

        (b) Frustration theory.

            [1] Attempts to communicate are interrupted by dysfluencies that are created by environmental pressures, such as loss of the listener's attention.

            [2] The child's communication behavior is punished, or receives little appropriate reinforcement; he notices his dysfluencies and begins to struggle with speech production.

        (c) Pressure theory.

            [1] Developmental pressures placed on the child who produces dysfluencies.

            [2] Pressures from conflicts in the home or high standards of performance that are difficult to meet in articulation, grammar, politeness, and conduct cause maladaptive behaviors.

            [3] As part of the syndrome, the child and others react negatively to the dysfluencies.

        (d) Neurotic theories.

            [1] Stuttering is defined as an outward manifestation of inner needs.

            [2] These needs are caused by defective relationships with the parents, resulting from such factors as overprotection, overdominance, or strict toilet-training methods.

        (e) Learning theories: stuttering is a learned behavior and therefore can be modified (Van Riper, 1970a).

  d Prognosis.

    (1) Prognosis is favorable, if therapy is begun as soon as the problem arises.

    (2) Approximately 80 percent of children who are believed to stutter will not exhibit dysfluencies in adulthood.

(3) The chance of complete remission generally decreases as an individual becomes a secondary stutterer.

e Evaluative procedures.

  (1) Iowa Scale of Attitude toward Stuttering by R. Ammons and W. Johnson (assessment of a speaker's opinion about stutterers and their feelings about various speaking situations).

f Treatment, therapy, or management.

  (1) Suggested methods of treatment vary considerably and are completely dependent on one's position regarding the presumed causation.

  (2) Van Riper (1972) suggests that the therapist must isolate and eliminate factors that contribute to the disorder.

    (a) The inability to find or remember the correct word.

    (b) The inability or doubt of ability to articulate correctly.

    (c) The fear of unpleasant consequences of communication.

    (d) The presence, threat, or fear of interruption by someone else.

    (e) The loss of the listener's attention.

  (3) Play therapy (Murphy and Fitz-Simons, 1960), creative dramatics (McIntyre and McWilliams, 1959), and parent and group counseling are often used to minimize presumed pressures.

  (4) Psychoanalysis has been used, with questionable results (Wyatt and Herzon, 1962).

  (5) Behavior modification and operant conditioning techniques have been effective in removing and decreasing the frequency and intensity of stuttering (Goldiamond, 1968; Martin, 1968; Van Riper, 1970b).

2 Cluttering.

a It is unclear whether cluttering is a type of rhythm disorder, a form of stuttering, or a forerunner of stuttering.

b Characteristics.

  (1) Speed of speaking is excessive, like "a hot potato in the mouth" or "verbal salad."

  (2) Sentence structure is disorganized.

  (3) Speech is garbled with syllables and sounds that are slurred or omitted.

  (4) Excessive repetitions occur.

c Postulated causes.

  (1) Heredity.

  (2) Neurological impairment of some form.

    d Therapy.

        (1) Improvements can be made when a speaker is told to stop and slow down in speaking.

        (2) Therapies used to deal with stuttering are believed to be effective in dealing with cluttering.

C Voice or phonation disorders.

  1 Characteristics.

    a There are marked deviations from generally accepted local standards in voice quality, pitch, intensity, and flexibility.

    b This group of speech problems represents the lowest incidence of speech disorders among children.

    c They are difficult to correct in children, since the speech mechanism and vocal quality of a young child are still developing and changing even beyond adolescence.

  2 Types.

    a Vocal quality disorders.

        (1) Hypernasality, i.e., excessive nasal emission during speech.

            (a) Characteristics.

                [1] Hypernasality is often combined with tension in vocal production resulting in a "twang."

                [2] Hypernasality may be consistent throughout speech or vary with content.

            (b) Causes.

                [1] Functional causes.

                    [a] Speech sounds found in certain regions of the country are imitated.

                    [b] Whining behavior is rewarded.

                    [c] Fatigue or low energy levels can also be causes.

                [2] Organic causes.

                    [a] Paralyzed soft palate resulting from condition like poliomyelitis.

                    [b] Congenitally short palate.

                    [c] Perforations in palate.

        (2) Hyponasality or denasality, i.e., failure to produce adequate nasal sounds: oral equivalent sounds are substituted for nasal sounds, i.e., /b/, /d/, and /g/ are substituted for /m/, /n/, and /ng/, respectively.

            (a) Extreme deviations in amount of tissue in the oral-nasal areas.

            (b) Swollen adenoids or swollen oral-nasal tissues from cold or allergies.

        (3) Harsh, husky, or breathy voice.
            (a) Causes.
                [1] Excessive tension or muscle strain in laryngeal area.
                [2] Growth on vocal cords (nodules) due to vocal abuse or excessive yelling.

b Pitch disorders.
    (1) Characteristics.
        (a) Pitch level too high or too low.
        (b) Pitch breaks, spontaneous changes, or intermittent interruptions.
        (c) Falsetto, i.e., combined disorder of pitch and quality reflected in an abnormally high-pitched voice.
    (2) Presumed causes.
        (a) Deliberate attempt to escape the pitch breaks and hoarse or husky vocal characteristics of adolescence.
        (b) Glandular difficulties preventing normal growth of the larynx.

c Intensity disorders.
    (1) Characteristics.
        (a) Speech too loud or too soft.
        (b) Loss of voice (aphonia).
    (2) Causes.
        (a) A loud voice may indicate a demand for attention or that the speaker has a hearing disorder.
        (b) Speech that is too soft may also result from a hearing problem, feelings of unsureness, or from psychosocial imitations.
        (c) Aphonia is often caused by laryngitis, but this occurs only temporarily.
        (d) True, long-term aphonia is caused by severe organic conditions in the oral area, such as paralysis or growths.

d Flexibility.
    (1) Characteristics.
        (a) Stereotyped inflections, e.g., the voice drops in pitch and loudness after every pause.
        (b) Monotone: lack of variation in vocal pitch and loudness.
    (2) Possible causes.
        (a) Emotional conflict in the environment.
        (b) Lack of physical energy due to sickness or fatigue.
        (c) Inability to hear normal variations in pitch and loudness.

       (d) Pitch level that normally is either too high or too low so that the speaker does not have an adequate range to vary.

3 Evaluative procedures: in most cases, the child is referred to a physician for medical diagnosis or to a speech therapist, if applicable.

4 Therapy.

    a Nonorganic causes.

       (1) Train the client to hear and distinguish vocal variations in himself and in others.

       (2) Find an acceptable voice (rather than teach a new one) in the person's repertoire and establish it until it is consistently exhibited.

    b Organic causes: medical diagnosis and treatment are provided.

IV TYPES OF LANGUAGE DISORDERS, THEIR CHARACTERISTICS, CAUSES, AND TREATMENT.

  A General definition and conditions.

    1 Speech and language disorders are intimately interrelated.

    2 Wood (1964) defines language as "an organized system of linguistic symbols (words) used by human beings to communicate on an abstract level."

    3 Language disorders (dysphasia) are usually meant to apply to all disorders of symbolic formulation or expression.

  B Types.

    1 Delayed verbal communication.

      a Characteristics.

        (1) The child does not acquire speech or the oral expression of language at the predicted "normal" time or with a standard degree of accuracy.

        (2) This condition can be present even when the child's articulation and general speech production are quite normal for a child his age.

      b Causes.

        (1) Organic.

          (a) Hearing loss associated with a congenital or an acquired physically based problem.

          (b) Brain damage.

          (c) Gross glandular irregularities.

        (2) Functional.

          (a) Poor teaching or child-rearing procedures to stimulate verbal communication.

          (b) Emotional problems.

          (c) Negativism toward communication models.

        (d)   Environmental deprivation, such as the child's not being spoken to at home or not being encouraged to label things, etc.

        (e)   Poor speech and language standards in the home.

   c Examples of evaluative procedures.

        (1)   Illinois Test of Psycholinguistic Abilities (ITPA) by S. A. Kirk and J. J. McCarthy (ages 2 to 9 years; tests in various areas of language development and performance).

        (2)   Northwestern Syntax Screening Test (NSST) (ages 3 to 11 years; used as screening test for syntax only).

   d Prognosis.

        (1)   The future outlook is good for disorders that are due to functional causes.

        (2)   Some severe, organically based, disabilities often remain after speech and language therapy.

           (a)   Significant all-encompassing articulation disorders.

           (b)   Extreme difficulty in school with certain skills in reading and writing, difficulties with visual perception, poor coordination, or poor psychomotor performance.

   e Some general principles regarding therapy.

        (1)   The therapist should only reward gestures that are accompanied by utterance, not silent gestures when verbal utterances are desired.

        (2)   He should encourage verbal imitative behavior through appropriate reinforcement.

        (3)   He should teach the child the sound alphabet if these skills are not already developed.

           (a)   Use of such procedures as rhymes and word plays.

           (b)   Use of the monokinesthetic method, i.e., one locates the muscles of the child's face and body in the correct position in order to aid the youngster to produce proper sounds and proper timing.

        (4)   Use of parallel talk with a therapist or with the parents will help a child to verbalize his thoughts.

2 Aphasia: the partial or total failure to develop use of language for oral communication.

   a Types (Telford and Sawrey, 1972).

        (1)   Sensory or receptive aphasia: the person seems not to understand spoken (or sometimes written) language.

        (2)   Motor or expressive aphasia: the person seems to be unable to speak (or sometimes to write) properly.

        (3)   Conceptual aphasia: the person has difficulty formulating generalizations or classifications or both.

      (4)   Global or mixed aphasia: all language forms are affected.

b Causes: presumed to be organic, caused by brain dysfunction or damage.

c Developmental characteristics frequently observed in children with aphasia (Lundeen, 1972).

      (1)   Infants are silent and exhibit little babbling.

      (2)   The child's sentence formation is usually delayed; however, words may appear in a normal way at an appropriate time.

      (3)   Common sounds may be reversed, e.g., "saw" and "was" or "on" and "no."

      (4)   Gestures are often not used.

      (5)   Response to sound is inconsistent.

      (6)   The child shows tendencies toward perseveration and distractibility.

d Illustrative evaluative procedures.

      (1)   Ammons Full-Range Picture Vocabulary Test (FRPV) by R. B. Ammons and H. S. Ammons (ages 2 years and over; sample of 85 words presented to which the child responds by pointing to the picture that shows the meaning of the word presented by examiner).

      (2)   Peabody Picture Vocabulary by L. M. Dunn (ages 2 years and 6 months to 18 years; 150 words are ordered according to increasing difficulty; the subject chooses one of four pictures that best represents the word named by examiner).

e Prognosis.

      (1)   The prognosis for a young child is good.

      (2)   In a prelinguistic child, if the dominant left cerebral hemisphere is injured, the right cerebral hemisphere will presumably take over the usual language functions.

      (3)   Recovery from delayed speech, however, is seldom complete.

f Therapeutic procedures illustrated.

      (1)   Parallel talking is often used in which the child and therapist tell what he is doing in simple words and phrases.

      (2)   The child is taught to echo words and noises consistently.

      (3)   The child is encouraged to stop what he is doing and to reorganize his activities.

      (4)   The youngster is taught to shift from one kind of symbolization to another, e.g., from writing a word to spelling it aloud.

      (5)   Sequences of movements are presented with the request to reproduce the sequences in proper order.

V   MULTIPLE SPEECH AND LANGUAGE DISORDERS.
  A   Cleft-palate speech.
    1   Characteristics of the cleft palate.
      a   A cleft lip or cleft palate or both are created when the two halves of the lip or the bony upper gum ridge or the two halves of the hard and soft palates fail to grow together and unite in a normal fashion by the third month of prenatal development.
      b   A cleft lip or palate or both, if left unrepaired, can adversely affect speech production.
        (1)   The disability prevents pressure from building up in the mouth for the proper articulation of certain sounds.
        (2)   It creates excessive resonance since air escapes through the nose because of inadequate closure between the oral and nasal cavities.
    2   Characteristics of cleft-palate speech.
      a   Articulation disorders.
        (1)   Distortion of consonant sounds because of nasal emission.
        (2)   Substitutions of sounds.
        (3)   Omission of sounds.
      b   Rhythm disorders: faltering or hesitations that may be due to the child's anxiety surrounding the significant speech disorders that result from air leakage.
      c   Vocal disorders: usually hypernasal if they occur.
    3   Types of cleft palate.
      a   Cleft of the prepalate, that is, the upper lip and alveolar process (upper front tooth ridge).
        (1)   Partial cleft (incomplete).
        (2)   Total cleft (complete).
      b   Clefts of the palate: both hard and soft palates.
        (1)   Partial cleft.
        (2)   Total cleft.
      c   Clefts of both the prepalate (lip) and palate.
        (1)   Partial cleft.
        (2)   Total cleft.
    4   Presumed causes.
      a   The hereditary cause of certain forms of clefts has been verified.
      b   Factors in the prenatal environment may cause clefts.
        (1)   Malnutrition in the pregnant mother.
        (2)   Certain drugs such as cortisone or other types of teratogenic agents.
        (3)   Fetal anoxia or other forms of maternal-fetal trauma.
        (4)   Mechanical injuries.
        (5)   X ray or other types of irradiation.

   (6) German measles or other types of infectious diseases in the mother.

5 Evaluative procedures.

 a The usual articulation tests.

 b Nasal and airflow measures.

 c Examinations by members of a team that includes various medical specialists as well as speech therapists, psychologists, educators, and so on.

6 Typical therapy.

 a The cleft lip is usually closed surgically during the first 3 months after birth; the palate is closed within the first 2 years of life to minimize the development of future speech problems.

 b When surgery is not used, the palate is closed off with a special dental prosthesis called an "obturator."

 c Goals of speech therapy for this condition are usually established during the evaluative stage and might include various forms of therapy to deal with specific problems.

   (1) Nasal emission and defective articulation.

   (2) Disorders in rhythm of speech.

   (3) Weak air pressure and airflow.

   (4) Inactive tongue tip, lip, and jaws.

B Speech disorders associated with cerebral palsy.

1 Characteristics and causes.

 a Cerebral palsy is caused by brain injury which usually occurs prenatally or in early life.

 b Nearly 90 percent of persons with cerebral palsy have significant speech disorders.

 c Problems, other than motor disorders, common to this syndrome include hearing loss, sensory and perceptual deficits, mental retardation, behavior problems, and dental anomalies.

 d Types or classifications of cerebral palsy.

   (1) "Spasticity" involves some muscles which are usually tense and in the use of which a person's voluntary movements are jerky.

   (2) "Athetosis" is characterized by writhing movements when voluntary motion is attempted and typically involves the extremities and the muscles of the trunk, neck, and head.

   (3) "Ataxia" involves a lack of balance and coordination.

2 Types of communication disorders that frequently occur among the cerebral-palsied.

 a Articulation disorders.

   (1) The person often experiences difficulty in twisting the tongue in order to produce complex sounds such as /s/, /z/, /th/, /ch/, and /r/.

   (2) Unintelligible speech is due to slurring of sounds.

        (3) Omissions, distortions, and substitutions of sounds are frequent.

  b Vocal disorders.

        (1) Excessive tension in the laryngeal area of the cerebral-palsied often produces abnormal voices.

        (2) The child's voice may be husky, hypernasal, or monotonic.

  c Rhythmic problems.

        (1) Faulty breathing and breath control.

        (2) Timing affected by frequent respiratory disorders.

        (3) Spasmodic or abnormally explosive patterns of speaking.

3 General evaluative procedures.

  a The ability of the cerebral-palsied person to follow instructions is assessed.

  b A comparison is often made of the child's language concepts and compared to those of other children of the same age.

  c Use is made of specific evaluative procedures such as those listed for articulation, vocal and rhythmic disorders.

4 Illustrations of therapeutic procedures.

  a Develop language skills.

        (1) Encourage vocalizations.

        (2) Teach concepts.

        (3) Provide opportunities to interact with others and generally to explore the environment.

  b Improve the breathing patterns and motor control of the child.

        (1) Teach good posture.

        (2) Teach control of breathing and respiration.

        (3) Provide opportunities to exercise vocal musculature.

  c Improve the articulation skills.

        (1) Teach proper tongue movements.

        (2) Teach control of swallowing, chewing, and sucking movements.

        (3) Improve the functions of the lips and jaws.

  d Improve phonation.

        (1) Teach variations in loudness.

        (2) Teach variations in pitch.

  e Alleviate the stigma attached to cerebral palsy by improving the child's swallowing and eliminating behaviors like drooling.

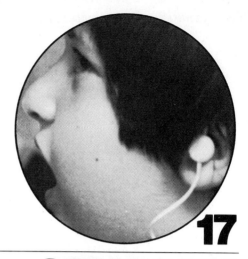

17

SENSORY PROBLEMS

HEARING

I NORMAL STRUCTURE AND FUNCTION OF THE AUDITORY SYSTEM (SEE FIGURE 17-1).
  A Outer ear.
    1 Pinna or external portion.
    2 Auditory canal.
    3 Eardrum or tympanic membrane: boundary between outer ear and middle ear.
  B Middle ear (serves to conduct sound vibrations to inner ear).
    1 Ossicles: chain of three small bones.
      a Parts.
        (1) Malleus (hammer).
        (2) Incus (anvil).
        (3) Stapes (stirrup).
      b Function: transmission of vibrations from eardrum to oval window of the inner ear.

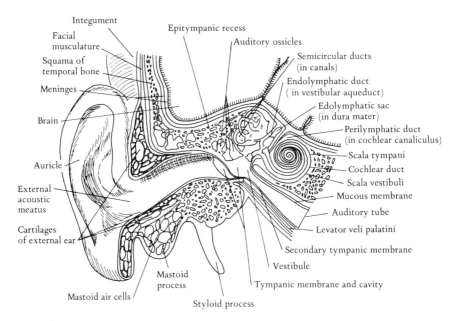

FIGURE 17-1 Normal structure of the auditory mechanism [From Edwards, L. T., and Gaughran, G. R. L., *Concise Anatomy.* (3d ed.) New York: McGraw-Hill, 1971, p. 314.]

    2 Eustachian tube.
       a It connects middle ear with nose and throat.
       b It allows outside air to enter, equalizing air pressure on both sides of the eardrum.
  c Inner ear or labyrinth.
    1 Parts.
       a Nonacoustic labyrinth comprised of the semicircular canals (organs for balance).
       b Acoustic labyrinth.
          (1) Vestibule or central portion of inner ear opening into semicircular canals on one side and cochlea on other side.
          (2) Cochlea: location of sensory cells or organ of Corti.
    2 Sound waves are transmitted from eardrum to create vibrations in the fluid of the inner ear.
       a Vibration of the fluid activates cilia on the organ of Corti; each cilium is attached to a nerve fiber.
       b The nerve impulse travels through the eighth cranial nerve (the auditory nerve) to the brain stem.

II AUDITORY DISORDERS.
  A Incidence of auditory disabilities.
    1 Estimates vary because of differences in defining the disability and differences in testing methods.

2 One estimate is that at least 5 percent of school-age children have hearing levels outside of the normal range in at least one ear and that one or two out of every ten in this group require special education (based on a study of Pittsburgh schoolchildren [Silverman and Lane, 1970]; children in special schools for the deaf are not included in this estimate).

3 The U.S. Office of Education estimates that for 1971–1972, 0.575 percent of school-age handicapped children are deaf and hard of hearing (U.S. Office of Education, 1971).

4 Although deafness is often a part of many multiple handicapped conditions, an accurate estimate of incidence is not available.

B Classification of auditory disorders (Myklebust, 1964).

1 Degree of hearing impairment, based upon degree of hearing loss in decibels (db) as measured by an audiometer using ISO standard (International Standard Organization) (Davis and Krantz, 1964).

a Deaf: hearing loss is so severe that the sense of hearing is nonfunctional and the development of normal spoken language is prevented.

b Hard of hearing or partially hearing (see Table 17-1): sense of hearing is defective but functional, so that development of spoken language is not precluded. This category includes five levels with varying degrees of decibel loss.

(1) Slight: 27 to 40 db.

(2) Mild: 41 to 55 db.

(3) Marked or moderate: 56 to 70 db.

(4) Severe: 71 to 90 db.

(5) Extreme: 91 db or more.

2 Age at onset (Committee on Nomenclature of the Conference of Executives of American Schools for the Deaf, 1938).

a Deafness.

(1) Congenital deafness.

(a) Those born deaf.

(b) Sense of hearing is nonfunctional for the ordinary purpose of life.

(2) Adventitiously deaf children are born with normal hearing but their sense of hearing becomes nonfunctional later because of accident or illness.

(3) People are adventitiously hard of hearing when an acquired hearing loss is not severe enough to prevent functional hearing with or without a hearing aid.

3 Physical origin or site of the defect.

a Conductive hearing loss: hearing loss due to obstructions or lesions in the outer or middle ear which block the transmission of sound vibrations to the inner ear.

b Sensory-neural hearing loss: caused by damage of the inner ear.

      c Central or perceptual hearing loss: caused by defects in auditory nerve pathways affecting the transmission of impulses from the brain stem to the auditory area of the cortex of the brain.

      d Endogenous impairment: caused by a genetic defect, congenital impairment, or developmental deviation.

      e Exogenous or adventitious impairment: caused by postnatal environmental factors, e.g., physical insult, disease, or toxins.

C Types and causes of auditory disorders.

   1 Conductive hearing loss: obstruction in the outer or middle ear.

      a Congenital malformations such as atresia or closure of the external canal.

      b Impacted wax in the external canal, preventing sound waves from reaching middle ear.

      c Obstruction from the insertion of a foreign body, such as a bean, in the ear.

      d External otitis: a pimple or boil in the skin of external canal.

TABLE 17-1   RELATION OF DEGREE OF IMPAIRMENT TO EDUCATIONAL NEEDS

Average of the Speech Frequencies in Better Ear	Effect of Hearing Loss on the Understanding of Language and Speech	Educational Needs and Programs
Slight (26–40 db)	May have difficulty hearing faint or distant speech. May experience some difficulty with the language-arts subjects.	Child should be reported to school principal. May benefit from a hearing aid as loss approaches 40 db (ISO). May need attention to vocabulary development. Needs favorable seating and lighting. May need speech reading instruction. May need speech therapy.
Mild (41–55 db)	Understands conversational speech at a distance of 3–5 feet (face to face). May miss as much as 50 percent of class discussions if voices are faint or not in line of vision. May exhibit limited vocabulary and speech anomalies.	Child should be referred to special education for educational follow-up. Individual hearing aid by evaluation and training in its use. Favorable seating and possible special class placement, especially for primary children. Attention to vocabulary and reading. Speech reading instruction. Speech conservation and correction, if indicated.

Source: Adapted from Illinois Commission on Children (1968).

TABLE 17–1 CONTINUED

Average of the Speech Frequencies in Better Ear	Effect of Hearing Loss on the Understanding of Language and Speech	Educational Needs and Programs
Marked (56–70 db)	Conversation must be loud to be understood. Will have increased difficulty in group discussions. Is likely to have defective speech. Is likely to be deficient in language usage and comprehension. Will have limited vocabulary.	Child should be referred to special education for educational follow-up. Resource teacher or special class. Special help in language skills: vocabulary development, usage, reading, writing, grammar, and so on. Individual hearing aid by evaluation and auditory training. Speech reading instruction. Speech conservation and correction. Attention to auditory and visual situation at all times.
Severe (71–90 db)	May hear loud voices about 1 foot from the ear. May be able to identify environmental sounds. May be able to discriminate vowels but not all consonants. Speech and language defective and likely to deteriorate.	Child should be referred to special education for educational follow-up. Full-time special program for deaf children, with emphasis on all language skills, concept development, speech reading, and speech. Program needs specialized supervision and comprehensive supporting services. Individual hearing aid by evaluation. Auditory training with individual and group aids. Part time in regular classes only as profitable.
Extreme (91 db or more)	May hear some loud sounds but is aware of vibrations more than tonal pattern. Relies on vision rather than hearing as primary avenue for communication. Speech and language defective and likely to deteriorate.	Child should be referred to special education for educational follow-up. Full time in special program for deaf children, with emphasis on all language skills, concept development, speech reading, and speech. Program needs specialized supervision and comprehensive supporting services. Continuous appraisal of needs in regard to oral and manual communication. Auditory training with group and individual aids. Part time in regular classes only for carefully selected children.

e Otitis media: inflammation or infection of the middle ear.

    (1) This condition commonly develops from a cold in the head. Nasal secretions back up and infect the eustachian tube so that the air pressure in the middle ear is no longer equalized and a partial vacuum is created, causing impairment in hearing.

    (2) This condition may be caused by the puncturing of the eardrum with a dirty instrument, such as a hairpin, which causes infection.

f Infection in the middle ear caused by infected adenoids, tonsils, or sinuses.

g Cholesteatoma: a cyst lined internally with skin located in the middle ear.

h Blockage of the eustachian tubes caused by allergies.

i Otosclerosis.

    (1) This disease causes a growth of bone tissue around the stapes, producing fixation of the stapes; thus, vibrations are not effectively transmitted to the fluid of the inner ear.

    (2) This condition is usually hereditary.

    (3) It begins in youth but usually is not noticed until adolescence or the early twenties.

    (4) It rarely advances to severe hearing impairment.

j Accidents and injuries, such as fracture of the skull, bullet wounds, etc.

2 Sensory-neural or inner-ear impairments.

a Drugs, poisons, and allergens may affect the structure of the inner ear.

b Bacterial and viral infections.

    (1) Maternal rubella: rarely a cause of total deafness but may result in severe hearing impairment.

    (2) Encephalitis.

    (3) Diseases, such as measles, mumps, influenza, meningitis, which affect the respiratory system and result in high temperatures may cause damage to nerve fibers.

c Rh and other incompatibilities.

d High-intensity noise, such as from a gun shot or certain toys (toy missiles and rockets), may damage hearing.

e Blows to the head may cause hearing losses of varying degrees.

f Birth injury: prematurity, prolonged labor, or difficult delivery are all associated with the possibility of auditory impairment.

g Metabolic and endocrine disorders, e.g., hypothyroidism (cretinism).

h Hereditary deafness.

i Presycusia: hearing loss due to advancing age.

3 Causes of central deafness or hearing loss (auditory-perceptual hearing loss): lesions in auditory pathways are thought to produce receptive aphasic language disorder, i.e., the inability to understand language symbols.

a Diseases such as encephalitis, meningitis, and multiple sclerosis.

b Injuries.

c Toxins, e.g., carbon monoxide poisoning.

d Birth injury and anoxia.

e Brain tumors and cysts.

4 Tests and evaluative procedures.

a Pure-tone audiometry.

   (1) Procedure.

   (a) The audiometer creates pure tones of known intensity and frequency.

   [1] The intensity is the amplitude or loudness of the sound wave measured in decibels (db).

   [2] The frequency or wavelength is the number of vibrations or cycles per second (cps) or measured as Hertz (Hz); the greater the frequency, the greater the pitch.

   (b) Range of intensity and frequency to which the human ear can respond

   [1] Intensity: up to 130–140 db.

   [2] Frequency: from 16–20 Hz to as high as 20,000–30,000 Hz.

   (c) The results are recorded graphically on an audiogram (usually) made to record frequencies from 125 to 8,000 Hz.

   (2) Tests

   (a) Air conduction audiometry.

   [1] The stimulus is presented at various intensities and frequencies through headphones.

   [2] Frequencies from 125 to 8,000 Hz, which encompass all speech sounds and most sounds in man's environment, are presented at intervals.

   [3] The whole auditory system is tested as tones are transmitted through the entire system.

   [4] Hearing thresholds can be charted for each ear by this method.

   (b) Bone conduction audiometry.

   [1] Sound is transmitted directly through the temporal bone to the inner ear.

   [2] Stimuli therefore are not transmitted through the outer and middle ear.

[3] Hearing impairment is thus located in the sensory-neural mechanism or cochlea of the inner ear.

(c) When both air and bone conduction thresholds indicate impairment, nerve damage is often inferred.

b Speech audiometry.

(1) Ability to hear and understand speech is tested.

(2) Measures.

(a) Speech reception threshold (SRT): comparison with the normal population of the person's ability to hear speech as measured in decibels.

(b) The speech discrimination score measures understanding and discrimination between various parts of speech.

c Physiological audiometry (employed when the person cannot report reception of sound, e.g., with very young children or the severely retarded and disturbed).

(1) Noisemakers are used to elicit startle or orienting reflexes or awakening from sleep in neonates.

(2) Electrodermal audiometry (EDA).

(a) Galvanic skin response (GSR) is employed: conduction of a small current across palm; perspiration elicited by conditioning.

(b) Slight electric shock is preceded by a tone.

(c) Conditioned response to the tone is established.

(d) The person will produce galvanic skin response when he is able to hear the tone.

(3) Electroencephalic audiometry (EEA).

(a) This method uses the electroencephalogram (EEG).

(b) The EEG pattern changes between waking and sleeping.

(c) The electroencephalic response (EER) to auditory stimuli is recorded.

(d) This method can be used with very young children but is not limited by age.

d Operant conditioning audiometry (Dix and Hallpike, 1947; Meyerson and Michael, 1960).

(1) A sound is presented to the child.

(2) The child is conditioned to perform a response when the sound is presented.

(3) Reinforcement such as candy or the illumination of pictures (Dix and Hallpike's "peepshow") is used to establish and maintain responses.

    e Tuning fork tests.
       (1) Description.
          (a) The tuning fork can vary pitch systematically.
          (b) The test is used to distinguish between conductive and sensory-neural hearing loss.
       (2) Types.
          (a) Rinne test: bone conduction is compared to air conduction.
          (b) Weber test: the bone conduction of both ears is compared.
          (c) Schwabach test: the bone conduction of the patient is compared with the bone conduction of a normal listener.
    f Informal tests.
       (1) Watch test: a watch is placed close to the ear and slowly removed until the person is unable to hear it.
       (2) Whisper test to test auditory acuity: the tester stands 20 feet from the person being tested and whispers; person tested must repeat what was whispered.

D Treatment and management of auditory disorders (Davis and Fowler, 1970; Walsh, 1970).
    1 Medical and surgical aspects.
      a Medical treatment of infections, blockages, and diseases resulting in impaired hearing.
      b Preventive medicine (conservation of hearing).
        (1) Screening audiometry is widely employed to detect hearing problems in children.
        (2) Prevention of hazardous noise exposure is becoming increasingly important.
      c Surgical treatment.
        (1) Middle ear and mastoid.
          (a) Removal of tonsils or adenoids which prevent proper ventilation of the ear and therefore contribute to infection.
          (b) Mastoidectomy: removal of mastoid cells, if other methods are not feasible, to promote adequate draining of pus from infected middle ear.
        (2) Repair of tympanic drum perforations.
        (3) Fenestration: a new oval window is made in the semicircular canal, is closed with a membrane which picks up sound waves, and bypasses the eardrum and the immobile stapes.
        (4) Mobilization of stapes: bone matter that has been preventing action of the stapes is broken away.

2 Hearing aids.
   a Types of electric hearing aids.
      (1) Wearable.
      (2) Portable or desk type.
      (3) Group.
   b The hearing aid cannot compensate totally for hearing loss; the quality of sound is often distorted.
3 Language training.
   a Speech reading or lipreading.
      (1) The speaker's words are comprehended by visual attention to lip movements.
      (2) The visual modality is used to acquire language.
      (3) The child who is deaf or hard of hearing can learn oral speech by imitating the lip movements, facial expression, and gestures of people talking.
   b Manual language, i.e., the manual alphabet, is used.
   c There is controversy as to which of these three approaches is best for developing language in deaf children (Moores, 1970; Quigley, 1969; Stuckless and Birch, 1966).
      (1) Oral method: the use of speech reading and the use of any hearing, reading, and writing skills acquired prior to deafness.
      (2) Combined approach: the use of the oral approach and finger spelling, i.e., the teacher spells a word manually while saying it.
      (3) Simultaneous approach: the use of the oral approach with finger spelling and the use of manual signs (signs which indicate a word, rather than spelling it).
3 Education programs.
   a Residential school.
   b Special classes.
   c Special provisions in regular classes.
   d Parent teaching programs (McConnell and Horton, 1970): parents used as "teachers" of their young deaf children in their own home.
   e Nursery and kindergarten programs for children with hearing disorders.

VISION

I NORMAL STRUCTURE AND FUNCTION OF THE VISUAL SYSTEM (SEE FIGURE 17-2).
   A Parts of the visual system.
      1 Protective parts.
         a Conjunctiva: the thin membrane covering the eyelids and part of the sclera.

    b Sclera: the white part of the eye; a tough, protective covering.

    c Choroid: the vascular layer which lines the sclera and provides nourishment for the retina.

    d Eyelashes.

    e Eyebrows.

    f Bony eye socket.

2 Refractive structures (focus light rays on the retina).

    a Cornea: the transparent layer of eyeball.

    b Aqueous humor: the clear fluid which fills the anterior and posterior chambers and maintains intraocular pressure.

    c Anterior chamber: the space between the cornea and the iris.

    d Posterior chamber: the space between the iris and the lens.

    e Canal of Schlemm: the canal located at the connecting point of the cornea and the sclera, where the aqueous humor is excreted after circulating.

    f Iris: the colored membrane behind the cornea and the front of the lens which regulates the amount of light coming into the eye.

    g Pupil: the opening at the center of the iris.

    h Crystalline lens: the transparent, colorless body held by a suspensory ligament at the front of the eyeball that focuses light rays on the retina.

    i Vitreous body: the transparent, colorless, gelatinous material filling the chamber behind the lens.

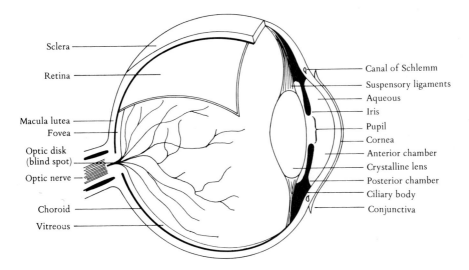

FIGURE 17-2 Normal structure of the visual mechanism. [From Joint Study Committee of the American Health Association and the National Society for the Prevention of Blindness, Inc. *Teaching about Vision.* (2d ed.) New York: National Society for the Prevention of Blindness, Inc., 1972.]

3 Receptive structures.
   a Retina: the innermost, sensitive layer of the eye, consisting of nerves and receptors (rods and cones) that connect to the optic nerve.
   b Optic nerve: the nerve that carries messages from the retina to the brain.
   c Optic disc: the normal blind spot at the point where the optic nerve enters the retina.
   d Fovea: the center of vision or fixation point, a small depression in the retina.
   e Macula lutea: the area of the retina surrounding the fovea where there is less acute central vision.
4 Directive group: muscles of the eye.
   a Internal rectus: moves the eye in the direction of the nose.
   b External rectus: moves the eye toward the temple.
   c Superior rectus: moves the eye upward and outward.
   d Inferior rectus: moves the eye downward and outward.
   e Superior oblique: moves the eye downward and inward.
   f Inferior oblique: moves the eye upward and outward.
B Function of the visual system.
   1 Light rays pass through the cornea, the aqueous humour, the pupil of the iris, and the lens.
   2 The pupil contracts or dilates so that more or less light enters according to the brightness of the object viewed.
   3 The cornea and the lens bend the light rays to focus on the retina.
   4 The rays pass through the vitreous body and stimulate the rods and cones of the retina, thereby creating a photochemical response.
   5 The impulse is carried by the optic nerve to the brain.

II VISUAL DISORDERS.
   A Incidence of visual disorders.
      1 The U.S. Office of Education estimates that approximately 0.1 percent of school-age children have visual disorders (Bureau of Education for the Handicapped, 1969, 1970).
      2 Estimates range as high as 25 percent (this figure includes defects that are correctable and which require no special education).
      3 The estimate is generally that from .01 to .04 percent of children with visual disorders are blind and from .06 to .14 percent have partial vision.
      4 Children with visual disorders are the smallest group of exceptional children.
   B Classification of visual disorders.
      1 Legal classification (National Society for the Prevention of Blindness, 1966). Classification is usually based on standards of the Snel-

len chart. The symbol 20/20 means the person can distinguish at 20 feet what the normal eye can distinguish at 20 feet. A person with 20/200 vision can distinguish at 20 feet what the normal eye can distinguish at 200 feet.

    a Blind: persons with central visual acuity of 20/200 or less in the better eye with best correction; or visual acuity of more than 20/200, if there is a field defect, in which the widest diametic of visual field subtends an angle no greater than 20 degrees. A person with a field defect may be able to read some print but is considered legally blind because of his restricted field of vision.

    b Partially seeing: persons with visual acuity greater than 20/200 but not greater than 20/70 in the better eye with best correction.

  2 Classification for educational purposes.

    a Blind: children who cannot read print but who can learn to read braille.

    b Partially seeing: children who can read print under special conditions.

    c Major causes of visual disorders. (See Table 17-2 for the percentage of blind schoolchildren according to site and type of eye defect.)

        (1) Infectious diseases.

            (a) Rubella.

            (b) Conjunctivitis.

            (c) Syphilis.

        (2) Injuries.

        (3) Poisonings (includes excessive dosage of oxygen as in retrolental fibroplasia).

        (4) Tumors.

        (5) Heredity factors.

        (6) General diseases.

        (7) Nutritional deficiencies.

C Major visual disorders (types, causes, and treatment).

  1 Disorders of the protective structures, e.g., trachoma, which is a serious form of conjunctivitis or pink eye, and affects the cornea, conjunctiva, and eyelid.

  2 Refractive errors.

    a Myopia or nearsightedness.

        (1) Characteristics and cause.

            (a) Light rays are bent and focused in front of the retina because the eyeball is too long or the lens too thick and curved.

            (b) The person easily sees objects which are near but cannot see objects at a far distance.

TABLE 17-2 CAUSES OF BLINDNESS

Site and Type	Percent
Eyeball in general	24.8
Structural anomalies	23.4
Multiple anomalies	5.5
Myopia	4.9
Glaucoma (Infantile)	4.6
Albinism	4.2
Coloboma	0.9
Anophthalmos and microphthalmos	1.2
Aniridia	0.7
Other	1.4
Other general affection to eyeball	1.4
Conjunctiva (ophthalmia neonatorum)	0.3
Cornea	1.8
Lens	12.1
Cataract	11.5
Dislocated lens	0.6
Uveal tract	4.8
Retina	40.4
Retrolental fibroplasia	33.0
Retinal and macular degeneration	4.4
Retinoblastoma	1.7
Other	1.3
Optic nerve, optic pathway, and cortical visual centers	9.5
Optic nerve atrophy	8.6
Other	0.9
Other specified affection	3.7
Not reported	2.6
Total, all causes *Percent*	100.0
Number	7,757

From: Hatfield, E. M. Causes of blindness in school children. *Sight-Saving Review*, 1963, **33**, 218–223.

      (c) Nearsightedness may cause postural problems because the person must bend in order to see objects at a close distance.

      (d) Nearsightedness usually begins at 6 to 8 years.

  (2) Treatment: eyeglasses with concave lens.

b Hyperopia or farsightedness.

  (1) Characteristics.

      (a) Light rays are bent and focused behind the retina because the eyeball is too short or the lens too thick and flat; thus light rays do not bend enough to focus properly on the retina.

      (b) Persons can see objects better at a far distance than close up.

      (c) Farsightedness can occur at any age.

  (2) Treatment: eyeglasses with convex lens.

   c Astigmatism.
- (1) Characteristics and cause.
    - (a) Astigmatism results from an irregularity in or a defective curvature of the cornea or the lens.
    - (b) Diffusion of light rays on the retina results; sharp focus is impossible and vision is blurred.
- (2) Treatment: eyeglasses or contact lenses.

   d Presbyopia: loss of ability to focus sharply on objects close by; usually found in older people and is due to the normal aging process.

3 Disorders due to defects in muscle functioning.
- a Amblyopia or "lazy eye."
    - (1) Characteristics.
        - (a) Reduction of visual acuity in one or both eyes.
        - (b) Disruption in learning to coordinate both eyes to focus on fine features of objects in central vision.
        - (c) Use of only one eye for seeing or alternation of eyes focusing on objects.
    - (2) Cause: faulty alignment of the eyes due to muscular inadequacies or imbalance; one eye is turned inward or outward in relation to the other.
    - (3) Treatment.
        - (a) Glasses.
        - (b) Surgery.
        - (c) Patching.
        - (d) Combination of the above plus eye exercises.
- b Strabismus: crossed eyes or squint.
    - (1) The eyes fail to focus on the same object at the same time.
    - (2) The condition is caused by faulty muscle coordination.
    - (3) Usually one eye turns inward toward nose and the other eye focuses on the object.
- c Heterophoria.
    - (1) Deviation of the eyes is not apparent.
    - (2) Visual fusion is impaired, or two images (an image from each eye) is fused into a single image.
    - (3) The condition is caused by faulty muscle balance.
- d Nystagmus: quick jerky movements of eye related to albinism or brain injury.

4 Disorders in the receptive structures of the visual system.
- a Retrolental fibroplasia: detached retina (in later stages) caused by the subjecting of premature infants to excessive amount of oxygen.

    b Retinitis pigmentosa: deterioration and atrophy of the retina due to heredity.

    c Optic atrophy: deterioration of the nerve fibers connecting the retina to the brain.

5 Cataracts (leading to blindness in the adult population).

    a Characteristics.

        (1) The lens becomes opaque due to a growth of cataract "film."

        (2) Visual acuity is lost.

    b Causes.

        (1) Heredity.

        (2) Drugs.

        (3) Injury.

        (4) Disease.

    c Treatment: removal of the cataract through surgery; glasses are then prescribed.

6 Glaucoma.

    a Drainage of the aqueous fluid is obstructed, thereby causing damage to the eye from a buildup of fluids.

    b Treatment.

        (1) Surgery in acute cases.

        (2) Eye drops and oral medication to control buildup.

7 Albinism.

    a Characteristics.

        (1) Absence of pigment in hair, skin, iris, and choroid.

        (2) Refractive errors.

        (3) Loss of some visual acuity.

        (4) Nystagmus.

        (5) Photophobia: excessive sensitivity to light.

    b The cause is hereditary.

D Evaluative procedures for visual disorders.

1 Teacher/tester observations of some general indicators of eye problems.

    a Rubbing the eyes frequently.

    b Holding books or objects too close to the eyes.

    c Squinting or frowning.

    d Complaining of eyes itching or burning or of dizziness and blurred vision.

    e Swollen, red, or encrusted eyes.

2 Screening devices (National Society for the Prevention of Blindness, 1969).

    a Snellen Chart.

        (1) This measures distant-field acuity.

        (2) It uses standard letters or the letter "E" and different sizes and positions of figures.

      (3) Criteria for referral to ophthalmologist when using the Snellen Chart.

         (a) Kindergarten through third grade: vision of 20/40 or less.

         (b) Fourth grade and above: vision of 20/30 or less.

  b Plus-lens test for hyperopia: the child's vision is tested while he is wearing a pair of convex lenses called "plus" lenses.

  c Tests for muscle balance or ability of eyes to work together.

      (1) Use of lens called a Maddox rod, use of a stereoscope, or use of color to present different images to each eye, i.e., to cause fusion to be disassociated.

      (2) Measurement of relationship of two images as seen (unit of measure is a prism diopter).

  d Tests for depth perception: stereopsis or visual perception of three-dimensional space.

  e Tests for color discrimination.

      (1) Hardy-Rand-Rittler Pseudoisochromatic Plates Test.

      (2) Ishihara Test.

  f Massachusetts Vision Test: battery of three tests (visual acuity, plus lens, and muscle balance).

E   Management of visual disorders

  1 Principles for teaching blind children (Lowenfeld, 1973).

    a Individualization: the program should be geared to the child's individual needs.

    b Concreteness: knowledge about concrete objects should be obtained through hearing and feeling.

    c Unified instruction: all areas of instruction should be related to each other so total education is integrated.

    d Additional stimulation: the child should use sensory-motor-kinesthetic equipment for learning about environments. Systematic stimulation should be provided.

    e Self-activity: the child should be encouraged to perform most activities himself, rather than having someone do them for him.

  2 Special instructional materials.

    a Braille reading or touch reading (see Figure 17-3).

      (1) Combinations of six dots are ordered in a cell, two dots wide and three dots high:

           .   .

           .   .

           .   .

      (2) The dots are embossed on heavy manila paper and are arranged from left to right.

      (3) The person reads the braille with one hand.

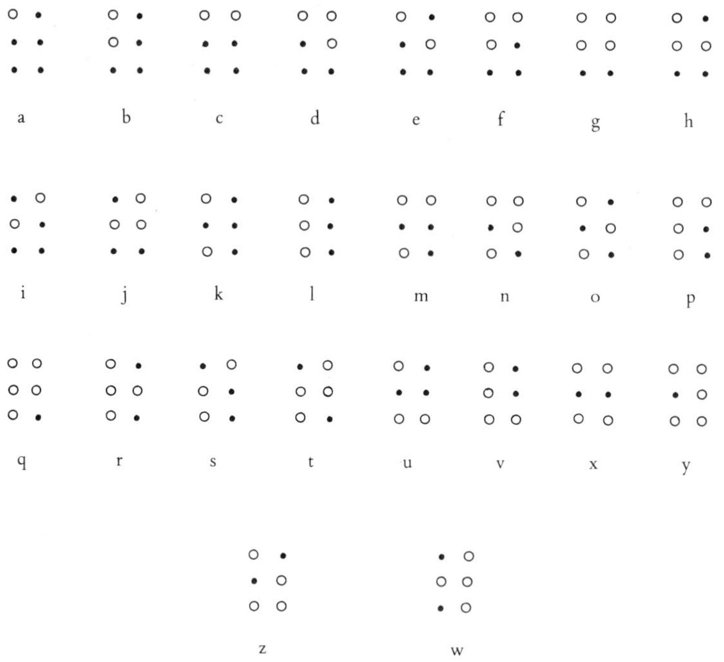

FIGURE 17–3   The alphabet in Grade I braille.

(4)   Standard English braille was developed in about 1950 and has been used since then.

b Braille writing.

(1)   Braille typewriter.

(2)   Handwritten braille with special stylus and slate.

c Typing: for communication with the sighted.

d Abacus: for computations.

e Tapes, records, and talking-book machines.

f Large type or print for partially sighted persons.

g Visual aids may be used.

(1)   Magnifiers.

(2)   Telescopic and microscopic lenses.

h Dictaphones and record players.

i Adjustable desks: adjustment for angle (to avoid glare), height, position.

j Chalkboards: gray or green chalkboards because they reflect more light.

k Pencils and paper: large lead pencils and nonglare (cream-colored, unglazed) paper.

l Embossed and relief maps.

3 Technological aids.

  a Optacon: converts print into 144 pins which when activated produce a vibratory image of the letter on the reader's finger.

  b Computer translations of braille.

  c MIT braille emboss: use of computer with telewriter so person can request material by phone and receive it in braille by teletypewriter.

  d Ultrasonic aid, Russell Pathsounder, and laser cone: function to warn the person of obstacles by vibrations and sounds

  e Compressed speech: doubles word rate without producing distortions.

  f Possibilities of artificial vision: prosthetic device in the occipital cortex which receives input and stimulates the brain.

4 Special environment.

  a Lighting controlled to avoid glare but maximize contrast between object and surroundings.

  b Noise: prevention of distracting noise since, without vision, there is a greater dependence on hearing.

  c Adjustable furniture and equipment.

5 Self-help and living skills.

6 Listening skills.

7 Physical education.

8 Orientation and mobility.

  a Cane travel developed and codified by Hoover (1947).

  b Instruction of mobility skills in the home and the school (Suterko, 1973).

  c Teaching object perception (Ammons, Worschel, and Dallenbach, 1953; Supa, Cotzin, and Dallenbach, 1944).

9 Educational settings.

  a Residential school.

  b Full-time special class.

  c Cooperative special class.

  d Resource room.

  e Itinerant teacher: individual instruction.

  f Teacher consultant: child enrolls in regular classes and receives services indirectly through the consultant.

  g Home instruction.

18

MOTOR PROBLEMS

I NORMAL DEVELOPMENT OF MOTOR SKILLS.
   A The period from birth to 6 weeks.
      1 Reflexive behavior.
         a Sucking.
         b Swallowing.
         c Grasping, i.e., tight closing of the hand when stimulated.
         d Coughing.
         e Pupillary reflex: contraction of the pupils in reaction to bright lights.
         f Babinski reflex: extending the big toe and fanning out the others following stimulation.
         g More reflex: head thrown back, arms apart, legs extended, then arms brought back.
         h Tonic neck reflex: head turned to side, arm on that side extended, other arm flexed.
      2 Approximate body size and proportions.
         a Height: 20 inches.
         b Weight: 7½ pounds.

     c Head is one-fourth of body length with the trunk approximately one-half the remaining total body length.

3 The child is able to lift the head and chin when he is placed face downward in a prone position.

4 The youngster retains a ring placed in his hand.

5 The perceptual-motor development of an infant is typically characterized by the following.

     a This infant visually pursues the movements of someone else at 1 or 2 weeks of age.

     b Oculomotor muscles are coordinated for depth perception and visual fixation.

B The period from 6 weeks to 3 months.

1 The child's body size averages 22 inches in height and 10 pounds in weight.

2 The youngster is able to hold his chest up when he is placed in a prone position.

3 The head is held erect and steady, the tonic neck reflex has disappeared, and the child's first reaching movements are in response to objects.

C The period from 3 to 6 months.

1 Children at this age average 24 inches in height and weigh 14 pounds.

2 They can typically sit with support, turn from side to back, roll from back to front, exhibit complete control of the head, and bend and use the arms for self-support.

D The period from 6 to 9 months.

1 Children at this age can usually sit alone without support, stand with support, crawl, and grasp objects.

2 At 28 weeks the child uses the palm in grasping, at 8 months he can pick up a pellet with the thumb and fingertips, and at 36 weeks the forefinger is used in grasping.

E The child who is 9 to 12 months of age is able to raise himself to a sitting position, pull up to a standing position, take steps when supported, begin to creep on hands and knees at about 40 weeks, and have the thumb and forefinger function together.

F The child who is 12 to 18 months can usually climb, stand alone, walk alone, sit alone, and throw a ball.

G Abilities of the 24-month-old.

1 The child can transfer weight from the heel to the toe of the foot, stand alone on either foot, and take some steps on tiptoe.

2 The child can run but lacks complete ability to stop or turn quickly.

3 The child can climb stairs by marking time (one foot forward only).

4 The child can jump off the floor with both feet and jump down from a chair.

5 The child can kick a ball.

6 The child can hold writing instruments, manipulate objects, and build a block tower of six cubes.

H The child who is between 3 and 4 years of age can usually extend his arms and twist his trunk, walk on tiptoe 3 yards, run smoothly with speed, ascend stairs using alternating feet, jump 12 inches, hop on one foot for about seven steps, skip on one foot, ride a tricycle, and perform some small motor movements.

I Characteristics of children 4 to 5 years of age.
1 Height: 42 inches. Weight: 39 pounds.
2 Ability to walk in an adult fashion.
3 Control over starting, stopping, and turning.
4 Ability to descend stairs using alternating feet, jump rope, hop on one foot, and catch a ball in the arms.

J Children who are 5 to 6 years of age can walk on tiptoe a long distance, jump 28 to 30 inches, hop ten or more steps on one foot, climb easily, skip on alternating feet, and catch a ball with both hands.

K Children who are 6 to 7 years of age are usually 46 inches tall and weigh 48 pounds; they exhibit a mature throwing pattern and are able to write correctly from left to right.

II TYPES OF MOTOR DISORDERS IN CHILDREN.
 A Cerebral palsy.
  1 Frequency.
   a It is estimated that 550,000 children and adults in the United States have cerebral palsy.
   b The prevalence is approximately 103 per 1,000 school-age children.
  2 Prominent characteristics.
   a Motor disability resulting from brain damage (most characteristic problem).
   b Other disorders often found: sensory defects, vision and hearing disorders, speech and language disorders, mental retardation, psychological problems, perceptual and behavioral disorders.
  3 Five different classification approaches.
   a Types.
    (1) Spasticity.
     (a) This accounts for 40 to 60 percent of the total cerebral-palsied population.
     (b) The motor cortex and the pyramidal tract of the brain are injured.
     (c) Spasticity is characterized by loss of control of the voluntary muscles.
     (d) The flexor and extensor muscles contract simultaneously.
     (e) The movements are jerky and poorly coordinated.

       (f)   Victims exhibit hypertonicity, i.e., excessive muscle tension or contraction of the muscle fibers while the muscles are at rest.

  (2) Athetosis.

       (a)   Athetosis accounts for 15 to 20 percent of all cerebral-palsied people.

       (b)   There are brain lesions in the extrapyramidal system (located in the forebrain or the midbrain).

       (c)   Athetosis is characterized by jerky, involuntary, slow, irregular, and twisting movements.

       (d)   Involuntary movements occur when deliberate, voluntary exertion is made, thus hindering normal muscle activity.

       (e)   The throat and diaphragm muscles are often involved; therefore, drooling frequently occurs.

       (f)   Major problems occur most frequently in the hands, then in the lips and tongue, and least often in the feet.

  (3) Ataxia.

       (a)   Ataxia is caused by a lesion in the cerebellum, i.e., that part of the brain which controls muscle coordination and balance.

       (b)   It is characterized by disturbance of balance.

       (c)   Movements are awkward.

       (d)   Walking motions are such that the individual appears to be dizzy.

       (e)   The victim of ataxia falls easily.

       (f)   The condition is often not diagnosed until the child begins to walk.

  (4) Tremor.

       (a)   Tremor is caused by injury to the extrapyramidal system.

       (b)   The condition is characterized by involuntary movements of the flexor and extensor muscles.

       (c)   It differs from the athetoid condition in that athetoid movements are large and changeable, whereas tremor movements are small and rhythmic.

  (5) Rigidity.

       (a)   Rigidity is caused by injury to the extrapyramidal system.

       (b)   The rigid cerebral-palsied person is characterized by resistance to movements of the flexor and extensor muscles, i.e., the limbs are rigid and hard to bend.

       (c)   Rigidity is constant in some instances, intermittent in others.

       (d)   Victims are able to perform only slow movements.

b Number and location of limbs involved.
   (1) Monoplegia: one limb is affected (the condition is very rare).
   (2) Hemiplegia: one arm and one leg (on the same side of the body) are affected.
   (3) Triplegia: three limbs are affected (this, also, is very rare).
   (4) Paraplegia: both legs are affected, but not the arms.
   (5) Quadriplegia: four limbs are affected.
   (6) Diplegia: four limbs are affected, but more involvement usually occurs in the legs.
   (7) Double or bilateral hemiplegia: four limbs are affected, but there is more involvement of the arms than the legs.
c Time of onset or manifestation (this is subjective and hypothetical).
   (1) Prenatal (before birth).
   (2) Natal (during birth).
   (3) Postnatal (after birth).
d Degree of involvement (very subjective, no specific criteria have been developed for each category).
   (1) Slight or mild.
   (2) Moderate.
   (3) Severe.
   (4) Very severe.
e Extent and nature of brain damage or other disorders often involved.
   (1) Hearing disorders.
   (2) Visual disorders.
   (3) Perceptual disorders.
   (4) Intelligence and learning disorders.
   (5) Speech disorders.
4 Causes.
   a Prenatal (before birth).
      (1) Inherited conditions.
      (2) Condition of mother during pregnancy.
         (a) Infections, e.g., German measles, syphilis, meningitis, or encephalitis.
         (b) Anoxia (lack of oxygen) in the brain, cord twisted around neck of fetus, severe anemia of mother, placenta separated too early, shock, critical cardiac condition.
         (c) Rh blood incompatibility.
         (d) Irradiation.
   b Natal or perinatal (during birth).
      (1) Problems with cord and placenta, causing anoxia.

    (2) Mechanical injuries from difficult delivery.

    (3) Improper anesthesia.

  c Postnatal (after birth).

    (1) Injury to skull from accidents.

    (2) Infections, e.g., meningitis, encephalitis, or influenza.

    (3) High fevers, as from typhoid or diphtheria, causing anoxia.

    (4) Toxic factors, i.e., lead poisoning or carbon monoxide poisoning.

    (5) Strangulation.

    (6) Brain tumors.

5 Treatment and management of cerebral palsy.

  a Prominent physical therapy theories (McDonald, 1964).

    (1) Therapy of Winthrop Phelps (1940).

        (a) Emphasis is on the treatment of individual muscles.

        (b) The treatment program focuses on fifteen phases or modalities.

            [1] Massage.

            [2] Passive motion, i.e., the therapist shows the child the correct motion by moving his body through the motion. No voluntary action is made by the child.

            [3] Active assisted motion, i.e., the therapist moves child's body through the motion with some effort from him.

            [4] Active motion, i.e., the child voluntarily performs a motion without physical assistance.

            [5] Resisted motion, i.e., the child's movements are resisted by manual force of the therapist.

            [6] Conditioned motion, i.e., the child is taught a rhyme which becomes the stimulus for performing a certain motion whenever the rhyme is sung.

            [7] Automatic or confused motion, used to strengthen the muscles which cannot contract voluntarily by applying resistance to other muscle groups.

            [8] Combined motions, i.e., the child is taught motions which combine movements at two joints.

            [9] Rest: special equipment (e.g., braces) is used to control motion and thus conserve the person's energy.

            [10] Relaxation, i.e., use of a systematic program to teach muscle relaxation.

            [11] Motion from relaxed position.

[12] Balance training.

[13] Reciprocation, i.e., the capability of moving both arms or legs in opposite directions at the same time.

[14] Reach, grasp, and release.

[15] Skills, e.g., self-help skills like dressing and feeding.

(2) Therapy of Karl and Berta Bobath (1954).

    (a) There are four levels of integration of motor function.

        [1] Spinal.

        [2] Brain stem.

        [3] Midbrain.

        [4] Cortical.

    (b) Usually therapeutic activities are shifted from the spinal level to the cortical level as the child matures; lower-level reflexes then come under inhibition control by higher centers.

    (c) Cerebral palsy is viewed as brain damage resulting in failure to inhibit lower-level reflexes.

    (d) Motor movements of the cerebral-palsied are limited to reflexes, e.g., flexor, withdrawal reflex, extensor reflex, and tonic neck reflex.

    (e) Sensory stimulation input is shunted into the synaptic channels created by control of the spinal, brain-stem, and midbrain reflexes.

    (f) Law of shunting.

        [1] Muscles that are contracted or elongated send impulses to the central nervous system, which processes the impulses and regulates which muscles should be inhibited and which activated.

        [2] The law of shunting is that the central nervous system reflects the state of of the body's musculature.

        [3] Tonic reflexes continue (i.e., certain muscles are contracted and certain muscles are elongated most of the time), so that the central nervous system produces and fixes stereotyped motor movements.

    (g) The Bobaths advocate the use of reflex inhibiting patterns (RIPS), i.e., the child's body is positioned so that the muscles which were contracted are elongated and those that were elongated are contracted.

    (h) This method should be used by all involved in treatment, including speech, physical, and occupational therapists.

(3) Therapy of Margaret Rood (1956).
  (a) There are two types of muscles.
    [1] Heavy work muscles such as those that maintain posture.
    [2] Light work muscles.
  (b) Reflexes and motor activities are pressured to develop normally in a certain sequence.
  (c) Since sensory stimulation creates muscle activation, the light work muscles are activated by the brushing of skin sensory receptors.
  (d) Heavy work muscles are activated by the application of pressure to the muscles.
  (e) Ice and warm applications are also used for stimulation.
(4) Therapy of Herman Kabat and Margaret Knott (Knott and Voss, 1956).
  (a) The normal actions of a person involve the movement of a group of muscles, not a single muscle.
  (b) Treatment is directed at activating the greatest number of muscles with each effort.
  (c) Use is made of proprioceptive neuromuscular facilitation techniques in which resistance is applied by the therapist against the movement made by the child.
  (d) By this method mass movement patterns are reinforced.
(5) Therapy of Temple Fay (1955).
  (a) The cerebral-palsied child produces many reflex pattern movements.
  (b) Therapy is aimed at developing muscles and better coordination of muscle groups.
  (c) The method is based on the phylogenetic plan in which the patient goes through the motions of a fish, then an amphibian, a reptile, a quadruped, and a biped (swimming, then crawling, then balance).
  (d) The method that is used is patterning, i.e., primitive movement patterns found in man such as crawling, are produced by the organization of reflex movements to produce these patterns.
b Equipment used in treatment.
  (1) Uses of bracing.
    (a) To supply support.
    (b) To prevent or remedy deformities.
    (c) To regulate involuntary movements.

       (2) Special equipment.
          (a) The relaxation chair can be adjusted so that the child is in better postural position.
          (b) The standing table allows the child to stand in a box-like structure which furnishes support but allows movement.
          (c) Stabilizers help to produce standing balance.
          (d) Other devices used include canes, crutches, and parallel bars.
    c Orthopedic surgery.
    d Drug therapy.

B Epilepsy.
    1 Incidence.
      a Estimates are that 0.5 percent of the population is afflicted with epilepsy; the majority are children.
      b Prevalence is approximately 1 or 2 per 1,000 school-age children.
    2 Characteristics.
      a There is a functional disturbance of the normal pattern of electrical discharge of the brain cells.
      b Damaged cells discharge electrical energy at an excessive rate and produce seizures.
      c Seizures that are characteristic of epilepsy are always recurrent.
      d Epilepsy constitutes a motor disorder only when a seizure is occurring.
      e A major problem associated with epilepsy is the difficulty in gaining social acceptance of the condition by others.
    3 Classification.
      a Origins.
        (1) Primary or idiopathic epilepsy.
          (a) The origin is unknown; the areas of the brain that are damaged cannot be located.
          (b) Abnormal electrical discharge and convulsive behavior are present.
        (2) Secondary or symptomatic epilepsy.
          (a) Convulsions are due to a known pathological condition in the brain.
          (b) Brain dysfunction may be due to infections, toxins, injury, or congenital abnormalities.
      b Types of seizures.
        (1) Grand mal.
          (a) Most frequent type of seizure.
          (b) Stages.

        [1]   Aura.
           [a]   The warning stage may be characterized by auditory, olfactory, or visual experience, e.g., flashes of lights or different colors may be seen.
           [b]   The warning stage may come within an instant before loss of consciousness or may occur within a few seconds, allowing the person to prepare for the seizure.
        [2]   Tonic phase.
           [a]   Consciousness is lost.
           [b]   Muscles become stiff and contracted.
           [c]   This phase may last from a few seconds to several minutes.
        [3]   Clonic phase.
           [a]   This is the convulsive stage.
           [b]   There is a series of violent contractions and relaxations of the muscles.
           [c]   This phase usually lasts two or three minutes.
        [4]   Coma.
           [a]   Contractions decrease.
           [b]   The person relaxes and typically goes into a deep sleep.
           [c]   "Status epilepticus" refers to recurring grand mal seizures without the recovery of consciousness.

(2)   Petit mal.
    (a)   There is a loss of consciousness for a few seconds to a half minute.
    (b)   The petit mal begins and ends quickly; there is no aura.
    (c)   The person may jerk suddenly, drop something, or stare blankly.
    (d)   The condition is found more frequently in younger children.

(3)   Jacksonian.
    (a)   Jerking begins in an arm or a leg or on one side of the face and advances to other parts of the body.
    (b)   If the whole body is encompassed, it creates a grand mal.
    (c)   The condition is rarely found in children.

(4)   Psychomotor.
    (a)   This is a poorly defined category with no specific associated behaviors.

        (b) Behavior may range from sitting still to extremely violent activity.

        (c) There is no loss of consciousness but the person appears to be unaware of his behavior.

        (d) The problem is also characterized by amnesia.

        (e) It is rarely found in children.

4 Causes of brain damage resulting in epilepsy.

    a Some professionals believe that genetic factors cause idiopathic epilepsy.

    b Mechanical injuries during the natal or postnatal periods.

    c Infections.

    d Anoxia.

    e Toxins.

    f Tumors.

    g Maldevelopment of brain tissue.

5 Treatment and management of epilepsy: medical.

    a Drug therapy (sedative and anticonvulsant drugs).

    b Surgery in some cases.

6 Prognosis.

    a Grand mal: the prognosis is good if adequate control is established by drugs.

    b Petit mal: this often ceases by 20 to 30 years of age.

C Spina bifida.

  1 Incidence: approximately 2 to 4 per 1,000 children.

  2 Characteristics.

    a There is a congenital defect in spinal development.

    b Closure of the spine is incomplete, leaving an opening.

    c Hydrocephalus (increased cerebrospinal fluid in the skull, creating excess pressure and enlargement of the skull) often accompanies spina bifida.

    d In more severe cases paralysis of the lower limbs and loss of control of the bladder and the sphincter occurs.

  3 Types.

    a Spina bifida occulta.

      (1) There is no neurological impairment.

      (2) A partial cleft may be found in the lumbar region.

      (3) There is no meningeal sac (tumorlike sac).

    b Meningocele lesion.

      (1) There is no neurological impairment.

      (2) The meningeal sac is present with no neural tissue protruding into it.

    c Myelomeningocele lesion.

      (1) There is neurological impairment.

      (2) Neural tissue protrudes into the meningeal sac.

    4 Treatment and management of spina bifida.
       a Surgical closure of spinal lesion within first 48 hours.
       b Physical therapy, bracing, and use of special equipment to assist in walking.
  D Muscular dystrophy.
    1 Characteristics.
       a This is a progressive disease involving the voluntary muscles.
       b Fatty tissues replace muscle tissues as the muscles degenerate, but the child appears healthy.
       c Muscular dystrophy is usually not diagnosed until child is ready to walk.
       d More males than females are afflicted (estimates are from three to six times more males).
       e Few children with this condition live to adulthood.
    2 Cause: hereditary.
    3 Types.
       a Childhood muscular dystrophy.
         (1) Onset at around 3 years old.
         (2) Pseudohypertrophic or Cuchenne type: enlargement of muscles due to fatty tissue.
       b Juvenile muscular dystrophy.
         (1) Onset around teenage or twenties.
         (2) Males and females afflicted equally.
         (3) Slow wasting of face and shoulder muscles and muscles of upper arm.
    4 Treatment and management of muscular dystrophy.
       a Physical, occupational, and speech therapy for muscle use and strengthening.
       b No successful treatment available to reverse the condition.
  E Poliomyelitis.
    1 Characteristics and cause.
       a It is also known as "infantile paralysis."
       b It is caused by a virus.
       c Paralysis results if the gray matter of the spinal cord is affected.
    2 Treatment and management: medical (Salk vaccine).
  F Other motor disorders (crippling conditions of joints, muscles, or bones).
    1 Classification according to cause.
       a Congenital.
         (1) Clubbed feet or hands.
         (2) Congenital amputation.
         (3) Scoliosis-lateral curvature of the spine.
       b Acquired: caused by infectious disease, injury, or other environmental factors.

(1) Mild functional motor problem.
    (a) Locomotor pattern deviations, e.g., deviations in the running pattern such as failure to alternate sides, jerkiness, whipping of the leg or the foot in or out.
    (b) Balance pattern deviations, e.g., deviations in standing or sitting patterns, such as weight shifted more to one side than the other or one part of the body twisted (e.g., the trunk) with regard to the rest of the body.
    (c) Pattern deviations in handling objects, e.g., throwing or catching deviations such as loss of balance while throwing or catching, inability to control the object, inability to adjust to different speeds or heights in catching the object.

(2) Severe functional motor problems, e.g., amputation or loss of limb.

  c Combination of causal factors (e.g., congenital dislocation of the hip).
    (1) Genetic: 7 females are afflicted with this condition for every 1 male.
    (2) Environmental.
      (a) Prenatal: intrauterine breech posture (hips flexed, knees extended).
      (b) Postnatal: maintaining infant in a position with hips extended and adducted, such as from tight swaddling or a cradle board.

2 Classification according to limbs involved.
  a Monoplegia: one limb.
  b Hemiplegia: both limbs on same side of body.
  c Triplegia: three limbs.
  d Paraplegia: both legs.
  e Quadriplegia: four limbs.
  f Diplegia: four limbs, with more involvement of legs.
  g Double or bilateral hemiplegia: four limbs, with more involvement of arms.

3 Treatment and management.
  a Physical and occupational therapy.
  b Special equipment for mobility.
  c Prosthetic devices for amputees.

III EVALUATIVE PROCEDURES FOR MOTOR DISORDERS.
  A Bayley Scales of Infant Development by Nancy Bayley (1935).
    1 Ages 2 to 30 months.
    2 Three parts.
      a Mental scale.

   b Motor scale: measures range from gross motor skills such as sitting and standing to fine motor skills such as grasping an object.

   c Infant behavior record.

  B Denver Developmental Screening Test by W. K. Frankenburg and J. B. Dodds (1966).

   1 Infants and preschool, ages 2 weeks to 6 years.

   2 Tested individually.

   3 Areas of development tested.

    a Gross motor.

    b Fine motor: adaptive, language, and personal-social.

   4 Used as screening device to detect delays in development.

  C Lincoln-Oseretsky Motor Development Scale (Western Psychological Services; Sloan, 1951).

   1 Ages 6 to 14 years.

   2 Individual test of various motor skills.

  D Marianne Frostig Developmental Test of Visual Perception.

   1 Ages 3 to 8 years.

   2 Measures five factors of visual perception.

    a Eye-motor coordination.

    b Figure-ground discrimination.

    c Form constancy.

    d Position in space.

    e Spatial relationships.

  E The Purdue Perceptual Motor Survey by E. G. Roach and N. C. Kephart (1966).

   1 Ages 6 to 10 years.

   2 Designed to assess perceptual-motor development of those abilities necessary for academic success.

   3 Areas.

    a Balance.

    b Body image.

    c Perceptual-motor function.

    d Ocular control.

IV PROMINENT THEORIES OF PERCEPTUAL-MOTOR DEVELOPMENT.

  A Kephart's perceptual-motor theory (1967).

   1 This theory states that normal perceptual-motor development is necessary so that the child can build concepts of world.

   2 Four major groups of motor patterns are focused upon: locomotion, contact, balance and maintenance of posture, and receipt and propulsion.

  B Getman's visumotor model (1965).

   1 This model is concerned with visual development and learning.

2 Each successive stage of development is dependent upon learning the previous stage.

C Patterning theory of neurological organization by Doman and Delacato (Delacato, 1966).

1 The maturation of the individual occurs in the same developmental stages as the development of the species in the evolutionary process.

2 Patterning is the manipulation of a child's body into positions of the various developmental stages until neurological organization is produced.

D Barsch's movigenic theory (1967, 1968): learning related to motor skills.

E Frostig's visual perception learning theory (Frostig and Horne, 1964).

GLOSSARY *

ABO system   Classification scheme for blood typing to indicate the presence or absence of A or B antibodies. Thus, an "A" individual has anti-B; a "B" individual has anti-A; an AB individual has neither A nor B antibodies; and an "O" individual has both antibodies.

Albinism   A condition of no or spotty pigmentation of the skin and iris.

Alexia   Inability to read written or printed language, although there is no organic visual pathology.

Amblyopia   Weakness of vision without any apparent change in the structure of the eye itself.

Amniocentesis   A procedure for analyzing factors in the amniotic fluid that may indicate the presence of problems for the offspring.

Anoxia   Lack of oxygen or the disturbance of bodily functions resulting from lack of oxygen.

Aphonia   Loss or disturbance of the capability of producing appropriate sounds.

* The glossary was prepared with the assistance of Peter Picuri, Pennsylvania State University.

Astigmatism   Irregular refraction causing blurred vision.

Athetoid   The name given to someone with athetosis, a neuromuscular disability found in the cerebral-palsied; characterized by slow, squirming, twisting, purposeless movements.

Athetosis   A form of cerebral palsy marked by involuntary, wormlike movements.

Atoxia   A form of cerebral palsy marked by an impairment of muscular coordination which makes it difficult to walk or maintain balance.

Audiometry   The evaluation of hearing ability, usually made by the use of standardized testing and devices.

Aura   A sensation that precedes the onset of an epileptic attack.

Autosome   An ordinary chromosome as opposed to a sex-determining chromosome.

Babinski reflex   The involuntary extension and fanning of the toes upon stimulation of the sole of the foot.

Behavior modification   The practice of applying behavior principles to educational, therapeutic, and social problems; a technology built upon principles of operant and respondent conditioning.

Blindness   A state of severe visual impairment in which there is no measurable or useful vision.

Brain-injured   Characterizing one who before, during, or after birth has received an infection of the brain, which prevents or impedes normal brain functioning and which may be related to disturbances in sensing, responding, and learning.

Cataract   A condition of the eye in which the lens of the eye is clouded, resulting in dimming of vision.

Cerebral palsy   Any one of a group of disorders affecting control of the motor system and due to brain damage.

Chromosomes   Very small bodies in the nucleus of a cell which carry the genes or hereditary factors.

Cleft palate   A congenital failure in development of the roof of the mouth, often associated with cleft lip.

Compulsion   A rigidly enacted behavior often resembling the "fixed," ritualistic behaviors of animals.

Congenital   present at birth.

Crippled   Characterizing orthopedic impairment that interferes with the normal functions of the bones, joints, or muscles.

Cystic fibrosis   A hereditary disorder producing a generalized malfunction of the pancreas leading to numerous organic and functional deficiencies.

Deafness   A condition in which one has sustained severe impairment of the hearing; nonfunctional for normal purposes.

Decibel   A relative measure of the intensity of sound; hearing loss is measured in decibels.

Developmental period   That time period during which major, relatively stable characteristics of the individual are established; frequently designated as that interval between conception and 18 years of age.

Deviation From a social view, any departure from the norm sufficient to produce differential social consequences.

Diabetes mellitus Disorder of pancreatic insulin production resulting in excessive amounts of glucose in the blood and in the urine.

Diplegia Paralysis affecting similar parts of both sides of the body.

Disability A deviation in body or functioning that results in functional inadequacy in view of environmental demands.

Discriminative stimuli Mark the time or place when an operant behavior will have reinforcing consequences and, thus, sets the occasion for a behavior.

Dysarthria Disorder of articulation due to a loss of control and coordination of the muscular movements of tongue, lips, jaw, and palate required for speech.

Dyslalia Any of the disorders in the articulation of speech not due to damage of the central nervous system.

Dyslexia Inadequate reading skill.

Dysphemia Any speech disorder due to a psychoneurotic condition having no known organic base.

Echolalia Repetition of words or phrases spoken by others.

Ectomorphic A term for body types characteristically tall and thin, fragile and lightly muscled.

Electroencephalogram An instrument used to measure changes in the electric potential of different areas of the brain; the record of such measurements.

Encephalitis Viral infection of the brain.

Endogenous Internally or biologically caused.

Endomorphic A term for a body type characteristically generally soft and round, with relatively underdeveloped bone and muscle tissue.

Environmentalism A nonbiological view which believes that one's physical environment is responsible for the kind, direction, and rate of development.

Epilepsy A group of nervous diseases in which the person has seizures; related to disorders in the brain's electrical activity; may be present at birth or developed after illness or injury.

Etiology The study of the causes of a disorder.

Eugenics A branch of science which attempts to improve the human race through controlled heredity.

Exceptional individual Any person whose physical attributes or functioning deviate from the norm sufficiently to evoke or require differential interpersonal or environmental response or arrangements.

Exogenous Externally or environmentally caused.

Formative assessment Frequent evaluation designed to provide feedback to permit adjustments in educational or therapeutic programing, e.g., progress checks.

Frustration Emotional tension resulting from the blocking of a desire or need; a subjective state experienced under conditions of ratio strain , i.e., sparse or absent reward for continued effort.

Galactosemia Disorder of carbohydrate metabolism in which the absence of a particular enzyme prevents the normal transformation of galactose to glucose, resulting in damage to tissue.

Genetic counseling Advice provided to parents and potential parents on the probabilities of hereditary assets and liabilities, based on a detailed medical pedigree, pregnancy histories, and certain laboratory tests.

Genotypic language Terminology relating to hypothesized and generalized "states" or "conditions" alleged to be the underlying causes of observable problems.

Germ cell The male sperm or female ovum, which carries the genetic materials.

Gestational Pertaining to the period of pregnancy.

Glaucoma Pressure inside the eyeball caused by the forming of fluid in the front portion of the eyeball.

Grand mal seizure Epileptic seizure consisting of several phases in which the person loses consciousness, thrashes about, stiffens, and goes into a deep relaxed state.

Handicap The burden imposed socially on an individual by virtue of judgment of functional or somatic difference.

Hard of hearing Characterizing condition in which one's sense of hearing is defective, but is functional.

Hemiplegia Paralysis affecting one half of the body.

Heterophoria Imbalance of the external muscles of the eyes.

Hydrocephalus Presence of excess cerebrospinal fluid within the brain resulting in damage to brain tissue; frequently results from spinal injury.

Hyperkinetic Pertaining to condition characterized by excessive motor activity, inattention, and impulsivity.

Hypernasality Speech sounds which should be emitted through the mouth being emitted instead through the nasal cavity. This often occurs in partial or complete paralysis of the soft palate.

Hyperopia Farsightedness; rays focus behind the retina.

Hypertonicity Abnormal tightness of a muscle not at work.

Impairment Actual tissue damage.

Interactionism The view that the development of a child is a cumulative and progressive product of the continuous interaction between heredity and environment.

Jacksonian seizure A type of epilepsy in which there is no loss of awareness but a definite series of attacks affecting a certain area of the body, spreading out from a focal point to one whole side of the body.

Jaundice Disorder of the liver resulting in yellowish pigmentation of the skin, tissue, and body fluids.

Kernicterus Damage and pigmentation of the basal ganglia and other portions of the brain caused by the same pigments related to jaundice.

Learning Relatively permanent changes in behavior as a result of experience.

Mastoid Cells of the temporal bone in the ear.

Mesomorphic A term for body types characterized by developed muscles and bones and strong, tough bodies resistent to injury.

Metabolism The use of energy by the body; all the physical and chemical processes needed by the organism for its maintenance.

Modalities Ways of sensing and responding; thus, visual, auditory, tactile, verbal, motor, etc. capabilities.

Mongolism A condition, most frequently of hereditary origin, in which one has certain physical characteristics, such as a flattened skull, an oblique eye slit, a fissured tongue, a horizontal palmar crease, and stubby fingers and toes; almost always associated with mild to moderate intellectual retardation.

Monoplegia Paralysis affecting one body part.

Moro reflex Reflex occurring in young infants when their supporting surface is jarred; the infant's arms and legs become drawn up in a pattern described as the clasping or embrace reflex.

Muscular dystrophy A condition characterized by weakness of the skeletal muscles with increasing deformity as the disease progresses.

Myopia Nearsightedness; parallel rays come to a focus in front of the retina.

Neonate The child from birth to 1 month.

Neurologically handicapped Refers to authenticated damage or dysfunction of the brain resulting in an array of possible physical and behavioral deficiencies; frequently, however, also refers to a syndrome of deficiency presumably and inferentially due to brain damage or dysfunction.

Neurologist Medical specialist in the diagnosis and treatment of disorders of the nervous system.

Normality Statistical average or, more often, a socially defined range of acceptability with respect to physique or behavior or both.

Normalization The concept that the educational and therapeutic goal for exceptional individuals must be normal functioning and status, and that procedures employed in attaining the goal must be as close to normal as is feasible.

Nystagmus Involuntary rapid movement of the eyeball.

Ontogeny Development of the individual from conception onward.

Operant conditioning A learning process in which the behavior of the subject is modified as a consequence of his own behavior. Behaviors which "operate" on and thus change the environment are themselves changed by the new environment.

Ophthalmologist Medical specialist in the diagnosis and treatment of diseases of the eye.

Orthopedics The area of medicine concerned with bones, joints, and muscles. Also, the area of surgery dealing with the correction of deformities and the treatment of chronic diseases of the joints and spine.

Otolaryngologist   Medical specialist in the diagnosis and treatment of diseases of the ear, nose, and throat.

Otologist   Medical specialist in the diagnosis and treatment of diseases of the ear.

Paraplegia   Paralysis affecting the lower half of the body and both legs.

Perinatal   Occurring at or pertaining to the time of birth.

Perseveration   Inappropriate repetition of behavior; continuation of a behavior in the absence of the appropriate or intended stimulus.

Petit mal seizure   Mild and quite brief epileptic seizure in which there may be only a slight loss of consciousness.

Phenotypic language   Terminology relating to objectively measurable behaviors, characteristics, and variables subject to manipulation for purposes of positive intervention.

Phenylketonuria (PKU)   A hereditary metabolic disease transferred through genetic action; resulting in a lack of the necessary enzyme for oxydizing phenylalanine, which in turn promotes accumulation of phenylpyuric acid with resulting mental retardation.

Phobia   Irrational (out-of-context) reaction to stimuli with avoidance or escape responses; behavior may appear "irrational" or inappropriate when the person responds to stimuli others do not consider important.

Phylogeny   Evolutionary or racial development of a related group of organisms; development of species characteristics as opposed to individual characteristics (ontogeny).

Postnatal   Occurring after birth.

Predeterminism   A concept which holds the belief that if the environment is free and permissive, "innate" potentials, latent talents, and natural goodness will unfold as the child grows.

Preformationism   A view which states that all an individual is or ever will be is preformed at conception.

Prenatal   Occurring or existing before birth.

Presbyopia   A condition in which distant objects can be seen clearly, but no distinct picture of nearby objects can be obtained; this is caused by a restriction of accommodation due to inelasticity of the lens of the eye.

Prognosis   Prediction of the course and end of a disorder.

Prosthesis   An artificial replacement of an absent part of the body; adaptation of the environment to minimize sensory and response difficulties.

Pseudo mental retardation   False, not genuine mental retardation; frequently, but inappropriately, used as a retrospective diagnosis to "explain" marked improvement in intellectual functioning; a necessary concept when one assumes the irreversibility of retardation.

Psychometrics   Evaluation of psychological functioning, especially learning, usually done by means of standardized objective testing.

Psychomotor seizure   A form of epileptic seizure consisting of purposeful but inappropriate acts. A difficult form to diagnose and control.

Psychosis Term used to describe any of several extreme syndromes involving excessive withdrawal, aggression, or self-abuse that preclude normal, constructive functioning; usually of unknown origin.

Quadriplegia Paralysis affecting all four body limbs.

Regression Inappropriate return to attributes and behaviors characteristic of an earlier period of development.

Reinforcement A procedure for strengthening a response involving the immediate presentation of a consequence that acts to build the response frequency, duration, or intensity, or all three.

Reinforcer A stimulus which by its occurrence immediately after a behavior strengthens that behavior.

Reliability Degree to which a test or other instrument of evaluation measures consistently whatever it purports to measure; consistency across persons, tests, or time.

Resource-room specialist A special educator employed to provide special assistance to exceptional children and others in regular and special classes through the use of specialized materials and methods.

Retardation Slowness or delay in the acquisition of physical or behavioral characteristics relative to norms for these characteristics.

Retrolental fibroplasia A disease of the retina, in which an overgrowth of vascular tissue forms behind the lens of the eyes, occurring in premature infants because of excess oxygen.

Rheumatic fever A chronic infection of the connective tissues of the body, affecting the joints, heart, and blood vessels.

Rh incompatibility Parental difference in a certain blood group factor (first discovered in Rhesus monkeys) that can result, for example, in an Rh-negative mother's producing antibodies against a father-contributed Rh-positive factor present in the fetus; resulting in agglutination of blood with serious consequences for the baby and the mother.

Rigidity A diagnostic classification of cerebral palsy characterized by stiffness and immobility.

Rubella German measles, especially hazardous to the fetus during the first 3 months of pregnancy.

Self-management The practice of applying principles of behavior to one's own activities in order to achieve self-selected objectives.

Shaping The practice of reinforcing only those behaviors that progressively move in the direction of the desired final performance and extinguishing (not reinforcing) all other responses.

Sickle-cell anemia An inherited abnormality of the red blood cells (with cells shaped like "sickles," rather than spheres) resulting in severe anemia, predominantly, but not exclusively found in persons of African ancestry. Parents who are "carriers" of the disorder may discover this through a sample test and receive counseling relative to treatment and the desirability of reproduction.

Social maladjustment A syndrome in which one's social behavior is sufficiently deviant that he cannot participate in "normal" activities with others; usually involves violation of social norms and codes of conduct.

Sociogram A technique which evaluates the social movement and distance of a person within a given group.

Somatopsychology The study of the impact of bodily deviation on behavior.

Spasticity Excessive tension of the muscles making control of the muscles difficult.

Special education The profession concerned with the arrangement of education variables leading to the prevention, reduction, or elimination of those conditions that produce significant defects in the academic, communicative, locomotor, or adjustive functioning of children.

Speech pathologist One who is engaged in the study of the disorders of speech and language usually responsible for diagnosing a speech problem and supervising the therapy.

Spina bifida (Occulta) A defect of closure in the posterior bony wall of the spinal canal that is not accompanied by associated spinal cord or meninges pathology.

Strabismus Deviation of the axis of the eyes, which the person cannot overcome, making single binocular vision impossible.

Stuttering A speech impediment in which the normally smooth flow of words is disrupted by rapid repetition of words, hesitations, or breathing spasms or all three.

Summative assessment Single, end-of-sequence evaluation, e.g., year-end achievement tests and final exams.

Syphilis Contagious venereal disease.

Tabula rasa (blank slate) A view that suggests that the mind is blank at birth and that a child is born with no storehouses of memories, instinctive thoughts, or cognitive processes.

Target behaviors Specific, explicitly stated behaviors selected for modification.

Tremor Involuntary shaking or unsteadiness, especially of the extremities.

Triplegia Paralysis affecting three body limbs.

Validity The extent to which a test or other measuring instrument fulfills the purpose for which it is used.

REFERENCES

Abeson, A., & Berenson, B. *Physical environment and special education: An interdisciplinary approach to research (final report).* Arlington, Va.: Council for Exceptional Children, 1970.

Abeson, A., & Blacklow, J. *Environmental design: New relevance for special education.* Arlington, Va.: Council for Exceptional Children, 1971.

Allen, G. Patterns of discovery in the genetics of mental deficiency. *American Journal of Mental Deficiency,* 1958, **62,** 840–849.

American National Standards Institute, Inc. American National Standard Specifications for Making Buildings and Facilities Accessible to, and Usable by, the Physically Handicapped. October, 1961; reaffirmed, 1971.

American Psychiatric Association. *Diagnostic and statistical manual for mental disorders.* Washington, D.C.: APA, 1952.

Ammons, C. H., Worchel, P., & Dallenbach, K. M. Facial vision: The perception of obstacles out of doors by blindfolded and blindfolded-deafened subjects. *American Journal of Psychology,* 1953, **66,** 519–553.

Anthony, E. J. The behavior disorders of children. In P. H. Mussen (Ed.), *Carmichael's manual of child psychology.* Vol. 2. (3d ed.) New York: Wiley, 1970. Pp. 667–764.

Apgar, V. A proposal for a new method of evaluation of the newborn infant. *Anesthesia and Analgesia,* 1953, **32,** 260–267.

Ausubel, D. P. *Theory and problems of child development.* New York: Grune & Stratton, 1958.

Ausubel, D. P., & Sullivan, E. V. *Theory and problems of child development.* (2d ed.) New York: Grune & Stratton, 1970.

Bacon, H. K., Child, I. L., & Barry, H. A. A cross-cultural study of correlates of crime. *Journal of Abnormal and Social Psychology,* 1963, **66,** 291–300.

Baer, D. M., & Wolf, M. M. The reinforcement contingency in preschool and remedial education. In R. Hess and R. Bear (Eds.), *Early education: Current theory, research and action.* Chicago: Aldine, 1968. Pp. 119–129.

Bailey, J., & Meyerson, L. Vibration as a reinforcer with a profoundly retarded child. *Journal of Applied Behavior Analysis,* 1969, **2,** 135–137.

Bandura, A. *Principles of behavior modification.* New York: Holt, 1969.

Bandura, A., & Walters, R. H. *Adolescent aggression.* New York: Ronald Press, 1959.

Bandura, A., & Walters, R. H. *Social learning and personality development.* New York: Holt, 1963.

Bank-Mikklesen, N. E. Model service models: A metropolitan area in Denmark-Copenhagen. In R. B. Kugel and W. Wolfensberger (Eds.), *Changing patterns in residential services for the mentally retarded.* Washington, D.C.: President's Committee on Mental Retardation, 1969. Pp. 227–254.

Barber, T. X., Forgione, A., Chaves, J. F., Calverly, D. S., McPeake, J. D., & Bowen, B. Five attempts to replicate the experimenter bias effect. *Journal of Consulting and Clinical Psychology,* 1969, **33,** 1–14.

Barker, R., Dembo, H., & Lewin, K. *Frustration and regression: An experiment with young children.* Iowa City: University of Iowa Press, 1941.

Barker, R., Wright, B., & Gonick, M. *Adjustment to physical handicaps and illness: A survey of the social psychology of physique and disability.* New York: Social Science Research Council, 1946.

Barnett, C. D., Ellis, N. R., & Pryor, M. Learning in familial and brain-injured defectives. *American Journal on Mental Deficiency,* 1960, **64,** 894–897.

Barsch, R. H. *Achieving perceptual-motor efficiency.* Vol. 1. Seattle, Washington: Special Child Publications, 1967.

Barsch, R. H. *Enriching perception and cognition,* Vol. 2. Seattle, Washington: Special Child Publications, 1968.

Bateman, B. An educator's view of a diagnostic approach to learning disorders. In J. Hellmuth (Ed.), *Learning disorders.* Vol. 1. Seattle: Special Child Publications, 1965. Pp. 219–239.

Bayley, N. The development of motor abilities during the first three years. *Monograph of Society for Research in Child Development,* 1935, **1,** 1–26.

Bayley, N. *Bayley scales of infant development: Birth to two years.* New York: Psychological Corporation, 1969.

Beach, F. A., & Jaynes, J. Effects of early experience on the behavior of animals. *Psychological Bulletin,* 1954, **51,** 239–263.

Becker, W. C. Consequences of different kinds of parental discipline. In M. L. Hoffman and L. W. Hoffman (Eds.), *Review of child development research.* Vol. 1. New York: Russell Sage, 1964. Pp. 169–208.

Becker, W. C., Engelmann, S., & Thomas, D. R. *Teaching: A course in applied psychology.* Chicago: Science Research, 1971.

Bellak, L., & Bellak, S. S. *Manual: Children's apperception test.* New York: C.P.S. Co., 1949.

Bereiter, C., & Engelmann, S. *Teaching disadvantaged children in the preschool.* Englewood Cliffs, N.J.: Prentice-Hall, 1966.

Berkowitz, L. *Aggression: A social psychological analysis.* New York: McGraw-Hill, 1962.

Berkowitz, P., & Rothman, E. *The disturbed child.* New York: New York University Press, 1960.

Bernstein, B. Social class and linguistic development: A theory of social learning. In A. H. Halsey, F. Anderson, and C. A. Anderson (Eds.), *Education, economy and society.* Glencoe, Ill.: Free Press, 1961. Pp. 288–314.

Bernstein, B. A socio-linguistic approach to socialization: With some reference to educability. In J. Gumpery and D. Hymes (Eds.), *Research in socio-linguistics.* New York: Holt, in press.

Berry, M. F., & Eisenson, J. *Speech disorders, principles and practices of therapy.* New York: Appleton-Century-Crofts, 1956.

Bijou, S. W. A functional analysis of retarded development. In N. Ellis (Ed.), *Research in mental retardation.* New York: Academic Press, 1966.

Bijou, S. W., & Baer, D. M. The laboratory-experimental study of child behavior. In Paul H. Mussen (Ed.), *Handbook of research methods in child development.* New York: Wiley, 1960. Pp. 140–197.

Bijou, S. W., & Baer, D. M. *Child development: Readings in experimental analyses.* New York: Appleton-Century-Crofts, 1967.

Birch, H. Boldness and judgment in behavior genetics. In M. Mead, T. Dobzhansky, E. Tobach, and R. E. Light (Eds.), *Science and the concept of race.* New York: Columbia, 1968.

Blatt, B. Some persistently recurring assumptions concerning the mentally subnormal. *Training School Bulletin,* 1960, **57,** 48–59.

Blatt, B., & Kaplan, F. *Christmas in purgatory.* Boston: Allyn and Bacon, 1967.

Bloom, B. S. *Stability and change in human characteristics.* New York: Wiley, 1964.

Blum, G. S. *Manual: The Blacky pictures.* New York: The Psychological Corporation, 1950.

Blumberg, A. *A pilot project for preparing special education teachers regarding new teaching methods (final report).* University of West Virginia, Morgantown, Washington, D. C.: Bureau of Elementary and Secondary Education (DHEW/OE), 1970.

Bobath, K., & Bobath, B. An assessment of the motor handicaps of children with cerebral palsy and their response to treatment. *American Journal of Occupational Therapy,* 1958, **21,** 19–36.

Bowlby, J. *Child care and the growth of love.* London: Penguin, 1951.

Bowlby, J., Ainsworth, M., Boston, B., & Rosenbloth, O. The effects of mother-child separation: A follow-up study. *British Journal of Medical Psychology,* 1956, **29,** 211–249.

Bowman, P. H., DeHaan, R. F., Kough, J. K., & Liddle, G. P. *Mobilizing community resource for youth.* Chicago: University of Chicago Press, 1956.

Braginsky, D. D., & Braginsky, B. M. *Hansels and Gretels: Studies of children in institutions for the mentally retarded.* New York: Holt, 1971.

Brazelton, T. Berry. *Infants and mothers: Differences in development.* New York: Delacorte Press, 1969.

Brown, F. W. Childhood bereavement and subsequent psychiatric disorder. *British Journal of Psychiatry,* 1966, **112** (491), 1035.

Bruner, J. S. The course of cognitive growth. *American Psychologist,* 1964, **19,** 1–15.

Bruner, J. S. On cognitive growth: I and II. In J. S. Bruner, R. R. Olver, P. M. Greenfield, et al. *Studies in cognitive growth.* New York: Wiley, 1966. Pp. 1–67.

Bureau of Education for the Handicapped. *Better education for the handicapped.* Annual Reports FY 1968 and FY 1969. Washington, D.C., 1969, p. 4; 1970, p. 4.

Bzoch, Kenneth R. (Ed.) *Communicative disorders related to cleft lip and palate.* Boston: Brown & Company, 1971, 1972.

Capobianco, R. J. Diagnostic methods used with learning disability cases. *Exceptional Children,* 1964, **31,** 187–193.

Carhart, R. Development and conservation of speech. In H. Davis and A. R. Silverman (Eds.), *Hearing and deafness.* (3d ed.) New York: Holt, 1970. Pp. 360–374.

Cassidy, V., & Stanton, J. An investigation of factors in the educational placement of mentally retarded children: A study of differences between children in special and regular classes in Ohio. U. S. Office of Education Cooperative Research Program, Project No. 043. Columbus: Ohio State University, 1959.

Cattell, R. B., Saunders, D. R., & Stice, G. *Handbook: Sixteen personality factor questionnaire.* Champaign, Ill.: Institute for Personality and Ability Testing, 1957.

Chaney, C. M., & Kephart, N. C. *Motoric aids to perceptual training.* Columbus, Ohio: Merrill, 1968.

Christoplos, F., & Renz, P. A critical examination of special education programs. *Journal of Special Education,* 1969, **3,** 371–379.

Claiborn, W. L. Expectancy effects in the classroom: A failure to replicate. *Journal of Educational Psychology,* 1969, **60,** 377–383.

Clark, A. D. B., & Clarke, A. M. Pseudo-feeblemindedness—Some implications. *American Journal of Mental Deficiency,* 1955, **59,** 507–509.

Cohen, J., & Struening, E. L. Opinions about mental health: Hospital social atmosphere profiles and their relevance to effectiveness. *Journal of Consulting Psychology,* 1964, **28,** 291–298.

Committee on Nomenclature, Conference of Executives of American Schools for the Deaf. *American Annals of the Deaf,* 1938, **83.**

Corwin, R. G. *A sociology of education: Emerging patterns of class, status, and power in the public schools.* New York: Appleton-Century-Crofts, 1965.

Council for Exceptional Children, *Physical facilities: Exceptional child bibliography series.* Arlington, Va.: Information Center on Exceptional Children, 1971.

Council for Exceptional Children. Proposed CEC Policy Statement on the Organization and Administration of Special Education. *Exceptional Children,* 1973, **39,** 493–497.

Cratty, B. J. *Perceptual and motor development in infants and children.* New York: Macmillan, 1970.

Craig, W. The child in the maladjusted household. *Practitioner,* 1956, **177,** 21.

Cronbach, L. J., & Gleser, G. C. *Psychological tests and personal decisions.* Urbana: University of Illinois Press, 1957.

Cruickshank, W., Bentzen, F., Rotsburg, F., & Tannhauser, M. *A teaching methodology for brain-injured and hyperactive children.* New York: Syracuse University Press, 1961.

Cruickshank, W. M., & Quay, H. C. Learning and physical design: The necessity for research and research design. *Exceptional Children,* 1970, **37,** 261–268.

Cummings, S. T., Bayley, H. C., & Rie, H. E. The effects of the child's deficiency on the mother: A study of mothers of mentally retarded, chronically ill, and neurotic children. *American Journal of Orthopsychiatry,* 1966, **36,** 595–608.

Davidson, M. A., McInnes, R. G., & Parnell, R. W. The distribution of personality traits in seven-year-old children: A combined psychological, psychiatric, and somatotype study. *British Educational Psychology,* 1957, **27,** 48–61.

Davis, H. Abnormal hearing and deafness. In H. Davis and S. R. Silvermann (Eds.), *Hearing and deafness.* (3d ed.) New York: Holt, 1970. Pp. 83–139.

Davis, H. Anatomy and physiology of the auditory system. In H. Davis and S. R. Silverman (Eds.), *Hearing and deafness.* (3d ed.) New York: Holt, 1970. Pp. 47–74.

Davis, H. Audiometry: Pure tone and simple speech tests. In H. Davis and S. R. Silverman (Eds.), *Hearing and deafness.* (3d ed.) New York: Holt, 1970. Pp. 179–184.

Davis, H., & Fowler, E. P. The medical treatment of hearing loss and the conservation of hearing. In H. Davis and S. R. Silverman (Eds.), *Hearing and deafness.* (3d ed.) New York: Holt, 1970. Pp. 140–148.

Davis, H., & Goldstein, R. Audiometry: Other auditory tests. In H. Davis and S. R. Silverman (Eds.), *Hearing and deafness.* (3d ed.) New York: Holt, 1970. Pp. 221–248.

Davis, H., & Krantz, F. W. The international standard reference zero for pure tone audiometers and its relation to the evaluation of impairment of hearing. *Journal of Speech and Hearing Research,* 1964, **7,** 7–16.

Delacato, C. H. *Neurological organization and reading problems.* Springfield, Ill.: Charles C Thomas, 1966.

Dennis, W. Infant development under conditions of restricted practice and of minimum social stimulation: A preliminary report. *Journal of Genetic Psychology,* 1938, **53,** 149–158.

Dennis, W. Causes of retardation among institutional children: Iran. *Journal of Genetic Psychology,* 1960, **96,** 47–59.

Dennis, W., and Dennis, M. G. The effect of cradling practices upon the onset of walking in Hopi children. *Journal of Genetic Psychology,* 1940, **56,** 77–86.

Deno, E. N. Special education as developmental capital. *Exceptional Children,* 1970, **37,** 229–237.

Deno, E. N. Strategies for improvement of educational opportunities for handicapped children: Suggestions for exploitation of EPDA potential. In M. C. Reynolds and M. D. Davis (Eds.), *Exceptional children in regular classrooms.* Minneapolis: University of Minnesota, 1971. Pp. 12–20.

Despert, J. L. *The emotionally disturbed child: An inquiry into family patterns.* New York: Doubleday, 1970.

Despert, L. Urinary control and enuresis. *Psychosomatic Medicine,* 1944, **6,** 294–307.

Deutsch, A. *The mentally ill in America: A history of their care and treatment.* (2d ed.) New York: Columbia University Press, 1949.

Deutsch, M., et al. (Eds.) *Social class, race and psychological development.* New York: Holt, 1968.

Deutsch, M., Fishman, J. A., Kogan, L. S., North, R. D., & Whitman, M. Guidelines for testing minority children. In D. Payne and R. McMorris (Eds.), *Educational and psychological measurement.* Waltham, Mass.: Blaisdell, 1967. Pp. 303–314.

Di Carlo, L. M. *The deaf.* Englewood Cliffs, N.J.: Prentice-Hall, 1964.

Dix, M., & Hallpike, C. S. The peepshow, *British Medical Journal,* 1947, **2,** 719–723.

Doll, Edgar A. *Clinical studies in feeblemindedness.* Boston: R. D. Badger, 1917.

Dollard, J., Doob, L. W., Miller, N. E., Mowrer, H. O., & Sears, R. R. *Frustration and aggression.* New Haven, Conn.: Yale, 1939.

Drillien, C. The incidence of mental and physical handicaps in school age children of very low birth weight. *Pediatrics,* 1961, **27,** 452.

Dunn, L. M. (Ed.) *Exceptional children in the schools.* New York: Holt, 1963.

Dunn, L. M. Special education for the mildly retarded: Is much of it justifiable? *Exceptional Children,* 1968, **35,** 5–22.

Dunn, L. M. (Ed.) *Exceptional children in the schools.* (2d ed.) New York: Holt, 1973.

Edgerton, R. B. *The cloak of competence: Stigma in the lives of the mentally retarded.* Berkeley: University of California Press, 1967.

Eichenwald, H. The pathology of reading disorders: Psycho-physiological factors. In M. Johnson and R. Kress (Eds.) *Corrective reading in the elementary classroom.* Newark, Del.: International Reading Association, 1967. Pp. 31–44.

Eisenberg, L. School phobia: A study in the communication of anxiety. *American Journal of Psychiatry,* 1958, **114,** 712–718.

Eisenson, J. *Stuttering: A symposium.* New York: Harper, 1958.

Eisenson, J., & Ogilvie, M. *Speech correction in the schools.* New York: Macmillan, 1971.

Elashoff, J. D., & Snow, R. E. A case study in statistical inference: Reconsideration of the Rosenthal Jacobson data on teacher expectancy. (SCRDT Technical Report 15.) Stanford, Calif.: Stanford University, School of Education, 1970.

EMR curriculum: A persisting life needs approach. Madison: Wisconsin State Department of Public Instruction, 1970.

Engel, M. The tin drum revisited. *Journal of Special Education,* 1969, **3,** 381–384.

Erikson, E. *Childhood and society.* New York: Norton, 1963.

Espenschade, A. S., & Eckert, H. M. *Motor development.* Columbus, Ohio: Merrill, 1967.

Eysenck, S. B. G. *Manual of the junior Eysenck personality inventory.* London: University of London Press, 1965.

Farber, B. Effects of a severely mentally retarded child on family integration. *Monographs of the Society for Research in Child Development,* 1959, **24** (2).

Fargo, G. A., Behrms, C., & Nolen, R. (Eds.) *Behavior modification in the classroom.* Belmont, Calif.: Wadsworth, 1970.

Farina, A., Allen, J. J., & Saul, B. B. The role of the stigmatized person in affecting social relationships. *Journal of Personality,* 1968, **36,** 169–182.

Farina, A., & Ring, K. The influence of perceived mental illness on interpersonal relations. *Journal of Abnormal Psychology,* 1965, **70,** 47–51.

Fay, T. The origin of human movement. *American Journal of Psychiatry,* 1955, **3,** 644–652.

Fenichel, C. Psycho-educational approaches for seriously disturbed children in the classroom. In N. J. Long, W. C. Morse, & R. G. Newman (Eds.), *Conflict in the classroom: The education of children with problems.* (2d ed.) Belmont, Calif.: Wadsworth, 1971.

Fernald, G. M. *Remedial techniques in basic school subjects.* New York: McGraw-Hill, 1943.

Fisher, D. C. *The Montessori manual for teachers and parents.* (Copyright 1913 by W. E. Richardson Co.) Cambridge, Mass.: Robert Bentley, 1964.

Fitts, W. H. *Manual: Tennessee self concept scale.* Nashville: Counselor Recordings and Test, 1965.

Fleming, E., & Anttonen, R. G. Teacher expectancy or my fair lady. *American Educational Research Journal,* 1971, **8,** 241–252.

Flitcher, S. S. F., & Welton, J. *Froebel's chief writings on education.* London: E. Arnold, 1912.

Fokes, J. Developmental scale of motor abilities. In B. Stephens (Ed.), *Training the developmentally young.* New York: John Day, 1971. Pp. 78–101.

Frankenburg, W. K., & Dodds, J. B. *Denver Developmental Screening Test.* Denver: University of Colorado Medical Center, 1966.

Franks, C. M. (Ed.) *Behavior therapy: Appraisal and status.* New York: McGraw-Hill, 1969.

Franks, C. M., & Wilson, G. T. *Annual Review of Behavior Therapy.* New York: Brunner/Mazel, 1973.

Freedman, J. L., & Doob, A. A. N. *Deviancy: The psychology of being deficient.* New York: Academic, 1968.

Friedlander, B. Z. The effect of speaker identity, voice inflection, vocabulary, and message redundancy on infants' selection of vocal reinforcers. Paper presented at the meeting of the Society for Research in Child Development, New York, March, 1967.

Fries, M. E., & Woolf, P. J. Some hypotheses on the role of the congenital activity type in personality development. *Psychoanalytical study of the child.* Vol. 8. New York: International Universities Press, Inc., 1953. Pp. 48–62.

Froebel, F. W. A. *Die Menschenerziehung, d. Erziehungsunterrichts u. Lehrkunst.* Leipsig: Weinbrack, 1826.

Frostig, M., & Horne, D. *The Frostig program for the development of visual perception.* Chicago: Follett, 1964.

Frostig, M., Lefever, D., Whittlesey, D., & Whittlesey, J. A developmental test of visual perception for evaluating normal and neurologically handicapped children. *Perceptual Motor Skills,* 1961, **12,** 383–394.

Gallagher, J. J. The future special education system. In E. Meyen (Ed.), *The Missouri conference on the categorical/non-categorical issue in special education.* Columbia, Mo.: University of Missouri, 1971.

Garner, A. M., & Wenar, G. *The mother-child interaction in psychosomatic disorders.* Urbana: University of Illinois Press, 1959.

Gay, M. J., & Tonge, W. L. The hate effects of loss of parents in childhood. *British Journal of Psychiatry,* 1967, **113**(500), 753–760.

Gearheart, B. R. (Ed.) *Education of exceptional children.* Scranton, Pa.: International Textbook, 1972.

Gesell, A. *The first five years of life.* New York: Harper, 1940.

Gesell, A. *Studies in child development.* New York: Harper, 1948.

Getman, G. N. The visumotor complex in the acquisition of learning skills. In J. Hellmuth (Ed.), *Learning disorders.* Vol. 1. Seattle: Special Child Publications, 1965. Pp. 49–76.

Glueck, S., & Glueck, E. T. *Unraveling juvenile delinquency.* New York: Commonwealth Fund, 1950.

Godfrey, B. B., & Kephart, N. C. *Movement patterns and motor education.* New York: Appleton-Century-Crofts, 1969.

Goffman, E. *Stigma: Notes on the management of spoiled identity.* Englewood Cliffs, N.J.: Prentice-Hall, 1963.

Goldfarb, W. Infant rearing as a factor in foster home replacement. *American Journal of Orthopsychiatry,* 1945a, **15,** 162.

Goldfarb, W. Psychological privation in infancy and subsequent adjustment. *American Journal of Orthopsychiatry,* 1945b, **15,** 247.

Goldiamond, I. Stuttering and fluency as manipulative operant response class. In H. N. Sloan and B. D. Macauley (Eds.), *Operant procedure in remedial speech and language.* Boston: Houghton Mifflin, 1968. Pp. 348–410.

Goldman-Eisler, H. The problem of "orality" and of its origin in early childhood. *Journal of Medical Science,* 1951, **97,** 765–782.

Goldstein, H. Construction of a social learning climate. *Focus on exceptional children.* Denver: Love Publishing Company, 1969, **1** (2). Pp. 94–114.

Goldstein, H., Moss, J. W. & Jordan, L. J. The efficacy of special class training on the development of mentally retarded children. U.S. Office of Education Cooperative Research Program, Project No. 619. Urbana: University of Illinois, 1965.

Goodman, P. The present moment in education. In R. Havighurst, B. Nengorten, and J. Falk, *Society and education: A book of readings.* (2d ed.) Boston: Allyn and Bacon, 1971.

Gordon, E. W. Methodological problems and pseudo issues in the nature-nurture controversy. In R. Cancio (Ed.), *Intelligence: Genetic and environmental influences.* New York: Grune & Stratton, 1971. Pp. 240–251.

Gordon, R. *The design of a preschool therapeutic playground: An outdoor learning laboratory.* New York: New York University Medical Center, Institute of Rehabilitation Medicine, 1972.

Gottesman, I. I. Personality and natural selection. In S. G. Vandenberg (Ed.), *Methods and goals in human behavior genetics.* New York: Academic Press, 1965. Pp. 63–80.

Gregory, I. Studies of parental deprivation in psychiatric patients. *American Journal of Psychiatry,* 1958, **115,** 432.

Griffiths, D. E. *Research in educational administration: An appraisal and a plan.* New York: Bureau of Publications, Teachers College, Columbia University Press, 1959, 18.

Guerney, B. G., Jr. *Psychotherapeutic agents: New roles for nonprofessionals, parents and teachers.* New York: Holt, 1969.

Guilford, J. P. The structure of the intellect. *Psychological Bulletin,* 1956, **53,** 267–293.

Gunzburg, H. C. The physical environment of the mentally handicapped. *The British Journal of Mental Subnormality,* 1972, **28**(34), 48–57.

Guskin, S. L., & Spicker, H. H. Educational research in mental retardation. In N. R. Ellis (Ed.), *International review of research in mental retardation.* New York: Academic Press, 1968. Pp. 217–278.

Hamilton, K. W. *Counseling the handicapped in the rehabilitative process.* New York: Ronald Press, 1950.

Hanson, M. Modifying the behaviors of the nondisabled child toward the physically disabled. Unpublished thesis, The Pennsylvania State University, 1974.

Hardy, M. P. Speechreading. In H. Davis & S. R. Silverman (Eds.), *Hearing and deafness.* (3d ed.) New York: Holt, 1970. Pp. 335–344.

Harlow, H. F. The development of affectional patterns in infant monkeys. In B. M. Foss (Ed.), *Determinants of infant behavior.* New York: Wiley, 1961. Pp. 75–88.

Harlow, H. F., & Zimmerman, R. R. Affectional responses in the infant monkey. *Science,* 1959, **130,** 421–432.

Harvey, J. To fix or to cope: A dilemma for special education. *Journal of Special Education,* 1969, **3,** 389–392.

Hathaway, S. R., & McKinley, J. C. *The minnesota multiphasic personality inventory manual.* (Rev. ed.) New York: Psychological Corp., 1951.

Heber, R., & Dever, R. Education and rehabilitation of the mentally retarded. In H. D. Haywood (Ed.), *Social-cultural aspects of mental retardation.* New York: Appleton-Century-Crofts, 1970. Pp. 395–423.

Heber, R. A. Modifications in the manual on terminology and classification in mental retardation. *American Journal on Mental Deficiency,* 1961, **65,** 499–500.

Hensley, G., & Patterson, V. W. (Eds.) *Changing patterns of professional preparation and services in special education.* Selected papers of a working conference (San Diego). Washington, D.C.: Office of Education, Bureau of Education for the Handicapped, 1970.

Hetherington, E. M., & Martin, B. Family interaction and psychopathology in children. In H. C. Quay & J. S. Werry (Eds.), *Psychopathological disorders in childhood.* New York: Wiley, 1972. Pp. 30–79.

Hewett, F. M. Educational engineering with emotionally disturbed children. *Exceptional Children,* 1967, **33,** 459–470.

Hewett, F. M. *The emotionally disturbed child in the classroom.* Boston: Allyn and Bacon, 1968.

Hewett, L. E., & Jenkins, R. L. *Fundamental patterns of maladjustment: The dynamics of their origin.* Springfield, Ill.: Green, 1946.

Hilleary, J. F. Building for all to use. *American Institute of Architects Journal,* 1970, 14 pp.

Hinshelwood, J. *Congenital word blindness.* London: H. K. Lewis, 1917.

Hobbs, N. Helping disturbed children: Psychological and ecological strategies. *American Psychologist,* 1966, **21,** 1105–1115.

Hoffman, R. B. *How to build special furniture and equipment for handicapped children,* Springfield, Ill.: Charles C Thomas, 1970.

Hoover, R. E. Orientation and travel techniques. *Proceedings of the American Association of Workers of the Blind,* 1947.

Hunt, J. McV. *Intelligence and experience.* New York: Ronald Press, 1961.

Hunt, J. McV. How children develop intellectually. *Children,* 1964, **11,** 89.

Hunt, J. McV. The psychological basis for using preschool enrichment as an antidote for cultural advantage. *Merrill-Palmer Quarterly,* 1964, **10,** 209–248.

ICTA Information Centre. *Aids for children: Technical aids for physically handicapped children,* Fack, S-16103, Bromma 3, Sweden.

Illingworth, R. S. *The development of the infant and young child.* (4th ed.) Edinburgh: E. & S. Livingstone, 1971.

Illinois Commission on Children. *A comprehensive plan for hearing impaired children.* Springfield, Ill.: Office of the Superintendent of Public Instruction, 1968.

Irwin, F. W. Stated expectations as functions of probability and desirability of outcomes. *Journal of Personality,* 1953, **21,** 329–335.

Iscoe, I. & Payne, S. Development of a revised scale for the functional classification of exceptional children. In E. P. Trapp and P. Himelstein (Eds.), *Readings on the exceptional child.* New York: Appleton-Century-Crofts, 1972. Pp. 7–29.

Isom, J. Paper presented at *The troubled child workshop: The neurologically handicapped.* University of Oregon, Eugene, Oregon, 1967.

Itard, J. M. G. *The wild boy of Aveyron.* Translated by G. and Murrel Humphrey. New York: Appleton-Century-Crofts, 1932.

Jenkins, R. L. Psychiatric syndromes in children and their relation to family background. *American Journal of Orthopsychiatry,* 1966, **36,** 450–457.

Jensen, A. R. Social class, race, and genetics: Implications for education. *American Educational Research Journal,* 1968, **5,** 1–42.

Jessor, R., & Readie, J. The influence of the value of an event upon the expectancy of its occurrence. *Journal of Genetic Psychology,* 1957, **56,** 219–228.

Johnson, A. Report of committee on colonies for segregation of defectives. Proceedings of the National Conference on Charities and Correction, 1903.

Johnson, G. O. Special education for the mentally retarded—A paradox. *Exceptional Children,* 1962, **29,** 62–69.

Johnson, V. M. Salient features and sorting factors in the diagnosis and classification of exceptional children. *Peabody Journal of Education,* 1975, in press.

Johnson, W. *Speech handicapped school children.* New York: Harper, 1956.

Jones, E. E., Hester, S. L., Farina, A., & Davis, K. E. Reactions to infavorable personal evaluations as a function of the evaluator's perceived adjustment. *Journal of Abnormal and Social Psychology,* 1959, **59,** 363–370.

Jones, M. C. The elimination of children's fears. *Journal of Experimental Psychology,* 1924, **7,** 382–390.

Jones, R. L. (Ed.) *Problems and issues in the education of exceptional children.* Boston: Houghton Mifflin, 1971.

Kagan, J. The determinants of attention in the infant. *American Scientist,* 1970, **58,** 298–306.

Kallmann, F. J. The genetic theory of schizophrenia. *American Journal of Psychiatry,* 1946, **103,** 309–322.

Kallmann, F. J. *Heredity in health and mental disorder.* New York: Norton, 1953.

Kanner, L. *Child psychiatry.* (3d ed.) Springfield, Ill.: Charles C Thomas, 1957.

Katz, S., & Rosenthal, D. (Eds.) *Transmission of schizophrenia.* London: Pergamon, 1968.

Keats, S. *Cerebral palsy.* Springfield, Ill.: Charles C Thomas, 1965.

Kehle, T. J. Teachers' expectations: Ratings of student performance as biased by student characteristics. Unpublished dissertation, University of Kentucky, 1973.

Kendall, D. C. The training of education personnel to work in the rehabilitation field. *Rehabilitation Digest,* 1970, **2**(2), 7–10.

Kephart, N. *The slow learner in the classroom.* Columbus, Ohio: Merrill, 1960.

Kephart, N. C. Perceptual-motor aspects of learning disabilities. In E. Frierson & W. Barbe (Eds.), *Educating children with learning disabilities.* New York: Appleton-Century-Crofts, 1967. Pp. 405–413.

Kidd, J. W. Toward a more precise definition of mental retardation. *Mental Retardation,* 1964, **2,** 209–212.

Kidd, J. W. Pro—The efficacy of special class placement for educable mental retardates. Paper presented at the 48th Annual Convention of the Council for Exceptional Children, Chicago, April 1970.

Kirk, S. A. *Early education of the mentally retarded: An experimental study.* Urbana: University of Illinois Press, 1958.

Kirk, S. A. *Educating exceptional children.* (2d ed.) Boston: Houghton Mifflin, 1972.

Klapp, O. *Heros, villains and fools.* Englewood Cliffs, N.J.: Prentice-Hall, 1962.

Klineberg, O. *Negro intelligence and selective migration.* New York: Columbia University Press, 1935.

Knott, M., & Voss, D. E. *Proprioceptive neuromuscular facilitation-patterns and techniques.* New York: Hoeber, 1956.

Kolstoe, O. P. Programs for the mildly retarded: A reply to the critics. *Exceptional Children,* 1972, **39,** 51–56.

Kugel, R. B., and Wolfensberger W. (Eds.) *Changing patterns in residential services for the mentally retarded.* Washington, D.C.: President's Committee on Mental Retardation, 1969.

Lachman, S. J. *Psychosomatic disorders: A behavioristic approach.* New York: Wiley, 1972.

Lerner, J. W. *Children with learning disabilities: Theories, diagnosis* and teaching strategies. Boston: Houghton Mifflin, 1971.

Levy, D. M. Finger-sucking and accessory movements in early childhood. *American Journal of Psychiatry,* 1928, **7,** 881–918.

Levy, D. M. *Maternal overprotection.* New York: Columbia University Press, 1943.

Lewis, E. D. Types of mental deficiency and their social significance. *Journal of Mental Science,* 1933, **79,** 298–304.

Lewis, H. *Deprived children.* London: Oxford University Press, 1954.

Liahy, A. M. Nature-nurture and intelligence. *Genetic Psychology Monographs,* 1935, **17,** 241–305.

Lilly, M. S. Special education: A teapot in a tempest. *Exceptional Children,* 1970, **37,** 43–49.

Lovaas, O. I., Schaeffer, B., & Simmons, J. Building social behavior in autistic children by use of electric shock. *Journal of Experimental Research in Personality,* 1965, **1,** 99–109.

Lowenfeld, B. Psychological considerations. In B. Lowenfeld (Ed.), *The Visually Handicapped Child in School.* New York: John Day, 1973. Pp. 27–60.

Lowrey, G. H. *Growth and development of children.* Year Book Medical Publication. (6th ed.) Chicago, 1973.

Lundeen, Dale J. "Speech disorders" in B. R. Gearhart (Ed.), *Education of the exceptional child—History, present practices and trends.* Scranton, Pa.: Intext Educational Publishers, 1972. Pp. 152–184.

MacFarlane, J. W., Allen, L., & Honzik, M. P. *A developmental study of the behavior problems of normal children.* Berkeley: University of California Press, 1954.

MacMillan, D. C. Special education for the mildly retarded: Servant or savant. In E. L. Meyen, G. A. Vergason, & R. J. Whelan (Eds.), *Strategies for teaching exceptional children.* Denver: Love Publishing Co., 1972. Pp. 17–36.

Maier, N. R. F. Frustration: *The study of behavior without a goal.* New York: McGraw Hill, 1949.

Manis, M., Houts, P., and Blake, J. Beliefs about mental illness as a function of psychiatric status and psychiatric hospitalization. *Journal of Abnormal and Social Psychology,* 1963, **67,** 227–233.

Marquis, D. P. A study of frustration in newborn infants. *Journal of Experimental Psychology,* 1943, **32,** 123–138.

Martin, R. "The experimental manipulation of stuttering behaviors." In H. N. Sloan, & B. D. Macauley (Eds.), *Operant procedures in remedial speech and language.* Boston: Houghton Mifflin, 1968. Pp. 325–347.

Martmer, E. E. (Ed.) *The child with a handicap.* Springfield, Ill.: Charles C Thomas, 1959.

McCarthy, J. J., & McCarthy, J. F. *Learning disabilities.* Boston: Allyn and Bacon, 1969.

McClearn, G. E. Genetic influences on behavior and development. In P. H. Mussen (Ed.), *Carmichael's manual of child psychology.* Vol. I. New York: Wiley, 1970. Pp. 39–76.

McConnell, F. Children with hearing disabilities. In L. M. Dunn (Ed.), *Exceptional children in the schools.* (2d ed.) New York: Holt, 1973. Pp. 351–412.

McConnell, J., & Horton, K. B. *A home teaching program for parents of very young deaf children (final report).* U.S.O.E., Bethesda, Maryland: Educational Resources Information Center Document Reproduction Service, 1970.

McCord, J., & McCord, W. The effect of parental role model on criminality. *Journal of Social Issues,* 1958, **14,** 66–75.

McCord, W., McCord, J., & Gudeman, J. *Origins of alcoholism.* Palo Alto: Stanford University Press, 1960.

McCord, W., McCord, J., & Howard, A. Familial correlates of aggression in nondelinquent male children. *Journal of Abnormal and Social Psychology,* 1961, **62,** 79–93.

McDonald, E. J., & Chance, B., Jr. *Cerebral palsy.* Englewood Cliffs, N.J.: Prentice Hall, 1964.

McIntyre, B. M., & McWilliams, B. J. Creative dramatics in speech correction. *Journal of Speech and Hearing Disorders,* 1959, **24,** 277–230.

McKusick, V. A., & Claiborne, R. *Medical genetics.* New York: H. P. Publishing Co., 1973.

Mearham, M. L., & Wiesen, A. E. *Changing classroom behavior: A manual for precision teaching.* Scranton, Pa.: International Textbook Co., 1971.

Mercer, J. Sociological perspectives on mild mental retardation. In H. Carl Haywood (Ed.), *Social-cultural aspects of mental retardation.* New York: Appleton-Century-Crofts, 1970. Pp. 378–391.

Meyen, E. L. *Developing units of instruction for the mentally retarded and other children with learning problems.* Dubuque, Iowa: Wm. C. Brown Company Publishers, 1972.

Meyerowitz, J. H. Self-derogation in young retardates and special class placement. *Child Development,* 1962, **33,** 443–451.

Meyerson, L., & Michael, J. L. *The measurement of sensory thresholds in exceptional children.* Houston, Texas: University of Houston, 1960.

Miller, W. B. Lower class culture as a generating milieu of gang delinquency. *The Journal of Social Issues,* 1958, **14**(3), 5–19.

Missouri Conference on the Categorical/Non Categorical Issue in Special Education. *Focus on exceptional children.* May 1971, 11–14.

Montessori, M. *Montessori method.* Translated by Anne E. George. New York: Stokes, 1912.

Montessori, M. *The Montessori elementary material.* (Copyright 1917 by Frederick A. Stokes Company.) Cambridge, Mass.: Robert Bentley, Inc., 1965.

Montessori, M. *The Montessori method.* (Copyright 1912 by Frederick A. Stokes Company.) Cambridge, Mass.: Robert Bentley, Inc., 1965.

Moores, D. F. Review of analysis of communicative structure patterns in deaf children by B. Tervoot and A. J. Verbeck. *American Annals of the deaf,* 1970, **115** (January), 11–15.

Morgan, W. P. A case of congenital word blindness. *British Medical Journal,* 1896.

Morris, P. R., & Whiting, H. T. A. *Motor impairment and compensatory education.* Philadelphia: Lea & Febiger, 1971.

Morse, W. C. Education of maladjusted and disturbed children. In N. J. Long, W. C. Morse, and R. G. Newman (Eds.), *Conflict in the classroom: The education of children with problems.* (2d ed.) Belmont, Calif.: Wadsworth, 1971. Pp. 330–336.

Mullen, F. A., & Itkin, W. Achievement and adjustment of educable mentally handicapped children. U.S. Office of Education Cooperative Research Program, Project No. OE-SAE-6529, Board of Education, Chicago, Illinois, 1961.

Muller, H. *Well planned town centers—A contemporary demand of the handicapped.* Bromma, Sweden: ICTA Information Centre, 1970.

Murphy, A. T., & Fitz-Simons, R. M. *Stuttering and personality dynamics.* New York: Ronald Press, 1960.

Murray, H. A. *Manual: Thermatic Apperception Test.* Cambridge, Mass.: Harvard University Press, 1943.

Mussen, P. (Ed.) Infancy and early experience. Part II. *Carmichael's manual of child psychology* (3d ed.) New York: Wiley, 1970. Pp. 287–656.

Mussen, P. H., Conger, J. J., & Kagan, J. *Child development and personality.* (3d ed.) New York: Harper, 1969.

Myers, Patricia, & Hammill, D. D. *Methods for learning disabilities.* New York: Wiley, 1969.

Myklebust, H. R. *The psychology of deafness.* (2d ed.) New York: Grune and Stratton, 1964.

National Society for the Prevention of Blindness. *Visual screening in schools.* Publication No. 257. New York: National Society for the Prevention of Blindness, 1969.

National Society for the Study of Education. C. Thoresen (Ed.), *Behavior modification in education.* Chicago: University of Chicago Press, 1972.

Neisworth, J. T. The educational irrelevance of intelligence. In Robert M. Smith (Ed.), *Teacher diagnosis of educational difficulties.* Columbus, Ohio: Merrill, 1969. Pp. 30-46

Neisworth, J. T., Deno, S. L., & Jenkins, J. R. *Student motivation and classroom management.* Lemont: Behavior Technics, 1973.

Neisworth, J. T., & Greer, J. Learning disability and mild mental retardation: Functional similarities for purposes of intervention. *Exceptional Children,* March, 1975.

Neisworth, J. T., & Smith, R. M. *Modifying retarded behavior.* Boston; Houghton Mifflin, 1973. Pp. 52–54.

Nellist, I. *Planning buildings for handicapped children.* Springfield, Ill.: Charles C Thomas, 1970.

Newbrough, J. R., & Kelly, J. G. A study of reading achievement in a population of school children. In J. Money (Ed.), *Reading disability: Progress and research needs in dyslexia.* Baltimore: Johns Hopkins Press, 1962. Pp. 61–79.

Newland, T. E. Psychological assessment of exceptional children and youth. In W. M. Cruickshank (Ed.), *Psychology of exceptional children and youth.* (3d ed.) Englewood Cliffs, N.J.: Prentice-Hall, 1971. Pp. 115–174.

Newman, H. H., Freeman, F. N., & Holzinger, K. J. *Twins: A study of heredity and environment.* Chicago: University of Chicago Press, 1937.

Niemoeller, A. F., Silverman, S. R., & Davis, H. Hearing aids. In H. Davis and S. R. Silverman (Eds.), *Hearing and deafness.* (3d ed.) New York: Holt, 1970. Pp. 280–332.

O'Leary, K. D., & Becker, W. C. Behavior modification of an adjustment class: A token reinforcement program. *Exceptional Children,* 1967, **33,** 637–644.

O'Leary, K. D., & O'Leary, S. G. *Classroom management: The successful use of behavior modification.* New York: Pergamon, 1972.

Orton, S. T. *Reading, writing and speech problems in children.* New York: Norton, 1937.

Osgood, C., Suci, G., and Tannenbaum, P. *The measurement of meaning.* Urbana: University of Illinois Press, 1957.

Parsons, T. The school class as a social system: Some of its functions in American society. In R. Havighurst, B. Neugarten, and B. Falk, *Society and education: A book of readings.* (2d ed.) Boston: Allyn and Bacon, 1971.

Patterson, G. R. Responsiveness to social stimuli. In L. Krasner and L. P. Ullmann (Eds.), *Research in behavior modification.* New York: Holt, 1965. Pp. 157–178.

Patterson, G. R., & Brodsky, G. A. A behavior modification program for a child with multiple problem behaviors. *Journal of Child Psychology and Psychiatry,* 1966, **7,** 277–295.

Pennsylvania Association for Retarded Children, Nancy Beth Bowman, et al. vs. Commonwealth of Pennsylvania, Davis H. Kurtzman, et. al. Court Action No. 71–42, June 18, 1971.

Perkins, W. H. *Speech pathology, an applied behavior science.* St. Louis: Mosby, 1971.

Peter, L. *Prescriptive teaching.* New York: McGraw-Hill, 1967.

Peterson, D. D. Children with physical disabilities and multiple handicaps. In B. R. Gearheart (Ed.), *Education of the exceptional child—History, present practices and trends.* Scranton, Pa.: Intext Educational Publishers, 1972. Pp. 243–273.

Phelps, W. M.: The management of the cerebral palsies. *Journal of the American Medical Association,* 1941, **117,** 1621.

Piaget, J. *The moral judgment of the child.* London: Routledge and Kegan Paul, 1932.

Piaget, J. *The psychology of intelligence.* New York: Harcourt, Brace, 1950.

Piaget, J. *The origins of intelligence in children.* New York: International Universities Press, 1952.

Piaget, J. *The language and thought of the child.* (Originally published, 1926). Cleveland: World Publishing, 1955.

Piaget, J. *The language and thought of the child.* (3d ed.) Translated by M. Gabian. London: Routledge, 1962.

Piaget, J. *The moral judgment of the child.* Translated by M. Gabian. New York: Free Press, 1965.

Piaget, J. *On the development of memory and identity.* Translated by Eleanor Duckworth. Worcester, Mass. Clark University Press, 1968.

Piaget, J. *The mechanisms of perception.* Translated by G. N. Seagrim. New York: Basic Books, 1969.

Piaget, J., & Inhelder, B. *The psychology of the child.* New York: Basic Books, 1969.

Porteus, S. D. *The practice of clinical psychology.* New York: American Book, 1941.

President's Committee on Mental Retardation. MR67: *A first report to the president on the nation's progress and remaining great needs in the campaign to combat mental retardation.* Washington, D. C.: U.S. Government Printing Office, 1967.

President's Panel on Mental Retardation. *A proposed program for national action to combat mental retardation,* 1962.

Provence, S., & Lipton, R. C. *Infants in institutions: A comparison of their development with family reared infants during the first year of life.* New York: International Universities Press, 1962.

Quay, H. C. Remediation of the conduct problem child in the special class setting. *Exceptional Children,* 1966, **32,** 509–515.

Quay, H. C. The facets of educational exceptionality: A conceptual framework for assessment, grouping and instruction. *Exceptional Children,* 1968, **35,** 25–31.

Quay, H. C., Morse, W. C. & Cutler, R. L. Personality patterns of pupils in special classes for the emotionally disturbed. *Exceptional Children,* 1966, **32,** 297–301.

Quay, H. C., and Peterson, D. R. Manual for the behavior problem checklist. Mimeo, 1967.

Quay, H. C., and Werry, J. S. (Eds.) *Psychopathological disorders of childhood.* New York: Wiley, 1972.

Quigley, S. P. *The influence of finger spelling on the development of language, communication, and educative achievement in deaf children.* Urbana, Ill.: Institute for Research on Exceptional Children, 1969.

Rees, L. The importance of psychological, allergic, and infective factors in childhood asthma. *Journal of Psychosomatic Research,* 1964, **7,** 253–262.

Reese, H. W., and Lipsitt, L. P. Sensory processes. *Experimental Child Psychology,* 1970, 33–62. (a)

Reese, H. W., and Lipsitt, L. P. Behavior modification: Clinical and educational applications. *Experimental Child Psychology,* 1970, 643–672. (b)

Reger, R., Schroeder, W., & Uschold, D. *Special education: Children with learning problems.* New York: Oxford University Press, 1968.

Reinert, H. R. The emotionally disturbed. In B. R. Gearheart (Ed.), *Education of the exceptional child—History, present practices and trends.* Scranton, Pennsylvania: Intext Educational Publishers, 1972. Pp. 215–242.

Reynolds, M. C. A framework for considering some issues in special education. *Exceptional Children,* 1962, **28,** 367–370.

Reynolds, M. C. Categories and variables in special education. In M. C. Reynolds and M. D. Davis (Eds.), *Exceptional children in regular classrooms.* Minneapolis: University of Minnesota, 1971. Pp. 51–63.

Rheingold, H. L. The modification of social responsiveness in institutional babies. *Monograph Social Research Child Development,* 1956, **21**(2).

Rheingold, H. L. The effect of environmental stimulation upon the social and exploratory behavior in the human infant. In B. M. Foss (Ed.), *Determinants of infant behavior.* New York: Wiley, 1961. Pp. 143–177.

Rheingold, H. L. Controlling the infant's exploratory behavior. In B. M. Foss (Ed.), *Determinants of infant behavior.* Vol. II. London: Methuen (New York: Wiley), 1963. Pp. 171–175.

Roach, E. G., & Kephart, N. C. *The Purdue perceptual-motor survey.* Columbus, Ohio: Merrill, 1966.

Robbins, M. P. A study of the validity of Delacato's theory of neurological organization. *Exceptional Children,* 1966, **32,** 517–522.

Roberts, E. Thumb and finger sucking in relation to feeding in early infancy. *American Journal Dis. Child,* 1944, **68,** 7–8.

Robinson, H. B., & Robinson, M. *The mentally retarded child: A psychological approach.* New York: McGraw-Hill, 1965.

Robinson, W. P. The elaborated code in working class language. *Language and Speech,* 1965, **8,** 243–252.

Robinson, W. P. Restricted codes in sociolinguistics and the sociology of education. Paper presented at Ninth International Seminar, University College, Dar es Salaam, December 1968.

Rood, M. S. Neurophysiological mechanisms utilized in the treatment of neuro-muscular dysfunction. *American Journal of Occupational Therapy,* 1956, 220–225.

Rorschach, H. *Psychodiagnostics.* New York: Grune and Stratton, 1951.

Rosen, B. M., Bahn, A. K., & Kramer, M. Demographic and diagnostic character-istics of psychiatric clinic outpatients in the U.S.A., 1961. *American Journal of Orthopsychiatry,* 1964, **24,** 455–467.

Rosenthal, D. Some factors associated with concordance and disconcordance with respect to schizophrenia in monozygotic twins. *Journal of Nervous and Mental Disorders,* 1959, **129,** 1–10.

Rosenthal, M. J., Finkelstein, M., Ni, E., & Robertson, R. E. A study of mother-child relationships in the emotional disorders of children. *Genetic Psychol-ogy Monographs,* 1959, **60,** 65–116.

Rosenthal, R., & Jacobson, L. Teacher expectancies: Determinants of pupil IQ gains. *Psychological Reports,* 1966, **19,** 115–118.

Rosenthal, R., & Jacobson, L. *Pygmalion in the classroom.* New York: 1968.

Ross, A. O. *The exceptional child in the family.* New York: Grune & Stratton, 1964.

Ross, A. O. Conceptual issues in the evaluation of brain damage. In J. L. Khanna (Ed.), *Brain damage and mental retardation: A psychological evaluation.* Springfield, Ill.: Charles C Thomas, 1968. Pp. 20–39.

Ross, A. O. *Psychological disorders of children: A behavioral approach to theory, research and therapy.* New York: McGraw-Hill, 1974.

Rubin, E. Z., Simon, C. B., & Betwee, M. L. *Emotionally handicapped children and the elementary schools.* Detroit, Mich.: Wayne State University, 1966.

Rubington, E., & Weinberg, M. *Deviance: An interactionist perspective.* New York: Macmillan, 1968.

Sarason, S. B. *Psychological problems in mental deficiency.* (2d ed.) New York: Harper & Row, 1953.

Sataloff, J. *Hearing loss.* Philadelphia: Lippincott, 1966.

Sawrey, G. M., & Telford, C. W. *Psychology of adjustment.* Boston: Allyn and Bacon, 1967.

Schmidt, B. G. Changes in personal, social and intellectual behaviour of children originally classified as feebleminded. *Psychological Monograph,* **60,** 5, 1–144.

Schwartz, L., Oseroff, A., Drucker, H., & Schwartz, R. *Innovative non-categorical interrelated projects in the education of the handicapped.* Proceedings of the Special Study Institute. Florida State University, Tallahassee, Florida. Washington, D.C.: Bureau of Education for the Handicapped, Project 19-1800, P.L. 91-230, 1972.

Sears, R. R., Whiting, J. W. M., Nowlis, V., & Sears, P. S. Some child rearing antecedents of aggression and dependency in young children. *Genetic Psy-chology Monographs,* 1953, **47,** 135–234.

Seguin, E. Idiocy and its treatment by the physiological method. Albany, N.Y.: Brandow, 1866.

Shaw, C. R., & McKay, H. D. *Juvenile delinquency and urban areas.* Chicago: University of Chicago Press, 1942.

Shields, J., & Slater, E. Heredity and psychological abnormality. In H. J. Eysenck (Ed.), *Handbook of abnormal psychology.* New York: Basic Books, 1961.

Shirley, H. A behavior syndrome characterizing prematurely born children. *Child Development,* 1939, **10,** 115–128.

Shirley, M. The first two years: A study of 25 babies. *Institute of Child Welfare Monograph,* Series 7, 1933, **2,** 47–72.

Silverman, S. R., & Davis, H. Hard-of-hearing children. In H. Davis and S. R. Silverman (Eds.), *Hearing and deafness.* (3d ed.) New York: Holt, 1970. Pp. 426–446.

Silverman, S. R., & Lane, H. S. Deaf children. In H. Davis and S. R. Silverman (Eds.), *Hearing and deafness.* (3d ed.) New York: Holt, 1970. Pp. 384–424.

Singer, R. N. *Motor learning and human performance: An application to physical education skills.* New York: Macmillan, 1968.

Skeels, H. M. Adult status of children with contrasting early life experience. *Monographs of the Society for Research in Child Development,* No. 3, 1966.

Skeels, H. M., & Dye, H. B. A study of the effects of differential stimulation on mentally retarded children. Proceedings of the American Association on Mental Deficiency, 1939, **44,** 114–136.

Skeels, H. M., and Harms, I. Children with inferior social histories: Their mental development in adoptive homes. *Journal of Genetic Psychology,* 1948, **72,** 283–294.

Skodak, M., & Skeels, H. M. A final follow-up study of one hundred adopted children. *Journal of Genetic Psychology,* 1949, **75,** 85–125.

Skinner, B. F. *Science and human behavior.* New York: Macmillan, 1953.

Slavson, S. R. *A textbook in analytic group psychotherapy.* New York: International Universities Press, 1964.

Sloan, W. The Lincoln-Oseretsky Motor Development Scale, *Genetic Psychology Monographs,* 1951, **60,** 183–252.

Smith, D. P., & Carrington, P. *The nature of reading disability.* New York: Harcourt, Brace, 1959.

Smith, M. E., Lecker, G., Dunlap, J. W., and Cureton, E. E. The effects of race, sex and environment on the age at which children walk. *Pediatric Seminar,* 1930, **38,** 489–498.

Smith, R. M. *Teacher diagnosis of educational difficulties.* Columbus, Ohio: Merrill, 1969.

Smith, R. M. *An introduction to mental retardation.* New York: McGraw-Hill, 1971.

Smith, R. M. *Clinical teaching: Methods of instruction for the retarded.* (2d ed.) New York: McGraw-Hill, 1974.

Sparks, H. L., & Younie, W. J. Adult adjustment of the mentally retarded: Implications for teacher education. *Exceptional Children,* 1969, **38,** 13–18.

Spitz, R. A. *Hospitalism psychoanalytic study of the child.* Vol. 1. New York: International Universities Press, 1945.

Stephens, B. (Ed.) *Training the developmentally young.* New York: John Day, 1971.

Stephens, T. *Directive teaching of children with learning and behavior handicaps.* Columbus, Ohio: Charles E. Merrill, 1970.

Stevens, G. D. *Taxonomy in special education for children with body disorders: The problem and a proposal.* Pittsburgh: Department of Special Education and Rehabilitation, University of Pittsburgh, 1962.

Strauss, A. A., Lehtinen, L. E. *Psychopathology and education of the brain injured child: I. Fundamentals and treatment.* New York: Grune and Stratton, 1947.

Stuart, R. B. *Trick or treatment: How and when psychotherapy fails.* Champaign, Ill.: Research Press, 1970.

Stuckless, E. R., & Birch, J. W. The influence of early manual communication on the linguistic development of deaf children. *American Annals of the Deaf,* 1966, **3,** (March), 452–460.

Supa, M., Cotzin, M., & Dallenbach, K. M. "Facial Vision": The perception of obstacles by the blind. *American Journal of Psychology,* 1944, **57,** 133–183.

Suterko, S. Life adjustment. In B. Lowenfeld (Ed.), *The visually handicapped child in school.* New York: John Day, 1973. Pp. 279–318.

Sutherland, J. M., & Tait, H. *The epilepsies—Modern diagnosis and treatment.* London: Livingstone, 1969.

Talbot, J. A. Community psychiatry in the army: History, practice and applications to civilian psychiatry. *Journal of the American Medical Association,* 1969, **210,** 1233–1237.

Tanner, J. M. The morphological level of personality. *Proc. R. Soc. Med.,* 1947, **50,** 301–303.

Tarnapol, L. (Ed.) *Learning disabilities.* Springfield, Ill.: Charles C Thomas, 1971.

Telford, C. W., & Sawrey, J. M. *The exceptional individual: Psychological and educational aspects.* Englewood Cliffs, N. J.: Prentice-Hall, 1967.

Telford, C. W., & Sawrey, J. M. *The exceptional individual: Psychological and educational aspects.* (2d ed.) Englewood Cliffs, N. J.: Prentice-Hall, 1972.

Terman, L. M. *The measurement of intelligence.* Boston: Houghton, Mifflin, 1916.

Tharp, R., and Wetzel, R. *Behavior modification in the natural environment.* New York: Academic Press, 1969.

Thomas, A., Chess, S., & Birch, H. G. *Temperament and behavior disorders in children.* New York: New York University Press, 1968.

Thompson, W. R. Early environment—Its importance for later behavior. In P. H. Hock and J. Zubin (Eds.), *Psychopathology of childhood.* New York: Grune & Stratton, 1955.

Thorndike, R. L. Book review in *American Educational Research Journal,* 1968, **5**(4), 708–711.

Thurstone, T. G. An evaluation of educating mentally handicapped children in special classes and in regular grades. U.S. Office of Education Cooperative Research Program, Proj. No. OE-SAE-6452, University of North Carolina, Chapel Hill, N.C., 1960.

Tizard, J. The role of social institutions in the causation, prevention and alleviation of mental retardation. In H. Carl Haywood (Ed.), *Social-cultural aspects of mental retardation.* New York: Appleton-Century-Crofts, 1970. Pp. 281–340.

Travis, L. E. (Ed.) *Speech pathology.* New York: Appleton-Century-Crofts, 1931.

Travis, L. E. *Handbook of speech pathology.* New York: Appleton-Century-Crofts, 1957.

Tredgold, A. F. *A textbook of mental deficiency.* (6th ed.) Baltimore: Wood, 1937.

Tredgold, A. F., & Soddy, K. *A textbook of mental deficiency.* (9th ed.) London: Baillière, 1956.

Ullman, L. P., & Krasner, L. A. *A psychological approach to abnormal behavior.* Englewood Cliffs, N.J. Prentice-Hall, 1969.

U.S. Department of Transportation. *Travel barriers.* Office of the Secretary, Washington, D.C., May 1970. P. 19.

U. S. Office of Education. *Estimated number of handicapped children in the United States, 1971–72.* Washington, D.C.: U.S. Office of Education, 1971.

Uzgius, I. C. Sociocultural factors in cognitive development. In H. Carl Haywood (Ed.), *Social-cultural aspects of mental retardation.* New York: Appleton-Century-Crofts, 1970. Pp. 107–112.

Van Riper, C. Historical approaches. In J. G. Sheehan (Ed.), *Stuttering research and therapy.* New York: Harper, 1970. Pp. 36–57. (a)

Van Riper, C. *Behavior modification: An overview in conditioning in stuttering therapy.* Memphis, Tenn.: Speech Foundation of America, 1970. (b)

Van Riper, C. *Speech corrections: Principles and methods.* (5th ed.) Englewood Cliffs, N. J.: Prentice-Hall, 1972.

Vygotsky, L. S. *Thought and language.* Edited and translated by E. Hautman and G. Vakar. Cambridge, Mass.: M. I. T. Press (c.1962), 1971.

Walker, H. M. *Walker problem behavior identification checklist manual.* Los Angeles, California: Western Psychological Services, 1970.

Walker, R. N. Body build and behavior in young children: I. Body build and nursery school teachers' ratings. *Monograph Society for Research on Child Development,* 1962, **27**(3), 1–94.

Wallin, J. E. W. Prevalence of mental retardation. *School and Society,* 1958, **86,** 55–56.

Walsh, T. E. The surgical treatment of hearing loss. In H. Davis and S. R. Silverman (Eds.), *Hearing and deafness.* (3d ed.). New York: Holt, 1970. Pp. 164–177.

Watson, J. B. *Behaviorism.* New York: Norton, 1925.

Waugh, K. W., & Bush, W. J. *Diagnosing learning disorders.* Columbus, Ohio: Charles E. Merrill, 1971.

Weiner, G. The effect of distrust on some aspects of intelligence test behavior. In D. Payne and R. McMorris (Eds.), *Educational and psychological measurement.* Waltham, Mass: Blaisdell, 1967. Pp. 181–185.

Wenger, M. A. Study of the significance of measures of autonomic balance. *Psychosomatic Medicine,* 1947, **9,** 301.

Werry, J. S. Organic factors in childhood psychopathology. In H. C. Quay & J. S. Werry (Eds.), *Psychopathological disorders in childhood.* New York: Wiley, 1972, 83–121.

Westlake, H., & Rutherford, D. *Cleft palate.* Englewood Cliffs, New Jersey: Prentice-Hall, 1966.

Whelan, R. The relevance of behavior modification procedures for teachers of emotionally disturbed children. In P. Knoblock (Ed.), *Intervention approaches in educating emotionally disturbed children.* Syracuse, New York: Syracuse University Press, 1966. Pp. 35–78.

White, B. Informal education during the first months of life. In R. D. Hess and R. M. Baer (Eds.), *Early education: A comprehensive evaluation of current theory, research and practice.* Chicago: Aldine, 1968.

White, B. L. *Human infants: Experience and psychological development.* Englewood Cliffs, N. J.: Prentice-Hall, 1971.

White, B. L., & Held, R. Plasticity of sensorimotor development in the human infant. In J. F. Rosenblith and W. Allinsmith (Eds.), *The causes of behavior: Readings in child development and educational psychology.* (2d ed.) Boston: Allyn and Bacon, 1966. Pp. 60–70.

Wiegerink, R. Organizational model for preparing future special educators. *Journal of Special Education,* Summer 1973, **7,** 205–216.

Wiegerink, R., and Currie, R. Project in-step: Training tomorrow's special educators. *Journal of School Psychology,* 1972, **10,** 135–139.

Wilkins, L. T. *Social deviance: Social policy, action, and research.* Englewood Cliffs, N. J.: Prentice-Hall, 1965.

Wolf, J. M. *Physical facilities for exceptional children in the schools.* Balboa, Canal Zone: Division of Schools, 1968.

Wolfensberger, W. Diagnosis diagnosed. *The Journal of Mental Subnormality,* 1965, **11,** 62–70.

Wolfensberger, W. A new approach to decision-making in human management services. In R. B. Kugel and W. Wolfensberger, *Changing patterns in residential services for the mentally retarded.* Washington, D.C.: President's Committee on Mental Retardation, 1969. Pp. 367–382. (a)

Wolfensberger, W. The origin and nature of our institutional models. In R. B. Kugel and W. Wolfensberger (Eds.), *Changing patterns in residential services for the mentally retarded.* Washington, D.C.: President's Committee on Mental Retardation, 1969. Pp. 59–172. (b)

Wolfensberger, W. *The principles of normalization in human services.* Toronto: National Institute on Mental Retardation, 1972.

Wolpe, J., & Lazarus, A. A. *Behavior therapy techniques: A guide to the treatment of neuroses.* London: Pergamon, 1966.

Wood, N. E. *Delayed speech and language development.* Englewood Cliffs, N. J.: Prentice-Hall, 1964.

Woodward, M. The application of Piaget's theory to research in mental deficiency. In N. R. Ellis (Ed.), *Handbook of mental deficiency.* New York: McGraw-Hill, 1963. Pp. 297–324.

Woody, R. *Behavioral problem children in the schools.* New York: Appleton-Century-Crofts, 1969.

Wyatt, G. L., & Herzon, J. M. Therapy with stuttering children and their mothers. *American Journal of Orthopsychiatry,* 1962, **32,** 645–659.

Yamamoto, K. *Teaching.* Boston: Houghton Mifflin, 1969.

Zaslow, R. W., & Breger, L. A theory and treatment of autism. In L. Breger (Ed.), *Clinical-cognitive psychology: Models and integrations.* Englewood Cliffs, N.J.: Prentice-Hall, 1969. Pp. 246–291.

Zigler, E. The nature-nurture issue reconsidered. In H. C. Haywood (Ed.), *Methods and goals in human behavior genetics.* New York: Academic Press, 1965. Pp. 81–110.

NAME
INDEX

NAME INDEX

SUBJECT INDEX

SUBJECT INDEX